PSYCHOLOGY IN ECONOMICS AND BUSINESS

Psychology in Economics and Business

An Introduction to Economic Psychology

by

GERRIT ANTONIDES

With an Introduction by W. Fred van Raaij

Second, Revised Edition

KLUWER ACADEMIC PUBLISHERS

DORDRECHT / BOSTON / LONDON

Library of Congress Cataloging-in-Publication Data

Antonides, Gerrit, 1951–
    Psychology in economics and business : an introduction to economic
psychology / by Gerrit Antonides ; with an introduction by W. Fred
van Raaij.
        p.   cm.
    Includes index.
    ISBN 0-7923-4107-4 (hb : alk. paper)
    1. Economics--Psychological aspects.   I. Title.
HB74.P8A64 1996
330'.01'9--dc20   96-19922

ISBN 0-7923-4107-4 (HB)
ISBN 0-7923-4108-2 (PB)

Published by Kluwer Academic Publishers,
P.O. Box 17, 3300 AH Dordrecht, The Netherlands

Kluwer Academic Publishers incorporates
the publishing programmes of
D. Reidel, Martinus Nijhoff, Dr. W. Junk and MTP Press.

Sold and distributed in the U.S.A. and Canada
by Kluwer Academic Publishers,
101 Philip Drive, Norwell, MA 02061, U.S.A.

In all other countries, sold and distributed
by Kluwer Academic Publishers Group,
P.O. Box 322, 3300 AH Dordrecht, The Netherlands.

Cover picture has been adapted from F. J. Gall and G. S. Spurzheim (1810) in D. Krech et al.:
Elements of Psychology. Copyright ©1982 by Alfred A. Knopf.
Reproduced by permission of McGraw-Hill, Inc.
The idea expressed in the cover picture is that different kinds of behavior are controlled by
separate parts of the brain. This hypothesis in phrenology is not assumed here but we assume
that mental processes are involved in economic and social behavior as considered in this book.

Printed on acid-free paper

Printed in the Netherlands

CONTENTS

PART II
INFORMATION PROCESSING IN A WIDER SENSE

PREFACE

A number of books on economic psychology have appeared in the past few years. The most recent publications are *Economic Psychology: Intersections in Theory and Practice*,[1] *The Economic Mind*,[2] *The Individual in the Economy*[3] and *Handbook of Economic Psychology*[4]. Why produce yet another book for this discipline? This question can be answered in various ways.

In a sense, this book is the answer in itself. Its presentation of research and theories is innovative in this field, at least to my knowledge. It attempts to structure the many theories emerging in the interdisciplinary science of economic psychology and to explain the background of the research.

The second answer is pragmatic. In our introductory course of economic psychology for economics students at Erasmus University Rotterdam we used several of the above mentioned books. Our experience with this material is that, when preparing our lectures, we had to collect many additional theories and experiments to present to our students. Furthermore, diagrams, figures and examples had to be culled from other sources or made by ourselves. It is not my intention to run down these publications since I think they provide an excellent treatment of a number of topics by specialists in economic psychology. The plan for the present book, however, emerged from our need to present an integrated introductory course for our students, showing the development of theories in economic psychology.

In the fall of 1989, a draft version became available to our students to prepare them for their exam. One of the complaints we heard was: "Why has it not been written in Dutch?" The answer coincides with the third reason for this book. Economic psychology is a growing discipline and an increasing number of economists all over the world are becoming interested in psychological factors in economic behavior. Since economists usually have no formal education in psychology, there may be a need for a presentation of psychological ideas with their application to economics. I hope that this book will satisfy this need to some extent.

The organization of the book is such that the main psychological theories are dealt with in Chapters 2 to 10. With the exception of Chapter 11, the remaining chapters are not usually dealt with in psychology textbooks. Chapter 11 deals with several theories associated with cognitive consistency which I consider the counterpart of rationality in economics. Cognitive consistency deals with man's ability to pass judgments, to form and change attitudes and to interpret his environment, whilst still retaining consistency of opinions and beliefs. It is a guiding principle explaining many types of behavior dealt with in the other chapters.

The structure of each chapter is such that one or two sections deal with the basic theory behind the issue. Several applications to economic behavior are considered in the remaining sections. Almost every chapter includes a box illustrating the chapter. Each section finishes with a conclusion and each chapter contains a summary. The glossary contains brief descriptions of the main concepts dealt with in the chapters.

The main sources drawn on when compiling the chapters were the *Journal of Economic Psychology*, the annual colloquia of the International Association for Research in Economic Psychology, the books mentioned above and our own personal files.

Acknowledgements

First of all, I wish to thank Fred van Raaij for providing me with a great many valuable comments on the draft version of the book and for letting me use his document files. In addition, I also wish to thank him for writing the introductory chapter. Grateful thanks go to Peter Kaderják for his comments on the draft version and to Marianne Warmerdam for her assistance in compiling the glossary. Finally, I wish to express my gratitude to Caroline van Tienen who skilfully corrected the English.

Preface to the second, revised edition

The development of economic psychology, behavioral economics and experimental economics has been very fast during the past five years. This provides the main reason for the revision. About half the revision has been based on publications in the *Journal of Economic Psychology* which seems to attract an ever increasing number of authors with an economic background. Although having originally developed as a branch of psychology, economic psychology seems to becoming an interdisciplinary science. This is also evident from joint conferences of the International Association for Research in Economic Psychology (IAREP) on the one hand and the Society for the Advancement of Socio-Economics (SASE) in Stockholm, 1991, the Gesellschaft für Experimentelle Wirtschaftsforschung in Frankfurt, 1992 and the Society for the Advancement of Behavioral Economics in Shefayim, Israel, 1986 and Rotterdam, 1994, on the other.

Several scientific trends in the field are apparent:

— There is an increasing interest in the economic psychology of financial behavior. This is evident from workshops held in Exeter, 1994 and Tilburg, 1993 and 1995.

— Also a growing field is experimental economics capturing a great variety of economic anomalies, such as deviations from game theoretic predictions, reference effects, endowment effects, status quo bias, mental accounting, self-control and time-inconsistent preferences. The ongoing series of 'Anomalies' in the *Journal of Economic Perspectives* is telling. A separately published volume of Anomalies appeared, titled *The Winner's Curse*.[5]

— Although they have not yet reached the advanced stage of the areas mentioned above, the areas of economic socialization and economic perceptions also enjoy a growing interest.

— A fascinating and growing area is negotiation behavior. Unlike the area of game theory, the research here is mainly descriptive.

The new research has been judged in the light of its contribution to economic psychological theory rather than by its contribution to specific themes or problems. It has been included by adding paragraphs and sections and a new chapter has been devoted to negotiations.

Applications of economic psychology to business are not yet impressive,[6] probably due to the existence of organizational psychology, a separate branch of psychology. Applications to experimental economics are increasing in number, however, and we have tried to do them justice in this respect.

Acknowledgements

Grateful thanks go to Gary Bolton, Robert East, Shlomo Maital, Sharmila Ramadhin, Nico van der Sar and Harry Susianto for reviewing some material. I thank Linda Schijvens and Dennis Goedhart for their assistance in editing the revised edition. Once again, I express my gratitude to Caroline van Tienen for correcting the English.

Notes

[1] MacFadyen and MacFadyen 1986.
[2] Furnham and Lewis 1986.
[3] Lea et al. 1987.
[4] Van Raaij et al. 1988.
[5] Edited by Thaler 1992.
[6] Van Witteloostuijn 1993.

CHAPTER 1

INTRODUCTION

Economists often neglect psychology. However, for economic policy to be successful, psychological factors are important. Do people trust the government enough to believe in its economic policy? Are consumers optimistic or pessimistic and how does this influence their spending, saving and borrowing? How are consumer attitudes toward products and brands affected by advertising? What outcomes do people consider to be fair, just or equitable?

We believe that psychology is an integral part of economics. Consumers, taxpayers, entrepreneurs and other economic agents base their decision making on their perceptions and evaluations of economic facts and their expectations about future developments.

Economic psychology is the science which describes, explains and predicts the economic behavior of individuals, small groups (e.g., households) and large categories of persons (consumers as a whole). Economic psychologists study economic behavior, i.e. the expenditure and saving of time, money and effort. They use mainly psychological theories and concepts. In this book, these psychological concepts and theories are explained for economists and managers. By doing this, one can demonstrate the importance of these concepts for economics and management.

In this introductory chapter, I wish to argue that psychology is indispensable to an understanding of economic behavior. In the extreme case, economics should be restructured to socio-economics[1] to include moral and affective dimensions, without which many economic behaviors cannot be understood. In a less radical approach, psychological concepts are added to economic concepts to reach a better understanding of economic behaviour. The least radical approach is to argue that psychological concepts add flavor to the economic approach, the latter remaining the core explanation of economic behavior. In this way psychology adds 'meat' to the 'bones' of economics. It will be obvious that the authors of both this chapter and the book favor the first and the second approach.

1

Socio-economics

Neo-classical economics is the world of utility maximization. Individual consumers and entrepreneurs are seen as utility maximizers who are rational, egoistic and individualistic. If this approach is taken to extremes, individual actors will free ride on others to maximize their own profit and to minimize their costs. Moral considerations, love, loyalty, altruism and commitment are not usually included in the utility functions.

A new type of economics has emerged: socio-economics.[2] Socio-economics can be defined as a type of economics, based on psychological, sociological, cultural and anthropological considerations. These social sciences have come to offer insights into individual and social behavior, decision and comparison processes, emotions, norms and values. This knowledge is not only useful but essential to fully understand economic behavior of people.

In fact, according to socio-economics classical micro-economics needs a complete overhaul in order to adopt this knowledge as a basis for understanding economic behavior. Three bridging questions have to be dealt with first: (1) What are the sources of human valuations, norms or goals? (2) How are the means to advance our goals chosen? Beyond rationality, including normative and affective dimensions? And (3), Who are the key actors? Individual persons or groups?

Neo-classical economics studies the mechanisms necessary to make an efficient allocation of resources. Nothing is wrong with this approach, except that it is a very partial representation of reality. People do not always have ordered wants; they also have moral commitments and norms which govern their economic behavior.

Decision-making is not necessarily rational. Due to mental constraints and moral considerations, not all alternatives are examined. Some decisions and behaviors run clearly against rational considerations. The knowledge that smoking may cause lung cancer does not deter all people from smoking. Many decisions are made on affective considerations and many habits are continued without careful consideration.

According to neo-classical economics, individuals are free-standing units, while in fact they are members of social groups and are influenced by referent persons in these groups.

Socio-economics puts sociological and psychological dimensions at the basis of the study of economic behavior, thus providing a wider scope of explanation than neo-classical economics.

Psychological concepts

In many instances, psychological concepts are added to economic concepts to explain economic behavior.[3] Katona added an index of consumer optimism/pessimism to income changes to explain consumer spending and saving at an aggregate level. He proved that the combination of the two gives a better prediction than income data or expectations data only. In marketing (research) psychological concepts were first added to economic concepts, e.g. price perception and price elasticity. Psychological concepts have now almost taken over economic concepts in consumer behavior.

The focus of this book is that economic actors are affected by motivational and personality factors, circumstances, expectations, social comparison processes, attributions, etcetera. Wärneryd gives an overview of these factors, a somewhat revised version of which follows:[4]

1. *Motivational factors*: biological, social and cognitive motivations, mostly seen as a discrepancy between an actual and a desired state (Chapter 3).
2. *Values and norms*, developed through socialization, guiding and constraining economic behavior (Chapter 6).
3. *Information processing* from the internal and external environment, combining information from memory with new information. Information processing includes encoding, transformation and retrieval from memory (Chapter 7).
4. *Attitudes* as an evaluative construct of individuals to judge objects, persons and ideas. Attitudes should be predictive of behavior (Chapter 6).
5. *Social comparison* of own input e.g. effort, output e.g. payment and situation with referent persons and social influence of others (Chapter 11.)
6. *Rules or heuristics* for combining information, weighting benefits and costs and assessing the value of choice alternatives (Chapter 7).
7. *Attributions* of success and failure to causes and learning from this for future behavior (Chapter 11).
8. *Affect* (emotional factors) in perception and evaluation of information and guiding behavior (Chapter 9).
9. *Bargaining* and negotiation processes in competitive games or in dividing group outcomes among group members (Chapters 14 and 15).
10. *Learning* processes, other than using rules or heuristics (Chapters 5 and 7).
11. *Expectations* as evaluations and uncertain knowledge of future events and developments (Chapter 8).

This list of concepts shows that economic behavior is governed by the same factors as other human behaviors. Economics, in as far as it is concerned with the economic behavior of individuals and groups, is largely based on psychological (and sociological) factors.

Psychology for a richer description

Some economists only grant psychology a role in order to provide a richer description of the situation than economic theory allows. Economics provides the theory and the measurement tools to explain economic behavior. Psychology provides additional evidence, anecdotes, examples and cases to give a better understanding of and feeling for the phenomena under study.

The approach whereby psychology is used to provide a richer description, tacitly assumes that the economic model is valid but that there is more to say about economic behavior than just costs and benefits. The additional information is considered merely illustrative, not essential. Psychology is therefore a qualitative addition to an essentially quantitative economic theory.

Obviously we do not favour this role for psychology. Psychology as a science has more to offer than additional evidence. Psychology plays a central role in economic behavior, rather than a peripheral one. Needless to say, psychology is a quantitative science in its own right. It is neither acceptable nor valid to give psychology purely an additional and illustrative role.

Process and outcome

The contribution of psychology is not limited to providing additional or alternative factors to explain economic behavior. Psychology can also be employed to describe processes. Not only the outcome of a decision process is relevant; the process itself teaches us how economic actors proceed in collecting information, comparing alternatives and selecting an alternative.

Katona's view of economic psychology is succinctly expressed in the following quotation:

> "... the basic need for psychology in economic research resides in the need to discover and analyze the forces behind economic processes, the forces responsible for economic actions, decisions and choices ... 'Economics without psychology' has not succeeded in explaining important economic processes and 'psychology without economics' has no chance of explaining some of the most common aspects of human behavior."[5]

Examples of these processes are:

1. *Information collection* from external sources. How many and what types of information sources are consulted? Which information is collected from these sources?
2. *Information integration*: Information on choice alternatives often consists of a number of attribute values. How are these attributes evaluated? How is the information on different attributes combined into an overall assessment of the alternatives? Which decision rules are used?[6]

3. *Attitude formation and change*: Depending on the level of involvement, the formation and change of attitudes may be a highly elaborated or a less elaborated process.[7] The ability and motivation to process information determines which level of elaboration can be expected.

4. *Attribution* of observation to causes is a type of layman science. People want to know the causes of behaviors and events in order to react more adequately on the next occasion. Causal attribution is essentially a process of combining information.

5. *Bargaining* is a process almost by definition. After a series of information exchanges the bargaining process leads to an outcome. How do people change their proposals to the other party? In which order do they raise the points for negotiation? What do they infer about the intention and position of the other party?

6. *Economic socialization* is a long-term process of children's education by parents, teachers and peers. Early experiences in youth may have strong effects later. Learning processes may take years before they result in (a change in) economic behavior.

Knowledge about the processes of economic behavior increases the explanatory and predictive power of scientific research. Knowledge not only of outcomes but also of the processes and mechanisms leading to these outcomes facilitates the prediction of new outcomes. This is partly an attribution problem.[8] If economic behavior can be attributed to circumstances and conditions, one is less certain about future economic behavior than when economic behavior can be attributed to internal causes (preferences).

These and other examples show that the study of processes is an important contribution of psychology. Economists are often only interested in predictions and not in the assumptions and processes underlying the predictions of outcomes. Friedman even asserts that assumptions do not matter, as long as the predictions are correct.[9]

We, however, are of the opinion that a correct prediction of outcomes is rather unlikely, unless the underlying processes are well understood. Knowledge of the underlying processes will largely increase the predictability of the outcomes and understanding of why economic agents reached these outcomes.

W. Fred van Raaij

Notes

[1] Etzioni 1988.
[2] Etzioni 1988.
[3] Katona 1975.

[4] Wärneryd 1988.
[5] Katona 1975, p. 9.
[6] Van Raaij 1988.
[7] Petty and Cacioppo 1986.
[8] Van Raaij 1986.
[9] Friedman 1953.

PART I

AN ECONOMIC PSYCHOLOGICAL PARADIGM

CHAPTER 2

ECONOMICS AND PSYCHOLOGY

2.1. Shared interests of economics and psychology

Psychology is commonly described as the study of mind and behavior. The behavior of interest here is economic behavior of people in our society. Although on several occasions we shall deal with the behavior of organizations or (small) groups, such as the family, the main object of study is the individual.

Traditionally, different fields in psychology can be distinguished, dealing with different types of behavior:

— The psychology of personality deals with the structure and measurement of the individual personality. Applications of this type of psychology are psychological testing and the treatment of abnormal behavior.

— Developmental psychology deals with the influence of upbringing and education on the subsequent personality and behavior. Applications are in educational counseling, remedial teaching and instructional techniques.

— Social psychology deals with individual behavior in a social group. Studies pertain among other things to the quality of social relations, the effects of power and leadership, the spread of information in a group, efficiency of group behavior and social dilemmas. Applications are in organizational counselling, information services and group decision making.

— Experimental psychology today deals mainly with cognitive behavior, including perception, learning, thinking and language. Applications are in man-machine relations, problem solving and artificial intelligence and education.

A special branch, economic psychology, has emerged from the fields mentioned above. Economic psychology deals with economic behavior including personal, cognitive and social factors. By including these factors, it offers explanations for behavior that is not explained, or simply not considered, by the economic approach. For example:

— in the long run, people frequently are not found to be happier when their incomes have increased;

— many people are saving money in a bank account while at the same time financing their car at a substantially higher interest rate;

9

- when asked to divide a sum of money between themselves and another person, a 50–50 split is very common, unlike the division expected from rational behavior;
- people report satisfaction with a very dull task for which they get little financial compensation;
- people frequently are willing to walk a mile to buy an article of dress which is $5 cheaper, but do not even think of visiting another city to look for a car which is $500 cheaper;
- in general, people consider providing services in exchange for affection from other people as more appropriate than giving money;
- goods are generally valued higher after they have been acquired than before they are owned.

Many of these 'inexplicable' behaviors are considered in this book.

Economic behavior is defined here as the behavior of individuals that involves economic decisions and the determinants and consequences of economic decisions.[1] Economic decisions deal with scarce resources such as money, time and effort. As many determinants and consequences of behavior are subjective, these fall within the scope of psychology. This constitutes one important difference from economics where only observable behavior or results of behavior are studied and not mental processes.

Although psychology in principle deals with all types of behavior, economic behavior is studied by only a minority of psychologists, notably industrial and organizational psychologists. Yet, the interest in economic psychology and consumer psychology is increasing, illustrated by a steady growth in membership of the International Association for Research in Economic Psychology, the Society for the Advancement of Behavioral Economics and the Association for Consumer Research over the last decade.

On the other hand, economics is gradually broadening its scope, to include, for example, welfare economics, the economics of health and education, economics of the family and the environment. This trend in imperialistic economics[2] is supplemented by the inclusion of psychological factors in economic models.

This provides a growing basis for the interdisciplinary science of economic psychology, combining the interest in economic behavior with the study of the mind. However, several barriers to interdisciplinary research do exist, one of which is the communication of psychological knowledge and methodology to economists and vice versa. Here, we shall attempt to communicate the basics of psychological theory as it might be relevant to economics, given the current state of affairs.

Section 2.2 shows the importance of economic behavior in everyday life. Section 2.3 considers the relevance of psychological insights for economic models (and the overcoming of their failures). Section 2.4 shows several economic psychological models structuring the antecedents and consequences of economic behavior.

Conclusion

Economic psychology and behavioral economics are converging in a wide range of human behaviors. The interdisciplinary scientific approach requires communication, understanding and application of both psychological and economic models and methodologies.

2.2. Economic actions in everyday life

An increasing number of activities in daily life turn out to be of interest to economics, as was argued above. Economics today is even concerned with such topics as mate selection and love in human relationships,[3] the birth of children and the addiction to drugs. To establish the significance of these activities and events, we shall consider the time spent on them and importance ascribed to them.

Time spent on economic activities

If we define activities in a paid job, voluntary work and household production as economic activities, then we can see from Table 2.1 that these take up 31–34% of available time. The information in Table 2.1 is derived from a time budget study in which a Dutch sample of participants meticuluously kept a diary for an entire week. Activities like feeding, housekeeping, shopping, child care, transportation (e.g. for travelling with children) were classified as home production. Activities like personal care, schooling (not for work), social and cultural visits, sports and relaxation were classified as leisure activities.

Importance of economic activities

There appears to be no reason for the lack of attention to economic activities in psychology. Economic activities are as important for life satisfaction as other types of activities. This is evident from a Swedish study in which participants rated the importance of 47 types of activities on a 13- point importance scale.[4] The mean importance of all activities was 6.7. Classifying certain types of activities as economic, as above, showed 32% of daily life activities to be economic with an average rating of 6.7 on the importance scale.

Table 2.1. Hours per week spent on daily life activities.

	Males	Females
Home production (*economic*)	21.1	45.3
Paid work (*economic*)	29.3	8.6
Voluntary work (*economic*)	2.3	2.2
Leisure time	59.8	55.1
Sleeping time	55.4	56.7
Number of participants	1878	1441

Source: Grift et al. (1989). The Hague: SWOKA.

People asked to report their personal wishes, hopes, worries and fears frequently mention economic items associated with 'a decent standard of living', 'housing', leisure time', 'modern conveniences', etcetera.[5] This finding also indicates the importance of economic achievements in everyday life.

Although the studies mentioned above suggest that about 30% of daily life activities are economic, a study using a sample of 94 students, suggests that not all economic activities are perceived as economic by the students.[6] A broadcasting signal, given irregularly five times a day during an entire week, received by the subjects, prompted for the completion of a questionnaire concerning the activity of the moment. Activities that took place for economic reasons or to fulfil material needs (according to the students) were classified as economic. In this way, only 9% of all reported activities are economic, including gainful employment, shopping, transportation, looking for a job and home-making. Considering the fact that the sample consisted of students, it is surprising how seldom education was reported as an economic activity. Either the students did not spend much time on their study or education was not regarded as an economic activity!

The studies reported above use direct information regarding the importance of economic activities. The importance of economic factors for life satisfaction can also be assessed indirectly, e.g. by investigating the statistical relations between general life satisfaction and economic factors.[7]

Conclusion

A substantial part of daily life consists of economic activities which appear to be as important for life satisfaction as non-economic activities. This legitimizes the psychological study of economic behavior as a separate branch of psychology.

2.3. Relevance of psychology for economics

The science of economics has been built upon several assumptions which deserve scrutiny.[8] The assumption of *rationality* in economics avoids the necessity of studying human thought processes. However, it merely generates norms for economic behavior, indicating what is to be expected if economic behavior is rational and seeks to maximize pecuniary gain. From a psychological point of view, this assumption is not realistic. For instance, it can be observed that people do not always choose the best alternative of those available. This is illustrated by the following example:

> "Mr. H. mows his own lawn. His neighbor's son would mow it for $8. He wouldn't mow his neighbor's same-sized lawn for $20."[9]

Such behavior is quite common in our society.[10]

Economics tries to explain changes of behavior as a result of changes in the structure of constraints, assuming preferences as given and stable over time.[11] Thus, economics is not the science of explaining preferences but of using preferences as *revealed* by actual choices. Since history has provided numerous examples of how people can be influenced by propaganda or 're-education', it would appear to be short-sighted to exclude from study the explanation of preferences. It seems somewhat strange, for instance, that economics theoretically includes expenditures on advertising but at the same time excludes the effects on consumer preferences.[12]

In the *psychological approach*, individual data are obtained in order to study the variation in behavior, after which aggregates, averages, and indexes maybe utilized.[13] Furthermore, information is obtained directly from the individual and does not rely on data from which behavior can only be studied after the act.

The psychological approach investigates all kinds of habits, attitudes and motivations, not only the profit-seeking. Finally, the *process* of attitude and motivational change is studied and the techniques that might induce the changes. Thus, the psychological approach is relevant to economics in that it provides a more realistic basis to explain behavior and behavioral change.

In a number of instances the economic paradigm does not seem to fit the observations of behavior.[14] Some of these instances are reported here.

In real life, economic theory predicts *free-riding*, the selfish behavior of taking only the benefits of collective outputs while not contributing to the inputs. Yet, it has been found that on average 40–60% of people voluntarily contribute to the provision of a public good. Examples are blood donation, giving information to strangers, helping old people, etcetera.

In experiments, it has been found that many people are not willing to sell their homes even though they could sell them at a high price. Nor would they ever buy a home at such a high price. This indicates that goods in a person's endowment are valued more highly than those not held in the endowment.[15] Economic theory does not have an explanation for this effect.

In applications of the economic model, the results frequently are not according to expectation. An example of this is *overjustification*, a phenomenon where the intrinsic motivation to an action is destroyed by a material reward. The effect of this is a decreased willingness to perform the same action without a reward.[16] As an illustration of the overjustification effect, consider an employee who gives a colleague a free lift to work in her car (e.g. for social reasons). Once the colleague starts to pay for the ride, the intrinsic reward (the social satisfaction) disappears or becomes less important. If she then stops paying, the owner of the car is less likely to offer the ride.

Usually, in the provision of public goods, the government and other institutions contribute in addition to private donations. The *crowding out* hypothesis concerns the idea that an increase (decrease) in public donations is compensated by a commensurate decrease (increase) in private donations. However, both in practice and in experiments, incomplete crowding out has been found. For example, in one study it has been found that a $10,000 increase in government funds for public radio resulted in only $0.15 decrease in average private donations.[17] A second study showed 72% crowding out in a public goods experiment in which a tax was levied in one condition and no tax in a second condition.[18] A third study found incomplete crowding out in a *dictator game*,[19] in which subjects could unilaterally alter a 18–2 distribution in favor of themselves in one condition or a 15–5 distribution in a second condition.[20] Although many subjects altered the distribution into a 10–10 split, on average only 74% crowding out was found in the latter study. That is, in the 18–2 condition, less subjects gave away 8 than subjects in the 15–5 condition gave away 5.

The examples above ask for improvement and enrichment of the economic model. Psychological motivations could be incorporated in preferences.[21] This means that economic behavior is not motivated solely by greed but that other motives, such as the need for stimulation, altruism, achievement, etcetera are also important.[22]

Another suggestion is to study processes instead of outcomes.[23] For instance, goods produced in a way not harmful to the environment may be valued more than better or cheaper goods, the production of which is harmful to the environment. Processes also play a part where people are dissatisfied with a good outcome because certain rules were not obeyed, e.g. by obtaining a salary not in agreement with the demands of the job. In equity theory, behavioral outcomes are judged in terms of inputs and outputs of actors.[24]

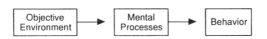

Figure 2.1. A basic economic psychological paradigm.

The assumption of stable preferences can be adapted to include preference dynamics. The adaptation of preferences may be explained by psychological learning theory.[25] In this way economic psychology may add or replace variables in economic models. Although psychological insights may be useful to economic theory, this does not mean that rational economic models are useless. The debate between economists and psychologists may be concluded with two *false* statements:

"1. Rational models are useless.
2. All behavior is rational."[26]

The psychological approach implies the use of data obtained *directly* from individuals. This approach offers the opportunity to study the individual perception of economic goods and services.[27] The world, as perceived by the individual, is evaluated subjectively, on the basis of which decisions are taken to behave in a certain way.[28]

The psychological approach to the study of economic behavior has given rise to several economic psychological models which are dealt with in the next section.

Conclusion

By including psychological variables and processes in economic models, several economic assumptions are adapted. This provides for a more realistic explanation of behavior and a wider range of behavior to be explained.

2.4. Economic psychological models of behavior

A *basic economic psychological paradigm* is displayed in Figure 2.1.[29] The arrows in the figure indicate the causal relationships between the elements in the boxes. It is assumed that the objective environment, including income, assets, employment opportunities and socio-economic status, influences the mental processes and subjective well-being of members of society, together with their economic attitudes and expectations. Attitudes and expectations regarding the personal situation and the economy as a whole influence economic behavior, i.e. consumer demand and saving. Considering the objective environment as stimuli (S) impinging on the individual, the mental processes as taking place within the organism (O), and the behavior as a response (R)

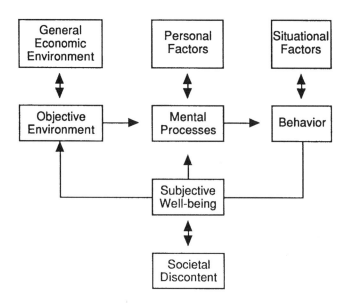

Figure 2.2. An extended economic psychological model.

of the organism, this model resembles a well-known scheme in the psychological school of behaviorism (*S-O-R*).[30] A feedback loop may be added to
this model, assuming the influence of economic behavior on the objective
environment.[31]

This model has been used to explain and forecast consumer demand
from survey information about income and economic attitudes.[32] It has been
claimed that the model is more successful than economic models in this
respect.[33]

More *extensive* economic psychological models include personal factors
and the attitude toward the economic and political system as a whole.[34]
See Figure 2.2. Besides the relationships present in the basic model, it is assumed that behavior influences subjective well-being, comprising satisfaction
with consumption, work, income, marriage, standard of living, awareness of
opportunities. Subjective well-being in turn influences the economic environment, e.g. by inducing new product design and development. Furthermore,
subjective well-being influences an individual's perception of the economic
environment, e.g. on the basis of confirmed and disconfirmed expectations
regarding consumer goods. Behavior is also assumed to have a direct effect
on the economic environment, e.g. in the economic relation of supply and
demand for goods and services.

Further relations are assumed:
– between the general economic environment and the personal economic

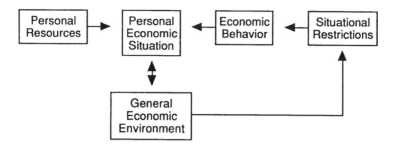

Figure 2.3. The structure of economic behavior on the objective plane.

situation (the objective environment). The general economic environment includes recessions and upswings, economic policy of the government, pollution, war and peace, criminality, etcetera.

— between personal factors and the mental process of perception, interpretation and decision making with regard to the economic environment. Personal factors include goals, values, aspirations, expectations, socio-demographic variables and personality characteristics.[35]

— between societal discontent and subjective well-being. Societal discontent includes one's general happiness or satisfaction with societal structures (political and cultural) and the economic system (capitalism, socialism, communism).

— between situational factors and economic behavior. Situational factors include unexpected events, e.g. accidents, illness, a bank refusing credits and anticipated situations such as a party or a weekend trip.

The extended model gives ample opportunity to supplement economic models explaining behavior. However, processes taking place at the objective level are not strictly separated from subjective or mental processes.

The paradigm used in the following chapters makes a distinction between objective and subjective factors and processes. This paradigm will be referred to as a *structural* paradigm, consisting of an objective and a subjective part. The *objective* part can be observed, measured independently and accounted for by statistical figures. The *subjective* part can be accessed directly by consulting the individual by means of questionnaires or other psychological methods or indirectly by inference from behavior. In general, economics deals with information and behavior on the objective plane, the structure of which is shown in Figure 2.3.

On the objective plane, situational restrictions include common economic restrictions, such as the budget restriction, restrictions of place and time, etcetera, which are assumed to influence (restrict) economic behavior, as defined in Section 2.1. This relationship is estimated, for example, in demand

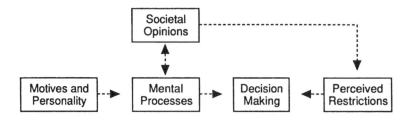

Figure 2.4. The structure of economic behavior on the subjective plane.

equations (explaining demand for goods and services from prices and income) and Engel curves (depicting the relation between expenditure on a particular item and income).

Economic behavior is assumed to influence the personal economic situation, e.g. paid employment generates a certain amount of income, buying commodities will increase the existing stock. This relation is similar to the feedback loop added to the basic model in Figure 2.1.[36]

Personal economic situations of many people together make up the general economic environment as shown, for example, in national statistics (e.g. GNP). On the other hand, the general economic environment influences the personal economic situation. For example, the tax system affects the economic situation for each person in a different way. This relation is similar to the relation between the general and the objective economic situation in Figure 2.2.

The general economic situation is assumed to influence the situational restrictions, for example the interest rate in a country may affect the mortgage limit of an individual, imposed by the bank.

Personal resources include the individual history, education, marital status, age, gender, etcetera. These go to make up the socio-demographic factors which play an important part in studies of marketing and consumer behavior. These factors are assumed to have a direct influence on the personal economic situation.

The subjective part of the structural model, shown in Figure 2.4, deals with mental factors influencing decision making. The relations between these factors are represented by dotted arrows, to distinguish them from the relations between the objective factors in Figure 2.3. Motives and personality are formed in early childhood, probably in combination with hereditary factors. These factors are assumed to influence the mental processes in different ways.[37]

Societal opinions include the modal opinions of a society concerning social, political, economic and cultural affairs. For example, common habits, conventions, ethics, expectations[38] and public images regarding people and

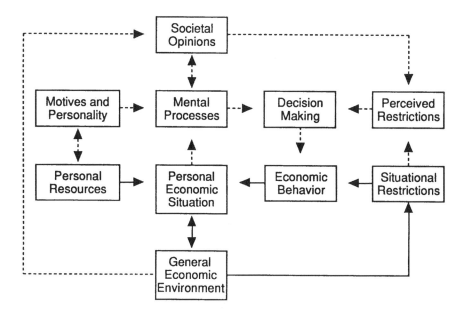

Figure 2.5. The structure of economic behavior on the objective and the subjective plane.

firms[39] are expressions of societal opinions. The societal opinions form a special part of the model. Societal opinions constitute the combined personal opinions of a group of people. Communication processes, the media and research organizations are used in the formation of societal opinions, for example in constituting the tone of the New York Stock Exchange market or the Index of Consumer Sentiment.[40] In mental processes, it is assumed that these societal opinions are compared with individual goals, motives and attitudes.

Mental processes might result in decision making, although this is not necessary. When you are reading this book, for example, many mental activities are taking place, usually not involving decision making.

Perceived restrictions pertain to internalized constraints affecting decision making. Several perceived constraints are derived from societal opinions, e.g. social norms.[41] Both subjective restrictions and mental processes are assumed to influence decision making. In decision making, the available information is combined and alternative behavior is compared and evaluated.[42]

The subjective plane is assumed to be connected to the objective plane by perception and interpretation of the world and the execution of decisions by taking action. (See Figure 2.5.) This is evident from the dotted arrows leading respectively from the personal economic situation to the mental processes and from decision making to economic behavior.

Three other relations are assumed:

— On the one hand, the socio-economic environment (the personal resources) influences personality, e.g. gender is known to relate to personality in various ways. On the other hand, motives and personality influence performance at school, the type of the job and the career (the socio-economic environment).

— The objective restrictions are perceived and supplemented by *subjective restrictions*. Subjective restrictions include, for example, psychological effort, physical energy and (internalized) social norms. These norms may well be influenced by social opinions.

— Apart from being the aggregation of individual opinions, the societal opinions are influenced by the general economic situation. For example, a high level of unemployment in society probably will lead to unfavorable opinions as regards the standard of living.

The structural paradigm presented above need not necessarily be a perfect representation of processes in reality or in the human mind. It merely serves as a research paradigm which can be used to integrate several types of research. The paradigms considered here also lack a structure containing the way people react to one another. Such a structure should capture the structure of interpersonal relationships, including how one's behavior depends on others and interpersonal communication.[43] The paradigms could be extended, for example in a third dimension for individuals, at the expense of simplicity, however.

To investigate the relationships indicated in the model economics uses a number of statistics compiled by a number of statistical organizations. Although these statistics are believed to represent objective facts, they are not always 100% reliable (e.g. unemployment statistics).

In the psychological approach, use is made of *direct measurements* of subjective phenomena. These include survey questionnaires, psychological tests, field observations, interviews, interpretations of behavior and reports of experiences (e.g. dreams), physiological measurements, etcetera.[44] In psychology, reliability and validity of measurements have been given much attention. Despite this, many economists are suspicious of subjective information and prefer not to use it at all. In our opinion, they throw out the baby with the bathwater, since psychological information is necessary to overcome the shortcomings and the lack of reality in economic science.

Conclusion

Economic psychological models have been extended and refined since the introduction of the basic behavioristic scheme. Objective relations, traditionally studied in economics, have been retained, while subjective relations have been added. A structural model, including both types of relations, offers a paradigm for studying the interrelations between economics and psychology in the following chapters.

Summary

Economic psychology has emerged from several psychological fields: experimental, social and developmental psychology and the psychology of personality. It deals with economic behavior including personal, cognitive and social factors. In this way, insight is gained into hitherto unexplained behavior. Economics and psychology can be said to combine interests in this interdisciplinary branch of science.

About 30% of available time is spent on economic activities, although people do not always classify these activities as intrinsically economic. Furthermore, economic activities are reported to be as important for life satisfaction as other activities.

By obtaining information on mental processes directly, economic psychologists are able to study them, whereas economics relies on assumptions regarding these processes. It appears that several economic assumptions should be expanded to include psychological variables and processes in explaining economic behavior.

Economic psychological models attempt to combine economic and psychological relationships. This has been accomplished by including variables from the psychological organism to the original behavioristic scheme. In addition, the relations between economic and psychological environments have been made explicit. The resulting paradigm may serve as a framework to deal with the topics in the following chapters.

BOX 2.1

MENTAL ECONOMICS

Subjective representations of the objective environment do not deal with a scientific model as represented in Section 2.4 but with mental models, assumed to exist in the human mind.[45] As an example, a mental scheme of the causes and effects of inflation has been constructed from information given by a number of individuals.

The subjects in the study were 18 psychology and 18 economics students. The psychology students fulfilled a course requirement by serving as subjects, the economics students were paid SEK30 (about $4).

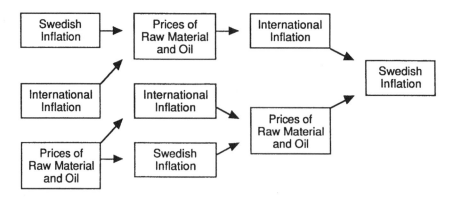

Figure 2.6. Mental structure of the causes of inflation. (Psychology students.) Adapted from Svenson and Nilsson (1986).

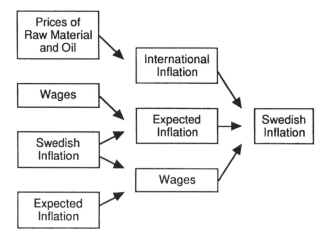

Figure 2.7. Mental structure of the causes of inflation. (Economics students.) Taken from Svenson and Nilsson (1986).

In one part of the experiment, the students were given a set of variables, related to inflation. For each of the variables, the students indicated its importance for influencing inflation and whether it caused an increasing or a decreasing rate of inflation. This was repeated for each of the variables, in order to show the importance and effect of each one in relation to the others.

From this information, there emerged a series of causal relationships. Figure 2.6 shows the relationships which were considered the two most important by at least five of the psychology students.

On comparing the mental structure of the psychology and the economics students with regard to the causes of inflation, the economists (see Figure 2.7) are seen to attach more weight to wages and the expected rate of inflation as major variables causing inflation than the psychology students. The economics students appear to have the expectational theory of inflation in mind.[46] Different perceptions and cognitive structures between individuals and groups is the rule rather than the exception in economic psychology.[47]

Notes

[1] Van Raaij 1981.

[2] Stigler 1984.

[3] Becker 1973, 1974.

[4] Gärling et al. 1987.

[5] See Section 10.1.

[6] Sjöberg 1985.

[7] This will be considered in Chapter 10.

[8] Hayes 1950.

[9] Thaler 1980, p.43.

[10] Rationality will be dealt with more extensively in Chapter 12.

[11] Meyer 1982.

[12] Preferences and attitudes will be dealt with in more detail in Chapter 6.

[13] Hayes 1950.

[14] Frey 1983.

[15] See Chapter 12.

[16] Several explanations for this effect are offered in Chapters 3 and 11.

[17] Kingma 1989.

[18] Andreoni 1993.

[19] See Chapter 14.

[20] Bolton and Katok 1995.

[21] Frey 1983.

[22] A selection of motives is considered in Chapter 3.

[23] Frey 1983.

[24] See Chapter 11.

[25] See Chapter 5.

[26] Thaler 1986, p. S283.

[27] This topic will be dealt with in Chapter 4.

[28] Subjective evaluation and decision making are dealt with in Chapter 6 and Chapter 7, respectively.

[29] Katona 1964.

[30] See Chapter 5.

[31] Van Raaij 1981.

[32] See Katona 1964 and Mueller 1963.

[33] Economic attitudes and expectations will be dealt with in Chapter 8.

[34] Strümpel 1976 and Van Raaij 1981.

[35] See Chapter 3.

[36] Van Raaij 1981.

[37] See Chapter 3.

[38] See Chapter 8.

[39] See Chapter 6.

[40] See Chapter 8.

[41] See Chapter 6.

[42] Decision making is dealt with in Chapter 7.

[43] See Chapters 14 and 15.

[44] Psychological methods of measurement are dealt with in Chapter 16.

[45] Svenson and Nilsson 1986.

[46] Lipsey and Steiner 1978, p. 737.

[47] In Chapter 4, scientific models of perception and cognitive structures representing the economic environment will be discussed.

CHAPTER 3

MOTIVATION AND PERSONALITY

3.1. The function of motivation and personality in economic behavior

In Chapter 2, it has been argued that motivation and personality are connected to personal resources and to subjective well-being, including preferences.

To explain how motivation may be connected to preferences, consider the following example. Jeanette, who is an ambitious unmarried young woman, striving for an opportunity to join the board of directors of her organization, is offered a more responsible position than she occupies now but only for a slightly higher salary. Jeanette prefers this position, since it takes her closer to the top. Ben, who is satisfied with a good, stable salary for him and his family and is not very ambitious, is offered the same type of position as Jeanette. Ben, however, does not prefer the offer, since he is not motivated to take the greater responsibility associated with the job, even if he is paid a slightly higher salary. In this case, the different preferences can be explained from a different motivation to *achieve* a higher position.

The relation between motivation and personal resources can be made clear by using the same example. Jeanette can fully employ her ambitions, since she does not have to care for a husband and children, contrary to Ben's personal circumstances. In this case, different circumstances (marital status) induce different motivations to make a career.

No sharp distinction will be made between motivation and personality. To the extent that motivational *dispositions* or *needs* are characteristic of the person over time, these are features of her personality. Thus, the achievement motivation, mentioned above, might be considered as part of the individual's personality if it is relatively enduring, not if it is only occasional.

An individual's personality influences behavior, although this might occur in an inconsistent way. Rather than influencing behavior in a stable and predictable way, the effect of personality may depend on the particular context of behavior.[1] For example, the need for achievement may be expressed in a working environment, but not in the field of sports. Contemporary psychology takes an interactionist position concerning the explanation of behavior. It is believed that both person and situation variables are necessary to understand

25

behavior. Although it is generally believed that global personality variables cannot efficiently explain specific behavior, they may explain broader categories of behavior in broader categories of circumstances, i.e. by abstracting from situation specific influences.[2] Furthermore, personality measures may be aggregated over time to obtain more reliable measures.[3] Alternatively, correlations between personality and behavior may be improved by correcting for unreliability of the measures.[4] The 'big five' personality dimensions may explain behavior in future economic psychological research:[5] emotional stability, extraversion, conscientiousness, agreeableness and openness.[6] Specific motivations may be described as vectors in the five-dimensional space in order to improve the compatibility of studies. This seems to constitute a methodological dilemma: on the one hand specific behavior may be explained efficiently by specific variables, at the expense of theoretical elegance, whereas on the other hand aggregate behavior may be explained efficiently by global personality dimensions, at the expense of practical relevance. Here we take a pragmatic point of view: since most studies in economic psychology include specific dimensions to explain specific behavior, the focus will be on a selection of the most promising and economically relevant motivational factors.

The distinction between person and situation variables is related to the motivational sources of behavior. If it is believed that an individual behaves in a certain way because internal, personal standards induce the behavior (e.g. accepting a job because of the personal work ethic), in the absence of any apparent external contingency, the motivation is said to be *intrinsic*.[7] By contrast, *extrinsic* motivation refers to environmental variables (e.g. salary associated with a job) inducing the behavior.

Using the distinction between intrinsic and extrinsic motivations, the *overjustification* effect can be understood better.[8] Consider the following example:

> "A boy on good terms with his parents willingly mows the lawn of the house. His father then offers to pay him a fee for each time he cuts the lawn. As a result, the boy now only mows the lawn when this payment comes forth – nor is he prepared to do any other type of housework for free."[9]

The original intrinsic motivation to mow the lawn has disappeared because of the extrinsic motivation provided by the money. The intrinsic motivation has been crowded out by the extrinsic motivation. Crowding out may result from a change in the *locus of causality*.[10] Whereas the behavior was caused by the intrinsic motivation first, the locus of causality has changed such that the individual now believes that it is caused by the cash reward. Classifying motivations as intrinsic or extrinsic involves internal or external attributions of behavior.[11]

Figure 3.1. Maslow's hierarchy of needs.

The overjustification effect has important consequences for the choice of efficient reward systems in work settings. Other areas of application are blood donation systems based either on monetary reward or on voluntary behavior and environmental management following the introduction of marketable permits and emission charges. Monetary reward or punishment frequently crowds out intrinsic motivation, thus leading to sub-optimal outcomes for society, known as the 'hidden costs of reward'.[12] Several conditions determining crowding out can be summarized as follows.[13] An extrinsic reward is more likely to replace the intrinsic motivation by an extrinsic motivation if:
— the relationship between the allocator and the beneficiary is personal;
— the behavior is interesting for the beneficiary;
— the beneficiary has extensive participation possibilities in defining a task;
— it is provided uniformly, i.e. disregarding the individual performance;
— it is contingent on task engagement and on the performance desired by the allocator.

In addition to the overjustification effect on the behavior concerned, there may be a spillover effect on other types of behavior, i.e. other housework in the example above. In the area of blood donation, the overjustification occurring in paid donations may spill over to other people donating voluntarily, i.e. unpaid donors will no longer contribute for free because other donors get paid.

A number of psychological motivations are distinguished in the literature. According to Maslow,[14] physiological needs are the most basic needs motivating behavior. For example, hunger motivates feeding behavior (e.g. shopping for food). Maslow assumes a hierarchy of motives (see Figure 3.1) in which physiological needs are subordinate to safety needs (e.g. needs for shelter, financial security). The third level consists of social needs (e.g. needs for friendship, affiliation), the fourth of self-esteem needs (e.g. needs for status, competence). The highest level comprises self-actualization, including the realization of one's full potential, e.g. being creative, content with life.

Maslow's assumption implies that lower needs have to be satisfied before higher needs become prominent. This assumption has not been substantiated by empirical research and appears to be invalid in many cases. For example, artists, philosophers and writers frequently reach self-actualization in their performances without satisfaction of physiological needs. In contemporary research, the assumption of a hierarchy of needs is relaxed in that different individual orderings or even equal importance of needs is assumed.

The distinction of needs is useful since it explains why people want goods and services or show particular behavior. The preoccupation with particular needs frequently characterizes an individual's personality, e.g. people striving for satisfaction of social needs are likely to be sociable.

There are several motivations important to the method of decision making, other than via the evaluation of product attributes. In this chapter, six types of motivations and personalities are selected from the economic psychological literature: need for achievement, locus of control, sensation seeking and risk attitude, altruism, time preference, cognitive style and life-style. These will be dealt with in the following sections.

Conclusion

Motivation applies to the determinants of behavior, which may be located in the organism (intrinsic motivation) or in the environment (extrinsic motivation). Stable motivational dispositions form part of the personality structure and characterize an individual's economic behavior. Attempts have been made to structure the distinguished motivations; the best known of these is Maslow's hierarchical system.

3.2. Need for achievement

A motivation that has frequently been investigated in relation to economic behavior is the *need for achievement* (or achievement attitude). The achievement attitude has been described as:

> "The need to accomplish something difficult, to master, manipulate or organize physical objects, human beings or ideas. To do this as rapidly and as independently as possible. To overcome obstacles and attain a high standard. To surpass oneself. To rival and outdo others. To increase self-regard by the successful exercise of talent."[15]

As is the case with many other psychological characteristics, the strength of the need for achievement may vary across individuals. This makes it necessary to develop a rather accurate measurement instrument to assess the individual strength of this need. The most important instrument to measure need for achievement (nAch) is the *Thematic Apperception Test* (TAT). The TAT procedure includes the presentation of several pictures about which subjects are asked to write a story. The stories should answer the following questions:

— What is happening? Who are the persons?

— What has led up to this situation? That is, what has happened in the past?

— What is being thought? What is wanted? By whom?

— What will happen? What will be done?

The subjects are told that the test measures their creative imagination and that there are no right or wrong answers. They should tell a story about the pictures as vividly and dramatically as possible. For each picture the story should be finished within four minutes, allowing one minute for each of the above questions. Some examples of the pictures used are:

— Two men ('inventors') in a shop working at a machine.

— Boy in check shirt at a desk, an open book in front of him.

— A father and a son looking out at a field.

— Boy with vague scene of activity in background.

The story contents are scored by *judges* in 12 categories, representing several facets of achievement motivation. A total of 11 categories is scored $+1$ each if they appear in a story and one category is scored -1 if it appears. Thus, the range of scores over four pictures is -4 to 44.[16] Examples of the scoring are given in Table 3.1.

Although the reliability of the test is far from perfect and the written stories require the subject to be literate and fairly articulate the TAT is favored as the only direct approach to the study of individual achievement motivation.[17] The direct questioning approach is considered disadvantageous since respondents could give *socially desirable* answers that would disguise their true achievement motives.

The need for achievement has been related to a number of economic phenomena, such as working performance resulting from different payment schedules, entrepreneurship and economic growth of societies.

In an experiment,[18] students competed for monetary rewards for those solving the largest number of arithmetic problems in a certain time allotted. Two different amounts were given as a reward in two experimental conditions: $1.25 and $2.50. In the low reward condition, subjects with a high nAch performed better than subjects with a low nAch. However, if the money reward was raised to $2.50, the performance of the subjects high in nAch remained about the same and the mean performances of the high and the low achievers were nearly equal.

Table 3.1. Scoring examples of the Thematic Apperception Test

−1.	Unrelated Imagery (UI) is scored for stories in which there is no reference to an achievement goal.
+1.	Achievement Imagery (AI) is scored for stories in which an achievement goal (success in competition with some standard of excellence) is included. Example: "He is trying to run faster".
+1.	Need (N) is scored if someone in the story states the desire to reach an achievement goal. Example: "He wants to do well".
+1.	Instrumental Activity (IA) is scored if the activity of at least one of the characters in the story indicates that something is being done to attain an achievement goal, whether successfully or unsuccessfully. Example: "He has been practising every day for a week".
+1.	Positive Anticipatory Goal State (Ga+) is scored if someone in the story anticipates goal attainment. Example: "He is thinking how great he will feel if he does".
+1.	Negative Anticipatory Goal State (Ga−) is scored if someone in the story anticipates frustration or failure with respect to the goal. Example: "He is thinking how badly he will feel if he fails".
+1.	Personal Obstacle or Block (Bp) is scored when the story mentions that the progress of goal directed activity is blocked by something for which the individual himself is responsible. Example: "He worries so much it slows him down".
+1.	Environmental Obstacle or Block (Be) is scored when the story mentions that the goal-directed activity is blocked by something in the environment. Example: "His mother thinks he is crazy to spend so much time running".
+1.	Positive Affective State (G+) is scored if someone in the story is described as feeling positive about goal attainment. Example: "He is happy he succeeded".
+1.	Negative Affective State (G−) is scored if someone in the story experiences an unpleasant feeling associated with failure to attain an achievement goal. Example: "He is unhappy he failed".
+1.	Nurturant Press (Nup) is scored when there are personal forces in the story which aid the character in his on-going achievement-related activity. Example: "His coach has given him some good advice on how to improve".
+1.	Achievement Theme (Ach Th) is scored when the achievement imagery is elaborated to become the central plot or theme of the story.

Composed from McClelland et al. (1953, pp. 110–138) and McClelland (1987, p. 192).

This indicates that offering money rewards to subjects high in nAch does not increase their drive, but may increase the performance of low achievers (cf. the example given at the start of this chapter). This result can be considered as an example of *overjustification* in that the monetary reward does not increase the motivating forces of subjects high in nAch.

Individuals high in nAch set *moderately difficult goals* for themselves, to maximize the likelihood of achievement satisfaction.[19] Too easy goals would be reached by everyone and would give no satisfaction; goals too hard to reach would most likely lead to failure and achievement dissatisfaction. This is consistent with the theory of optimal arousal levels.[20] The occupational aspirations of high and low achievers were examined to test this hypothesis.[21] It appeared that 81% of the vocational choices made by those high in nAch were confidently agreed to be realistic versus unrealistic, as compared with only 52% of the choices of those low in nAch. This should give subjects high in nAch a better start toward occupational success, since they would be more likely to pursue occupations that are realistic, given their education and abilities. The idea of an optimal level of task difficulty seems to be related to the hypothesis of an optimal level of stimulation.[22]

The relationship between the need for achievement and the careers of executives in a large company were examined over a three year period.[23] It was found that those with a high nAch received a larger number of promotions than those with low nAch scores.

The need for achievement of business executives in actual situations may also be related to nAch. On the basis of laboratory findings, is was hypothesized that business executives would score higher than professionals on need for achievement (see also Box 3.1).[24] Studies in a number of countries, including socialist Poland, bore out this expectation.

McClelland used the TAT procedure to examine the relationship between achievement needs and economic growth.[25] He made use of verbal material, available in contemporary as well as in ancient societies, to score the need for achievement. Prose material, such as children's readers, speeches, folktales, songs and so on, was scored according to the TAT procedure and related to available indices of economic activity, such as the consumption of electric power, the amount of coal imports, the number of independent artisans in a society, the number of patents and so on. Evidence has been found that increments in nAch precede economic development and decrements in nAch precede economic decline. McClelland's work is valued because it provides a *macro-psychological* theory of economic growth, despite later critiques in the literature.[26]

The TAT procedure has been applied to the reasons for migration given by immigrants living in an Austrian town.[27] It appeared that success motives,

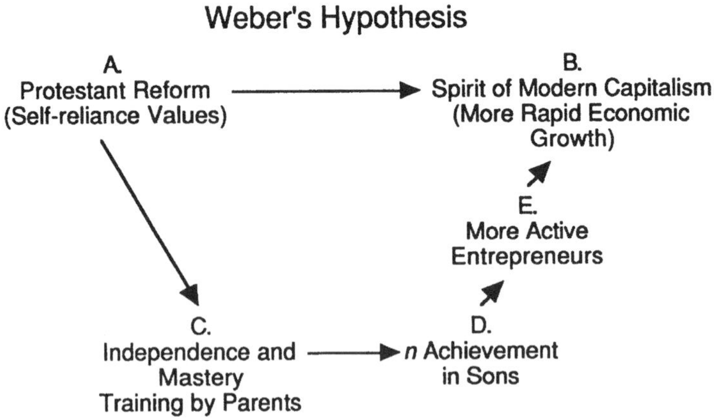

Weber's Hypothesis

A.
Protestant Reform
(Self-reliance Values) ─────────────▶ B.
                                      Spirit of Modern Capitalism
                                      (More Rapid Economic
                                      Growth)

                                      E.
                                      More Active
                                      Entrepreneurs

C.   D.
Independence and ────────▶ *n* Achievement
Mastery   in Sons
Training by Parents

Figure 3.2. Hypothesized effect of the Protestant Reformation on nAch and economic growth. From McClelland (1961).

as revealed by the TAT procedure, contributed to the explanation of the immigrants' wage rates in addition to a number of other factors.

The need for achievement is assumed to develop through independence and mastery training by parents during upbringing. Setting achievement demands on children at a moderately high level (neither too high nor too low) results in high achievement motivation.[28] This result supports Weber's hypothesis that capitalism was not invented by Protestants but that Protestant business people and workers were more energetic and entrepreneurial than Roman Catholics.[29] This might have been induced by the process depicted in Figure 3.2. The Protestant values favor early independence training and thus a high need for achievement. High nAch in turn breeds more active entrepreneurs, giving rise to a spirit of capitalism.

The developmental process considered above influences several motives to be dealt with below.

Conclusion

The need for achievement has a pervasive and enduring effect on individual behavior and on the economic development of a society. A powerful measurement technique, the Thematic Apperception Test, is used to assess nAch. Individuals high in nAch are intrinsically motivated to task performance and set moderately difficult goals for themselves. The nAch, like many other personality traits, develops during upbringing and affects the schooling and professional career.

3.3. Locus of control

A well-known phenomenon in gambling behavior is the ritual of dice-throwing, card shuffling, etcetera. This can be interpreted as generating an illusion of control over the outcomes of the game.[30] Moreover, it has been observed that people are less willing to wager after the dice have been thrown than before the throw.[31] Presumably they believe that being permitted to throw the dice themselves, i.e. to exercise their 'skill', will have some effect on the outcome.[32] Belief in the ability to exercise control over the environment is assumed to be characteristic of human beings but may be increased under some conditions. People's illusion of control over chance events may be increased by including in the situation elements usually associated with skill events, i.e. competition, choice, familiarity and involvement.[33] It was found that subjects in an experiment wager more if competition is low, as indicated by an inconfident opponent, than if competition is high, as indicated by a confident opponent. They value lottery tickets, selected by themselves, higher than tickets assigned to them by the experimenter. Tickets looking familiar were valued higher than tickets bearing unfamiliar symbols and characters. High involvement, as indicated by expending more effort and time, also induced higher ticket evaluations than low involvement. Although this behavior is explained by a natural tendency to control the environment and to avoid perceptions of having no control, errors in classifying the situations may also play a part. If more stimuli indicate a skill event than a chance event, a 'skill event' categorization is relatively likely.[34]

The psychological belief to exercise control over the environment has been labeled *locus of control* (LOC) in the psychological literature. When an individual action is followed by a result, not entirely *contingent* upon the action, typically it is considered the result of luck, chance, fate, as under the control of others or as unpredictable. If the event is interpreted in this way by an individual this is labeled a belief in *external control*.[35] If the person perceives that the event is contingent upon her own behavior, it is labeled a belief in *internal control*. The external control component has been distinguished according to whether events are contingent on powerful other people or on factors of luck and chance (see Figure 3.3).[36] Obviously, a person does not hold the same belief of control for each and every action taken. Also, the locus of control may change over time. However, the LOC is assumed to be relatively stable and, generally, people can be spotted somewhere on the internal-external continuum.

In Table 3.2 a number of statements are presented which were used in earlier versions of the *Internal-External Scale*. Of any pair of statements, subjects are forced to choose one. Each choice constitutes a subscore on the *I-E* scale, and the sum of the scores represents the individual locus of control.

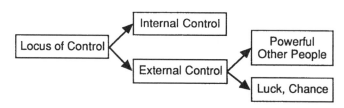

Figure 3.3. Distinctions of locus of control.

Table 3.2. A sample of locus of control statements.

I more strongly believe that:

1. a.   Many people can be described as victims of circumstances.
    b.   What happens to other people is pretty much of their own making.
2. a.   Much of what happens to me is probably a matter of luck.
    b.   I control my own fate.
3. a.   The world is so complicated that I just cannot figure things out.
    b.   The world is really complicated all right but I can usually work things out by effort and persistence.
4. a.   It is silly to think one can really change another's basic attitudes.
    b.   When I am right I can convince others.
5. a.   Most students would be amazed at how much grades are determined by capricious events.
    b.   The marks I get in class are entirely my own responsibility.

From Phares (1978, p.271). In: H. London and J.E. Exner Jr. (eds.) Dimensions of Personality. Copyright ©1978 by John Wiley and Sons, Inc. Reprinted by permission of John Wiley & Sons, Inc.

The final version of the scale has been constructed in such a way that the tendency to give socially desirable answers minimally affects the LOC score.

The locus of control has a pervasive effect on the performance of all kinds of behavior and on the evaluation of circumstances.

Generally, it has been found that internals exert more effort when a task is thought to be skill-demanding than when it is simply a matter of chance; externals do not differentiate as much between these two kinds of tasks. It has been found that internal tuberculosis hospital patients possessed more information about their physical condition and were more demanding of such information from both physicians and nurses. In a similar way, internals show more prophylactic dental behavior, use more seat belts in cars, take more preventive medical shots, participate more in physical fitness activity, etcetera.

People who are more internally controlled tend to be more open to information, take more initiatives, assume more responsibility and be more creative, if this is relevant to their manipulation and control over the environment, than those who are more externally controlled. The development of locus of control partly results from upbringing and education. In addition, there is a clear relationship with social class in that ethnic and minority groups that possess little access to social or economic power are more likely to have an external locus of control. The poorer an individual is, the more external forces (e.g. the state or management of the economy) are considered responsible for this situation.[37] In attribution theory, the conditions for reporting external causes of events are relevant, too.[38]

It has been shown that business leaders generally have a high degree of internal locus of control.[39] Top executives who are more internally controlled tend to pursue more product-market innovation, undertake greater risks and lead rather than follow competitors. Also, entrepreneurs tend to be more internally controlled.

Regional differences in locus of control have been examined in relation to striking differences in protective measures against tornados.[40] Although Alabama and Illinois are annually struck by equally large numbers of severe tornados, many more tornado-related deaths occur each year in Alabama. It appeared that Alabamans tended to be much more fatalistic or external in their responses[41] than people from Illinois. People in Illinois make more active efforts to protect themselves from tornados, listening to the radio for warnings and retreating to a safe place in the event of an approaching tornado.

Conclusion

The LOC can be distinguished in internal and external beliefs regarding control over one's own behavior and the environment. This influences self-protecting behavior, information seeking and entrepreneurial behavior. LOC is related to the causal attribution of events.[42] An important conclusion from the LOC research seems to be that people with belief in internal control can be motivated to perform better if the outcomes of their behavior are made contingent upon their own efforts (or if they can be led to believe so).

3.4. Sensation seeking and risk attitude

In economics, it has been assumed that man strives for the satisfaction of his needs, thus creating utility, and minimizes his efforts to obtain goods and services. If all needs are satisfied, boredom begins and people start looking for all kinds of stimulation.[43] Economics has no explanation for this phenomenon, nor does it take into account the possibility of joyful productive activity. Many jobs are not exclusively performed to obtain financial rewards but to experience the thrill and the challenge of the task demands.

Table 3.3. Selected items from the Sensation Seeking Scale

For each of the following items decide which of the two choices best describes your likes and feelings. If neither choice applies, choose the one that most describes you. Answer all items.

1. a. I like the tumult of sound in a busy city
   b. I prefer the peace and quiet of the country.
2. a. I dislike the sensations one gets when flying.
   b. I enjoy many of the rides in amusement parks.
3. a. I would like a job which would require a lot of traveling.
   b. I would prefer a job in one location.
4. a. I often wish I could be a mountain climber.
   b. I can't understand people who risk their necks climbing mountains.
5. a. I get bored seeing the same old faces.
   b. I like the comfortable familiarity of everyday friends.
6. a. I like to explore a strange city or section of town by myself, even if it means getting lost.
   b. I prefer a guide when I am in a place I don't know well.
7. a. I find people that disagree with my beliefs more stimulating than people that agree with me.
   b. I don't like to argue with people whose beliefs are sharply divergent from mine, since such arguments are never resolved.
8. a. I prefer more subdued colors in decoration.
   b. I like to decorate with bright colors.
9. a. When I have nothing to do or look at for any length of time, I get very restless.
   b. I often enjoy just relaxing and doing nothing.
10. a. Most people spend far too much money on life insurance.
    b. Life insurance is something that no man can afford to be without.
11. a. I don't like to drink coffee because it overstimulates me and keeps me awake.
    b. I like to drink coffee because of the lift it gives me.
12. a. The worst social sin is to be rude.
    b. The worst social sin is to be a bore.
13. a. The most important goal of life is to live it to the full and experience as much of it as you can.
    b. The most important goal of life is to find peace and happiness.
14. a. If I were a salesman, I would prefer working on commission if I had a chance to make more money than I could on a salary.
    b. If I were a salesman, I would prefer a straight salary rather than the risk of making little or nothing on a commission basis.
15. a. I like sharp or spicy foods.
    b. I prefer foods with a minimum of seasoning.

How to score your answers. Count one point for sensation seeking for each of the following: 1a, 2b, 3a, 4a, 5a, 6a, 7a, 8b, 9a, 10a, 11b, 12b, 13a, 14a, 15a.
If you answered eleven or more items this way, you probably have a strong motivation for sensation seeking. If you answered five items or less this way, you probably have a weak motive for sensation seeking. If you responded this way six to ten times, you are probably in the average range of sensation seekers. The older one gets the more sensation seeking scores go down. These items represent an abbreviated version of Zuckerman's Sensation Seeking Scale.
From Zuckerman, M., Sensation Seeking ©1979 Lawrence Erlbaum Associates, Hillsdale, NJ.

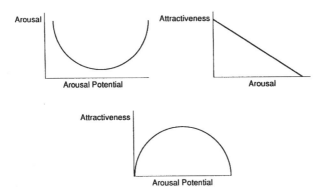

Figure 3.4. The relations between collative properties, arousal and attractiveness. From Berlyne (1963, pp. 318–319). In: S. Koch (ed.) Psychology: A Study of a Science. Copyright © 1963 by McGraw-Hill. Reproduced by permission of McGraw-Hill, Inc.

Boredom has been empirically investigated in experiments with sensory deprivation. If people are disconnected from the environment by impeding their sight, hearing and other senses, they first become bored, then anxious and finally experience hallucinations and delusions. However, the period before these experiences occurred varied across people. To measure the need for stimulation or optimal levels of stimulation, a questionnaire was devised.[44] In Table 3.3 a sample of items of this *Sensation Seeking Scale* (SSS) is presented.

The theory of exploratory behavior assumes the existence of an optimal level of stimulation which is most attractive to people. Stimuli with *collative* properties, such as novelty, surprisingness, change, ambiguity, incongruity, blurredness and power may induce uncertainty, which are able to produce *arousal*[45] in the human organism.[46] A lack of collative properties, e.g. with sensory deprivation or near the perceptual threshold,[47] as well as an overabundance of them, e.g. with information overload,[48] causes high arousal, which is experienced as uncomfortable. An intermediate amount of collative properties produces a low level of arousal, which is assumed to be most attractive to people.[49] (See Figure 3.4.)

The assumption that moderate amounts of collative stimuli (and a low level of arousal) are most attractive has implications for the marketing of holiday parks, movies, tours, etcetera. On the one hand, these services should offer neither too much nor too little novelty and surprise. On the other hand, a low level of arousal should be guaranteed (e.g. by stressing relaxation and comfort).

The scores on the SSS have been found to show a significant correlation between various kinds of risk taking behavior and risky professions. The SSS correlates with subjects' proportions of bets made at the highest risk options in a card drawing game. The SSS differs significantly between skydivers and controls, between firemen, riot squad police (volunteers), racing car drivers, parachutists, snowmobilers and a control group composed of civil servants and college students. Further differences have been found between patrolmen and sheriff's deputies and a group of jailers, between professional and para-professional volunteers working in crisis intervention centers and professionals working in more traditional academic and clinical roles and between volunteer groups of divers engaged in underwater rescue and salvage work, volunteer groups of fireman who also took risks without being paid for doing so, and students at an institute of technology. The SSS also correlates with students' reported preferences for streaking (taking off one's clothes and running through a public place), a popular activity in the seventies.

In economic psychological experiments with lotteries,[50] the SSS might explain the subject's choice between the sure and the uncertain alternatives, although this has not yet been tested.

In social dilemma situations,[51] the SSS might explain the choice between strategies, corresponding with cooperative and competitive solutions to the situation. In situations where the best outcome depends on the behavior of others, the probability of the other's strategies is important. Thus the risk attitude is likely to affect behavior in social dilemma situations. This possibility has still to be investigated, however.

Although the SSS has been correlated with trivial activities, the implications for economic *risk attitudes* are interesting. It can be assumed that the SSS relates to, *inter alia*, taking insurance, investment behavior, entrepreneurship and tax evasion. Attitudes of risk aversion and risk seeking might increase the explanation of behavior from economic variables alone.

A final remark has to be made regarding the perception of the risky option at hand. Mountaineering, for example, is considered a dangerous activity by many people and presumably preference for it is related to the risk attitude. However, a self-confident young man in excellent physical condition might consider mountaineering merely as a sportsmanlike activity, devoid of risk. In the latter case, preference for mountaineering is probably less related to the risk attitude. This possibility may arise in entrepreneurial behavior, since entrepreneurs are very alert to the discovery of opportunities and information and appear to suffer less from biases in information processing.[52] An undertaking, normally considered risky in the usual sense (including financial institutions financing the project), may be perceived as having a relatively high probability of success by entrepreneurs, because of their greater information and experience in this area.

Conclusion

Sensation seeking applies to the desired level of stimulation in performing behavior. It appears that a moderate exposure to collative stimuli produces the lowest level of arousal which is most attractive. The perception of stimulating or risky alternatives further determines what is the optimal level of stimulation for an individual. Sensation seeking also influences the type of professional activities.

3.5. Altruism

In many situations, for example in traffic, cooperative behavior is required rather than the pursuit of immediate advantage for oneself. In social relationships, such as the family, the behavior of an individual benefits from the influence of others. In many instances, for example blood donation, people behave selflessly in the interest of others. These modes of behavior are based largely on altruistic motivations, the strength of which may vary across people and across situations.

In economics, *altruism* has been formally accounted for by including the utility of others in the utility function of an individual.[53] An interesting example to show two different ways in which another person's state may affect utility is the following.

"The masochist begs the sadist: 'Torture me!'
'No!' says the sadist."[54]

In a 'love-based' approach, individual 1's utility is affected by individual 2's utility. This approach is expressed in the quotation above. In an 'altruism-based' approach, individual 1's utility is affected by 2's objective state variables, such as income, health, etcetera. The latter approach implies that some weight is given to the other's outcomes. In this approach, sadists should torture because the masochists' pain would increase their utility.

A simple version of this idea has been examined in psychology,[55] distinguishing the outcome P of a person and the outcome O of another individual. The altruistic motivation with respect to the other person is captured by the weight, a, given to O. The individual's preference toward the joint outcome of the two persons can be characterized by $P + aO$. If a equals 1, the person strives for a maximal sum of outcomes for herself and for the other person. This results in cooperative behavior. If a equals 0, the person strives for a maximal outcome for herself, ignoring the other's outcome. This results in individualistic behavior. If a equals -1, the person strives for a maximal difference between the two outcomes in her own favor. This results in competitive behavior.

In practice, a will take values anywhere on the $(-1, 1)$ interval, indicating a certain degree of altruistic motivation. The weight, a, is not assumed to be constant but may vary according to whether the other person is a relative, a friend, a stranger or an antagonist. Furthermore, a may depend on the outcome involved. For example, one may be altruistic with small services but not with money.

It has been attempted to measure the degree of altruism by asking subjects for their preferences toward a distribution of salary (or grades) between themselves and others.[56] Subjects preferring the same salary for themselves and for others were classified as cooperative. A preference for a salary difference was classified as competitive. If the salary of others was not correlated with preferences for one's own salary, this was classified as individualistic. It appeared that subjects were more altruistic toward friends than toward strangers and more altruistic toward strangers than toward antagonists. What is more, in general, social science students showed more altruism. Business students are more strictly concerned with maximizing their own welfare, regardless of other people's. Large differences between self-interested behavior by economists and non-economists exist.[57] Economists are more likely to free-ride in ultimatum bargaining games, Prisoner's Dilemma games[58] and charitable giving. Training in economic theory (notably game theory) seems to increase self-interested behavior.

In general, a is assumed to vary between -1 and 1. However, a may exceed these values, for example if one values one's own outcomes less than the other's. This may only occur if the other person sets a higher value on her own outcome. If both partners in a social relationship do this, the result will be a 'combat de générosité'. A generalization of this framework adds a weight, b, to an individual's own outcomes, so that she evaluates $bP + aO$.[59] The weight b may also be assumed to vary between -1 and 1 (actually, the scale of the weights is not important). This may be represented graphically in a two-dimensional space, consisting of outcome axes of two individuals (see Figure 3.5).

Altruism also has been used to explain incomplete crowding out.[60] A model of impure altruism was developed in which individuals not only contribute to a public good because they receive their share of it but also because they may obtain utility from their gift per se, like a *warm glow*.[61] The pure altruism model holds that people are concerned with the final distribution only. Consequently, in Bolton and Katok's experiment, all who choose 10–10 in 18–2 would choose 10–10 in 15–5; gifts of 8 and 5 respectively. In contrast, the impure altruism model posits that at least some people receive utility – a warm glow – from the actual act of giving a gift, and the amount of utility is influenced by the size of the gift. Consequently, some who choose to donate

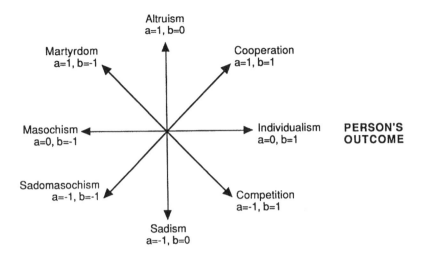

Figure 3.5. Classifications of preferences for own and other's outcomes. Composed by permission from Lurie, S., ©1987 American Psychological Association and C.G. McClintock, R.M. Kramer and L.J. Keil 1984, New York: Academic Press.

8 in 18–2 could donate more than 5 in 15–5. Indeed, no one in the 18–2 treatment gave more than 8, but three people in the 15–5 treatment gave more than 5.[62]

Altruism is associated with biological instincts, empathy and social norms such as social responsibility, equity (fairness) and reciprocity.[63] Learning processes may enhance altruistic behavior, e.g. by reward and punishment or by imitation of a model.[64]

In economic psychology, altruism has been related to helping behavior,[65] voluntarism,[66] gifts and charitable donations and behavior in social dilemma situations and negotiations. The framework presented above makes it possible to study more diverse types of behavior, including competition and individualism.

Conclusion

Altruism implies a particular weight associated with outcomes of another individual. This affects the preferred distribution of money (or income), the probability of cooperative behavior, charitable donations, among others. In economics, the assumption of utility maximization is retained by including the other individual's outcomes in the utility function.

3.6. Time preference

In economics, intertemporal choice is implied in dynamic models of consumption. The question of consuming now or saving and investing in order to consume more later is a fundamental economic question faced by individuals, families, corporations and entire nations.

A person is said to exhibit a *general time preference* if, when confronted with a potential stock of resources to be allocated over periods of time in the future, she allocates those resources in such a way that the time distribution is skewed toward or away from the present.[67] A *positive time preference* is a preference for allocation of resources in or near the present. A *negative time preference* is a preference for delaying the allocation of resources.

Time preference can be related to the psychological concept of willingness to delay gratification.[68] It has been observed in experiments that children vary with respect to the willingness to defer a reward (e.g. a certain amount of candy) in order to receive a greater reward (e.g. a larger amount of candy) at some later point in time. Furthermore, it is assumed that *delay of gratification* can be learned in the course of socialization (especially from parents and peers by means of *social learning*[69]) beginning at a very early age. Delay of gratification has a very pervasive and stable effect on behavior. It was observed, for example, that a preschool child's ability to delay gratification for pretzels or marshmallows is related to her socially competent behavior some twelve years later.[70]

In society, the measure of the willingness to save a sum of money now in order to receive a greater amount of money in the future is the interest rate. An interest rate of 7% per annum, for example, indicates that in general people are willing to save $100 in order to receive $107 a year later. Many people, however, are not willing to save at this interest rate but demand, for example, $130 a year later. This corresponds to a *subjective interest rate* of 30% per annum. The greater the subjective interest rate, the greater the positive time preference will be. In studies of consumer behavior regarding capital goods, subjective interest (or discount) rates have been estimated at 25% per year for the purchase of air conditioners[71] and 21% for the replacement of washing machines.[72]

The measurement of time preference has been conducted in various ways, for example by the following type of question:

> "If offered $100 now or X dollars in six months, what would be the *smallest* amount of money (X dollars) you would accept rather than the immediately available $100?"[73]

Variations on this question include presenting the future amount and asking subjects for the current value and presenting both amounts and asking for the time period. An alternative measure of time preference is provided by forced choice items such as the following:

"Suppose you had a choice between a cash bonus of $100 today and $200 a year from now: which would you choose?"[74]

This question may be followed by others in a 'cascade' fashion, for example (if the subject chose $200):

"Suppose you had a choice between a cash bonus of $100 today and $175 a year from now: which would you choose?"

and so on until the subject chooses $100. The choices of respondents can be used directly as an indication of time preference or an *implicit interest rate* can be inferred from the answers.

These measures have been used in a number of experiments to study the effects of the amount of money, the length of the time period and whether the sum involved was associated with a gain or a loss.[75] Studies have also been made of the relationships between the implicit interest rate and socio-demographic variables on the one hand and other types of behavior on the other.

A decreasing implicit interest rate was found with increasing money amounts and with increasing time periods.[76] These results are contrary to the behavior of the market rental rate associated with a deposit's volume and the lending period. What is more, the implicit interest rate appeared to be lower for losses than for gains, indicating a greater willingness to delay losses than to delay gains. Experiments conducted with students in economics and finance yielded an average implicit interest rate of 14.3% per annum, which compares favorably with the annual interest rates in Israel on bank loans and savings linked to the U.S. dollar (15% and 10% respectively) at that time.[77] An experiment with subjects not trained in economics or finance, showed implicit interest rates varying from 35% to 139% on average in the various question types.[78] Different rates of time preference with different amounts and time intervals were replicated in a Dutch survey, too.[79]

The probability of taking the money now versus taking it in the future was related to the implicit interest rate and a number of socio-economic variables.[80] According to expectations, the probability of taking the money now (indicating positive time preference) decreases with the implicit interest rate of the 'cascade' questions asked, and increases with the implicit interest rate revealed by the other type of questions mentioned above.[81] Moreover, positive time preference was lower (for males) at higher ages and at a higher level of education of the parent. The expected inflation had a positive effect on the probability of taking the money now. However, the explained variance of time preference by the variables included in the analyses was not very impressive.

Table 3.4. Implicit discount rate and income.

Income class	Implicit discount rate (in %)
less than $6,000	89
$6,000–$10,000	39
$10,000–$15,000	27
$15,000–$25,000	17
$25,000–$35,000	8.9
$35,000–$50,000	5.1

From Hausman (1979). Copyright 1979. Reprinted by permission of RAND.

Time preference has also been investigated with respect to health related behavior.[82] Activities or physical condition such as smoking, overweight, delay of dental checkups, physical exercise and the use of seat belts are presumably related to time preference with respect to health. Actually, small correlations were found between these health related behaviors. The relations between time preference and health related behaviors are either not significant (except for smoking) or in the wrong direction. It has been concluded that even if there is a common factor at work across behaviors, there are also other factors that are specific to particular behaviors.

Fisher has already mentioned the effect of income on the time preference.[83] He suggested that a small income, other things equal, tends to produce a high rate of *impatience*, partly from the thought that provision for the present is necessary both for the present itself and for the future as well and partly from lack of foresight and self-control.

Impatience may depend on age and social class because young people have yet to master the techniques of *self-control*.[84] Class differences are expected in as much as these techniques are transferred in upbringing. Fisher's suggestion has been substantiated by research showing a subjective implicit discount rates decreasing with income.[85] (See Table 3.4.)

Fisher also mentions the time shape of the income stream as influencing impatience. People expecting an increased income in the future value extra consumption in the present more than extra consumption in the future, resulting in a high subjective discount rate. This suggestion is consistent with Katona's assumption regarding saving behavior of consumers. During a recession, net savings are predicted to grow because people are strongly motivated to save. During an upswing, net savings will decline because people are less strongly motivated to save.[86]

The implicit discount rate has also been estimated from replacement decisions regarding a consumer durable.[87] The implicit discount rate has been

Table 3.5. Implicit discount rate according to current and expected financial position.

	Expected position	
	Pessimistic	Optimistic
Current position (saving)	9.6%	32.4%
Current position (not saving)	27.6%	42.0%

From Antonides (1990).

distinguished according to whether the subjects were able to save from their income or not and whether they held *optimistic or pessimistic expectations* regarding their future financial situation.[88] The results in Table 3.5 appear to be according to Fisher's suggestions. The results imply that advanced replacement of a durable is more likely if the implicit discount rate is high.

A general paradigm has been proposed to account for differences in time preference.[89] It deals with evaluations (e.g. gains or losses) and expectations (e.g. uncertainty) regarding the outcomes that are discounted on the one hand and with external (e.g. physical, environmental) and internal factors (e.g. knowledge, attitudes, motivations) influencing the evaluations and expectations, on the other hand. The paradigm can be used to integrate experimental findings and to stimulate further research.

Conclusion

Time preference refers to the preference for allocating resources either in the present or in the future. The concept is associated with the willingness to delay gratification and with the ability to save. Measurements involve the estimation of the subjective interest rate, which appears to be associated with socio-demographic characteristics and economic expectations. Time preference in economic behavior has been generalized to other types of behavior, however with inconclusive results.

3.7. Cognitive style

Several psychological theories are concerned with the characteristic way people regard their environment. Whereas economics assumes that people are able to assess their environment correctly, in actual fact the ability to differentiate the environment and integrate the information varies across people. This variation might lead to different economic behavior, even if individual circumstances and preferences are the same. The ability to differentiate and integrate information facilitates the processing of information, decision

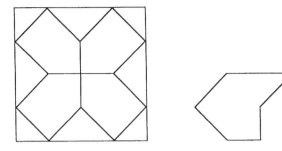

Figure 3.6. An example of figures used in the Embedded Figure Test. Source: Psychological Laboratory, State University of Utrecht, The Netherlands.

making and problem solving.[90] It can be assumed to accelerate learning and adaptation to new environments.

Several measures of cognitive differentiation have been developed. The *Rod and Frame Test* (RFT) measures a subject's susceptibility to environmental influences on her judgment.[91] In the RFT, the subject is seated in a darkened room in front of a luminous rod surrounded by a luminous square frame. Both the square frame and the subject's chair can be tilted to the left and to the right. The subject is asked to adjust the rod to the vertical position, while the frame and the seat remain in the tilted position. The degree of deviation from the true vertical is a measure of the subject's *field-dependence*, that is the extent to which the subject is influenced by the environment in her opinion regarding the vertical position of the rod.

Another measure of cognitive differentiation is the *Embedded Figure Test* (EFT). In the EFT, subjects are asked to locate a simple geometric figure within a more complex one. (See Figure 3.6.) Several pairs of simple and complex figures are presented and cognitive differentiation is measured as the total time needed to locate the simple figures.[92]

Yet another measure of cognitive differentiation is the *Figure Drawing Test*.[93] In this test, subjects are asked to draw a male and a female figure. These figures are scored by judges with respect to the presence or absence in the figures of a number of features, e.g. buttons, rings, boot-laces. The more differentiated the figures, the more the subject is assumed to differentially perceive the environment.

A test of cognitive differentiation developed in social psychology is the *Interpersonal Discrimination Test*.[94] In this test, subjects are asked to rate a number of persons from their close environment (e.g. parents, relatives, friends) along ten dimensions such as outgoing-shy, friendly-unfriendly, etcetera. Individuals who rate their set of persons in a similar way on several dimensions are designated cognitively simple, whereas those who rate these persons as differently on each dimension are designated as cognitively complex.

The cognitive differentiation concept has been found to influence the performance of cognitive tasks.[95] It can be assumed that cognitively complex individuals are more able to extract information out of a complex environment, to integrate more of this information in a meaningful way and in general to progress in rational decision making. A simple cognitive style might induce simplifying strategies of information processing.[96]

Field-dependence was found to develop during early childhood and to be very stable over time. Mothers fostering the development of differentiation in their children and mothers giving evidence of a developed body concept tend to have children who show articulacy of experience of the field, a developed body concept and a sense of separate identity.[97] Field-independence increases with age and appears to be present more frequently in males than in females.

The cognitive differentiation concept is relevant to consumer behavior.[98] Cognitively complex individuals are expected to be more active in their search for information and to form more accurate impressions of products and people. They also include both liked and disliked stimuli in their evaluation of products and services. Therefore they can be assumed to purchase products and services that are unlikely to prove unsatisfactory. Cognitively simple individuals might be more susceptible to one-sided persuasive communication (e.g. in ads). Cognitively complex individuals prefer more balanced information about goods and may even become intolerant of information totally congruent with existing beliefs. This suggests that messages aimed at changes in attitudes toward products and services should be designed in different ways depending on the audience to be reached.

The research considered above does not suggest which of the *cognitive style* tests are related most directly to economic behavior. Different aspects of cognitive style might relate to different aspects of economic behavior. These relations, however, still have to be investigated.

An interesting question is the theoretical relationship between cognitive style and various personality dimensions from the literature. In one study, people were classified as rational or emotional persons by using a variety of scales, such as 'Verstandes- und Gefühlsmenschen', disciplined, conscientious and introvert versus impulsive, easy-going and extravert.[99] Obviously, these scales are relevant to the style of information processing and decision making. Another dimension capturing the personal motivation to think about a problem and to expend cognitive effort, is the *need for cognition*.[100] The need for cognition is assumed to influence the likelihood of cognitive elaboration in information processing.[101] Further research may show the theoretical relationships between these concepts.

Conclusion

Cognitive style refers to the ability to differentiate the environment and integrate the information. It has been measured in different ways, e.g. the Rod and Frame Test, the Embedded Figure Test, the Figure Drawing Test, and the Interpersonal Discrimination Test. In short, it concerns the perception of cognitive and social stimuli, including the perception of consumer information.

3.8. Life-style

The motivations and personality traits considered above are general in that they affect many types of behavior. The study of this may be sufficient for the theoretical development of psychology; however, for practical purposes it may be advantageous to have traits that are more specifically related to a particular kind of behavior, e.g. the purchase of a specific brand product. A more practical classification of people can be achieved by describing their various *life-styles*, incorporating patterns of living and ways of spending time and money.

The VALS system distinguishes nine American life-styles which are characterized by certain values, demographics and buying patterns.[102] (See Figure 3.7.) The theoretical basis of VALS is Maslow's hierarchy.[103]

Two consumer types, the survivors and the sustainers, are need-driven. The survivors, for example, are characterized by a struggle for survival, are distrustful, socially misfitted and ruled by appetite. Their demographic characterization is poverty-level income, little education, many minority groups and a high incidence of slum dwelling. The buying pattern is price dominant, focused on basic necessities to satisfy immediate needs.

Three other types, the belongers, emulators and achievers, are outer directed and generally buy with awareness of how other people might evaluate their consumption.

The inner-directed consumers comprise four types, the I-Am-Me, the experiential, the socially aware and the integrated. Their lives are directed more toward their individual needs than toward values oriented to externals. Their numbers are small but increasing and they may be important as trend setters.

The *segmentation* considered above is only one possibility. Other classification schemes have been developed, e.g. for the unemployed, for students, for special markets like the market for fancy goods, second-hand articles, cars, etcetera. Most of the life-style traits have been measure by means of self-reports in questionnaires. Lastovicka (1982) lists more than a hundred different life-style traits and notices that the superabundance of these traits presents problems with respect to the validity of the concepts. Wells (1975) also has critical remarks regarding the reliability and validity of life-style

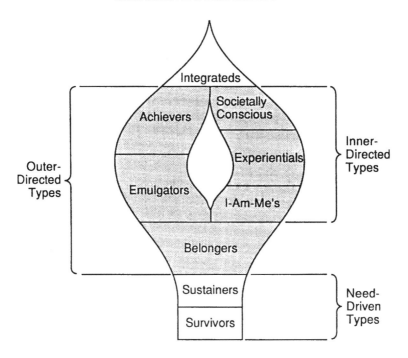

Figure 3.7. The nine VALS segments. Source: SRI International, Menlo Park, California.

traits and measurements.

The study of life-styles or *psychographics* is relevant to marketers and consumer researchers.[104] Psychographics is better able to provide lively descriptions of types of people that can be used in advertising, publishing, innovative production, etcetera, than demographic or personality classifications alone. Psychographic measures refer to the activities, interests and opinions (AIO's) of consumers.[105]

As an example, the demographic and psychographic profiles of heavy users of shotgun ammunition may be compared.[106] The man who spends at least $11 per year on shotgun shells differs from the non-buyer in that he tends to be younger, lower in income and education and more concentrated in blue collar occupations. He is also more apt to be living in rural areas, especially in the South. However, the demographic picture leaves unanswered a number of questions, for example:

— Is the hunter attracted by violence in general?
— Is the hunter also a fisherman or is he a camper?
— Is he a regular patron of discount stores?

A psychographic profile reveals that hunting is associated with fishing, camping, outdoor work, do-it-yourself activities and attraction to violence.

This suggests, for example, that promotional activities such as advertising are expected to be more successful in the neighborhood of camping and fishing sites and in action and adventure magazines.

Conclusion

Life-style refers to the specific activities, interests and opinions (AIO's) of individuals rather than to their general dispositions. Since the AIO's are associated more closely with consumer goods, psychographics is a practical market segmentation device.

Summary

A selection of motivations and personality traits, studied in economic psychology, has been presented in this chapter. These are assumed to influence the perception and evaluation of goods, services and outcomes of individual behavior. In economic psychology, it is assumed that motivations influence the utility function. In later chapters, it will be considered how these motivations and traits relate to utility functions and to the formation of attitudes.

In Section 2.4 it has been assumed that motivation and personality are related to socio-demographic variables. These relations have not been considered extensively in this chapter. Generally, motivational dispositions are shaped by upbringing and education. Motivations are assumed to influence economic behavior via their effect on mental processes such as perception, information processing, attitude formation and expectations.

With respect to motivational and situational influences on behavior, their interaction is assumed in contemporary psychology. This is evident from the combined effects on behavior of:
- nAch, goal setting and overjustification;
- LOC and task demands;
- sensation seeking and collative stimuli;
- differential altruism toward different people;
- time preference and financial situation;
- cognitive style and the amount and type of information.

From the motivation and personality research, it has become clear that great variation across individuals exists. This partly explains differences in economic behavior.

BOX 3.1

LEE IACOCCA

The former general manager of Ford (and later Chrysler), Lee Iacocca, can be considered not only as an excellent manager, but also as an interesting personality. From his autobiography, it is clear that he is highly motivated toward achieving. He gives several examples which show how his father served both as model and as stimulator in striving to achieve.

"With all my extracurricular activities, I still managed to graduate twelfth in a class of over nine hundred. To show you the kind of expectations I grew up with, my father's reaction was: "Why weren't you first?" To hear him describe it, you'd think I flunked!"[107]

Then he tells:

"I was also motivated by the pressure from my father that was typical among immigrant families, where any kid who was fortunate enough to attend college was expected to compensate for his parents' lack of education. It was up to me to take advantage of all the opportunities they never had, so I had to be at the top of my class."[108]

In his early years at Ford, Iacocca had to acquire experience with several sections of the firm:

"I even spent four weeks on the final assembly line. My job was to attach a cap to a wiring harness on the inside of a truck frame. It wasn't hard work but it was tedious as hell. My mother and father came to visit one day and when my dad saw me in overalls, he smiled and said: "Seventeen years you went to school. See what happens to the dummies who don't finish first in their class?""[109]

One aspect of the achievement motivation is to set high goals:

"I did much better in these subjects, finishing my last year with straight A's. My goal was a 3.5 grade average so I could graduate with high honors. I made it by a hair – ending up at 3.53. They say that this generation is competitive. You should have seen us at work!"[110]

Iacocca seemed hardly satisfied with his accomplishments which were to serve as motivators to breed still higher aspirations. After Henry Ford made Iacocca head of the Ford Division, the following goal was set:

"I was thrilled by the promotion but I could see that it put me in a delicate position. On the one hand, I was suddenly running the company's elite division. Henry Ford had personally entrusted me with the crown jewels.

On the other hand, I had bypassed a hundred older and more experienced people on my way up the ladder. Some of them, I knew, were resentful of my quick success. In addition, I still had no real credentials as a product man. At this point in my career there was no car that people could point to and say: "Iacocca did that one.""[111]

A few years later, the Mustang was introduced. This proved to be a real hit in the car market.

Being achievement orientated is generally considered a stable personality trait. Iacocca demonstrates that it remains active even in hard times:

"But if you really believe in what you're doing, you've got to persevere even when you run into obstacles. When I finished sulking, I doubled my efforts and worked even harder. In a few months I had my old job back. Setbacks are a natural part of life and you've got to be careful how you respond to them. If I had sulked too long, I probably would have got myself fired."[112]

Clearly, not everyone with a high performance motivation reaches the top. However, it appears to be a favorable condition to achieve success.

Notes

[1] Mischel 1968.

[2] Epstein and O'Brien 1985.

[3] Epstein 1979, 1980.

[4] Lastovicka and Joachimsthaler 1988, Epstein and O'Brien 1985, see also Section 16.5.

[5] Brandstätter 1993.

[6] McCrae and Costa 1987.

[7] Deci and Ryan 1980.

[8] See Section 2.3.

[9] Frey 1994, p.335.

[10] Deci and Porac 1978.

[11] See Section 11.3.

[12] Lepper and Greene 1978.

[13] Frey 1993.

[14] Maslow 1954.

[15] Murray 1938, p.164.

[16] See Byrne 1966, p.294.

[17] McClelland 1961.

[18] Atkinson 1958.

[19] Atkinson 1958.

[20] Berlyne 1963, see Section 3.4.

[21] Mahone 1960.

[22] See Sections 3.4 and 9.2.

[23] Andrews 1967.

[24] McClelland 1961.

[25] McClelland et al. 1953.

[26] Wärneryd 1988.

[27] Winter-Ebmer 1994.

[28] McClelland 1987.

[29] Weber 1904/1930.

[30] Lea et al. 1987.

[31] Strickland et al. 1966.

[32] Cohen 1960.

[33] Langer 1975.

[34] See Section 12.3 regarding the categorization of gains and losses.

[35] Rotter 1966, p. 1.

[36] Levenson 1973.

[37] Strümpel 1976.

[38] See Section 11.3.

[39] Wärneryd 1988.

[40] Sims and Baumann 1972.

[41] That is, they made more external attributions, see Section 11.3.

[42] See Section 11.3.

[43] Scitovsky 1976.

[44] Zuckerman 1978.

[45] General excitation, see Chapter 9.

[46] Berlyne 1963.

[47] See Chapter 4.

[48] See Chapter 7.

[49] The relationship between level of arousal and task performance will be considered in Section 9.2.

[50] For example, Kahneman and Tversky 1979, see also Chapter 13.

[51] See Chapter 14.

[52] Wärneryd 1988, see also Chapter 7.

[53] Becker 1981.

[54] Bolle 1992, p. 509.

[55] Sawyer 1965.

[56] Sawyer 1965.

[57] Frank et al. 1993.

[58] See Chapter 16.

[59] Lurie 1983.

[60] See Section 2.3.

[61] Andreoni 1989.

[62] Bolton and Katok 1995, see Section 2.3.

[63] Lea et al. 1987, Batson et al. 1988.

[64] See Chapter 5.

[65] Latané and Nida 1981.

[66] Unger 1991.

[67] Yates 1972.

[68] Mischel 1974.

[69] See Chapter 5.

[70] Mischel 1984.

[71] Hausman 1979.

[72] Antonides 1990.

[73] Thomas and Ward 1979, cited in Fuchs 1982, p. 97.

[74] Fuchs 1982, p. 97.

[75] Fuchs 1982, Maital et al. 1986, Thaler 1981, Benzion et al. 1989.

[76] Benzion et al. 1989.

[77] Benzion et al. 1989.

[78] Thaler 1981.

[79] Daniel 1994.

[80] Fuchs 1982.

[81] Thomas and Ward 1979.

[82] Fuchs 1982.

[83] Fisher 1930.

[84] Thaler and Shefrin 1981, see Section 12.6.

[85] Hausman 1979.

[86] Katona 1974.

[87] Antonides 1990.

[88] See Chapter 8.

[89] Jungermann 1988.

[90] See Chapter 7.

[91] Witkin et al. 1962.

[92] Witkin et al. 1979.

[93] Harris 1963.

[94] Bieri 1955.

[95] Span 1973.

[96] For example, *satisficing*, see Chapter 7.

[97] Witkin et al. 1962, pp. 366–367.

[98] Pinson 1978.

[99] Schmöelders, cited in Brandstätter 1993.

[100] Cacioppo and Petty 1982.

[101] See Section 9.4.

[102] Values And Life-Style, Mitchell 1983.

[103] See Section 3.1.

[104] Wells 1975.

[105] Engel et al. 1986.

[106] Wells 1975.

[107] Iacocca 1984, p. 18.

[108] Iacocca 1984, p. 22.

[109] Iacocca 1984, p. 32.

[110] Iacocca 1984, p. 23.

[111] Iacocca 1984, p. 49.

[112] Iacocca 1984, p. 40.

CHAPTER 4

PERCEPTION

4.1. Psychophysics

The perception of stimuli in the environment has been studied extensively by physiologists and psychologists. Economists generally are not concerned with perception of commodities.[1] However, implicitly, perceptions may be included in the utility function. In the economic psychological paradigm,[2] perceptual processes deal with the transfer of information from the objective part of the model (the objective economic situation and situational restrictions) to the subjective part (mental processes and subjective restrictions).

The psychology of perception has dealt with perceptual constancy (e.g. why a door retains its perceived shape while it swings open), perceptual adaptation (e.g. why, after some time has elapsed, we can perceive objects in a dark room) and perceptual illusions and ambiguities (e.g. the well-known portrait of the young and the old woman), among others. However, these phenomena are not very relevant to economic theory, in contrast with theories on the perception of the size and the amount of stimuli.

The earlier experiments on perception dealt with *discrimination* of stimuli, to be considered in this section. Later, interest shifted toward processes of *judgment* (to be dealt with in Section 4.2), from which it is only a small step toward *evaluation* (to be dealt with in Chapter 6). Several applications of perception theory concern the perception of prices (Section 4.3), money and inflation (Section 4.4), economic activities and resources (Section 4.5) and risk (Section 4.6).

Two different aspects of discrimination of physical stimuli have been studied: *absolute thresholds* and *difference thresholds*.

The intensity of physical stimuli has to exceed a certain value in order to be perceived by human individuals. This value is the absolute threshold, defined as the stimulus intensity at which in 50% of the cases the stimulus is perceived and in the other 50% not perceived. In other words, the probability of detecting a stimulus at the threshold level is 50%. The thresholds have been studied in *signal detection theory*. It appears, for example, that the absolute threshold of the human olfactory organ is one drop of perfume diffused throughout six

Table 4.1. Weber's fraction for various senses.

Type of discrimination	Weber's fraction
Changes in brightness	1/60
Changes in weight	1/50
Changes in loudness	1/10
Changes in salty taste	1/5

From Saccuzzo (1987).

rooms. In addition to the sensitivity to absolute stimulus values, the perception of stimulus differences has also been studied in psychological laboratories.

Ernst Weber (1795–1878) presented his subjects pairs of two slightly different weights. After lifting the weights, the subjects stated whether the weights were different or not. By this method Weber discovered that the *just noticeable difference* (j.n.d.) of the weights is a constant fraction of the stimulus intensity (the absolute weight). For example, *Weber's law* implies that a subject, just able to perceive the difference between 50 grams and 51 grams (Weber's constant being 1/50 in this case), will just be able to perceive the difference between 150 grams and 153 grams. Weber's law has been tested with a great variety of stimuli perceived by the human senses, e.g. with intensity of light and sound and with variations in pitch, flavor and taste. Weber's constant differs across the senses, as reflected in Table 4.1. The application of Weber's law is restricted to the perception of stimulus differences. It says nothing about the absolute magnitude of subjective sensations.

Gustav Theodor Fechner (1801–1887) related the perceived difference to the objective difference by equating the j.n.d. to the *unit of sensation* (by assumption). Since the j.n.d. is a constant, the unit of sensation is a constant and does not depend on the magnitude of sensation. This crucial assumption, combined with Weber's law, implies the relation between the magnitude of physical stimuli and the magnitude of sensation. Fechner's law, derived from the assumption above, states that the magnitude of sensation is a logarithmic function of the stimulus intensity.[3] In Figure 4.1, the increase of sensation from 50 to 60 grams equals the increase of sensation from 150 to 180 grams. *Fechner's law*, however, has not produced conclusive evidence in experimental research.

Stevens gives an intuitive example from which it becomes directly clear that Fechner's law cannot be true.[4] He notices that the apparent length of a line (according to perceptual judgment) is very nearly a linear function of physical length. Two meters look about twice as long as one meter (see Figure 4.2) and thus its perceived length should contain twice as much j.n.d.'s (units of subjective length). At the same time, Weber's law is known to hold

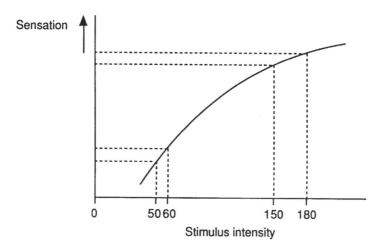

Figure 4.1. The relation between sensation and stimulus according to Fechner.

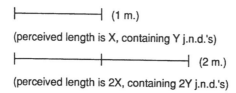

Figure 4.2. Stevens' argument concerning the perception of length.

fairly well for length, so the j.n.d.'s ought to get larger at greater lengths. Putting these two contradictory facts together, it turns out that the j.n.d. is not constant in subjective size.

Stevens assumed that equal objective stimulus ratios produce equal subjective ratios, in agreement with the results shown in Figure 4.2, i.e. $1m/2m$ equals $Y/2Y$. This corresponds with an exponential relationship between sensation and stimulus magnitude (see the Appendix for a derivation of this *power law*). This assumption has been favored in a number of experimental tests with different kinds of stimuli.[5] In Figure 4.3, an example is presented of the relationship between sensation, transformed to a logarithmic scale and loudness of sound in decibels (which is a logarithmic scale). Since the power law is exponential, the relationship is linear on a log-log scale. Both the logarithmic and the exponential (the exponent being positive and less than one) functions are consistent with the hypothesis of decreasing marginal utility in economics. The perception theories are briefly characterized in Table 4.2.

The explained variance (R^2) in the psychophysical relationships by means of the power law in most instances resulted in 0.95 or more.[6] It is concluded

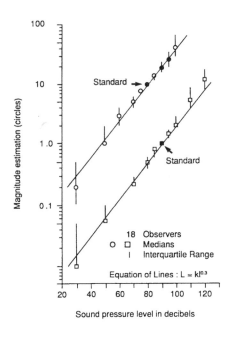

Figure 4.3. Illustration of the power law in the perception of sound magnitude. From Stevens (1957).

Table 4.2. Brief characterization of perception theories.

Theory	Object of study	Main assumption
Signal detection	Absolute thresholds	Threshold stimulus is detected 50% of the time
Weber's law	Difference thresholds	j.n.d. is constant fraction of stimulus intensity
Fechner's law	Stimulus-sensation relationships	j.n.d. is unit of sensation
Steven's law	Stimulus-sensation relationships	Stimulus ratio is proportional to subjective ratio

that the power law is assumed to hold for a variety of psychophysical relationships, although the shape of the functional relationship may differ between different senses and different stimuli.

Conclusion

The psychology of perception deals with lawful relationships concerning the discrimination of stimuli. An important result is the relation between sensation and stimulus intensity, either taking the form of Fechner's or Stevens' law.

BOX 4.1

A PSYCHOPHYSICAL CLASSROOM EXPERIMENT

In a classroom experiment at Erasmus University including 181 subjects, the psychophysical laws of Fechner and Stevens were tested with three different sets of stimuli:

— A line of standard size was projected and assigned an arbitrary length of 10. Next, 8 different lines were shown consecutively in addition to the standard line. Subjects were asked to write down the perceived lengths of the lines compared to the standard length.

— A square of standard area was projected and assigned an arbitrary size of 10. Next, 8 different squares were shown consecutively in addition to the standard square. Subjects were asked to write down the perceived sizes of the squares compared to the standard size.

— A circle of standard area was projected and assigned an arbitrary size of 10. Next, 8 different circles were shown consecutively in addition to the standard circle. Subjects were asked to write down the perceived sizes of the circles compared to the standard size.

Table 4.3. Objective and subjective sizes of three stimulus sets. (Standard errors of estimates between parentheses.)

	Lines objective lengths (cm)	Lines subjective lengths	Squares objective area (cm^2)	Squares subjective sizes	Circles objective area (cm^2)	Circles subjective sizes
1	4.6	3.61	6.76	1.72	7.07	1.56
2	5.3	4.06	9.61	2.42	9.08	2.27
3	6.0	4.75	12.25	2.61	12.57	2.59
4	7.5	6.20	19.36	3.58	19.64	3.87
5	9.0	7.49	28.09	5.46	28.27	5.38
6	10.5	8.55	37.21	7.66	38.48	6.98
7	12.0	10.00	49.00	10.00	50.27	10.00
8	13.5	11.28	64.00	11.20	63.62	10.98
9	15.8	13.15	86.49	12.37	84.95	12.57

Table 4.3 shows the objective sizes of the stimuli and the average subjective sizes reported by the subjects.

Next, psychophysical relationships between the averaged perceptions and the objective stimulus sizes were estimated by means of OLS regressions.

Table 4.4. Estimated psychophysical relations regarding three stimulus sets.

	Subjective size (linear relation) $Y = a + bX$	Subjective size (Fechner's law) $Y = a + b \ln X$	Log-subjective size (Stevens' law) $\ln Y = a + b \ln X$
Lines			
Constant (a)	−0.370	−8.764	−0.343
Stimulus size (b)	0.860	7.629	1.063
R^2	0.999	0.972	0.998
Squares			
Constant (a)	1.251	−8.212	−1.049
Stimulus size (b)	0.146	4.499	0.827
R^2	0.941	0.934	0.982
Circles			
Constant (a)	1.011	−8.395	−1.159
Stimulus size (b)	0.150	4.516	0.852
R^2	0.965	0.932	0.990

Y = subjective size, X = objective size

The results are shown in Table 4.4. Although the R^2's of the log-log regressions in the right-hand column cannot be compared directly with the other R^2's because the dependent variable is different, a Box-Cox transformation[7] shows that they are clearly superior to the linear relations in the case of the squares and circles (for lines, the linear relation is slightly superior). In this respect, the results can be interpreted as favoring Stevens' law.

4.2. Perceptual judgment

A number of researchers are not strictly concerned with perception or discrimination of stimuli. Frequently, this stems from the fact that stimuli have been presented in numbers. Strictly speaking, with numbers discrimination will always be perfect, since everyone can distinguish, say, 100,000 from 100,001, although the difference is only 0.001%. However, these researchers, too, felt that the sensation of a relatively small difference should be less than a relatively large difference. Thus, they started to study psychophysical relationships between stimuli, expressed in numbers and sensations in terms of liking, disliking, good and bad, high and low, etcetera. Strictly speaking, many of these sensations are evaluations or attitudes.[8]

The power law has been applied in relating social stimuli to the magnitude of sensations.[9] As an example subjects were asked to estimate the liking or

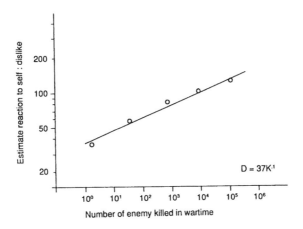

Figure 4.4. Dislike of number of enemy killed in wartime. From Hamblin (1973).

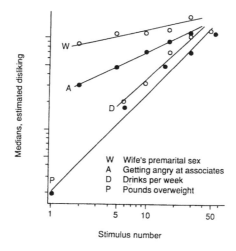

Figure 4.5. Dislike of four social stimuli. From Hamblin (1973).

disliking of particular numbers of enemy killed in wartime.[10] Ratio scales have been used in estimation by instructing the subjects to rate a stimulus at 20 if it was liked twice as much as another stimulus with a rating of 10 (the number 10 was arbitrarily assigned to one of the stimuli). In Figure 4.4, the aggregate results of 21 U.S. Navy seamen for dislike of number of enemy killed in wartime are presented in log-log scales. It appears that the data are approximated by the power function, given in the lower right part of the figure.

In Figure 4.5, estimated dislike of a number of social stimuli, expressed in numbers, is presented for the same sample mentioned above.

In these and other experiments, it appears that the power law, describing the psychophysical relationship between numbered stimuli and sensation gives a very good fit to the empirical data. The same applies to the liking and disliking of wage rates and for the reported degree of poverty associated with levels of income.[11] A number of different shapes of the psychophysical relationship between income evaluation and income level have been investigated.[12] The results favor the logarithmic and lognormal functions against a number of alternatives, including the power law.[13]

Other types of sensations, such as the degree of status, prestige or respect, have also been related to numbered stimuli. Psychophysical relations have been reported between perceived status and amount of income, status and years of schooling and status and years of acculturation.[14]

The psychophysical method has been used to find the money equivalence of non-monetary events.[15] After presenting ratio scales associated with a variety of (monetary and non-monetary) stimuli and estimating the psychophysical functions, the utility of money and the utility of events could be compared. In this way, it was possible to calibrate the (monetary and non-monetary) values of a consumer product of brand X and similar competitive brands in a test market.

In the experiments above, the absolute judgments were found to vary with the stimulus magnitudes. However, there appears to be substantial variation across people regarding the perception of social stimuli, which cannot be explained that easily. The variation in the judgments of 225 members of a consumer panel regarding the similarity of 12 activities was investigated: bowling, going shopping, golf, handicrafts, gardening, TV viewing, snow-mobiling, playing bridge, swimming, reading, visiting friends and going to movies.[16] While allowing for measurement errors, it appeared that there was significantly greater variation in the similarity judgments than could be expected by chance. These differences could hardly be explained by the subjects' familiarity with the activities, the subjects' personal values in life or by demographic characteristics. Section 4.6 considers the psychological similarities and disparities of economic activities in more detail.

Van Praag tries to explain the variance of judgments from a different angle.[17] He states that individuals make judgments according to their own standards with respect to the stimuli involved. For example, a judgment regarding the level of income is likely to depend on their own income and financial needs. This approach deals with the measurement of individual perception functions, in contrast with the experiments considered above. In a survey of 600 households in the Boston area, individuals were asked to state at which annual after-tax income they consider themselves respectively poor, nearly poor, just getting along, living reasonably comfortably, living very comfortably and prosperously. It appears that the income associated with the judgment 'poor' is higher if their own income is higher, if they have had more years of schooling and if their family size is larger (with the other levels of judgment the results are more or less the same). They explain this result from the fact that the own income level is used as a standard against which incomes are judged as sufficient or insufficient. Other standards used in income judgments are education and family size.

Perceptual standards have been examined with other stimuli as well.[18] With respect to age, it appears that one's own age functions as a perceptual standard in judgments of whether people of different ages are perceived as young, somewhat young, middle-aged, somewhat old or old. With increasing age, one tends to shift the perception of young ages from 'somewhat younger' to 'young', for example. Males and females have different standards on average, in conformity with the longevity of women compared to that of men. (Other standards relate to education and family size.) With respect to education, it appears that one's own years of schooling function as a perceptual standard in judgments regarding different amounts of schooling. For example, someone finishing a Ph.D. may consider 12 years of schooling a small amount, whereas someone who only completed secondary school may consider this a large amount. The *Evaluation Question Approach* has two main advantages:[19]

– discriminating power is high because respondents choose their own metric, unlike labeled scales in which respondents are forced to choose one of several labels;
– the respondent selects the appropriate range of response, unlike most psychological scales that present the same stimulus range to a number of different subjects.

Perceptual standards might also exist with respect to prices. What price is perceived as high or low may depend on a standard, reflecting the 'fair' price of a commodity, according to an individual. For example, items that are purchased infrequently, like houses or kitchens, are likely to be associated with a reference price that was paid in the past. In many instances, this reference price is not in agreement with current prices. Salesmen are usually apt to suggest a new reference price, which might be too high, of course. Reference prices may substantially influence consumer judgment and choice when combined with the framing of information about the product.[20]

Perceptual standards may be included in *adaptation level* which has been defined as a power function of average stimulus intensities and background stimuli.[21] For example, the adaptation levels in a weight judgment task varied according to whether the weights were presented in an ascending or descending order (different stimulus intensities) or whether or not the task was preceded by judgments of a much heavier weight (background stimuli). Psychological judgment in adaptation level theory is a function of both the stimulus value and the adaptation level, as shown in the Appendix. Evidence for the effect of the adaptation level has been shown concerning a wide variety of stimuli, including psychophysical, social, verbal and traumatic stimuli.

Conclusion

Perceptual judgments relate to the magnitude of sensation rather than to the ability to discriminate between stimuli. This makes perceptual judgments applicable to numbered stimuli which play an important part in economics. Perceptual judgments can be explained to some extent by individual perceptual standards and adaptation levels which may be related to economic variables.

4.3. Price perception

One economic application of perception theory is in the area of consumer prices. The study of price perception by consumers has concentrated on the absolute and difference thresholds, considered in Section 4.1.

Analogous to the discrimination of number differences, it seems hardly justified to assume an absolute threshold of price, since an extremely low price can always be discriminated from a zero price. In marketing, however, the price threshold concerns the price at which consumers are unwilling to buy a certain product.[22] The probabilities of buying a product have been investigated at different prices.[23] Consumers were asked if they would take a certain product if the price were ...... If the answer was "Yes", a similar question was asked with a different price and so on. If the answer was "No", the consumer was asked whether she thought the product was too expensive or too cheap. Upper and lower price limits for the acceptable price range of products were discovered. These limits have been found for a number of different products by several researchers.[24]

The sensitivity of consumers to price differences has also been examined in marketing. In general, with price increases above the lower limit of an acceptable price, the probability of buying increases in a sample of consumers. However, with prices just below the upper limit of acceptable price, the probability of buying increases as the price decreases. (See Figure 4.6.) The intersection of both probability-of-buying curves corresponds with the 'optimal' price, since at both higher and lower prices part of the consumer market will lose interest in buying the product.

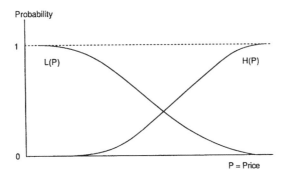

Figure 4.6. Probabilities of judging products as too cheap or too expensive to buy. From Gabor and Granger (1966).

The shape of the curves in Figure 4.6 appears to be lognormal, from which is was concluded that the subjective price scale of the consumer is logarithmic and that the deviation of a particular consumer's price attitude from the average is distributed normally.[25] The logarithmic subjective price scale supports Fechner's law, considered above (and Weber's law, since is is implied by Fechner's law). However, it was noticed that the ratio of price difference and price is not constant over the entire price range (as required by Weber's law) and that it differs according to the type of product involved.[26]

Fechner's law was tested by relating the perceived quality of products (sensation) to the logarithm of price.[27] Testing four products, stable logarithmic relationships have been found, with different values of the constant. This research seems to support Fechner's law. However, there is much evidence against the existence of a *price-quality relationship*,[28] which undermines the validity of Fechner's law in the area of price perception.

Several authors have obtained results contradicting Weber's law. For example, consumers perceive 15% changes better for a 55¢ product than for a 15¢ product.[29] The probability of consumers changing to a 2¢ lower priced gasoline brand is higher if the price is 42¢ than if it is 28¢, contradicting Weber's law, too.[30] As an alternative, consumers may compare price offers to a 'fair' price (which can be considered as a reference price or perceptual standard).[31] With a low 'fair' price, the consumers in the experiment above react adversely to a further price increase at 42¢, whereas they are quite tolerant to an increase at 28¢. There is still no valid test of the applicability of Weber's law to pricing.[32]

Conclusion

The perception of prices has been related to purchase behavior. Two opposing views concern the probability of whether a purchase is related to the magnitude of sensation or to the concept of a 'fair' price, which serves as a perceptual standard of judgment. This problem is still awaiting a solution.

4.4. Perception of money and inflation

Another application of perception theory is with respect to inflation. The perception of inflation may be assumed to follow the psychophysical laws considered above. This implies that a price increase is only perceived if it exceeds the just noticeable price difference. Furthermore, the ratio of perceived inflation and the price level should be constant, according to Weber's law and, according to Fechner's law, the perceived inflation should consist of a constant number of j.n.d.'s, irrespective of the level of inflation.

The implications of the psychophysical laws for the perception of inflation have been tested by using data from thrice-yearly surveys in the European Community in the years 1974–1982. The survey question concerning the perceived inflation reads:

> "Compared to what they were 12 months ago, do you think that prices in general are now: lower/about the same/a little higher/moderately higher/ much higher/don't know?"[33]

The observations with "don't know" answers were excluded from the sample. It has been assumed that the individual perceptions of inflation are normally distributed across people in eight countries of the EC. The distribution function of perceived inflation is depicted in Figure 4.7.

It is assumed that the mean of this distribution corresponds with the average perceived inflation and the observations indicating about the same prices as last year correspond with a zero level of inflation. The shaded areas in Figure 4.7 correspond with the j.n.d. around the zero level of inflation and with the j.n.d. around the level of inflation associated with moderately higher prices in the sample, respectively.

From the proportions of observations giving the different answers to the survey question, it has been possible to estimate the j.n.d.'s, the mean perceived level of inflation and the level of inflation associated with moderately higher prices.

In Table 4.5, the actual average inflation rate and its standard deviation over the years 1974–1982 are presented for eight countries in the EC. Table 4.6 shows the estimated values associated with the parameters in Figure 4.7.

It appears from these results that the perceived level of inflation, μ, exceeds the j.n.d. around zero to a significant degree. In some countries, the rate

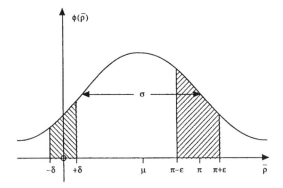

Key: ρ = mean perceived inflation
        μ = average perceived inflation in sample survey
        σ = S.D. of perceived inflation in sample survey
        π = moderate rate of inflation
        δ = j.n.d. in inflation around zero
        ε = j.n.d. in inflation around π

Figure 4.7. The distribution of inflation perceptions. From Batchelor (1986).

Table 4.5. Mean and standard deviation of consumer price inflation in eight European economies, 1974–1982. (Standard deviations between parentheses.)

Country	Inflation
Italy	17.2 (3.8)
Ireland	16.4 (4.5)
United Kingdom	15.4 (5.1)
France	11.6 (2.1)
Denmark	11.0 (2.8)
Belgium	8.2 (3.4)
The Netherlands	7.1 (2.1)
Germany	4.8 (1.4)

From Batchelor (1986).

Table 4.6. Estimated parameters of perceived price inflation.

Country	μ	σ	π	δ	ε	ϑ
Italy	17.1	6.7	10.3	1.3	4.1	4.7
Ireland	16.3	6.7	8.8	1.6	1.9	5.4
United Kingdom	15.3	7.1	13.8	2.4	4.0	4.6
France	11.7	4.6	7.8	1.3	2.1	5.2
Denmark	11.0	5.0	10.0	2.7	2.4	4.0
Belgium	8.1	3.2	4.4	0.7	1.6	4.8
The Netherlands	7.0	2.8	4.5	0.7	1.9	4.5
Germany	4.8	2.3	5.2	1.0	1.2	4.9

From Batchelor (1986).

of inflation is perceived as moderately high, since it is in the range of a j.n.d. around π, associated with moderately higher prices. This means that the perceived price level in the sample is more likely to be perceived as moderately higher than the year before than as being the same as before.

The estimated difference thresholds, δ and ε, vary across countries and across years, which contradicts the constant difference threshold in Weber's law. The number of j.n.d.'s, ϑ, contained in the inflation rate perceived as moderately high, varies across countries and across years. On average, 4–5 j.n.d's are contained in the perception of a moderate degree of inflation. This is interpreted as contradicting Fechner's law. The above-mentioned results pertain to the aggregate survey information regarding the proportion of subjects giving a particular answer and may not be valid for individual threshold estimates.

An interesting phenomenon associated with inflation is the perception of money size. An early study had already found that children tended to estimate coins as larger than their real size, the effect being stronger for the higher valued coins.[34] As inflation makes money less valuable, the subjective size of British coins might be judged as smaller after a period of inflation than before. Ten and five pence coins, having the same nominal value and the same diameter after the decimalization of British currency as two and one shilling coins before, were examined with regard to their subjective size.[35] The mean estimated diameters of the coins are presented in Table 4.7.

These results support the negative relationship between inflation and subjective money size. Similar results have been obtained regarding the estimated size of paper money.[36] Subjects overestimated the size of the old pound note (which was withdrawn in 1979) and underestimated the size of the new one. Different results were obtained with subjective estimates of the sizes of Israeli currency, which was changed in 1980 and again in 1985, because of high

Table 4.7. The effect of inflation on
estimated coin size.

	Old coin	New coin
$2s/10p$	29.8 mm	28.5 mm
$1s/5p$	23.5 mm	21.9 mm

inflation.[37] The hypothesis of underestimation of coins due to inflation was not supported in their experiment.

Conclusion

The theory of perception has been applied to the phenomenon of inflation. It might be assumed that the probability that consumers and labor unions take actions, and the scale of the actions, are related to the perceived level of inflation. As with purchase behavior, the perception of inflation is not exactly according to Fechner's law. Alternative evidence of perceived inflation comes from the estimated size of coins and paper money.

4.5. Perception of economic activities and resources

In psychology, there is some research tradition regarding the perceptual basis of economic activities and social resources. The aspects of activity perceptions were investigated by means of ratings scales.[38] Polish employees, self-employed and farmers were asked to rate 30 economic activities on 12 bipolar scales regarding the effort, knowledge and resources required and the perceived profitability, prestige, legality, benefits, delay of consequences, newness, riskiness, sensibility and pleasure. The twelve scales could be reduced to four underlying dimensions, constituting the *perceptual space* of the average participant in the survey. There were virtually no differences in the perceptual spaces across the different groups, indicating the generality of the perceptual structure.

The four dimensions and the activities associated with them were:
— social comfort and prestige, associated positively with giving to charities, educating children and being a priest and negatively associated with cheating on taxes, giving bribes and begging;
— newness and financial resources required, associated positively with buying stocks, running a casino, owning a newspaper and investing in production and negatively associated with being a priest, being employed as a teacher, being employed in a factory and being employed in an office;
— knowledge and effort required and profitability, associated positively with

being employed as a manager, having more than one job, being an owner of a bank, and being an owner of a newspaper and negatively associated with buying luxurious goods, giving money to charities and giving bribes;

— delay of consequences, associated positively with being a scientist, running a farm and educating children and negatively with being a priest, saving energy, running a casino and working abroad.

The survey also included similarity sorting as a different technique of eliciting perceptions of activities from the subjects. However, the perceptual structure resulting from this technique differed from the one reported above.

In a cross-cultural study, the perceptual spaces regarding economic activities in Poland, Hungary, United Kingdom and the Netherlands were studied, using similar scales and activities as in the study mentioned above.[39] Two perceptual dimensions were found (excluding a scale concerning delayed consequences), which were interpreted as a social values dimension and an economic dimension, indicating perceived costs and benefits. Hardly any differences in perceptual structure were found across the four countries. This points to the *cultural invariance* of economic perceptions (limited to the four countries involved, however).

Both of the studies above used statistical techniques based on the averaged perceptions of activities in the sample, i.e. the three-mode data (subjects × activities × scales) were reduced to two-mode data (activities × scales). The data of the latter study were re-analyzed using three-mode data analysis.[40] Three perceptual dimensions were found: economic versus social values, delay of consequences and a relaxation-exertion dimension. Furthermore, slight differences in perceptions across the four countries were found. A graph of the activity perceptions in two-dimensional space (excluding the relaxation-exertion dimension) is shown in Figure 4.8. It appears that, in addition to using different measuring techniques, different methods of analysis may also result in different types of perceptual spaces.

In consumer research and marketing, a number of different product classification schemes have been distinguished. In one study 108 products were evaluated on 18 different scales in a Dutch sample of 180 consumers.[41] The 18 scales were reduced to three dimensions, forming a perceptual space of consumer products. The three dimensions were involvement and values associated with the products, utility or functionality of the products and routine buying behavior regarding the products. The products, clustered by means of the 18 different scales, were perceived as follows. Refreshment goods were perceived as low involvement, low utility goods, purchased routinely. Utilities and external care products were perceived as low involvement, high utility goods, purchased routinely. Durables were perceived as high involvement, moderate utility goods, purchased infrequently. Cultural goods were

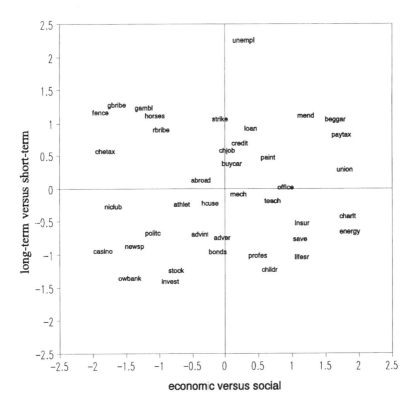

Key:

Charit	Giving to charity	Energy	Saving energy
Casino	Being an owner of a casino	Union	Being a member of a union
Pay tax	Paying taxes	Chetax	Cheating on taxes
Beggar	Giving money to a beggar	Niclub	Being an owner of a nigthclub
Gbribe	Giving bribes	Owbank	Being an owner of a bank
Insur	Buying property insurance	Politc	Being an politician
Unempl	Being unemployed	Newsp	Being an owner of a newspaper
Gambl	Gambling in the casino	Invest	Investing in an enterprise
Horses	Gambling on horse racing	Childr	Educating children
Stock	Buying shares	Profess	Studying for a new profession
Strike	Going on strike	Rbribe	Receiving bribes
Loan	Taking loans	Bonds	Buying government bonds
Credit	Using credit	Teach	Being employed as a teacher
Buycar	Buying a car	Save	Putting money in the bank
Mend	Repairing old clothes	Lifesr	Buying life insurance
House	Buying a house	Athlet	Being a professional athlete
Abroad	Working abroad	Office	Being employed in an office
Chjob	Changing workplace		
Fence	Being a 'fence' for stolen property		
Advint	Advertising products in an international fair		
Adver	Advertising products in the mass media		
Mech	Being employed as a car mechanic		
Paint	Being employed as a house painter		

Figure 4.8. A two-dimensional perceptual space of economic activities. From Veldscholte et al. (1995).

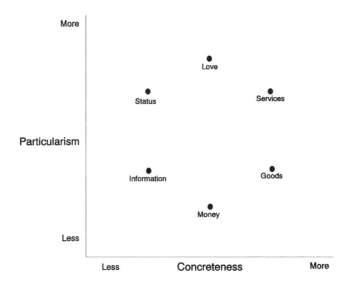

Figure 4.9. Structure of economic and social resources. Reprinted with permission from U.G. Foa (1971) Interpersonal and Economic Resources, *Science* 171, 345–351.

perceived as moderate involvement, moderately low utility goods, purchased infrequently.

An interesting idea associated with the perceptions of goods and services is their appropriateness in social exchange. In social exchange, economic resources, such as money, goods, services and information may be exchanged for the social resources of status and love. However, some resources will be perceived as more similar and more appropriate for exchange than others. Foa elicited the probabilities of returning a resource in exchange of each of the others in a sample of students.[42] For example, he asked "What is the proper compensation you wish to have in exchange for giving information to a person?" Information was most likely to be exchanged for status and money and less likely to be exchanged for love and services. The exchange probabilities could be fitted by two dimensions, capturing the perceptions of the resources. The first dimension distinguishes concrete resources such as goods and services from abstract resources such as information and status. The second dimension distinguishes particularistic items such as love and affection from general items such as money. This classification of resources is shown in Figure 4.9.

The two-dimensional space of economic and social resources was found in five different countries and cultures: Israel, Philippines, Mexican Americans, Sweden and the United States.[43] This points to the cultural invariance of the perceptual space of resources.

Conclusion

In addition to the quantity of sensation, considered in the preceding sections, the quality of sensation frequently is described in a low-dimensional perceptual space. Although the dimensions may vary according to the stimuli perceived, there are indications that their variability across countries is small.

4.6. Risk perception

Modern industrial societies and their governments are becoming increasingly aware of the technological hazards and this has inspired research in this area.[44] Economic analysis has yielded an overall positive relationship between the objective hazards of events (probabilities of fatalities per hour of exposure) and their objective benefits (average amount of money spent on the activity or the average contribution of the activity to annual income).[45] However, a different study showed a slightly negative relationship between perceived risk and perceived benefits, both measured by psychophysical methods.[46] This implies that the maximization of the ratio of objective benefit and risks by the government and technical engineers may not be understood by the citizens. This raises the question of what psychological aspects of risks should be distinguished.

In two different surveys, people were asked to rate a number of events on subjective scales associated with different aspects of risks.[47] Typically, they find a two-dimensional perceptual risk space. The first factor is interpreted as 'Dread Risk' or 'Severity', which is associated with uncontrollability, global catastrophy, fatal consequences, high risk to future generations, etcetera. Nuclear events, handguns and aviation score high on this factor, whereas home appliances, caffeine and power mowers score low. The second factor was interpreted as 'Technological Risk' or 'Unknown Risk', which is associated with lack of knowledge, delayed consequences, newness, etcetera. Chemical and biochemical technologies score high on this factor, whereas car accidents, swimming, mountain climbing and handguns score low (both studies were carried out in the US). Perceived risk appeared to be associated most with the 'Dread Risk' factor. Unfortunately, a scale concerning the (perceived) likelihood of the events was excluded.

An interesting idea regarding the acceptability of risks is the following.[48] The utility of events is assumed to be a marginally decreasing function of expected benefits, whereas the disutility is assumed to be a marginally increasing function of the expected losses. This assumption is based on the idea that the total utility of an event is a function of good and bad characteristics and that good things satiate and bad things escalate.[49] The balance of the two utilities shows an inverted U-shape for correlated benefits and losses (see

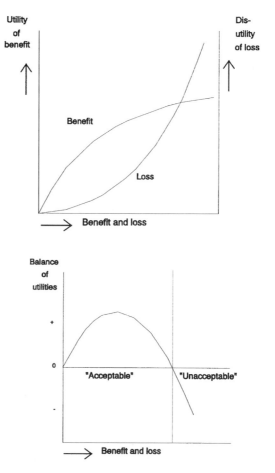

Figure 4.10. Utilities of benefits and losses. Adapted from *Acta Psychologica* 45, Vlek and Stallen, "Rational and Personal Aspects of Risk", pp. 273–300, (1980) with kind permission of Elsevier Science NL, Sara Burgerhartstraat 25, 1055 KV Amsterdam, The Netherlands.

Figure 4.10). The latter function is also known as a single-peaked preference function. If we consider the perceived benefits and perceived risks for 30 events[50] as positive and negative utilities, respectively, we should be able to state the acceptability of events. The balance of benefits and losses was calculated by subtracting the mean judgment of risk from the mean judgment of benefit for each activity. Although the perceived benefits and losses are correlated slightly negatively, it may be assumed that the acceptability of events is judged approximately as shown in Table 4.8. Indeed, since the time of the study, anti-lobbies have started for smoking, alcohol, spray cans and handguns, reflecting the unacceptability of these activities and technologies.

Table 4.8. Acceptability of activities and technologies.

Highly acceptable	Moderately acceptable	Hardly acceptable
Electric power	Contraceptives	Mountain climbing
Prescription antibiotics	Large constructions	Hunting
Vaccinations	(dams, bridges, etc.)	Spray cans
Railroads	Bicycles	Motor vehicles
Surgery	Swimming	Private aviation
X-rays	Food preservatives	Alcoholic beverages
Home appliances	Power mowers	Motorcycles
Fire fighting	High school football	Smoking
Commercial aviation	Skiing	Nuclear power
Police work	Food coloring	Handguns
Pesticides		

Acceptability decreases from top to bottom.
Compiled from Fischhoff et al. (1978) by permission of Kluwer Academic
Publishers.

Other examples of events including good and bad characteristics, leading
to a single-peaked preference function, are situations or activities including
exciting and boring elements such as jobs[51] and approach-avoidance conflicts
such as buying behavior.[52]

It should be stated that the risk acceptability figures are based on opinions
of the population, which may be quite different than the opinions of those
involved in the activities. For example, experienced mountaineers may consider their sporting activity as more beneficial and less risky than the general
population.[53]

Obviously, risk is associated with the concepts of probability and uncertainty. The acceptability of risk was found to be correlated negatively with
the perceived value of negative events and with the perceived moral value
associated with the risk concerned.[54] Acceptability of risks was also found to
be related to children's moral values of the risks concerned.[55] This research
shows that risk is associated both with cognitive and affective psychological
components.

Furthermore, the risk of being assaulted and falling ill with AIDS was
judged higher when it was considered affecting society than when it was
considered affecting people in general and it was judged the lowest when it
was considered affecting the own person.[56] One explanation is that problems
transcending one's own responsibility become general or societal problems,
which are considered more important. Alternatively, one could be relatively
optimistic about personal risks because of 'belief control'.[57] The wish to
control may induce the underestimation of unsafe situations.[58] People view

themselves as personally immune to hazards.[59] Nuclear fuel experts evaluated
the levels of risk regarding a number of technologies as less serious than
samples of students and retired persons.[60] Here, too, opinions may have
been biased by control beliefs. The psychology of risk will be taken up in
Chapter 13, which deals with decision making under uncertainty.

Summary

Perception theory is based on the study of absolute perceptual thresholds.
Weber, Fechner and Stevens studied the perception of stimulus differences
which resulted in lawful relations between the magnitude of sensation and
stimulus intensity.

The perception of numbered stimuli involves perceptual judgments regarding social stimuli. The psychophysical relationships appear to apply to
these stimuli, too. Important concepts, explaining individual judgments to
some extent, are the perceptual standard and the adaptation level which might
be related to socio-economic and situational variables.

Perceptual judgments have been applied to the perception of prices and
inflation. Regarding these phenomena, psychophysical laws do not always
account for opinions and behavior, although the application of perceptual
standards might improve the explanatory power of these laws.

Perceptions of economic activities, resources and risks may be distinguished qualitatively. The perception of economic activities seems to be
based on dimensions reflecting economic values, social values and delay of
consequences. Resources are perceived as more or less particularistic and as
more or less concrete. Risks are perceived as more or less severe and as more
or less known. Different psychometric techniques have been used to reveal
the perceptual dimensions, leading to different results in some instances.

Appendix

The assumptions, underlying the different psychophysical laws, can be for-
malized as follows.

Weber's law states that a difference in stimulus size, $d\phi$, is just noticeable
if its ratio to the stimulus size, ϕ, equals a constant, K:

$$d\phi/\phi = K \tag{1}$$

Fechner's law assumes that the just noticeable difference, (1), equals the
subjective unit of sensation, $d\psi$, which is constant:

$$d\psi = K \tag{2}$$

$$d\phi/\phi = d\psi \tag{3}$$

Integrating both sides in (3) yields Fechner's law, relating the magnitude of sensation to the stimulus intensity:

$$\psi = C \ln \phi \tag{4}$$

with C a constant of integration.

Stevens assumed that equal stimulus ratios produce equal subjective ratios. This is equivalent to assuming that the ratio of an additional stimulus magnitude, $d\phi$ (e.g. an extra meter in Figure 4.2) and the original stimulus magnitude ϕ equals the ratio of the additional j.n.d.'s associated with the additional stimulus magnitude, $d\psi$ (the extra Y j.n.d.'s in Figure 4.2) and the original subjective stimulus value, ψ:

$$d\phi/\phi = d\psi/\psi \tag{5}$$

Integrating both sides of (5) yields the power law, relating the magnitude of sensation to the stimulus intensity:

$$\psi = A\phi^B \tag{6}$$

with constants A and B.

Helson's modification of Fechner's law in equation (7) amounts to:

$$\psi = C \ln \phi - C \ln AL \tag{7}$$

with AL the adaptation level.

Notes

[1] See Section 4.2 for an exception.
[2] See Section 2.4.
[3] See the Appendix to this chapter for a derivation of Fechner's law.
[4] Stevens 1957.
[5] Stevens 1957, Ekman 1959.
[6] Hamblin 1973.
[7] See Maddala 1977, p. 317.
[8] See Chapter 6.
[9] Hamblin 1973 and Saris et al. 1977.
[10] Hamblin 1973.
[11] Rainwater 1974.
[12] Van Herwaarden and Kapteyn 1979.
[13] See Chapter 10.
[14] Hamblin 1973.
[15] Galanter 1990.
[16] Ritchie 1974.
[17] Van Praag et al. 1988.
[18] Van Praag et al. 1988.

[19] Van der Sar and Van Praag 1993.

[20] See Chapter 13.

[21] Helson 1964.

[22] Gabor and Granger 1966, Monroe 1973.

[23] Gabor and Granger 1966.

[24] See Monroe 1973.

[25] Gabor and Granger 1966.

[26] Monroe 1973.

[27] Cooper 1970.

[28] Maynes 1980, 1983, Geistfeld 1982, Geistfeld et al. 1979, Sproles 1977, Dardis and Gieser 1980.

[29] Uhl 1970.

[30] Kamen and Toman 1970.

[31] Monroe 1973.

[32] Monroe 1973. Thaler 1980 offers yet another explanation which will be considered in Chapter 12.

[33] Batchelor 1986, p. 278.

[34] Bruner and Goodman 1947.

[35] Lea 1981.

[36] Furnham 1983.

[37] Leiser and Izak 1987.

[38] Tyszka 1994.

[39] Antonides et al. 1996.

[40] Veldscholte et al. 1995, Kroonenberg 1983.

[41] Antonides 1995.

[42] Foa 1971.

[43] Foa et al. 1982.

[44] Slovic et al. 1984.

[45] Starr 1969.

[46] Fischhoff et al. 1978.

[47] Fischhoff et al. 1978 and Slovic et al. 1984.

[48] Vlek and Stallen 1980.

[49] Coombs and Avrunin 1977, see also Chapter 12.

[50] Fischhoff et al. 1978.

[51] See Section 3.4.

[52] See Sections 5.5 and 9.2.

[53] Wärneryd 1988b, see Section 3.4.

[54] Sjöberg and Winroth 1986.

[55] Sjöberg and Torell 1993.

[56] Drottz-Sjöberg 1991.

[57] Van Raaij 1986, p. 367.

[58] See Section 3.3.

[59] Fischhoff et al. 1981.

[60] Svenson and Karlsson 1989.

CHAPTER 5

LEARNING

5.1. Introduction

Learning has been defined as a relatively permanent change in behavior that occurs as the result of practice.[1] The phrase 'relatively permanent' excludes changes in behavior due to temporary influences such as fatigue, drugs or adaptation. When learning is defined as resulting from practice, changes due to maturation, disease or physical damage can be excluded.

The type of learning that has most frequently been investigated in economic psychology is *learning by conditioning*. In this type of learning, the likelihood of a particular behavior is increased by associating it with a reinforcement. The principles of conditioning will be dealt with in the next two sections.

Since learning by conditioning only involves the relations between environmental stimuli and behavioral response, ignoring activities taking place in the organism during learning, the paradigm of conditioning is frequently referred to as the *S-R* model of learning. Other types of learning deal with biological, cognitive and social processes interacting with the environmental stimuli and responses of the organism. Hence, these types of learning are studied within the *S-O-R* paradigm, to be dealt with in Section 5.4.

Learning theories may explain economic preference formation and habitual economic behavior (e.g. routine purchase behavior). A common type of learning, economic socialization, is dealt with in Section 5.5. The effects of positive and negative outcomes of behavior are considered in Section 5.6.

In the context of the economic psychological paradigm,[2] the theories of learning by conditioning are associated with economic behavior, situational restrictions and (changes in) the personal economic situation in the objective plane. The learning theories, dealing with processes within the organism, also deal with the mental processes and decision making parts of the model in the subjective plane.

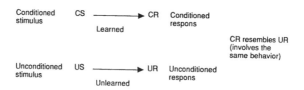

Figure 5.1. The classical conditioning process.

5.2. Classical conditioning

The Russian physiologist Pavlov has studied automatic reflexes occurring during the intake of food. When food is placed in the mouth of a dog, salivation is the automatic reaction to this stimulus. This reflex is described as an *unconditioned response* (UR) to an *unconditioned stimulus* (US).

In these experiments, Pavlov tapped the salivary duct of a dog to measure the strength of the response. Accidentally, he noticed that the dog started salivating not only at the sight of the food but also at the entrance of the experimenter into the room. This behavior was examined experimentally. It appeared that after repeated presentation of a light signal followed by the presentation of food, the dog started salivating in response to the light signal alone. Technically speaking, if a *conditioned stimulus* (CS) is repeatedly followed by an unconditioned stimulus (US), the preliminary unconditioned response (UR) becomes conditioned to the CS. This process is depicted in Figure 5.1. Salivation upon presentation of the light signal is then called a *conditioned response* (CR). This learning process is described as *classical conditioning* and the unconditioned stimulus is considered a *reinforcement*. Although some results have been obtained with presenting the CS after the US (backward conditioning) and presenting them simultaneously, presenting the CS before the US (forward conditioning) appears most effective.[3]

Several features of the learning curve can be distinguished. The intensity of the CR is increased during classical conditioning. (This means that more saliva is excreted in each conditioning trial, as shown in Figure 5.2.) Also, the CR is following more quickly after presentation of the CS, and the likelihood of the response increases during the process.

After classical conditioning has taken place, repeated presentation of the CS, without presentation of the US, leads to a decreased likelihood and a decreased intensity of the CR, which eventually disappears. This process is called *extinction*. *Spontaneous recovery* of the conditioned response may occur after some time delay, disappearing after more extinction trials. (See Figure 5.3.)

Classical conditioning is assumed to be largely responsible for human be-

Figure 5.2. The learning curve in the acquisition stage. From Hilgard et al. (1971).

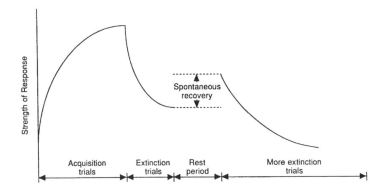

Figure 5.3. Acquisition and extinction of a conditioned response. Figure from Introduction to Psychology, Fifth Edition by E. Hilgard and R. Atkinson, copyright ©by Harcourt Brace Jovanovich, Inc., reprinted by permission of the publisher.

havior, not only by positive reinforcement but also by negative reinforcement (cf. reward and punishment in upbringing and education). A famous example is the experiment with "Little Albert", an 11-month-old child.[4] A pet rat (the CS) is paired with banging a metal bar behind Albert's ear (the US), resulting in startled crying (the UR) by Albert. Later presentation of the pet rat, without producing the banging, induces fear of the rat, evident from the startled crying response (the CR). This experiment of emotional conditioning shows how easily *phobia* (irrational fears) can be established and probably subjective reactions toward particular products or people as well. It has been observed that children in radiation or chemical therapy for cancer develop aversions to flavors of ice cream, e.g. chocolate or vanilla, they had eaten just before medication.[5] This occurred in spite of their knowledge from earlier medications that it was the medication and not the ice cream that caused their nausea.

Not only conscious behavior but responses controlled by the *autonomic nervous system* can be conditioned as well. An insulin shock (an overdose of the hormone regulating the amount of blood sugar) generally results in unconsciousness. This unconditioned stimulus and response have been used in a classical conditioning experiment in which the conditioned stimulus was a light signal.[6] If, after the learning trials, rats were injected with a solution of physiological salt instead of insulin, the conditioned response (unconsciousness) could be observed. By the same procedure, goose-flesh on a subject's hand, put in cold water, can be conditioned to a buzzer. These experiments indicate that emotions can be conditioned as well.

Several important phenomena in classical conditioning should be mentioned here, including stimulus generalization, stimulus discrimination and secondary reinforcement.

Stimulus generalization occurs if the conditioned response occurs after the presentation of a slightly different stimulus from the CS, for example a light signal of slightly different intensity or color. It has been found that the more similar the test stimulus is to the conditioned stimulus, the greater the generalization. Stimulus generalization is used in sales promotion by showing consumers a brand product (e.g. in an ad), which serves as the CS in combination with a number of favorable stimuli (the US). A favorable attitude toward the brand (the CR) is established by repeated presentation of the stimuli. It is assumed that the favorable attitude is generalized from the ad to the actual sales condition (e.g. in the shop).

Stimulus discrimination occurs if the conditioned response is not seen after the presentation of a slightly different stimulus from the CS, for example a light signal of a slightly different color. Since the usual reaction to a slightly different stimulus is stimulus generalization, stimulus discrimination has to be learned. Stimulus discrimination can be learned by linking the US exclusively to a particular signal, e.g. a yellow light, and not to a slightly different signal, e.g. an orange light. Very fine discriminations can be learned but this cannot be pushed to extremes. A dog, taught to discriminate between a luminous circle and an ellipse, began to bark if the axes of the ellipse reached a ratio of 9:8. The dog began to squeal and wriggle in its room and tried to use its teeth to tear off the apparatus connected to its skin, if this situation lasted longer. This behavior has become known as experimental neurosis.

Once the classical conditioning has been completed, the conditioned stimulus may serve as a reinforcement itself. For example, the light signal, mentioned above, may be used as an unconditioned stimulus in a new classical conditioning process in which it is paired with a new conditioned stimulus, e.g. a buzzer, to elicit the response upon the sound of the buzzer. The light signal in this example serves as a *secondary reinforcement* in the latter second-order conditioning process. Some conditioned stimuli have been associated with a very large number of responses. Examples of these are money, grades, praises, smiles, pats on the back, etcetera. These are called *generalized reinforcers* of which money is the most powerful economic incentive.

A predictiveness view on classical conditioning

It seems as if conditioning is taking place unconsciously, as a function of CS-US pairings only. However, subjects appear to take the information value of the CS into account, i.e. the extent to which the CS predicts or signals the occurrence of the US.[7] If the US also appears in the absence of the CS, the information value of the CS is reduced and the likelihood of the CR is diminished. For example, if a jingle (US), paired with a brand name (CS) in a commercial, is frequently heard elsewhere, the information value of the brand name disappears. In other words, the covariation of CS and US (or their contingency) is crucial in establishing the conditioning:

> "The notion of contingency differs from that of pairing in that it includes not only what events are paired but also what events are not paired."[8]

In Chapter 11, the covariation principle will be considered again in connection with attribution theory.

Conclusion

The learning process of classical conditioning is based on repeated pairings of a natural reinforcer, the unconditioned stimulus, with an unrelated stimulus. After the learning process, the conditioned stimulus elicits the conditioned response. An important result of classical conditioning is the effect of secondary reinforcement, in which arbitrarily selected conditioned stimuli have acquired reinforcing value. Generalized reinforcers are important means to influence economic behavior. Classical conditioning requires the covariation of conditioned and unconditioned stimuli.

5.3. Operant conditioning

In classical conditioning, the conditioned stimulus is presented before or simultaneously with the unconditioned stimulus. In *operant conditioning* or instrumental learning, the reinforcement is contingent on the occurrence of the response to be learned.

The difference with classical conditioning can be illustrated as follows. A dog can be conditioned to raise its paw (the UR) by giving it an electric

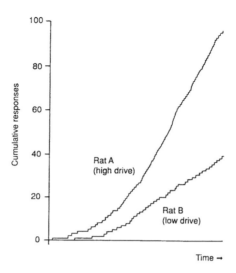

Figure 5.4. Operant conditioning of differently motivated rats. From Hilgard et al. (1971).

shock (the US) after or simultaneously with the sound of a bell (the CS). Note that delivery of the shock is not contingent on the dog's response: the dog is not able to avoid the shock. The instrumental learning situation can be established by attaching the electrode to the floor on which the dog's paw is resting. When the leg is raised, contact with the shock electrode is broken. The sound of the bell can then be used as a signal that shock is imminent. In this situation, the dog is able to avoid the shock by raising its leg. The (negative) reinforcement has been made contingent on the dog's behavior.

The *avoidance or escape response* is based on the negative reinforcement of an electric shock. In the same way, an appetitive or approach response can be learned by using a positive reinforcer like food or water. These responses have been studied extensively in the Skinner box, named after B.F. Skinner, who did important work in this area. The Skinner box is an experimental cage in which an animal is confined. If a rat presses a lever in the box, a food pellet or a sip of water appears in a cup next to the lever. In experiments with pigeons, an illuminated disc is used at which the animal may peck with its beak. As in classical conditioning, the *operant response* becomes more likely after a series of reinforcement trials. Furthermore, the learning motivation of the animal, experimentally manipulated by keeping it more or less hungry, influences the learning speed. (See Figure 5.4.)

In operant conditioning, the reinforcement is only presented after a particular behavior has been shown. For example, a pigeon is reinforced only after it has pecked the bottom of the box to the right. The learned response can be further changed by only reinforcing if a second behavior has been shown, for example turning around after pecking the bottom of the box, turning around, making a bow only when the light is on, etcetera. The process by which the animal is reinforced selectively for gradually more sophisticated behavior at successive stages is called *shaping*.

Shaping occurs frequently in everyday life, for example in language learning. At first, a baby is reinforced by a smile from her mother for any verbal utterance, resulting in many verbal utterances. Then, only utterances resembling the word "mama" are reinforced. Later, the child is taught to say "mama" only to her mother. By this time, the meaning of the word has been learned.

An important application of operant conditioning in education is *programed instruction*, to which Skinner made important contributions.[9] In programed instruction, teaching material is presented in small units, after each of which a student is prompted to give a response to ensure her proper understanding. Typically, the response consists of filling in a blank with the correct word, to answer a question, etcetera. The knowledge and insight of the student is continuously shaped in programed learning since each piece of teaching material builds upon knowledge acquired in earlier parts of the program. (See Figure 5.5.)

Learning by operant conditioning may sometimes go unnoticed by an individual. For example, subjects talking with an experimenter were given only reactions like "You're right", "I agree" or "That's so", to statements in which they gave an opinion of their own, for example "I think . . . ", "I believe . . . ", etcetera. After a time, the subjects were putting forward significantly more of their own opinions. When reinforcement by the experimenter stopped, the subjects' talk became normal again.[10]

Another example is *biofeedback*, in which subjects can be taught to slow down their respiration, heartbeat or blood pressure by operant conditioning techniques.

The frequency and intensity of the learned or operant response have been found to vary as a function of the *schedule of reinforcement*. Four schedules have been examined extensively: fixed and variable interval and fixed and variable ratio schedules.

The *fixed interval* schedule consists of regular reinforcement after a fixed period of time, e.g. one minute. Typically, response rate decreases immediately after a reinforcement and increases at the end of the time interval (prior to the reinforcement, see Figure 5.6). An example of this is the regular payment of salary by the end of the month.

In the *variable interval* schedule, the mean time interval for reinforcement is constant. However, in one instance the reinforcement may follow closely after the previous one and in another instance may be given relatively late.

Cover the answer column with a slider, read one frame at a time, write the answer in the blank, and then move the slider to uncover the correct answer.

1. Several stimuli are able to produce specific behavior, e.g. the sight of food produces salivation, a blow of cold air produces shivering. Since the response occurs spontaneously, the stimuli are called *unconditioned stimuli* (US) and the behavior is called the _____ response.   unconditioned

2. If the unconditioned stimulus (US) is preceded by an unrelated stimulus a number of times, e.g. by the sound of a bell, the organism becomes conditioned to it. The unrelated stimulus is called the _____ stimulus.   conditioned

3. The repeated pairing of *unconditioned* (US) and *conditioned* stimuli (CS) is called the _____ process.   conditioning

4. After a number of pairings of CS and US, the response occurs after presentation of the CS alone. The conditioning process has established a _____ response.   conditioned

5. Ivan Pavlov, a Russian physiologist, was the first to discover the process of conditioning. Hence, it is called *classical conditioning*. During classical conditioning, the US is presented _____ the CS.   after
Therefore, the US is called a *reinforcement*.

6. After classical conditioning, the _____ is followed   conditioned stimulus
by the response, whether or not the US (or reinforcement) is   (CS)
provided.

7. The process of *operant conditioning* is based on the principle of reinforcement, given after a response has occurred. In operant conditioning, the response is not conditioned preceded by a

_____.   conditioned stimulus

8. In operant conditioning, the reinforcement is made contingent on the behavior. The organism shows a response in order to get a reward. Hence, the process has also been called *instrumental*

_____.   conditioning

9. In operant conditioning, the response is strengthened by repeated rewards. It is said that the _____ response   operant
becomes more likely after a series of reinforcements.

10. Usually, the operant response is not the end of the learning process. In the course of the process, reinforcement is given after a slightly different _____. The continuous change   response
in the selection of the target behavior (to be reinforced) is called *shaping*.

11. By shaping, the operant response can become very sophisticated.
B.F. Skinner, the inventor of this technique, taught pigeons
to play a ping-pong game by consequent _____ of   reinforcement
selected behavior.

12. An application of operant conditioning is *programed
instruction*, in which students are gradually introduced into
a particular field of knowledge. After offering the students a
small piece of knowledge, they are prompted for an
_____ response.   operant

13. The operant response in programed instruction is reinforced
by the experience of success or failure upon discovery of the
correct response. By gradually _____ the knowledge in   shaping
small steps, students can be taught such items as the principles
of conditioning, for example.

14. One important difference between classical and operant
conditioning is that, in classical conditioning the most important
things happen _____ a response is made; in operant   before
conditioning, they take place _____ a response is made.   after

15. In classical conditioning, the key aspects of learning
occur between two _____, a CS and a US; in operant conditioning, stimuli
the key aspects of learning occur in the association of the
organism's response with the _____.   reinforcement

Figure 5.5. An example of programed instruction.

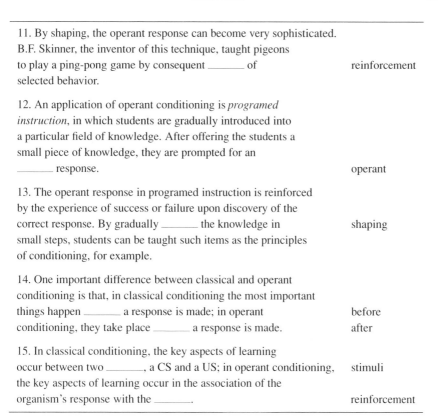

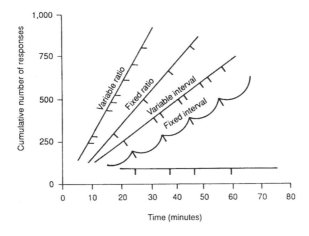

Figure 5.6. The effectiveness of reinforcement schedules after conditioning. From Skinner
(1961).

This procedure ensures a steady rate of operant responses. An example of this is the drawing of government securities.

The *fixed ratio* schedule is based not on the time interval between reinforcements but on reinforcement given after each of a particular number of responses, e.g. in payments proportional to the number of units produced.

In the *variable ratio* schedule, the average number of responses after which reinforcement is given is held constant. In the latter schedule, the likelihood of reinforcement is equal after each response. The ratio schedules may lead to very high response rates (in the variable ratio schedule, it may be even higher than with continuous reinforcement of each response). An example of this is gambling, with fixed probabilities of winning or losing. If the ratio of reinforcement to response becomes too low, however, this may lead to extinction of the operant response.

The effectiveness of the different schedules of reinforcement can be distinguished according to the effect on the learning process and on the maintainance of the behavior learned. It appears that the schedules most similar to continuous reinforcement, i.e. the fixed schedules (if the intervals and ratios are not too large), are most effective during the learning process. However, the ratio schedules are more effective in maintaining behavior than the interval schedules, once the behavior has been learned. (See Figure 5.6.)

The partial reward schedules appear to be more successful than the continuous reward schedules. This is explained by assuming the frustrating (motivational) effect of non-reward.[11] The effect was shown by an experiment in which rats had to run through alley 1 to obtain food in box 1, after which they had to run through alley 2 to obtain food in box 2. First, rats were trained to run through the alleys on a continuous reward schedule. Secondly, continuous reward of running in alley 1 was changed into partial reward. Partial reward of running in alley 1 was followed by faster running through alley 2 than continuous reward of running through alley 1. This was also true for rats that were never rewarded in the first stage. It appeared that frustration (not obtaining an expected reward) motivated running in alley 2.

Conditioning processes are assumed to be very powerful in practice. Skinner assumed that even a political system could be successfully based on the behavioristic scheme.[12] In "Walden Two", he sketched a utopian society that could be engineered through behavioral control. Criminality could be systematically extinguished and cooperative, humanistic behavior could be encouraged through reinforcement. In this way, everyone could live a prosperous life under the control of positive reinforcement.

Reflections on the motivating aspects of rewards

In Chapter 3, overjustification has been considered, assuming crowding out of intrinsic motivations by the provision of external rewards. However, learning theory assumes that rewards will increase the likelihood of behavior with regard to its baseline probability, even after rewards have been terminated. On the face of it, overjustification and learning theory constitute a paradox. This point is related to the dual nature of rewards.[13]

Firstly, it has been stated that learning theory has frequently been tested using animals. In contrast with animals, humans make inferences about the causes of behavior from the situation.[14] Secondly, except for the extinction phase, intrinsic and extrinsic motivations cannot be distinguished since intrinsic motivation is only revealed from spontaneous behavior, i.e. without giving reward. Thirdly, intrinsic motivation is associated with interesting tasks, not dull tasks frequently used in learning experiments. Thus, the paradox may only exist for humans, performing interesting tasks without obtaining rewards.

Furthermore, rewards are assumed to include two aspects, a controlling and an informational aspect. The controlling aspect of rewards is evident when they are given to induce the behavior per se, irrespective of the quality of performance, like piece rate payment of factory workers. The controlling aspect generally may crowd out intrinsic motivations. The informational aspect conveys information about a person's competence in performing the task and about the degree of self-determination or freedom in conducting the behavior. An example of the informational aspect of rewards is a bonus given to a worker for good performance. The informational aspect generally may enhance or crowd in intrinsic motivations. The relative salience of the two aspects determines the type of motivation elicited.

Conclusion

The process of operant conditioning plays an important part in the adaptation of individuals to their environment. Useful, adaptive behavior is reinforced while useless behavior is not. The idea of manipulating this process is applied in education and upbringing, in labor and other economic contexts and in political systems. Several reinforcement schedules are effective in influencing behavior.

In human learning, the control function of rewards should be distinguished from their information function, the former being consistent with the overjustification effect and the latter fostering internal behavior motivation.

5.4. Other types of learning

Learning may take place by different mechanisms. The theories of classical and operant conditioning are not concerned with cognitive processes underlying behavior. In the behavioristic approach, learning is studied in terms of stimuli and responses and the subject is treated as a *Black Box*. As we stated at the start of this chapter, there exist other theories of learning. A general paradigm in which the organism is made the object of study is the Stimulus-Organism-Response (*S-O-R*) scheme. This scheme enables us to study processes in the organism.

In *cognitive learning*, behavior changes may occur as a result of insight. For example, chimpanzees with no experience of how to reach bananas attached to the ceiling of a room were observed to make a pile of three boxes and climb up to grab a banana from the ceiling.[15] Typically, in this kind of experiment insight occurred suddenly after a certain period of trial and error. Human beings frequently show the same kind of behavior in problem solving, e.g. in choosing the most satisfying food item, buying the best insurance, taking the best decision for a company, etcetera. The mental processes in this case involve reasoning, imagination and creative thinking.

Another instance of cognitive processes in learning is the cognitive map, developed in *latent learning*. It has been observed that rats running through a maze without reinforcement learn more quickly in later reinforcement trials than rats without experience with the maze. Thus, the knowledge of the maze was applied to the learning process of finding the food in the right place. This has been interpreted as latent learning, in which a cognitive map of the maze is developed.[16] Latent learning can hardly be explained by classical behavioristic theories, since mental processes (i.e. memory) are involved. A cognitive map of a country and its infrastructure may be very helpful in the search for a suitable location of a factory, an office or a holiday destination.

Biological mechanisms play a part in the development of the central nervous system to promote learning in early childhood. For example, Piaget's theory of child development is based on maturation processes that are completed in a certain order.[17] Not until one stage of development is completed do learning processes in the following stage take place. The following qualitatively different stages are distinguished:
- Sensorimotor stage.
  Coordination of sensory experiences with physical actions. Age range from birth to two years.
- Preoperational stage.
  Representation of the world with words and images and increased symbolic thinking. Inability to perform mental exercises. For example, the concept of weight conservation, the awareness of the same weight of an object

appearing in different forms (e.g. a clay ball which is stretched in the form of a snake), cannot be acquired before the so-called concrete operation stage. In this stage the child is egocentric in that it cannot distinguish between its own and someone else's point of view. Age range from 2 to 7 years.

— Concrete operational stage.
Logical reasoning about concrete events and classification of objects into different sets. Inability to reason in the abstract. Age range from 7 to 11 years.

— Formal operational stage.
Reasoning in more abstract and logical ways. Age range from 11 to 15 years.

Research into economic socialization indicates that development of economic reasoning in children proceeds broadly speaking along the lines of the Piagetian stages.[18]

Biological processes in old age have a different impact on learning, frequently reducing the learning capabilities.

In *social learning* it is assumed that behavior is not only learned by conditioning but also by observing and utilising the results of other people's behavior and by devising cognitive plans and strategies of learning.[19] Observational learning involves four conditions. The first condition implies that attention is paid to another person who is under observation (the model). It appears that warm, powerful, atypical individuals generally get more attention than do cold, weak, typical individuals. Secondly, the model's behavior has to be remembered in order to be reproduced by the observer. A simple verbal description or a vivid image of what the model did assists retention. Thirdly, the observer is able to reproduce the model's behavior better if the requisite physical possibilities are available (e.g. physical strength if the model is a strong person). Finally, imitative behavior is more likely if the model is rewarded for a particular behavior. Reinforcement of the model takes the form of a (vicarious) reinforcement for the observer.[20] Economic examples of social learning may involve imitation of successful entrepreneurs or managers, innovators (e.g. in fashion), scientists, sportsmen, etcetera.

Conclusion

Several theories have developed as alternatives to the theories of learning by conditioning. Cognitive theories deal with mental processes in the organism. Biological theories deal with the organism's maturation processes. Social learning deals with learning by observation of other people. In these theories, the Black Box approach is replaced by an interest in processes taking place within the organism.

5.5. Economic socialization

Economic socialization includes consumer socialization, which has been defined as:

> "... processes by which young people acquire skills, knowledge and attitudes relevant to their functioning as consumers in the market-place ..."[21]

The relevance of studying consumer socialization is to predict adult behavior, development of consumer education programs, more effective marketing directed at young people, and understanding family behavior and intergenerational behavior.[22]

Many researchers have concentrated on children's understanding of the principles behind conventional (adult) economic behaviors such as working and spending, borrowing and lending, investing and saving.[23] However, the study of real economic behavior of children, such as saving up to buy gifts, the use of money boxes, marble games and swopping, should give better insights into the precursers of adult economic behavior.

A study in the first tradition dealt with children's understanding of a shop-keeper's profit taking, and consumer saving and borrowing.[24] It appeared that full understanding of these issues increased with the children's age (6–11 years) and mother's education. This points to the important role of the mother as a socializing agent. A socialization study across ten countries was reported in a special issue of the *Journal of Economic Psychology*.[25] The findings support the effect of age in children's understanding of economic behavior, e.g. how prices are determined, how salaries are allocated and how investments are made. Country effects in children's understanding were less easily interpreted. Regarding economic attitudes, e.g. causes and consequences of wealth and unemployment, differences across countries (North/South) were found but age effects were negligible.

Studies in the second tradition deal with children's spending behavior in a shop under controlled conditions. The effect of experience and responsibility with regard to money on spending behavior was investigated in an experimental shop.[26] Children of 6, 8 and 10 years old were provided either with $4.00 in cash or with a credit card worth the same amount (actually, this card was a debit card). To the extent that children lack understanding of monetary exchange, they were expected to spend more on credit than in cash.

On average, more money was spent in the credit card condition than in the cash condition. Although the older children had more money and knew more about credit, age did not explain the difference in spending. However, it appeared that getting general allowance rather than specific payment for household chores significantly decreased the difference in spending across the two conditions. Furthermore, it appeared that children getting an allowance had a better knowledge of prices than the other children, especially at the age of 6. The authors attributed the effect of allowance to a greater responsibility for the money they receive, greater efforts and higher sophistication in dealing with it.

A second experiment studied the source of money spent in the shop and several other factors in more detail.[27] In addition to allowances, conditions were included in which the children obtained $4.00 either as a gift or as a compensation for a cleaning job, an attractive versus an unattractive shop, heavy-handed versus gentle consumer guidance by the parents, and high versus low expectations of the parents regarding the children's age at which they should be able to act alone.

Some validation of the effect of allowances in the first study was found in positive correlations between payment for chores and heavy-handed guidance and between payment for chores and lower economic expectations. This indicates that allowance versus payment for chores reflects the style of education. On average, children spent more in the attractive than in the unattractive store. Further analyses revealed that this effect was greater for children who obtained allowance, who were high on the gentle guidance variable, whose mothers had high expectations and were paid for the cleaning job in the experiment than for the other children. Again, it appeared that the style of education affected the rationality of spending.

Several findings from studying 'children economies' may be summarized:[28]

− In the 'marble economy', 'capitalists' providing marbles could be distinguished from 'workers' who were experts in playing with the capitalists' marbles. Usually, the capitalists take the greater share of the proceeds.
− The value of marbles is subject to local supply and demand rather than commensurate with shop prices.
− 'Scrambling', throwing all the marbles in the air to be collected by the other children, seems to be a status-enhancing act.
− Swopping seems to be a favorite activity at age 9 or 10 and may include items such as pencils, toys, erasers, stickers, football cards and food. Even 'bad swops' may occur deliberately, as a gesture of friendship.

Although economic socialization studies are still in their infancy, several learning principles may be relevant here. Conditioning principles should contribute to experience, cognitive learning should be stimulated by gentle guidance and giving allowances and social learning should be relevant in children economies.

Conclusion

Although earlier research on economic socialization focused on the time and the order of mastering economic concepts, more recent research has dealt with the effects of guidance and upbringing styles on economic behavior and on behavior in 'child economies'. Longitudinal research should learn whether different economic socialization processes lead to different adjustments to adult economic life.

5.6. A conflict model of purchase behavior

Economic demand for goods is explained from maximizing the utility function under a budget constraint, assuming rational consumer behavior. However, in many instances the rationality hypothesis cannot be maintained. For example, the effectiveness of the variable ratio schedule of reinforcement considered above cannot be explained in economic terms. In a model by Alhadeff,[29] the notions of rationality and utility are dispensed with and substituted by lawful relations of behavior, such as those considered above. Unless indicated otherwise, this section has been based on Alhadeff.

Purchase behavior typically can be considered as an operant response, since the reinforcement takes place after the behavior response has occurred. Generally, reinforcement in purchase behavior is given continuously (after each purchase goods or services). It appears from psychological research into operant conditioning that continuous reinforcement induces a steady rate of responses.

In economics, goods are assumed to provide utility because of consumer tastes, needs and wants. In the learning model of buying behavior, utility has been replaced by reinforcement, which has been defined as the stimulus that strengthens the response, either being the approach toward a particular behavior (in case of a positive reinforcement) or the avoidance of a behavior (with negative reinforcement). Depending on the type of reinforcement, a classification of goods has been drawn up including primary commodities, secondary commodities and escape/avoidance commodities.

A *primary commodity* functions as an unconditioned stimulus, providing a positive reinforcement, for example items of food and drinks.

An *avoidance commodity* is based on the avoidance of a negative reinforcer. Examples of these are aspirin (to avoid headaches), umbrellas and raincoats (to protect one of becoming drenched), air conditioners (to escape or avoid extreme temperatures and humidity), etcetera.

A *secondary commodity* functions as a conditioned stimulus, paired with a positive reinforcer, for example status goods like jewelry or cars. In the past, these goods have been paired with other persons' approval and esteem (considered as unconditioned stimuli). Some commodities serve as generalized reinforcers, since these have previously been paired with several unconditioned stimuli. For example, clothes can be considered generalized reinforcers, since these provide warmth and protection, as well as a particular status between people in society. Because of stimulus generalization, a large number of commodities may function as secondary reinforcers, although actually not all of these may have been paired with unconditioned stimuli in the past.

The classification of commodities above is related to the distinction of tranformational and informational commodities (cf. Box 9.1).[30] *Transformational commodities* convert a baseline utility level into a utility increase. In ads, these commodities are generally accompanied by positive stimuli such as a happy family, a beautiful woman, soft music, etcetera.[31] Transformational commodities include the primary and secondary commodities mentioned above. *Informational commodities* (the above mentioned avoidance goods) convert negative feelings into neutral feelings. In ads, information regarding the effectiveness of these commodities is provided frequently.

The consequences of buying behavior are both positively reinforcing and aversive. The positively reinforcing consequences strengthen *approach behavior* (making the operant buy response more likely); the aversive consequences associated with the loss of money strengthen *avoidance behavior* (making the buy response less likely). Purchase behavior is the outcome of these two incompatible behaviors. The model to be discussed henceforth has been called a conflict model.[32]

The strength of the approach behavior is a function of several variables:

— The level of deprivation of the subject regarding the primary reinforcement influences the strength of the approach behavior for primary commodities. For secondary commodities, the strength of the approach behavior depends on the associated primary reinforcer. For example, the need for a taxi depends on the need for food in the restaurant. To get to the restaurant one requires a taxi.

— The reinforcement schedule of the primary reinforcement affects the strength of approach behavior. In most purchase behavior, the continuous schedule prevails. However, the intermittent schedules play a part when acquiring financial assets or commodities which are being purchased for the first time, e.g. innovative goods, a dinner in a new restaurant, etcetera.

— The delay between purchase and reinforcement influences the strength of approach behavior. This is not assumed to be an important variable in purchase behavior, although delay may occur in the ordering and delivery of a car or furniture, for example.

— The quantity and the quality of reinforcement has been found to influence approach behavior significantly.

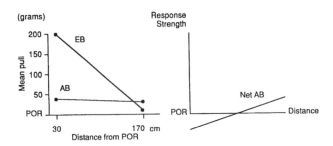

Figure 5.7. Strength of approach and escape behavior of rats. From Davis Alhadeff, Microeconomics and Human Behavior. Copyright ©1982 The Regents of the University of California.

The strength of avoidance behavior is a function of essentially the same variables that determine the strength of approach behavior. The loss of money in the purchase of commodities is a negative consequence in at least three senses: in the past, loss of money has frequently been associated with disapproval (by parents, friends, etcetera). It is associated with the impeded or blocked access to other positive reinforcers (depending on the size and stability of the budget) and it implies a loss of a direct positive reinforcer, in that losing money in itself is painful (e.g. as compared to payments by means of credit cards).[33]

In an experimental setting, the strength of approach (escape) behavior of rats toward (away from) a positive (negative) reinforcer has been measured.[34] After being trained to run down an alley to obtain food at the end, the rat was fitted with a light harness that did not interfere with its movement. At different distances from the food point, the rat was restrained and the pull strength exerted on the harness was measured. At 30 cm from the food, the pull strength was 56.5 grams, whereas it was 40.9 grams at 170 cm. The approach strength thus varied positively with proximity to the positive reinforcer. The escape strength was measured in a different series of experiments with electric shocks serving as negative reinforcements. At 30 cm from the shock point, the pull strength exerted on the harness was 198.4 grams. At 170 cm, only four rats (out of twenty) exerted pull strength, being 10 grams on average. These results are graphically presented in Figure 5.7. The strength of approach behavior relative to the strength of the escape behavior is presented as the *net response strength* in the figure. Although Figure 5.7 suggests linear approach and avoidance functions, they may actually be concave and convex functions, respectively, since 'good things satiate and bad things escalate'.[35] Consequently, the net response strength may actually be represented as a single-peaked preference function.[36]

These experiments bear implications for consumer behavior, since the strength of approach behavior relative to the strength of the escape behavior can be considered as the likelihood that a commodity will be purchased. The electric shocks used to measure escape behavior in these experiments are analogous to the commodity's price. The net response strength as a function of the negative reinforcer is analogous to the demand curve in economics.

Alhadeff puts restrictions on the effectiveness of reinforcers. Beyond the *satiation point*, a reinforcer may no longer be an effective determinant of approach behavior. Likewise, the budget constraint limits the effectiveness of the negative reinforcement of a money loss. Several other extensions of the model will not be dealt with here. The model may serve as a paradigm to integrate the psychological theory of learning and the economic theory of consumer demand but is still awaiting further empirical testing.

Conclusion

Alhadeff's model mainly deals with purchase behavior, based on conditioning processes. The balance of positive and negative reinforcement has been assumed in order to explain economic behavior. A classification of commodities has been proposed, based on these reinforcing qualities.

Summary

Learning processes are extremely important in adaptive behavior of human beings. Two mainstreams in psychological learning theory can be distinguished: behaviorism, based on the analysis of stimuli and responses and theories, dealing explicitly with organismic processes.

Behaviorism mainly deals with changes in behavior due to conditions in the environment. Classical conditioning is concerned with the pairing of stimuli before the occurrence of a response. Operant conditioning is based on reinforcement contingent on behavior.

Other types of learning deal with cognitive, biological and social aspects of mental processes taking place in learning. Probably, no single learning theory can account for the many different instances of learning and possibly a combination of approaches is most practical. However, different styles of guidance and upbringing may lead to different types of economic socialization.

An attempt to apply behavioristic learning principles to economic behavior is made by Alhadeff, who considers the benefits of commodities as positive reinforcements influencing behavior and the prices as negative reinforcements. These reinforcements induce respectively approach and avoidance tendencies regarding the commodities the balance of which determines behavior.

BOX 5.1

TOKEN ECONOMY

A *token economy* can be described as a closed system in which the behavior of its participants may be rewarded by means of tokens. Tokens, in the form of metal or plastic chips, stamps, printed papers, punched cards or merely points, are worthless in themselves but may be exchanged for commodities which have some value for the participants.

Token economies have been developed frequently in psychiatric wards and in classrooms to encourage normal behavior or educational achievement, respectively. The tokens serve as conditioned stimuli, giving access to unconditioned stimuli of various kinds, such as a room of one's own, a pass to walk on the grounds or to visit a nearby town or even an extra religious service. The conditioned stimuli are used as secondary reinforcements in operant conditioning of target behaviors, such as self-care, eating of meals, etcetera.

The tokens may be given as rewards for different behaviors of different people. For example, in a classroom, one pupil may be given a token for good performance in writing, another pupil for gymnastics and so on. To prevent mutual exchange of tokens, *personalized tokens* may be used. There is overwhelming evidence that target behaviors change when a token economy is introduced.[37] These changes generally persist as long as the token system is maintained. In addition, social interaction between inmates and between inmates and staff is enhanced by the token system. Token economies have frequently and often with substantial success been introduced in the back wards of institutions with severe and chronic psychiatric patients for whom there is no real hope of a cure.

Interestingly, several outcomes of token economies relevant to economics may be reported.[38]

— Since token rewards lead to increased rates of specific target behaviors, in economic terms the rewards increase the supply of labor to the jobs for which they are paid. Increase of token reward for some jobs leads to more labor supply to the high-paid jobs. However, raising real income by raising all token pay rates together may lead to a reduction in total labor supply.

— Raising the token price of commodities generally reduces the quantities purchased. More sophisticated studies, taking into account the whole demand system of commodities that can be purchased by tokens, show that the effects of token income on purchasing are consistent with economic expectations.

— The saving of tokens has been found to increase with token income and token earnings to decline with accumulated savings. In a token economy for pre-delinquent boys, token 'interest' was deemed necessary to encourage saving, while in a preschool token economy, children were observed lending tokens at interest to each other.

— Two other phenomena, giving tokens away and token gambling, are frequently observed, as this occurs with money in real life.

— Although in token economies consumption is decoupled from production and prices and wages are entirely under the control of institution authorities, studies have been made of macroeconomic issues such as economic growth and income inequality.

It appears that growth of the token economy is encouraged by staff, since it is the index of the clients' degree of commitment to the therapeutic system. If token earnings increase, either the price of commodities should be increased (causing inflation) or the supply and the variety of commodities should be increased to prevent token economy decline.

Studies concerning token income inequality have shown that the Gini coefficient (an economic measure of income inequality) compares quite reasonably with Gini coefficients found in the U.S. economy. Another analog with the real economy is that female token earnings averaged 70% of male earnings, only slightly more than the typical values in Western societies.

The principle of token economies is operant conditioning. This not only has therapeutic effects, it also facilitates the study of reinforcement schedules of interest to psychologists and changes in incomes and prices of interest to economists. In conclusion, much economic behavior is very probably induced by reinforcement-like processes. That is, in the real economy as in the token economy, reinforced behavior patterns contribute substantially to our economic behavior.

Notes

[1] Hilgard et al. 1971.
[2] See Figure 2.5.
[3] McSweeney and Bierley 1984.
[4] Watson and Raynor 1920.
[5] Bernstein 1978.
[6] See Sawry et al. 1956.
[7] Rescorla 1968, 1988.
[8] Rescorla 1968, p. 1.
[9] Skinner 1954.
[10] Verplanck 1955.

[11] Amsel 1958, 1962.

[12] Skinner 1948.

[13] Deci and Porac 1978 and Deci and Ryan 1980.

[14] See also Section 11.3.

[15] Kohler 1925.

[16] Tolman 1948.

[17] In Ginsburg and Opper 1969.

[18] See Stacey 1982, Furnham and Lewis 1986 and Sevón and Weckström 1988.

[19] Bandura 1986.

[20] See Section 5.2.

[21] Ward 1974, p. 2.

[22] Ward 1974.

[23] Webley and Lea 1993.

[24] Nakhaie 1993.

[25] Leiser et al. 1990.

[26] Abramovitch et al. 1991.

[27] Pliner et al. 1994.

[28] Webley and Lea 1993.

[29] Alhadeff 1982.

[30] Rossiter and Percy 1987.

[31] Wells 1981.

[32] See Section 9.1 for different types of conflicts.

[33] The different reinforcing value of out-of-pocket money and opportunity costs is considered in Section 12.3.

[34] Brown 1948.

[35] Coombs and Avrunin 1977.

[36] See also Section 4.6.

[37] Lea et al. 1987.

[38] Lea et al. 1987.

CHAPTER 6

ATTITUDE

6.1. Development of the attitude concept

In behavioristic learning theory, the cognitive and affective processes of the human mind are not considered. In social psychology, however, these processes have been studied in depth. Cognitive and affective reactions to the environment are combined into the individual's attitude toward objects and actions in the world. An *attitude* can be considered as an individual predisposition to evaluate an object or an aspect of the world in a favorable or unfavorable manner.[1] Attitudes are important in the individual's adaptation to the environment. By the learning process, positive attitudes are associated with the satisfaction of needs and negative attitudes are associated with negative reinforcements.[2]

Attitudes perform several psychological functions for human beings. In the *functional* theory of attitudes, instrumental, ego-defensive, value-expressive and knowledge functions are distinguished.[3]

An important function of attitudes in economic behavior is the *instrumental* or *utilitarian* function. According to this function, attitudes serve as a means to an end, for example, an entrepreneur favoring a liberal party in order to improve the circumstances of the enterprise. Attitudes can be expressed in various ways, for example verbally, in which case we speak of opinions, unconsciously by means of physiological changes (e.g. heart rate, dilation of the pupil, etcetera) or by taking actions (e.g. voting for the liberal party).

The *ego-defensive* function of attitudes is to keep one's self-perception in agreement with reality. For example, a person insecure about her own worth may hold favorable attitudes toward conspicuous consumer goods, since by owning these items she can regard herself as superior to other people.

The *value-expressive* function of attitudes is to express oneself in terms of attitudes (or actions) that are consonant with personal values, e.g. engage in entrepreneurial behavior while fostering strong liberal values. This function of attitudes may also be applied to consumer satisfaction resulting in a favorable attitude toward a product.[4] In this case, attitudes develop after the purchase, whereas the instrumental function implies that behavior follows the attitude, given the restrictions.[5]

The *knowledge* function of attitudes is to structure one's experiences so as to be consistent with one's former knowledge structure. For example, by adding reasons for income inequality to the consciousness of one's own wealth. Another aspect of the knowledge function of attitudes is that attitudes can be considered as summarized information (chunks) concerning behavioral alternatives or objects in the environment. This may considerably speed up decision making and action, since the information processing stage can be omitted.[6]

Attitudes have directive influence on behavior toward objects with which it is related.[7] The object is said to have some undifferentiated positive (or negative) value for the individual. This value is represented in a one-dimensional space, disregarding qualitatively different aspects of the object. An example of such an attitude might be the global favorable evaluation of gambling, leading to many visits to the casino.

This idea has been developed further by Lewin,[8] who distinguishes *valences* as regions within the life space of an individual that attract or repulse that individual. In addition, he assumes that the strength of the valence as well as the distance of the person to the valence determine the psychological force acting upon the individual. The distance of an individual to a valence, in our view, might be interpreted psychologically as the saliency of aspects of the environment for an individual.[9] This implies that irrelevant aspects (for example, alternatives not in the choice set of the individual), are not taken into consideration. Lewin, by assuming numerous different valences in the life space, assumes that the psychological forces form a resultant force which determines the direction and intensity of the attitude. An example of this might be a shelf in a supermarket containing different types of soft drinks. Each brand has some valence, although some brands are disregarded by a consumer (these brands being psychologically distant). The different brands of soft drinks exert psychological forces on the consumer, eventually forming the resultant force which determines the purchase action.

Later, Tolman elaborated upon the psychological structure underlying actions.[10] According to Tolman, people make cognitive distinctions which they value, according to their relevance for satisfying personal needs. Lewin, too, assumes that valences tend to reduce tensions in the human being. Tolman assumes an inner psychological structure, organized as a *matrix of beliefs and evaluations*, which determines selection of (preference for) possible behavior. (See Figure 6.1). Tolman goes one step further than Lewin in differentiating aspects of an object. Beliefs and values no longer concern the object as a whole but involve particular aspects of them, for example the food, the service, the price of food in a restaurant instead of the restaurant as a whole. Each aspect

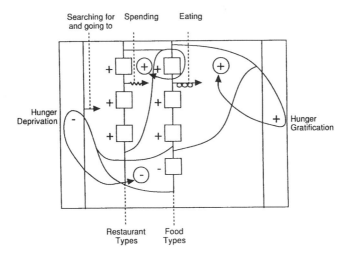

Figure 6.1. Belief-value matrix regarding eating in a restaurant. From Tolman (1951).

may be valued for its need-satisfying properties for an individual.

Since aspects of the environment satisfy individual needs, the values of these aspects can be considered as *importance weights*, associated with the aspects. Important aspects of the environment are generally assumed to contribute more to the total evaluation of an object than less important aspects. The evaluation of aspects, or importance weights, is assumed to be related to the need state of an individual. Underfed individuals, for example, will evaluate the nutritional aspects of food more positively in general than individuals who consumes their meals regularly. The importance aspect of attitudes may be related to Cattell's concept of ergic tension.[11] Ergic tension refers to the strength of an independent basic motivational factor.[12] The motivations are assumed to influence the evaluation of aspects of the environment in a variety of ways. Individuals with a negative time preference, for example, will evaluate delayed benefits of life insurance more positively than individuals with a positive time preference.

Evaluative and cognitive responses to an object together constitute the attitude.[13] The cognitive responses pertain to the *perceived instrumentality* of the aspects in satisfying different needs. The perceived instrumentalities are stated as an individual's beliefs regarding the need satisfying content of the aspects. For example, an individual might believe that a bar of chocolate (an object) contains X grams of sugar (an aspect of the object). Furthermore, the individual may evaluate the intake of sugar as more or less beneficial, depending on her need state.

An attitude toward an object consists of the sum of beliefs, weighted by

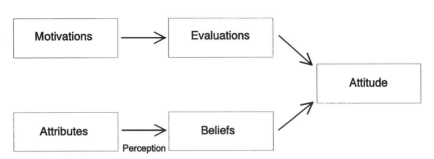

Figure 6.2. Attitude components and their determinants.

their importance, over all relevant aspects of the object. When the belief regarding an aspect is denoted by b, the importance of the aspect by e and the number of relevant aspects by I, the attitude, A, equals:

$$A = \sum_{i=1}^{T} b_i e_i.$$

This formal conception of attitude has been maintained by Fishbein, who characterizes a *belief* as the subjective probability that the object possesses a particular attribute and uses the evaluation of attributes instead of their importance.[14]

The beliefs regarding aspects of the environment are based on objective properties of an object, e.g. the amount of sugar in a bar of chocolate measured in grams. Since the perception of physical stimuli follows psychophysical laws,[15] a belief regarding an aspect can be considered as a sensation, associated with an objective quantity. The conception of attitude, based on evaluations and beliefs, is useful in practice, since beliefs can be stated even if objective measurement is not possible (for example, regarding the possible side effects of nuclear energy). Besides, perceived instrumentalities may be assumed to relate more directly to human behavior than objective measures of the contents of aspects. Figure 6.2 shows the relationships between the components of attitudes and their determinants.

The weighted summation of beliefs, constituting the attitude, obviously is only one possible formalization. In extending the psychology of perception to multiple stimuli, sensations may be related to multiple objective stimuli by means of a *multiplicative power law*.[16] For example, the perception of social status, ψ, has been related to several stimuli, ϕ, such as income, occupational and educational status as follows:

$$\psi = b \prod_{i=1}^{I} \phi_i^{c_i},$$

b and *c* being psychophysical constants. Evidence for composite power functions has been found with a number of sensations and stimuli in this line of research. The form of the composite power function is analogous to the Cobb-Douglas function in economics.[17] Alternative specifications of composite power functions include the additive power law[18] and the specification of subjective weights,[19] differing between stimuli and individuals.

In the psychology of perception, the coefficients of the power law are estimated from the relations between stimuli and reported sensations. The approach used in economics is to estimate the coefficients from relations between incomes, prices and demand for commodities. (See Section 6.2.) So, in social psychological attitude research, the evaluations and beliefs are measured *directly* by using survey questions or other psychological measurement techniques,[20] whereas in economics the relevant parameters are estimated *indirectly*. Several issues, related to the direct measurement of attitudes, are discussed in Section 6.3. Public attitudes or images are discussed in Section 6.4. The relation between attitudes and behavior is dealt with in Section 6.5.

Conclusion

Attitudes perform several psychological functions, of which the instrumental function serves to guide behavior. The development of the attitude concept involves a differentiation from a global concept to a combination of opinions regarding the attributes of an alternative. With multiple attributes, the attitude might be conceived as a composite power function of stimulus magnitudes (the objective values of the attributes).

6.2. Attitude and utility

In economics, the concept of utility is related to the psychological attitude in several respects.[21] The conceptual content of *utility* has been described as:

> "... some immediate sensation, which possibly cannot and certainly need not be analyzed any further. In the case of utility the immediate sensation of preference – of one object or aggregate of objects as against another – provides this basis".[22]

As in the global view of attitude,[23] utility is associated with the object as a whole and the qualities of the preference sensation are left unspecified. Both the attitude and the utility concept attach a common meaning to an unobserved phenomenon, assumed to influence behavior.

With the introduction of the *characteristics approach* in economics,[24] utility is assumed to be associated with aspects of commodities. In this approach, a utility function has been defined on amounts of characteristics rather than on quantities of goods and services. This change in the conception of utility is similar to Tolman's introduction of a belief-value matrix associated with objects in the environment. Human needs are assumed to be satisfied by the consumption of characteristics, or attributes, rather than by the consumption of commodities as such. By this approach, it can be explained why the consumer needs a particular brand of a commodity, why innovation of commodities takes place and why commodities disappear from the market.

Originally, characteristics were assumed to be objective, although consumers may have different perceptions of them. However, characteristics are combined to produce the *consumption services* from which consumers obtain utility.[25] For example, the number and the volume of cylinders in an engine, together with the weight of a car, combine to produce acceleration power. In this example, the characteristics as well as the service are objective, although the sensation of acceleration is subjective. The characteristics approach has frequently been applied to durable goods where characteristics are well-defined and are there for everyone to see.[26] In many commodities, however, characteristics are nebulous or present problems of definition and measurement, for example 'obsolescence' or 'style' of a commodity. In these cases, psychological measures of perceived attributes, or stated beliefs, which are consistent with the characteristics approach, can be used.[27]

In economic models of characteristics, the weights given to characteristics or product services, are estimated from consumer behavior. In psychological multi-attribute models, the weights are operationalized as evaluations or importances and are measured directly from consumers. The benefits of the psychological approach are that preferences can be explained directly from consumer information, that unobservable characteristics can be dealt with and that different opinions of consumers are taken into account. A disadvantage of psychological models is the amount of information needed from consumers. A summary of the differences between utility and attitude is presented in Table 6.1.

Another application of the characteristics model is the *hedonic price method*,[28] in which the prices of commodities are related to their objective characteristics. This amounts to demand functions for characteristics, from which the marginal prices of characteristics can be estimated.[29] Since the marginal price of a characteristic is assumed to be constant in a market, this represents the money value of a unit increase of a characteristic for the average consumer. Hedonic price relations can be used to make a price indication of a commodity with certain qualities. If the hedonic method is applied to the prices paid, the marginal prices can be considered as the relative importance weights of characteristics in a market.

Table 6.1. Differences between utility and attitude.

	Utility	Attitude
Global meaning	Preference	Value
Differentiation	Characteristics, services	Beliefs, perceived instrumentalities
Weights	Indirect estimates	Evaluations, perceived importances
Combination	(Non-)linear, multi-attribute	Weighted sum, composite power law
Function	Instrumental	Instrumental, knowledge, value-expressive, ego-defensive

Conclusion

The psychological concept of attitude is related to the economic utility. The multi-attribute approach is similar to the economic model in that it deals directly with perceived and weighted characteristics and services. The technique of revealed preferences in economics amounts to the estimation of perception and weight parameters from relations between characteristics and behavior.

6.3. Issues in attitude research

In this section, several theoretical and practical issues concerning attitudes will be dealt with. Attitude research is frequently carried out in marketing and in opinion research, and each time decisions have to be taken regarding the formulation of survey questions, the computation of attitude scores, the saliency of the attributes involved, the specificity of the attitude, the structure and specification of the attitude model and other variables than attitude explaining behavior. Several of these issues also pertain to the characteristics approach.

Formulation of survey questions

The formulation of survey questions regarding the multi-attribute attitude depends on the choice of the attitude model. Several models are based on a weighted combination of opinions regarding the attributes of an alternative, notably the *Fishbein model* and the *adequacy-importance model*. In the Fishbein model, the attitude toward a behavior is composed of a set of beliefs that performing the behavior leads to a set of consequences and of the evaluation of these consequences. In the Fishbein model, the belief that an attribute leads to a particular consequence is measured by a question of the following type:

"That a color television set of brand *A* will have an expected lifetime of 10 years is:"

very   very
likely ____ : ____ : ____ : ____ : ____ : ____ : ____ unlikely
     +3   +2   +1   0   −1   −2   −3

The evaluation of a consequence is measured by a survey question of the following type:

"Buying a color television set with an expected lifetime of 10 years is:"

very   very
good ____ : ____ : ____ : ____ : ____ : ____ : ____ bad
     +3   +2   +1   0   −1   −2   −3

Since the Fishbein model includes a probability and an evaluation measure of each attribute, it can be conceived as a variant of an expected utility model.[30]

In the adequacy-importance model,[31] the attitude toward an alternative (e.g. a commodity or an act) is composed of a set of evaluations of how satisfactory the alternative performs on a set of attributes and of the importance of these attributes. In the importance model, the satisfaction with an attribute is measured by a question of the following type:

"A color television set of brand A having an expected lifetime of 10 years is:"

very   very
satis-   unsatisfactory ____ : ____ : ____ : ____ : ____ : ____ : ____ factory
     +3   +2   +1   0   −1   −2   −3

The attribute importance is measured by the following type of question:

"An expected lifetime of 10 years for a color television set is:"

very   very
im-   unimportant ____ : ____ : ____ : ____ : ____ : ____ : ____ portant
     +3   +2   +1   0   −1   −2   −3

In some instances, where the probability that an object possesses an attribute is out of the question, the subjective probability measure in the Fishbein model appears to be unrealistic. For example, the probability that a car of brand A, type X, has fuel injection, can in practice only be zero or one. In such cases, the adequacy-importance model would be more appropriate. Obviously the seven-point response scales, running from −3 to +3, can be

Table 6.2. Evaluation of a brand by two individuals.

Attributes	Individual I			Individual II		
	b	e	$b \times e$	b	e	$b \times e$
Reliability	0.8	5	4.0	0.6	4	2.4
Expensiveness	0.5	2	1.0	0.4	1	0.4
Lifetime	0.3	5	1.5	0.4	5	2.0
Energy efficiency	0.4	3	1.2			
Good style	0.2	4	0.8			
Attitude (Σbe)			8.5			4.8
Averaged ($\Sigma be/N$)			1.7			1.6
Normalized ($\Sigma be/\sigma e$)			0.45			0.48

replaced by others, e.g. by five-point scales or nine-point scales. Furthermore, the range of the scales can be adjusted. For example, an evaluation scale might run from zero to one in agreement with utility scales, frequently applied in empirical economics. A natural probability scale should also be defined on the $(0, 1)$ interval.

Computation of attitude scores

The opinion regarding an object's attribute comprises a belief that the attribute is associated with a certain outcome (e.g. a belief that fluoride in the toothpaste of brand X protects the enamel) and the weight associated with an attribute comprises the evaluation or the importance of the outcome (e.g. the favorableness of enamel protection). The probability that the attribute is associated with the outcome (b) can be measured on the $(0, 1)$ probability scale (e.g. $b = 0.8$). The outcome can be evaluated on a good-bad N-point scale, for example running from 1 to 5 (e.g. $e = 4$). The products of b and e are computed for each attribute (e.g. $0.8 \times 4 = 3.2$). In Table 6.2, belief and evaluation scores regarding brand attributes are presented for two individuals. A summation of the $b \times e$ products yields the attitude toward the alternative.

In Table 6.2, the two individuals use different numbers of attributes, some of which are evaluated positively and some negatively. Negatively evaluated attributes (expensiveness) can be compensated by positively evaluated attributes. The attitudes show a relatively large difference, which is somewhat reduced by taking the average over the attributes used. There has been some question about whether the *summed or averaged* measures should be used.[32] For brand comparisons within an individual, this is not a problem since the attitude scale is the same up to a constant. Across individuals, however, the brand comparisons may be different for summed and averaged scales. Frequently, in survey research, a fixed number of attributes is presented to all respondents, in which case adding or averaging is not a problem.

Another issue with respect to the computation of attitudes is *normalization* of the importance weights (dividing each weight by the sum of the weights). It might be assumed that one individual attaches more weight to the attributes than another individual. This poses problems to a comparison of attitudes between different individuals. Again, for brand comparisons within individuals, normalization is not a problem, since the rank order of alternatives is preserved. As a conclusion, normalization needs to be considered for brand comparisons across individuals.[33]

Saliency

The saliency of attributes refers to the actual utilization of attributes in the evaluation of choice alternatives. Due to restrictions on the information handling capacities of human beings,[34] the number of attributes actually used varies between five and nine.[35] The number of salient attributes may vary across individuals, may depend on the object associated with the attitude, on the time available in the formation of the attitude and on the degree of involvement with the object. A practical way of eliciting the salient attributes is to ask subjects to list the attributes of an object. The first five to nine attributes in the list are assumed to be the salient ones. In a sample of individuals, the *modal salient attributes* may be defined as the most frequently mentioned attributes in the sample.

Several criteria for the relevancy of characteristics may be stated, which might be considered as salience criteria.[36] A *universal characteristic* of commodities is considered irrelevant if the maximum quantity that can be obtained by spending the whole budget on one commodity (group) is small in relation to the maximum quantity that can be obtained by spending the whole budget on other commodities. For example, energy-efficiency in electric clocks may be regarded as an irrelevant characteristic because electricity consumption is low compared to electricity consumption of all other electric appliances.

A universal characteristic is considered irrelevant if the content of the characteristic, per dollar spent, is approximately uniform over the commodity choice set. For example, the age of a commodity is more or less inversely related to its price. According to the criterion, the age of a good is not a relevant characteristic.

A characteristic which is invariant in a group of commodities is irrelevant. For example, protective measures against corrosion are taken by all car industries nowadays. Anti-corrosion treatment is therefore no longer considered a relevant characteristic.[37] Although an irrelevant characteristic will not be

Table 6.3. A classification of constraints.

Resources
Income and prices
Available time
Physical and mental attributes
State of technique
Technology
Social technology
Standards
Codified norms
Informal norms and values
Self-imposed constraints

From Frey and Foppa (1986).

included in the choice model, individuals will pay attention to them, just to
check whether the relevance criteria apply.

Other variables explaining behavior

Generally, attitudes only partly explain behavior. Many circumstances might
interfere with the expression of an attitude in behavior. In economics, the
budget restriction can be considered a restriction upon purchase behavior.
In Becker's 'New Home Economics',[38] time is considered a restriction on
activities. In the extended Fishbein model, social norms is considered an extra variable in explaining behavior.[39] Social norms may be codified, that is
formally issued by law and sanctioned by the public authorities, or informal,
that is voluntarily adopted from other people (e.g. tax morality). Other *restrictions* include physical and mental constraints (such as age, health, strength,
intelligence, creative capacities), technical constraints, social constraints (e.g.
public regulations and social inventions, such as car-pooling or dating mechanisms) and *self-imposed constraints* (e.g. taking little cash and no checks
to guard against spending too much).[40] Table 6.3 shows a classification of
restrictions.

These restrictions and extra variables explaining behavior should be used
as an alternative to other proposals to obtain a better correspondence between
attitude and behavior.[41] In the example given above measures of attitude
toward the church (not stated in terms of behavior, however) should be supplemented by an individual's financial situation to explain donations to the
church and by available time and mobility to explain church attendance,

respectively.

Structure of the attitude model

Many different structures of attitude models exist. The global models of attitude do not have a differentiated structure at all. Typically, in this case, the attitude toward an object is characterized by a single statement or an evaluative score.

The multi-attribute models of attitude, considered above, are *compensatory* in that favorable attributes may compensate for unfavorable ones. The attributes in this model are considered to be independent, excluding the possibility that particular attributes are valued only in combination with other attributes. An example of dependent evaluations of attributes is the evaluation of the interior space in a car which may only be valued if it is not at the expense of the luggage space. In interactive attribute models,[42] attribute dependency is accounted for.

Compensatory attitude models demand a lot of information processing by a decision maker. Several models have been developed, dealing with simplified information processing.[43] These include the conjunctive and the disjunctive models, the lexicographic and the elimination by aspects (EBA) model. (See Box 6.1.)

The *conjunctive* attitude model assumes that all of the salient attributes of an object exceed minimum levels (*cutoffs*) in order to be evaluated positively. In this model, attributes below the minimum level cannot be compensated by attributes above this level. This can be considered as a satisficing assumption.[44] The cutoffs can be considered as aspiration levels of the consumer that should be met by the preferred product.

The *disjunctive* model assumes that objects are valued because of one or more outstanding characteristics. Objects with an outstanding attribute cannot be evaluated unfavorably because other attributes are negatively valued.

The *lexicographic* model assumes that evaluation of objects occurs in the salience order of attributes. If two or more objects obtain the same evaluation on the most salient attribute, the second most salient characteristic is used in comparing these objects, etcetera. An object obtaining the highest evaluation of the most salient attribute cannot be valued unfavorably because of less salient unfavorable attributes.

The *elimination by aspects* (EBA) model, like the lexicographic model, assumes that objects are compared on successive attributes. However, all objects below the cutoff value of the attribute are eliminated from the choice set of alternatives.

The multiple attribute models, considered earlier, have a relatively simple structure. Other possible specifications comprise factor-analysis of attribute evaluations,[45] application of the Minkowski metric to the products of beliefs and evaluations[46] and normalization of the importance weights.[47] Linear models appear to perform well, even if the true model is non-linear.[48] The reason for this is that the right predictor variables frequently have a conditionally monotone relationship with the criterion, which can at least be approximated by a linear model.

Attitude dimensions

Usually, only one dimension is assumed in attitude formation. This implies that the attitude can be expressed as a single combined score based on attributes on the same dimension. Each belief-evaluation product is considered an indicator of the same attitude construct, disregarding qualitatively different dimensions of attitude. For example, in classic multi-attribute models, esthetic qualities of an object are related to the same dimension as economic or practical qualities. Besides the fact that this may be unrealistic, a better prediction of behavior might be obtained if different dimensions are distinguished.[49]

Attitude change

Many agents in society may benefit from and are striving for changes in attitudes of other people. By changing consumer attitudes in favor of a particular brand, the market share and the firm's profit might increase. By changing citizens' attitudes toward litter and waste disposal, the government might be able to increase environmental health. Advertising has become an industry of its own and non-profit institutions, such as the government and pressure groups, such as Greenpeace are becoming aware of the need for powerful means to attitude change.

Since attitudes perform different functions[50] attitude change may be accomplished in different ways.

Using the instrumental function of attitudes, it makes sense to accomplish attitude change by providing information on particular consequences of behavior (e.g. on the use of a product with a particular set of attributes). This may include information about the causal effects of behavior. In general, this way of changing an attitude demands high involvement of an individual regarding the issue at hand.[51] An example of this method would be an advertising campaign concerning a food brand product. By stressing the nutritional qualities of the product, consumers' beliefs regarding the product might be changed. The attitude mainly changes by means of cognitive processing using this method.

A similar method of attitude change is based on the need satisfying properties of behavior. An appeal to specific needs should increase the importance
of specific behavioral consequences. This method may use emotional appeals
which can also be used in case of low involvement regarding the issue.[52] An
example of this method is an appeal to the necessity of a good night's rest
in combination with a particular pillow brand. In this way, attitudes might be
changed by changing attribute evaluations.

Different motivations are involved in these two modes of attitude change.
The opinion or belief regarding the attributes of a commodity is associated
with the extrinsic motivation to behavior (i.e. a purchase), whereas the attribute evaluation or importance is associated with the intrinsic motivation.[53]

Using the ego-defensive function, the attitude might be changed by an
appeal to an individual's self-perception.[54] By suggesting the appropriate
attributions of an individual's circumstances and behavior, attitudes may be
influenced. Example: "Your way of living requires unusual amounts of energy.
Can you still cope with it? Get an extra kick at Fitness Center Quick". A
somehow related method uses the value-expressive function of attitude. This
method appears to be more suitable in strengthening the attitude once the
behavior has been shown. By the process of cognitive dissonance[55] individuals
generally try to adjust their attitudes to their previous behavior. If, for some
reason, an individual becomes engaged in a different type of behavior, the
attitude toward this behavior might become more positive. For example,
consumer satisfaction might be enhanced by stressing the good qualities
and the large number of other people who purchased the product. This may
increase replacement purchases.

The knowledge function of attitudes might be employed in advertising
by creating a network of cognitions related to the issue at hand. A positive
attitude toward saving, for example, may be enhanced by relating savings
to future economic growth, to the possibility of large future purchases, to
security in old age or in hard times, etcetera. An attitude embedded in a
cognitive network will be resistent to change because the psychological costs
of changing the attitude become associated with the (even higher) costs of
changing the network.

Conclusion

A number of attitude models are distinguished, notably the compensatory
Fishbein and adequacy-importance models and the non-compensatory models, dealing with simplified information processing. Problems with these models include the saliency of attributes, the specificity and the computation of
the attitude and the structure of the attitude model. In addition to the attitude,

restrictions of several kinds play an important part in the explanation of behavior.

BOX 6.1

SIMPLIFIED CHOICE IN AN INFORMATION DISPLAY

The operation of the simplified choice rules, mentioned in Section 6.3, can
be illustrated by means of an *information display*, as regularly presented
by consumer organizations regarding different types of consumer goods. In
Figure 6.3a, the information given on micro-wave ovens is likely to produce
information overload. Figure 6.3b shows arbitrarily chosen cutoffs and an
arbitrarily imposed importance order of attributes for a particular consumer.

The conjunctive attitude model for each brand verifies whether all of the
attributes exceed their respective cutoff levels or not. Obviously, only brand
C meets all of the cutoffs.

The disjunctive model is based on one or more outstanding characteristics.
Brand B has many extra supplies and is very safe and thus is a likely candidate
to be preferred by this model.

The lexicographic model retains firstly the brands performing best on the
most important attribute (brands B and E appearing the most safe). Secondly
the model retains the brands performing best on the second most important
attribute (preparation/cooking). Since B and E have the same performance,
both are retained. Thirdly, B and E are compared on their thawing qualities
which are again equal. The fourth attribute in the importance order is comfort.
Here brand E performs best. It appears that brand E is preferred by the
lexicographic model.

The elimination by aspects model verifies whether the brands exceed the
cutoff point of the most important attribute. Only brand G is rejected. Secondly, the remaining brands are verified with respect to the second most
important attribute. All remaining brands equal the cutoff point. Next, the remaining brands are compared on thawing, the third attribute in the importance
order. Only brands C and H equal the cutoff point. Since brand H does not
meet the cutoff point for noise (the tenth attribute in the importance order),
C is preferred by the EBA model.

Since consumer organizations frequently provide overall product evaluations to facilitate brand selection, it may well be that brand F is recommended. Brand F is available at a reasonable price and performs well on
most attributes. The purchase of brand A is likely to be dissuaded.

	Brands							
	A	*B*	*C*	*D*	*E*	*F*	*G*	*H*
Price ($)	200	325	350	400	450	250	200	300
Volume (l)	11	16.5	18	27.5	15	13	17.5	18
Power adjustment	2	10	4	5	4	5	2	6
Extra supplies	-	++	+	+	+	p	p	+
Max. time (min.)	30	100	30	60	100	30	35	30
Safety	+	++	+	+	++	+	p	+
Preparation/Cooking	p	p	p	p	p	p	p	p
Thawing	-	p	+	-	p	p	-	+
Comfort	p	p	p	p	+	p	p	p
Noise	-	p	p	p	-	p	p	-

Figure 6.3a. Information display regarding micro-wave ovens.

	Cutoffs	Importance
Price ($)	≤ 500	5
Volume (l)	≥ 15	8
Power adjustment	≥ 2	6
Extra supplies	7 Max. time (min.)	9
Safety	+	1
Preparation/Cooking	p	2
Thawing	+	3
Comfort	p	4
Noise	p	10

Figure 6.3b. Cutoff points and attribute importances of a particular consumer.

Recapitulating, brand preference in the above hypothetical example might differ across the simplified attitude models as follows:

Model	Preferred Brand
Conjunctive	C
Disjunctive	B
Lexicographic	E
Elimination by Aspects	C
Overall recommendation	F

Since the scales of the attribute values are different, the attributes cannot be compared with one another, which is requisite in compensatory attitude models. Also, the attribute importance values have not been provided. If the scales were comparable and importance measures were available, a compensatory attitude model might have been applied, possibly yielding yet another preferred brand. Which attitude model is applied depends on the information available and on the willingness to take the trouble to apply the model to the information display. In many instances, even information displays are not available and decision making is seriously hampered.

6.4. Images

Images play an important role in economic and social behavior. A positive public image of a political candidate is likely to be associated with many votes for her nomination. Likewise, a favorable brand image is associated with a large market share of the brand. Candidates, firms, retailers, shopping centers and even the government have realized that their images may evoke different reactions from the public. Thus, public reactions might be manipulated by creating a particular image.

The image may be defined as a public attitude toward an object or agent in society. In this respect, images can be investigated in the same way as individual attitudes. Images can be viewed as more or less complex.[56] Images may be distinguished as general, holistic impressions or perceptions,[57] as a network of meanings and as a multi-attribute attitude, such as has been considered above. In the latter view of an image, beliefs and evaluations can be measured and combined into an attitude score. Given this information, an economic agent may try to improve the image by stressing favorable attributes in advertising campaigns and by changing the agent's policy with respect to less favorable attributes.

Frequently investigated images are those regarding stores and shopping centers. To measure the store image, the modal salient attributes are elicited in a sample of consumers by means of interviews or questionnaires. In the

Table 6.4. Example of a store's image profile.

Attribute	Importance	Store A	Store B	Store C
Price level	4.1	2.0	4.0	3.3
Assortment	3.6	3.6	1.5	4.4
Personnel	3.3	4.6	2.3	2.3
Atmosphere	2.9	3.0	3.5	1.1
Service	4.0	4.5	4.4	4.0
Quality	4.5	3.9	3.6	2.7

second stage, beliefs and evaluations regarding the attributes are measured in a consumer survey. Generally, the store will be interested in its image among the general public. Thus, customers and non-customers are included in the survey sample. Obviously, the sample should be selected in the neighborhood of the store, among consumers more or less acquainted with its existence.

In Table 6.4, a hypothetical example of images regarding three stores is presented. In the example, service of store A is believed to be of good quality (4.5 on a positive five-point scale), whereas its commodities are believed to be expensive (2.0 on a positive five-point inexpensive scale). Store C scores low on personnel quality and shop atmosphere, however, these attributes are relatively unimportant on average (on a five-point importance scale). The image profile, rather than the weighted sum of beliefs, provides detailed information regarding the store's retailing policy. Favorable attributes might be stressed by the store, whereas relatively unfavorable attributes might be improved (e.g. store A might occasionally introduce special offers).

The absolute measures of store image are relatively arbitrary, since linear transformations of the attitude scale have no consequences for the ordering of images. For this reason, absolute figures regarding store image are not very informative. In a free market, more information is contained in the image if the relative standing of the store among its competitors can be derived from it. For this reason, the image of a store should be compared with the image of other agents on the market, preferably measured on the same scale, as in the example of Table 6.4.

The general image measurement procedure described above can be refined in various ways. Since the image is assumed to be related to purchase behavior, it is important to measure the images of customers and non-customers of the store separately. These measurements might indicate different policy measures with respect to these separate groups.

In Figure 6.4, an image profile is presented for a selected sample of bakers' shops in the Netherlands. The stated opinions are from customers and non-customers, respectively. The non-customers in this case are customers

Attributes	Favorable		Neutral		Unfavorable
	5	4	3	2	1

Quality

Assortment

Price level

Service speed

Atmosphere

Location

Parking

Promotion

Opening hours

——— = customer of baker's store
------- = customer of supermarket

Figure 6.4. Image profiles of bakers' shops relative to supermarkets. Adapted from Haffner (1989).

of supermarkets where they usually buy their bakery products. The beliefs regarding the bakers' shops are expressed in relation to their most important competitors, the supermarkets.

From the profile of beliefs, it can be observed that the bakers' shops are judged to be much more expensive than supermarkets (as regards bakery goods) and have less promotional activities. Favorable attributes of bakers' shops are the quality and the assortment of products and the atmosphere in the shop. Furthermore, differences between customers and non-customers are noticeable, the bakers' customers holding relatively favorable beliefs toward the baker.

The evaluation profile (not presented in the figure) shows several differences between customers and non-customers of bakers' shops. These differences arise from different need states of the consumers. For example, the customers of the supermarket are assumed to experience more financial strain, reflected in more weight attached to the price of baker's goods (which in fact are more expensive).

The image of the bakers' shops considered above, in addition to economic variables like income and family size, explains the frequency of purchases in bakers' shops and supermarkets to a certain extent.

Conclusion

Images can be regarded as public attitudes toward objects or agents in society. The instrumental function of images seems to be most important in explaining and predicting mass behavior. The image profile indicates opportunities to influence the image. A useful distinction of the image could be according to the relation with the relevant object or agent (e.g. customer or non-customer).

6.5. The relation between attitudes and behavior

The classic publication by LaPiere highlights the fact that people do not always behave in accordance with their opinions (see Box 6.2).[58] This has raised the issue of predictability of behavior from knowledge about attitudes.

Since attitudes are frequently related to behavior, the level of generality of the attitude measurement should be in agreement with the level of generality of the behavior associated with the attitude.[59] In relating the attitude toward beer with the purchase of a specific brand of it, attitude questions should be asked with respect to the specific brand of beer, *not* with respect to beer or alcohol consumption in general. Contrarily, to relate the attitude toward beer with the purchase of beer in general, attitude questions should not refer to a specific brand of beer.

Several conditions have been stated that should be satisfied in order to obtain a high correspondence between attitude and behavior.[60] These conditions concern the elements of action, target, context and time associated with the attitude and the behavior to be predicted. In fact, the theory states that the more these elements correspond, the higher the correspondence of attitude and behavior. This section supplements Section 6.3 and is presented here to highlight the relation between attitudes and behavior.

The element of *target* relates to the object about which an attitude is stated, e.g. marijuana. If the statement only expresses the attitude toward marijuana, a successful prediction of specific acts in particular contexts at a particular time (e.g. smoking marijuana in the company of one's friends during the weekend) is not to be expected. However, if the behavior to be predicted is a *multiple-act criterion*, correspondence will be obtained to some extent. In this respect, an experiment concerning a range of 29 possible behaviors toward snakes, has been judged as successful.[61] In this experiment, the avoidance behavior of 48 male and female subjects was recorded using a psychological scale involving various interactions with a snake. These interactions ranged from 'approaching the snake in an enclosed glass cage' to 'passively permitting the snake to crawl in one's lap'. The correlation between the behavior and two measures of attitude toward snakes was 0.56 and 0.73 if these measures preceded behavior and 0.70 and 0.87 if measured after the behavior.[62]

The element of *action* relates to the behavioral act to be predicted, e.g. buying behavior or helping behavior. An attitude toward helping behavior in general will not be able to explain specific behaviors, such as helping a stranger who asks the way or helping a girl who is being raped and murdered.[63]

If both the elements of action and target correspond in the attitude measure and in the behavior the attitude may explain this *single-act criterion* to some extent.[64] Several studies have been reported in which a relatively high correspondence between this type of attitude and single-act behavior has been obtained. The attitude toward the personal use of birth control practices and self-reported behavior correlates 0.69 on average.[65] Correlation coefficients ranging from 0.46 and 0.72 were obtained between attitudes toward personal drinking of alcohol and self-reported behavior.[66] Similar results have been obtained regarding smoking,[67] yielding a correlation of 0.80.[68]

One exception is made regarding attitudes toward single-act criteria, namely voting behavior or petition signing.[69] Voting is not considered as a behavior but as an expression of an attitude toward a candidate. In this case, specification of the target element is assumed to be sufficient to explain the voting behavior.

Correspondence of the *context* element is assumed to improve the attitude-behavior relation further. For example, in the attitude toward buying a detergent of brand X in shop Y, a single-act criterion is specified in a particular context.

Specification of the element of *time* may further improve the attitude-behavior relation. For example, in the attitude toward buying a car in the next six months from the dealer where the last car was bought, all four elements have been specified and a high degree of correspondence with this specific behavior is to be expected.

There is one main problem with this theory. If all four elements are specified in an attitude statement, this statement can hardly be distinguished from a behavioral intention. In research, it has been shown that the effect of intention on behavior, next to attitudes, is not significant.[70] A better way to establish a high correlation between attitude and behavior would be to supplement the attitude with the appropriate restrictions.[71]

Several personality factors may mediate the relationship between attitudes and behavior:

- *Self-monitoring*, being the tendency to pay attention to other people's opinions about one's behavior, may contribute to the influence of social norms on behavior. Thus, people high on self-monitoring are more sensitive to the social consequences of behavior than to act in accordance with their own attitudes. By contrast, people low on self-monitoring will act more in agreement with their attitudes and the relationship between attitudes and behavior will be more consistent.

- The personal orientation with regard to taking action may influence the relationship between attitudes and behavior, too.[72] A high *action orientation* may facilitate behavior in agreement with one's attitudes.[73]

— The attitude strength, the confidence and certainty of one's attitudes may influence the attitude-behavior relationship. Indicative of attitude strength in the case of high involvement issues may be the knowledge acquired with respect to the issue. Both the attitude, knowledge and attitude-knowledge interaction may affect the intended choice of heating mode.[74] The need for cognition may have similar effects because it leads to more differentiated attitudes.[75]

Conclusion

The prediction of behavior from stated attitudes depends on corresponding elements of target, action, context and time. Furthermore, multiple acts can be explained to some extent with only target correspondence. If all four elements of behavior are specified in the attitude statement, it can hardly be distinguished from the behavioral intention. A more fruitful approach would be to supplement the attitude with the appropriate restrictions.

Summary

Attitude and utility theory both deal with individual sensations that are associated with behavior. In utility theory, the instrumental function of sensations is stressed. In attitude theory, the ego-defensive, the value-expressive and the knowledge function are distinguished in addition. Both the differentiated attitude and utility are based on attributes, characteristics or services of alternatives. Both assume objective qualities, perceptions and weights but a fundamental difference exists regarding the measurement or estimation of the relevant parameters. Psychology deals with perceptions and weights directly (the composed power law in perception theory being a notable exception), whereas economic models use these components indirectly.

Compensatory and non-compensatory attitude models are distinguished, pointing to the possibility of favorable attributes compensating for unfavorable attributes. Compensatory models are the Fishbein and the attribute-adequacy models; non-compensatory models include simplified ways of information processing, such as the conjunctive, the disjunctive, the lexicographic and the elimination-by-aspects models. Regarding the computation of the attitude, summation or averaging and normalization have to be considered. Furthermore, only salient attributes which can be selected on the basis of objective or subjective criteria are included. Several structures and dimensions of the attitude have been distinguished.

The correspondence of attitude and behavior can be improved in different ways. One way suggests the similarity of attitude measurements and behavior in four respects: action, context, target and time. Such specific attitude statements become very similar to behavioral intentions which are less successful in predicting behavior. Alternatively, the attitude approach, using direct information regarding the attributes, may be supplemented by the appropriate restrictions, which can be of a different nature.

Attitude changes can be accomplished by providing information corresponding with the functions of attitudes.

Images are similar to attitudes, however the former are defined as aggregate (public) attitudes, whereas the latter are individual. The image profile can be used to influence the public by improving unfavorable and stressing favorable attributes.

BOX 6.2

ATTITUDES VERSUS ACTIONS

The title of this box equals the title of an article by LaPiere in *Social Forces* in 1934.[76]

In the early thirties, LaPiere traveled through the United States accompanied by a young Chinese student and his wife. The Chinese couple has been described as charming and sociable; however, their race could not be disguised. The three of them were once accepted as guests without hesitation in the 'best' hotel in a small town noted for its narrow and bigoted 'attitude' toward Orientals. Two months later, LaPiere phoned the same hotel and asked if they would accommodate 'an important Chinese gentleman'. The answer was an unequivocal "No".

LaPiere became interested in this event and started a systematic study of visiting all kinds of restaurants, cafés, hotels, auto camps and 'Tourist Homes', scattered throughout the United States in the company of the Chinese couple. The arrival at these places had been varied in a number of ways: sometimes LaPiere approached the reception together with his guests but most of the time the latter negotiated for accommodation by themselves; sometimes they arrived at high-class establishments after a hard and dusty day and sometimes at inferior auto camps in their most presentable condition; sometimes they carried a lot of luggage and camping gear with them and sometimes they had no luggage at all. In total, they visited 184 restaurants and cafés and 66 hotels, etcetera and were refused at only one instance. This concerned a rather inferior auto camp in a small Californian town where they arrived in the early evening in a very dilapidated car piled full of camp equipment. The proprietor hesitated when LaPiere spoke to him alone and definitely refused them when

Table 6.5. Establishments' policies regarding acceptance of Chinese guests.

	Hotels etc. Visited		Hotels etc. not Visited		Restau- rants etc. Visited		Restau- rants etc. not Visited	
Total	47		32		81		96	
	1*	2*	1	2	1	2	1	2
Number replying	22	25	20	12	43	38	51	45
No Undecided:	20	23	19	11	40	35	37	41
depend upon cir- cumstances	1	2	1	1	3	3	4	3
Yes	1	0	0	0	0	0	0	1

*Column (1) indicates in each case those responses to questionnaires which concerned Chinese only. The figures in column (2) are from the questionnaires in which the above was inserted among questions regarding Germans, French, Japanese, etcetera.

Taken from LaPiere (1967). Reprinted from Social Forces, Vol. 13, 1934. Attitudes versus Actions. Copyright ©The University of North Carolina Press.

he became aware of the guests, saying: "No, I don't take Japs".

Six months after they had visited these establishments, LaPiere mailed a questionnaire to these and a number of other hotels and restaurants with an accompanying letter including a special and personal plea for response. In one version of the questionnaire the question "Will you accept members of the Chinese race as guests in your establishment?" was mixed with a number of similar questions concerning Germans, French, Japanese, Russians, Armenians, Jews, Negroes, Italians and Indians, in the other version the question was not further qualified.

The responses to this question are summarized in Table 6.5. At only one instance was the answer to this question "Yes", accompanied by a chatty letter describing the nice visit the woman proprietor had had from a Chinese gentleman and his sweet wife during the previous summer.

The result of this survey shows a lack of correspondence between intentions and behavior. Is this to be expected from the theory of corresponding elements?

Notes

1 Katz 1960.
2 See Chapter 5.
3 Katz 1960.
4 See Section 10.5.
5 See Section 6.3. For a discussion of this issue, see Pieters 1988.
6 See Chapter 7.
7 Allport 1967.
8 Lewin 1938.
9 See Section 6.2.
10 Tolman 1959.
11 Vodopivec 1992.
12 See Chapter 3.
13 Rosenberg 1956.
14 Fishbein 1966. See Section 6.3 for an example.
15 See Chapter 4.
16 Hamblin 1973 and Saris et al. 1977.
17 Deaton and Muellbauer 1980.
18 Saris et al. 1977 and Lehtinen 1974.
19 Lehtinen 1974.
20 See Chapter 15.
21 Antonides 1989.
22 Von Neumann and Morgenstern 1944, p. 16.
23 Allport 1967.
24 Lancaster's 1966.
25 Cude 1980.
26 Taylor 1975.
27 Ratchford 1979.
28 Griliches 1971.
29 Ratchford 1975.
30 See Chapter 13.
31 Sheth and Talarzyk 1973.
32 Fishbein and Ajzen 1975.
33 Wilkie and Pessemier 1973.
34 See also Chapter 7.
35 Fishbein and Ajzen 1975.
36 Lancaster 1979.
37 Lancaster 1979 mentions several other criteria which are not considered here.
38 Becker 1965.
39 Fishbein and Ajzen 1975.
40 These restrictions have been mentioned in Lesourne 1977 and Frey and Foppa 1986.
41 Ajzen and Fishbein 1977. See Section 6.5.
42 Carmone and Green 1981, Green and Devita 1975.
43 See Chapter 7.
44 See Section 7.4.
45 Bagozzi 1981.
46 Wilkie and Pessemier 1973.
47 Bass and Wilkie 1973.

[48] Dawes 1979.

[49] Bagozzi 1981.

[50] See Section 6.1.

[51] See Section 9.4.

[52] See Section 9.4.

[53] See Chapter 3.

[54] See Section 10.3.

[55] See Section 11.2.

[56] See the development of the attitude concept in Section 6.1.

[57] Poiesz 1989, see also Section 9.3.

[58] LaPiere 1967.

[59] Fishbein and Ajzen 1975.

[60] Ajzen and Fishbein 1977.

[61] Bandura et al. 1969.

[62] Aggregating over different behaviors has also been proposed by Epstein 1979, see Section 3.1.

[63] Latané and Darley 1970.

[64] Ajzen and Fishbein 1977.

[65] Kothandapani 1971.

[66] Veevers 1971.

[67] Janis and Hoffman 1970.

[68] Nisbett 1968.

[69] Ajzen and Fishbein 1977.

[70] See Section 8.2.

[71] Antonides 1989.

[72] Bagozzi et al. 1992.

[73] Kuhl 1982.

[74] Berger et al. 1994.

[75] Cacioppo and Petty 1982.

[76] Reprinted in Fishbein 1967.

CHAPTER 7

LIMITED INFORMATION PROCESSING

7.1. Information processing in consumer decision making

In Chapter 6, we were concerned with attitude models which demand different degrees of cognitive effort in a person's information processing. Many of these models are *normative* in that the model prescribes that decisions are based on optimal processing of information. Frequently, however, non-optimal information processing can be observed in everyday practice. *Descriptive* models of these observations claim to relate more closely to reality.

Normative models usually assume complete information about alternatives of choice and adherence to prescriptive axioms, such as *transitivity of preferences*.[1] Normative and descriptive models both assume that decisions are based on preferences and at least to some extent on information processing. This basic assumption has been questioned in the area of consumer research.

Olshavsky and Granbois summarize the evidence of instances where external constraints limit the consumer to a single alternative and where purchases are observed to occur without reliance on information.[2] They consider several stages in the allocation of the budget: spending on broad expenditure categories and saving, generic allocation (on product categories), store patronage and brand purchase.[3]

Broad categories

Regarding decisions of saving and spending, 87% of households operate without a financial plan[4] and only 36% of respondents were able to predict very accurately their savings six months later.[5]

Frequently, expenditures on certain products are interlocked with expenditures on other products. *Strategic items*,[6] such as an automobile, dictate expenditures on supplementary goods, such as gasoline, repair services and insurance. A free choice of the latter goods can hardly be assumed. In a survey, less than 25% of respondents reported plans regarding expenditures on specific goods and setting aside amounts for this purpose.[7]

A general conclusion from these results is that the majority of consumers are not deliberate choosers regarding spending on broad categories and saving of the budget.

Generic allocation

A summary of studies regarding purchases of durable goods and clothing, reports 20% to 25% of these purchases to be impulsive in that no deliberation or planning takes place.[8] In supermarkets, variety stores and drugstores, 33% to 50% of the purchases were not intended by the customer when entering the store.

Many people who are institutionalized (e.g. in hospitals, rest homes or military institutions) have no control over the type of food, clothing or furnishings they use. Apartment dwellers, college students living in dormitories and campuses and in many cases home buyers have little control over such items as fixtures, appliances and floor coverings.

At the level of generic allocation, in many instances there appears to be no consumer planning or deliberation regarding purchases.

Store choice

A review of studies regarding store patronage shows that purchases of durables frequently take place after a single store visit: for black and white television in 39% of the cases, for color television 50%, furniture 22%, carpet 27%, soft goods 75–80%.[9] It has been concluded that in general extensive store visiting and store evaluation do not take place.

Brand choice

Even the most specific level of budget allocation, the purchase of a particular brand of a good, has shown limited planning and deliberation. It appears that 15–33% of the buyers of major appliances had no prior information or received information from only one source.[10] Regarding purchases of cereals, candy and detergent in supermarkets, in 38–72% of the cases no apparent in-store choice process took place. Frequently, it has been observed from tape recorded conversations between customers and salesmen, that customers rely entirely upon the salesman's recommendation in the purchase of major appliances. Another example of choice on the basis of recommendation is that in 75% of the cases newcomers to a community select a physician on this basis.

The lack of information processing is evident from the consumer studies above. However, it appears to be a more general phenomenon that operates at

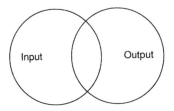

Figure 7.1. Variances of input and output variances in a communication system.

different levels of decision complexity. Several instances of limited information processing have been investigated in the literature. Section 7.2 deals with
the limited human information processing capacity, Section 7.3 with heuristics of information processing, Section 7.4 with the use of aspiration levels in
information processing and Section 7.5 with models of problem solving and
decision making.

Conclusion

From the research reported above it appears that in many instances and at
each level of the budget allocation only limited search, planning and deliberation regarding decisions take place. In these instances, normative and
descriptive models of decision making do not have any practical significance.
This result does not imply, of course, that information processing cannot be
modeled. To some extent economic behavior can be explained by decision
models, although these models frequently deal with non-optimal information
processing.

7.2. Information processing capacity

The processing of information can be considered within the framework of a
communication system.[11] Input information concerns environmental stimuli
impinging on the individual, output information concerns the response given.
If the variance of the input information is large, the individual is relatively
ignorant of the response to be given and the input is very informative. If
the information is perfectly received, the output variance equals the input
variance. Due to communication errors, however, the output variance will
only partly coincide with the input variance.

In Figure 7.1, the left and right circles represent the input and output
variances, respectively. The overlap of the circles denotes the covariance of
input and output or the amount of information correctly transmitted.

If the input variance increases from a small to a medium amount, the trans-

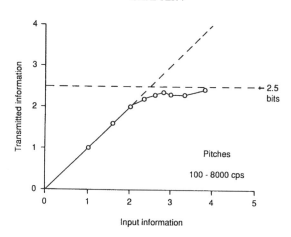

Figure 7.2. Transmitted information for pitches. From Miller (1956).

mitted information will increase, too. However, with a further increase from a medium to a large amount of input information, the amount of transmitted information will level off and reach an *asymptotic value*. The maximum amount of transmitted information equals the *channel capacity* of the communication system. An increase in the amount of information supplied can be obtained either by increasing the information speed per time unit or by increasing the number of choice alternatives.

The unit of information is the *bit* (an abbreviation of *binary digit*), which is the information needed to make a decision between two equally likely alternatives. If we must decide whether or not a family will buy a new car in the next year and if we know that the chances are 50–50, then we need one bit of information. Two bits are needed to decide among four equally likely alternatives, three bits to choose among eight and so on.

A number of experiments have been conducted to investigate the human information channel capacity. These experiments can be distinguished according to whether the information concerns *uni-dimensional* stimuli (e.g. the pitch of a tone) or *multi-dimensional* stimuli (e.g. a chord).

When tones of different frequency were presented to be identified by the listeners in an experiment, two or three different tones were never confused.[12] With four different tones confusions were quite rare but with five or more tones, the subjects frequently made mistakes. In Figure 7.2, the amount of transmitted information has been plotted against the amount of input information in bits. It appears that the asymptotic value of transmitted information in this experiment is about 2.5 bits. Thus, the channel capacity for communicating pitches amounts to six different tones.

Table 7.1.   Channel capacities for uni-dimensional stimuli.

Sense	Stimulus	Capacity
Hearing	Pitch	2.5
Hearing	Loudness	2.3
Taste	Salt concentration	1.9
Vision	Position of points on a line	3.2
Vision	Size of squares	2.2
Vision	Colors	3.1
Vision	Brightness	2.3
Touch	Location	2.8
Touch	Duration	2.3
Touch	Intensity	2.0

Adapted from Miller (1956).

This type of experiment has been varied with a number of different stimuli, associated with different senses. In Table 7.1, the channel capacity for these stimuli is presented in bits. On average, the channel capacity for different uni-dimensional stimuli is 2.6 bits, corresponding with about seven stimuli that can be distinguished.

After considering the limited human information capacity regarding uni-dimensional stimuli, one may wonder how people succeed in processing extensive multi-dimensional stimulus information.[13] People are able to distinguish thousands of words, objects, faces and so on. The answer is that people recode the extensive information in a smaller number of *information chunks*, each summarizing part of the information. A novice wireless operator, for example, receives endless strings of dit's and dah's without being able to make sense of it. Soon, strings of dit's and dah's are recognized as letters (chunks). Gaining more experience, strings of letters are *recoded* as words and strings of words as phrases. At the elementary level, only separate bits of information are processed. At more advanced levels, the number of bits per chunk has increased.

Another example of chunking is the number of binary digits that can be retained in memory (nine on average) compared to the number of decimal digits (eight on average). Yet much more information is included in decimal digits. In Figure 7.3, four recoding schemes of a series of 18 binary digits are presented (18 binary digits being far more than can be repeated back after a single presentation).

The first scheme recodes the binary digits to pairs: 00 is recoded as 0, 01 as 1, 10 as 2 and 11 as 3. The series of 18 digits has now been reduced to 9,

Binary Digits (Bits):																		
1	0	1	0	0	0	1	0	0	1	1	1	0	0	1	1	1	0

2:1									
Chunks	10	10	00	10	01	11	00	11	10
Recoding	2	2	0	2	1	3	0	3	2

3:1						
Chunks	101	000	100	111	001	110
Recoding	5	0	4	7	1	6

4:1					
Chunks	1010	0010	0111	0011	10
Recoding	10	2	7	3	

5:1				
Chunks	10100	01001	11001	110
Recoding	20	9	25	

Figure 7.3. Recoding a series of binary digits. From Miller (1956).

which is almost within the immediate span of memory.

The second scheme recodes the binary digits in chunks of three. A reduction to 6 octal digits is obtained as a result. This is well within the immediate span of memory. Further reductions are obtained in the third and fourth schemes.

Each of the schemes in Figure 7.3 was presented to the subjects in an experiment by Sidney Smith in the early 50's.[14] The schemes were studied until the subjects said they understood it; this lasted about 5 to 10 minutes. Next, the subjects were presented with a series of binary digits to be repeated back. It was expected that the more recoding implied by a scheme, the better the performance would be in repeating back the series of binary digits. Actually, the performance in each scheme was better than with the series of binary digits before but not as much as could be expected from the use of the schemes. This was explained from insufficient learning and practising with the schemes.

Upon failure of his subjects to perform according to expectations, Smith decided to learn the schemes himself. He drilled himself on each recoding successively and tested his own performance by repeating back series of binary digits. His actual performance was about that theoretically predicted under each recoding scheme. (See Figure 7.4.) With the 4:1 and 5:1 recoding schemes, Smith was able to repeat back series of 40 binary digits without error!

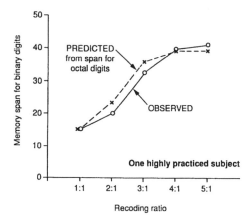

Figure 7.4. Expected and actual performance of repeating back series of binary digits. From Miller (1956).

BOX 7.1

AN INEFFICIENCY OF SHORT-TERM MEMORY

Series of digits have been used in studying the operation of short-term memory (STM). For instance, studies have been made as to whether items in STM can be accessed directly or serially. Several hypotheses were derived regarding the procedure that humans might be using to recall information from memory:[15]

1. *The Mind's Eye Sees All.* Under this procedure the mind is hypothesized to recall the entire memorized list and then to see if the test digit appears on the list. The entire list is called up as a whole and not, for example, processed serially from left to right. An implication of this hypothesis is that depending on where the test digit is in the list or on whether the test digit is or is not on the list, the reaction time will not vary. Thus, if the memorized list is 2, 4, 9, 10, 6, 1, 3, the reaction time should be the same whether the test digit is 2 or 3 or 7.

2. *The Self-Terminating Search.* The recall procedure hypothesized here is serial: each item on the list is called up individually from left to right; the subject compares the test digit with each member of the memorized list until she finds a match or comes to the end of the list. The implication of this hypothesis is that the reaction time will vary depending on where the test digit is in the memorized list; the later it is, the longer the reaction time. It also follows that negative responses will take longer than positive responses.

3. *The Exhaustive Serial Search.* This recall procedure is exactly like the
previous one save for the fact that the subject is hypothesized to go
through the entire memorized list before making any response, regardless
of where the test digit is in the list or whether it is or is not on the list.
The subject may have recognized a match early on but, to play safe,
goes through the whole list. As with the Self-Terminating Search, the
longer the list, the longer the reaction times. However, if this hypothesis
is correct and depending on where the test digit is on the memorized list,
response times will not vary.

It appeared that the mean reaction time varied with the length of the list
and that there was no difference in the reaction times for items on the list
and for items not on the list. Thus, the Exhaustive Serial Search hypothesis
was confirmed, while intuitively it concerns the least efficient access to STM.
This method makes sense if humans suspect that they are prone to making
recall errors.[16]

Recoding plays an important part in everyday processing of information.
For instance, an individual's name frequently serves as a summary of personality characteristics and past joint experiences with a person. A brand name
or the name of an economic transaction (e.g. lease) is often used as a short-
cut in information processing. With lack of recoding experience, however,
human information capacity appears to be limited. Excess of human information capacity frequently occurs in consumer decision making. Due to the
increasing number of consumption alternatives, advertisements and consumer
information, the consumer frequently experiences *information overload.*

An experimental study on information overload has been conducted in
which subjects were presented with information on a number of attributes for
a number of houses.[17] Experimental conditions included a different number of
attributes and a different number of houses, both varying from 5 to 25 (in steps
of 5). Each subject indicated the ideal value of each attribute, from which the
most preferred house could be inferred. The experimental task consisted of
listing the houses according to preference. A task result was scored as correct
if the most preferred house was closest to the ideal, otherwise the result was
scored as incorrect. The probability of a correct result was related to the
number of attributes and alternatives presented. It appeared that significantly
less correct results could be expected if the number of alternatives was 10 or
more and if the number of attributes was 15 or more. Furthermore, a self-
report measure of information overload appeared to be similarly related to the
number of attributes and alternatives. This indicates that information overload

occurs with stimuli exceeding these numbers.

Other indications of information overload in consumer choice have been provided by Jacoby.[18] It appeared from these studies that the number of subjects whose choices were predictable by a compensatory model decreased as the number of alternatives increased. Furthermore, the information processing time has been found to increase substantially as the number of alternatives increased from 4 to 16. The subjects had no experience of these experimental tasks. With more experience, it is conceivable that recoding of information may enable the subjects to overcome the effects of information overload. However, many economic decisions are taken infrequently and without much experience.

Conclusion

The channel capacity refers to limited information processing of uni-dimensional stimuli. With multi-dimensional or series of uni-dimensional stimuli, the capacity of information processing can be increased by recoding (chunking) the information. Recoding is facilitated by training and experience which is often lacking in economic decision making.

7.3. Heuristics in information processing

Sub-optimal information processing has been found not only in budget allocation and consumer choice but also in the making of cognitive judgments. In situations which are not transparent, inaccurate judgments are likely to be made on the basis of cognitive heuristics. Typically, in these situations relevant information is lacking rather than being superabundant.

The first heuristic to be dealt with applies to the binary choice experiment, in which subjects are rewarded with different probabilities for either of two possible responses. Suppose that the experimenter randomly rewards 'type A' behavior 1/3 of the time and 'type B' behavior the remaining 2/3. A rational strategy in this case is always showing 'type B' behavior (expected reward is 2/3 per trial). However, subjects match their behavior to the proportion of rewarded trials, in that they show 'type A' behavior one-third of the time and 'type B' behavior two-thirds of the time (expected reward is $1/3 \times 1/3 + 2/3 \times 2/3 = 5/9$ per trial). This heuristic has been called *event matching*.[19] An application of this heuristic in real life is the timing in catching a bus. Suppose the bus is late one-third of the time and is on time for the remaining two-thirds. A rational strategy would be always to go to the bus stop in time. However, due to event matching, this is not to be expected in practice. One explanation of this heuristic is *minimaxing regret*, i.e. minimizing the maximum expected loss. With an increasing probability of showing up in time

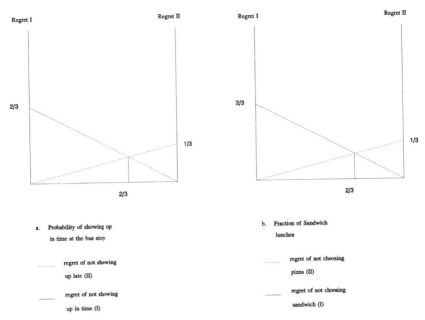

Figure 7.5. Minimizing regret in event matching and melioration.

at the bus stop, the attractiveness of showing up late increases. In other words, regret of not choosing the alternative behavior increases with the probability of showing up in time (see Figure 7.5a). Always showing up in time induces a regret of 1/3 (the payoff one could have had by showing up late). On the other hand, with an increasing probability of showing up late, the attractiveness of showing up in time increases. Always showing up late induces a regret of 2/3 (the payoff one could have had by showing up in time). Minimaxing regret results in choosing a probability of showing up in time at the intersection of the two lines in Figure 7.5a.

A similar heuristic, *melioration*, regards choices over time.[20] In order to show the similarity with event matching, let us assume that an individual values two menus, pizza and sandwich. The more sandwiches are consumed, the more the individual tends to value the pizza and vice versa (see Figure 7.5b). Melioration implies a choice of sandwich at a fraction corresponding to the intersection of the two preference lines which clearly is inferior to always choosing the highest valued alternative (sandwich). Melioration is assumed in situations where consumption of an alternative changes the value of all existing alternatives.

Melioration has implications for management.[21] Managers usually play tricks that guarantee short-term success. However, by doing this, the tricks become less successful. For example, short-term profit can be obtained by exhausting a firm's resources. However, doing this repeatedly will diminish resources such that no investments can be made and thus no more (short-term) profits will be obtained in the long run.[22] Box 7.2 contains an illustrative example of melioration applied to a tennis game.

Several heuristics in human judgment have been considered in the literature.[23] One of these is *judging by* the *availability* of information. For example, murders in New York City attract a lot of attention in the media each year. Thus, the incidence of murders has become readily available knowledge. If people are asked whether murders occur more frequently than suicides, the answer is likely to be affirmative. Actually, the number of suicides is greater but these get less attention in the media. The judgment in this case is said to be made by the heuristic of availability. A similar judgment is made regarding the probability of English words having an *r* as the first letter or an *r* as the third letter. Since words are stored lexicographically in human memory, the availability of words beginning with an *r* is much greater. So people judge these words to be more likely than words with an *r* as the third letter, whereas actually this is less likely.[24]

Availability of information about earthquake risk may affect insurance sales.[25] In 1990, retired business consultant and self-proclaimed climatologist Iben Browning claimed that there was a 0.5 chance that a severe earthquake would occur on the New Madrid fault during a two-day period centered on December 3, 1990. Although the New Madrid fault was a known catastrophic earthquake risk, the seismologists did not predict any risk changes, the probability of an earthquake being one in sixty thousand. A special conference was held to discredit Brown's claim. Nothing happened around December 3rd, except for the presence of hordes of reporters. However, sales of earthquake insurance increased dramatically (more than tripled in one year) due to the increased attention given to the earthquake risk.

In a different study, people were asked to estimate the frequency of a number of death causes in the United States.[26] It appeared that vivid causes that killed many people during a single occurrence were overestimated (e.g. being caught in a flood or tornado), whereas less vivid causes were systematically underestimated (e.g. dying of diabetes or heart disease). Furthermore, the estimation biases were highly correlated with attention in the media.[27]

The availability principle might operate on brand evaluation, too. Since in decision making the most recently acquired knowledge is the most available, this will operate to the advantage of well-known brands. The availability heuristic might also explain the *actor-observer bias* in attribution theory,[28] since environmental influences are more likely to be available to the actor, whereas personal influences are more available to the observer.[29] Hence, actors attribute failures to environmental influences and observers attribute failures to the person who is acting.

The heuristic of *representativeness* concerns probability judgments that an event or object belongs to a particular category. For instance, given the fact that John is a shy person, is it more likely that he is a librarian than a salesman or less likely? Since shyness is more associated with the image of librarians than with salesmen, common judgment is that John is probably a librarian. However, since there are many more salesmen than librarians, the probability that John belongs to the category of salesmen is actually much greater. Here, judgment is based on a mental model regarding certain professions.

Likewise, a brand with an image of reliability may benefit from the principle of representativeness in that a product failure of this brand is more likely to be attributed to factors of bad luck than to blame owing to the manufacturer.[30] For, according to the mental model, the quality of the product is essentially sufficient. Representativeness is based on a cognitive comparison of an event and a mental model regarding the event. Judgment is likely to be biased in the direction of the prevailing model.

This heuristic might also explain the *Halo effect* in which people are judged on the basis of a single favorable or unfavorable trait which is considered representative for the other qualities of an individual. Another common model of behavior is that it is intentional, e.g. an altruist showing altruistic behavior. The representativeness heuristic in this example implies that an altruistic act is attributed to an altruistic personality. The representativeness heuristic thus might explain the *corresponding inference* in attribution theory.[31]

Another heuristic is *anchoring*. In the absence of accurate information, judgments will be made on the basis of irrelevant frames of reference. An example of this is the following experiment. Subjects were first told the outcome of turning a wheel of fortune (running from 1 to 100). Next, they were asked which percentage of African countries belong to the United Nations. On average, those who got 10 from the wheel estimated the percentage at 25, whereas those who got 65 reported a percentage of 65. Obviously, there is no relation between the actual percentage and the result of turning a wheel of fortune.

The anchoring principle might operate in a number of economic situations, too. For instance, after inducing a favorable climate for business (e.g. by offering business partners a lunch), one can expect proposals to make a deal to be evaluated more favorably. In an experimental setting, it was found that in applying for a new job, the applicants' current salaries influenced their behavior in salary negotiations if there was incomplete information regarding the future salary scale.[32] In general, they demanded less (more) salary if their current salaries were lower (higher).

The heuristic of *simulation* uses as a basis for judgment the ease with which examples or scenarios can be reconstructed. The plausibility of the scenarios and the ease or difficulty of their construction serve as cues for judging the likelihood of outcomes. Thus, an entrepreneur might easily construct positive scenarios of an investment alternative whereas negative scenarios are less easily constructed. The simulation heuristic predicts a bias in the perceived likelihood of favorable outcomes of the investment. Scenarios need not always be one's own work but can be taken from similar situations or similar people in the same circumstances. Taking advice frequently may solve problems better and more efficiently than collecting the relevant information and making decisions on one's own. For example, many tax-payers visit advisers in fiscal matters and many consumers adopt the recommendations of consumer organizations to solve the purchase problem.

Another example of using scenarios is imitation of people who are apparently satisfied with their behavior. Regardless of the pros and cons of automatization of a company's administration, it will be obvious that competitive firms are quite satisfied with it and make more profit. The scenario might appear to be highly plausible and can be constructed easily; thus the likelihood of success might be overestimated under the simulation heuristic.

Imitation can be considered as an analogy. Analogies constitute another type of scenarios that can be used to solve problems. For example, computer chips have been used in space technology but have been built into household appliances in an analogous way. Another example is the TOTE model of human action as an analogue of a feedback model in engineering.[33]

A heuristic dealt with in the next section concerns the use of an *aspiration level* to simplify decision making. The aspiration level represents the desired utility level to be attained by behavior alternatives. The first alternative yielding the aspiration level is the preferred one in decision making.

A general principle is operating behind the use of the heuristics mentioned above.[34] Heuristics may be classified according to whether the events, objects or people to be judged are matched with a mental *prototype model* or with an *exemplar model* in the mind. Prototype models are abstractions of a number of stimuli, e.g. the consumer as a prototype of all people who purchase commodities for their personal use. An exemplar model implies that stimuli are associated with a number of similar stimuli stored in memory, e.g. a murderer associated with all murderers one has read about in the papers. Typically, the availability heuristic uses exemplar models of comparison in judgment, whereas the representativeness and simulation heuristics use abstractions as a comparison with stimuli to be judged. The anchoring heuristic might use both types of models in judgment according to the information provided. In the African nations example, the exemplar model is used but in judging a particular behavior as weird, the normal behavior serves as a prototype being

Table 7.2. A classification of cognitive heuristics.

Heuristic	Type of model
Event matching	Prototype
Melioration	Prototype
Availability	Exemplar
Representativeness	Prototype
Anchoring	Exemplar/Prototype
Simulation	Prototype
Aspiration level	Prototype

available for judgment. The event matching, melioration and aspiration level heuristics are mainly associated with prototype models.[35] This classification of cognitive heuristics is shown in Table 7.2.

The heuristics described above use the wrong cues in making judgments, thus frequently leading to non-optimal decisions. Typically, these heuristics are not applied in situations of information overload but rather in situations lacking the relevant information. Not all heuristics are detrimental to information processing. In a number of problems, several heuristics are conceivable that may produce solutions at least as good as those resulting from rational problem solving. In very difficult problems, for instance chess problems, it is not possible to collect information concerning all possible moves. Heuristics, such as 'protect the king' or 'set out the pieces', are frequently more useful in solving the problem. Likewise, aspiration levels are beneficial in that they protect men from too extensive a search for the optimal choice alternative.

Conclusion

Cognitive heuristics are applied in cases where relevant information is lacking rather than superabundant. A classification of heuristics can be made according to whether events, objects or people are represented by mental models or by exemplar information in the mind. Although cognitive heuristics may invoke biased decision making, the effort of information processing is reduced considerably.

BOX 7.2

HOW TO PLAY BETTER TENNIS?

This box has been taken from Erev, Maital and Or-Hof.[36]

The heuristic of melioration may be illustrated by studying the performance of a tennis player. To simplify matters, the player has available only two types of shots: a 'lob' (high soft shot over the head of the opponent) and a 'passing shot' (sharp flat return past the opponent). Both shots gain from surprise. However, lobs benefit more from surprise (infrequent use). The more each shot is used, the less effective it becomes. How many lobs should be played relative to the number of passing shots?

The objective of a tennis game is to maximize the probability of winning each point and by doing so maximize the probability of winning the match. Melioration in this context is based on an appealing intuitive decision rule, that turns out to be highly sub-optimal or non-rational.

Assume that your passing shot – a flat hard shot used to 'pass' your opponent, especially when he or she is up close to the net – has a known and constant probability of winning the point when it is used. It has no surprise effect and its probability of winning the point depends only on the quality of the shot itself, not on the frequency of its use.

The decision rule reported by Herrnstein which most people give, in one version or the other is the following.

> "As long as one shot is more effective than the other, I'd use it. When the other shot becomes more effective, I'd shift to that one. And so I'd oscillate from one shot to the other, *trying to switch to the one that is currently more effective*".
>
> "No one to whom I have presented the riddle has ever spontaneously noticed that the strategy I just characterized may be significantly suboptimal."[37]

The strategy reported is a special case of melioration. According to this strategy, tennis players choose their shots in order to equalize the average 'Rate of return' – i.e. the probability of winning a point – of both shots. This is in general suboptimal because it fails to take into account the fact that each time the lob is used, its surprise effect diminishes and hence the likelihood a lob will win a point in future diminishes, by a small but non-trivial percentage. This 'external' cost must be taken into account when choosing shots. But by equating average probabilities, we fail to take it into account.

Optimality implies equating two rates of return at the *margin*, not at the average. Melioration behavior will therefore result in our winning fewer matches than would be the case, if shot choice were fully optimal. This can be better understood by constructing a simple mathematical model.

Let the probability of winning a point with a lob be *pLOB* and the probability of winning a point with a passing shot be *pPASS*. Let xL be the proportion of shots that are lobs and hence $1 - xL$ be the proportion of shots that are passing shots. The overall probability of this player winning a point, on a decisive play, z, is a weighted average of *pLOB* and *pPASS*, with xL and $(1 - xL)$ serving as weights:

$$z = (pLOB)(xL) + (pPASS)(1 - xL) \tag{1}$$

If z is greater than 1/2, then if sufficient points are played, this player will win the match; if z is less, the player will lose. What is the appropriate strategy to achieve the objective of winning, in choosing lobs and passing shots? To simplify the problem, assume that *pLOB* is a decreasing linear function of *xLOB* because *the more lobs are used, the less surprising they are*, hence the less likely the lob is to win the point:

$$pLOB = a - b\,xL \tag{2}$$

Suppose also that the likelihood of winning a point with a passing shot is a constant, k and hence independent of xL (this assumption can be relaxed without in any way altering the conclusions):

$$pPASS = k \tag{3}$$

Melioration means allocating shots so that the likelihood of winning a point with a lob and with a passing shot are equal:

$$a - b\,xL = k \tag{4}$$

Solving for xL:

$$xL = (a - k)/b \tag{5}$$

This is the proportion of lob shots chosen, under the intuitively appealing melioration rule; it ensures that *pLOB* equals *pPASS* $= k$. The expected probability of winning the point, z, is found by substituting (5) into (1):

$$z = k \tag{6}$$

Optimizing implies *choosing xL in order to maximize the probability of winning the point, z*. The problem becomes:

$$\max_{xL} z = pLOBxL + k(1 - xL) \tag{7}$$

Substituting (2) into (7), the problem becomes:

$$\max_{xL} z = (a - b\,xL)xL + k(1 - xL) \tag{8}$$

Differentiating with respect to the decision variable, xL and equating to zero:

$$\mathrm{d}z/\mathrm{d}xL = 0 \rightarrow xL = (a - k)/2b \tag{9}$$

This implies that the *optimal proportion of lob shots is only one-half the proportion that melioration behavior chooses*. The reason is that maximizing behavior takes into account the 'external cost' that each shot imposes, by reducing the probability the next lob will be a (surprise) winner.

With $a = 1$, $b = 0.8$ and $k = 0.45$, the match will be lost when applying melioration. However, when the optimal proportion of lob shots is used, the weighted average probability of winning a point, z, equals 0.55 (readers should check this for themselves)[1] and the match is won. What proportion of lobs should be played in this case?

7.4. Aspiration levels in decision making

With increasing numbers of attributes and alternatives, the individual is likely to simplify the information processing. An important principle in the simplification of the process is *satisficing*.[38] With satisficing, the individual does not strive for the best alternative by optimally using all available information (such as in compensatory attitude models in specific choice) but is satisfied with the first alternative meeting her expectations. Thus, aspiration levels perform an instrumental function in directing the search process. Aspiration levels perform the same functions as attitudes in the decision process.[39]

In the allocation to broad expenditure groups, *aspiration levels* are assumed to play a part in the decision making, too. Standard economics assumes that the marginal utility of each dollar spent is equal in each direction of spending the budget.[40] Instead of taking this condition into account, satisficing assumes that consumers set aspiration levels for expenditures on particular goods.[41] In a survey regarding expenditures on 29 durables, they ask households to report whether they own these durables and which durables are still needed to be able to say: "Now I have an appropriate standard of living". The durables were weighted according to their estimated value to compute the equipment level (the actual degree of ownership) and the level of aspiration (the desirable degree of ownership), together constituting the consumption standard (see Table 7.3).

It appears that, although the equipment level varies positively with the level of household income, the level of aspiration is fairly constant, except for a remarkable drop at the highest income level. Thus, the income does not appear to explain the aspiration level. However, the survey deals with a limited number of durable goods while new desires may be present for other goods, not included in the survey.

---

[1] $xL = 11/32$.

Table 7.3. Consumption standard and income.

Total net income of household (monthly)	Equipment level (a)	Level of aspiration (b)	Consumption standard (a + b)	N
0–599	488	299	718	305
600–699	594	301	896	201
700–899	768	305	1073	488
900–999	878	287	1166	200
1000–1499	1006	303	1309	267
1500 and more	1190	207	1397	133
All households	785	279	1065	1594

From Schmöelders and Biervert (1972).

Table 7.4. Consumption standard and life-cycle of the household.

Life-cycle	Monthly income (a)	Equipment level (b)	Level of aspiration	Consumption standard (a + b)	N
Young people	826	875	461	1336	93
Young family	1034	980	415	1395	288
Normal family	1005	865	322	1188	440
Adult family	931	835	241	1076	383
Older people	699	536	134	671	364

From Schmöelders and Biervert (1972).

The level of aspiration for durable goods is found to depend on the life-cycle of the household (see Table 7.4), in that young families show a higher level of aspiration than older families.

The aspiration level not only depends on the current family status but on their economic expectations as well. The expected economic situation of the country one year ahead is found to relate positively to the level of aspiration, irrespective of the income level. (See Table 7.5.) This suggests that new desires are likely to show up if the economic situation is expected to improve. Thus, the aspiration level may be adapted to changed circumstances or revised expectations.

In a comparison of satisficing and maximizing, the individual welfare derived from expenditure on 28 durable goods was estimated by means of survey questions.[42] It appears that consumers demand a fixed amount of welfare from these goods (the aspiration level), whilst generating a willingness to spend a particular amount of money on them. This contradicts the economic

Table 7.5. Consumption standard and economic expectations of the household.

Expectations	Equipment level (a)	Level of aspiration (b)	Consumption standard (a + b)	N
Income up to 699 DM				
Better	605	341	947	73
Same	530	265	796	292
Worse	580	230	810	53
Income 700–999 DM				
Better	838	341	1179	154
Same	810	312	1122	408
Worse	746	204	951	55
Income 1000 DM and more				
Better	1137	281	1418	105
Same	1057	277	1334	235
Worse	988	269	1257	32

From Schmöelders and Biervert (1972).

hypothesis of utility maximization under a budget constraint.

Conclusion

The aspiration level constitutes a desired level of welfare and depends on family needs and economic expectations. The aspiration level simplifies decision making because the search for alternatives may be finished once a satisfactory alternative has been found. Aspiration levels may be revised in the light of new expectations and needs.

7.5. Models of information processing

In Chapter 6, consideration was given to compensatory and non-compensatory models of attitude. Section 7.3 dealt with heuristics in judgment and decision making. This section considers the conditions for using these models and heuristics and the structure of information processing.

A problem solving model describes the elements of the process that leads to a solution of the problem. The IDEAL model consists of five stages, shown in Table 7.6.[43]

In the first stage, problems are recognized and identified. This happens in a rather superficial way and does not go beyond the practical level at which the problem exists. For example, fixing a lamp to the wall may be identified

Table 7.6. The elements of IDEAL problem solving.

1.	*I*dentifying problems
2.	*D*efining and representing problems
3.	*E*xploring possible strategies
4.	*A*cting on a plan and looking at the effects
5.	*L*ooking back and evaluating the effects

as a problem since it requires physical effort. Identification does not deal with the causes of a problem.

In the second stage, the problem is defined more precisely and represented in terms of cause and effect. For instance, the reasons for the existence of the problem are separated from its symptoms. The problem might be split up in several sub-problems, e.g. the problem of a hard wall, the lack of physical power and the penetrating qualities of a screw. The sub-problems are sometimes defined in a sequential order, for example in the case of profit making by the firm. In this case, the firm may investigate problems of investment, product research and development, production and marketing sequentially.

The third stage deals with exploration of possible alternatives for action and application of a decision rule to select an alternative. For example, in the case of dissatisfaction with a product (a problem identification), this might be ascribed to a particular characteristic (a problem definition). Possible alternatives are replacing the product by another possessing at least the desirable characteristics of the present good and more satisfactory with respect to the unfavorable characteristic, making adjustments to the product to remedy the unfavorable attribute or purchasing additional items that can perform the service better than the product in use.

The exploration of alternatives sometimes demands creativity of the problem solver. A notable example is Maier's Two-String Problem,[44] in which a person's task is to tie two strings together. The strings hang down from the ceiling of a room at such a distance that the person cannot grasp both of them at the same time. There is miscellaneous equipment available, such as a table, a stick, a pair of pliers, etcetera.[45] Common solutions are tying one string to the table, grasping the other string and untying the first string or fishing for the other string with a stick. The most creative solution is the pendulum solution, in which the pliers are tied to one of the strings and are set to swing like a pendulum. While holding one string, the other string can be grasped when it swings over to the person. (See Figure 7.6.)

The fourth stage involves carrying out the decision and performing the plan of action. The last stage is looking back and evaluating the effects.

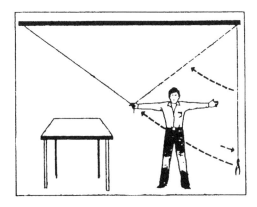

Figure 7.6. Maier's (1931) Two-String Problem. From Maier (1931).

If the problem is solved, the action can be stopped, otherwise the action continues or the problem is restated. The last two stages have been modeled before on the basis of neurophysiological principles.[46] The model is simply stated as a sequence of Test-Operation-Test-Exit (TOTE). For example, a test involves whether a screw is driven into the wall or not. If the test is negative, an operation is performed (driving the screw into the wall) and a second test is conducted. If the test is positive, the plan has been carried out and TOTE can be finished. Although this is a very simple model, it works on numerous sublevels of an action. For example, it is applied at the level of mental operations (Test lamp at the wall – Fix the lamp – Test lamp – Exit), at the level of the physical operation of turning the wrist to drive the screw (Test wrist – Turn wrist – Test wrist – Exit) and at the neural level (Test electric potential in the neuron – fire electric impulse – Test electric potential – Exit). More extensive models of decision making are described in the consumer behavior literature.[47]

In the second and third IDEAL stages, heuristics and information process-ing models can be applied extensively and several attempts have been made to describe how individuals cope with them. In Chapter 6, the attribute mod-els of attitude have been discussed along with several ways to combine the attribute information. A simple way to describe how individuals combine this information is the linear model in which the attribute judgments are weighted according to a linear function. It has been shown that in many cases the linear model can describe complex judgments very satisfactorily.[48]

One study compared the linear model to a computer program formalizing individual decision making.[49] After the mental process has been traced, the computer programer writes a program that simply imitates a number of items, usually checked by a decision maker in a sequential order. It appears that the process-tracing model and the linear model are about equally effective in explaining the individual judgments.

The IDEAL model of problem solving can be applied to consumer be-havior. The five steps of extensive problem solving in consumer behavior, problem recognition, search, alternative evaluation, purchase and outcomes correspond closely with the elements of IDEAL.[50]

Preferences for a number of decision rules were investigated, including compensatory and non-compensatory models of decision making regarding jobs and apartment offers.[51] It appeared that 75% of the subjects used two decision rules at least, mainly a combination of the conjunctive and one of the compensatory models. The conjunctive model[52] was used primarily regarding alternatives with very unattractive aspects. Also, the conjunctive rule was applied before the compensatory model in the choice process. The idea of a sequential order of decision rules has been elaborated and is shown in Figure 7.7.[53] It contains two non-compensatory rules followed by one compensatory rule.

Conclusion

Information processing models describe the structure and the order of the steps taken in decision making. The IDEAL model deals with the stages in decision making. Other models deal with the order and preference for combination rules. The latter models indicate that simplified rules are used to reject unacceptable alternatives and more complex rules to select the preferred alternatives from the remaining ones.

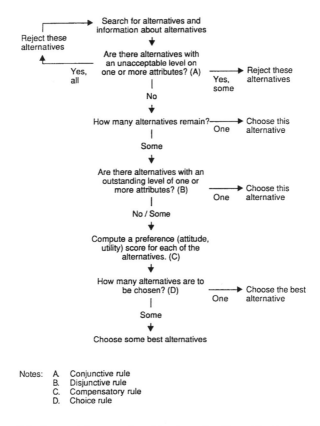

Figure 7.7. Sequential usage of combination rules. From Van Raaij (1986a).

Summary

Normative models prescribe how information processing has to proceed to select the most preferred alternative. In practice, however, people deviate considerably from the optimal way of information processing. Limited information processing has been found in consumer decision making as regards spending on broad expenditure categories and saving, generic allocation, store choice and brand choice.

Limited information processing has been investigated empirically with (series of) uni-dimensional stimuli and multi-dimensional stimuli. It appears that the channel capacity of communication sets a natural limit on the processing of uni-dimensional information. Multi-dimensional information and series of uni-dimensional stimuli can be summarized into recoded information chunks. By recoding, extensive information processing becomes possible and information overload can be thereby reduced. Recoding requires training and experience frequently not available in economic decision making.

If relevant information is lacking, cognitive heuristics are applied to decision making. The heuristics of event matching, melioration, representativeness, simulation and the use of aspiration levels are based on mental prototypes of events, objects and persons. The aspiration level has been found to depend on family needs and on economic expectations and can be revised according to circumstances. The availability heuristic is based on exemplar information in the mind. The anchoring heuristic can depend on prototypes as well as on exemplar information, according to the type of 'anchor' on which the judgment is based.

Models of information processing describe the steps taken in decision making and the order and preference for the combination rules dealing with elements of information. It appears that simplified rules are used first whereas more complex rules are applied to the remaining choice alternatives.

BOX 7.3

COMPUTER ASSISTED DECISION MAKING

Optimal decision making regarding multi-attribute alternatives requires a great deal of information processing and is likely to result in information overload. To facilitate decision making in these cases, the use of a computer might be helpful in keeping track of the process and carrying out the necessary computations. Several programs are available or in progress, according to the different type of decision making situation (e.g. individual or group), the type of model used (e.g. with subjective or inferred weights), style and organization. In Keeney and Raiffa,[54] the steps involved in assessing a multi-attribute utility function are considered and the computer program MUFCAP (multi-attribute utility function calculating and assessment package) is described.

Here, a program written for consumers and managers will be described in some detail.[55] The program was originally adapted from the MAUD program.[56] The program has been tested in several experiments dealing with choices of cars, political parties, holiday destinations and information suppliers. During its three years of development, the program has been rewritten several times (in BASIC, LISP and PASCAL) to adapt to different types of computers. The authors claim that the main benefits of the program are its advisory capabilities and its conscious raising properties whereby it makes the users aware of the reasons for their preferences. The following steps are followed in the program consecutively:[57]

Step 1: Identifying the choice alternatives
The program starts by asking the user to enumerate the alternatives she wants to consider in the choice process.

Step 2: Identifying the relevant attributes for making a decision between the alternatives
It is possible to prescribe the use of some attributes or to give free rein. A direct question can be used (for example: "Now, think of the different factors that are important to you in choosing your favourite holiday") or a more sophisticated procedure like the repertory grid.[58] In the repertory grid, the user is presented with triads of alternatives and asked whether she can indicate an alternative that differs from the other two. If the answer is in the affirmative, the program tries to determine the poles of the attribute that pinpoints the difference between the one alternative and the other two. Try-outs with a prototype of the program have shown that a number of users tend to introduce the same attribute more than once, so the program checks whether an attribute is mentioned with one or two of the poles that have already been determined. If so, the attribute can be deleted by the user.

Step 3: Assigning values or positions to the alternatives on the attributes
The next step requires the user to assign a value to each alternative on each attribute. This is accomplished by means of 7 or 9 point rating scales. These ratings can be given on the basis of information about the alternatives that the users have stored in their memory or on information obtained from different sources available to them during the session with the computer.

Step 4: Assigning the most preferred (or 'ideal') value to each attribute
In the fourth phase, the user has to indicate her most preferred value on each of the attributes, again represented by 7 or 9 point rating scales. In the case of 'the more the better attributes' (for example, comfort), the ideal point will be one of the extreme values; with attributes like left-right in the case of political parties the most preferred value on this attribute dimension will be somewhere in the middle for most decision makers. One of the key features of the program is the possibility for users to change things previously done. This is important as it has become clear from experiences with the program that for a number of users their decision process 'unfolds' itself during the session with the computer. As a result, they frequently want to change elements. In line with this, at the end of step 4 a table is presented displaying the values assigned to the alternatives and the ideal values, with the possibility of changing anyone of them for the user.

Step 5: Differential weighing of the attributes
The possibility of assigning different weights to the attributes is introduced in
the next step. This weighting is optional because not everyone wants to differentiate between the importance of attributes. If the user wishes to weight,
a mainly non-numerical technique is used for establishing weights. First, the
most and the least important attributes are identified. Next, the user has to
express the difference in importance between these two with a number, say
for example 4, meaning that the most important attribute is four times as important as the least important. The remaining attributes are scaled on a 7 or 9
point rating scale between least and most important attribute, scale positions
are indicated by characters instead of numerals. This procedure works very
well on the whole and has certain theoretical advantages over direct ranking
methods or fixed rating scales based on numerals.

Step 6: Presenting an advised preference order
To conclude the whole process the program calculates the values of the alternatives according to an additive multi-attribute choice model. The alternatives
rank ordered from lowest score to highest score are presented to the user. The
user can consider this advice and react accordingly. This whole question-
answer process between program and user is copied on a separate file. This
printed file serves at a later stage as a protocol for the researcher or the user.

Notes

[1] Becker and McClintock 1967. Several of these axioms are dealt with in Section 12.2.
[2] Olshavsky and Granbois 1979.
[3] These stages have been considered in Gredal 1966.
[4] Ferber 1973.
[5] Ölander and Seipel 1970.
[6] Arndt 1979.
[7] Hill 1963.
[8] Ferber 1973.
[9] Granbois 1977.
[10] Olshavsky and Granbois 1979.
[11] Miller 1956.
[12] Pollack 1952.
[13] Miller 1956.
[14] Cited in Miller 1956.
[15] Sternberg 1966, taken from Ulen 1987.
[16] Ulen 1987.
[17] Malholtra 1982.
[18] Jacoby et al. 1974a, 1974b.

[19] Simon 1959.

[20] Herrnstein and Prelec 1991.

[21] Erev and Maital 1996.

[22] Hayes and Abernathy 1980.

[23] Kahneman et al. 1983. An excellent review of cognitive heuristics is provided by Sherman and Corty 1984.

[24] See Ulen 1988.

[25] Johnson et al. 1993.

[26] Lichtenstein et al. 1978. See also Fischhoff et al. 1981.

[27] Combs and Slovic 1979.

[28] See Section 11.3.

[29] Sherman and Corty 1984.

[30] See Section 11.3.

[31] See Section 11.3.

[32] Daamen and Wilke 1994.

[33] See Section 7.5.

[34] Sherman and Corty 1984.

[35] These heuristics are not considered in Sherman and Corty 1984.

[36] Erev and Maital 1996.

[37] Herrnstein 1990, p. 360.

[38] Simon 1955.

[39] Starbuck 1963. See also Section 6.1.

[40] See, for example Deaton and Muellbauer 1980.

[41] Schmöelders and Biervert 1972.

[42] Kapteyn et al. 1979.

[43] Bransford and Stein 1984.

[44] Maier 1931.

[45] This resembles the situation of Kohler's apes, dealt with in Section 5.4.

[46] Miller et al. 1960.

[47] Engel et al. 1990.

[48] Dawes and Corrigan 1974 and Dawes 1979.

[49] Einhorn et al. 1979.

[50] Engel et al. 1986.

[51] Adelbratt and Montgomery 1980.

[52] See Section 6.3.

[53] Van Raaij 1986.

[54] Keeney and Raiffa 1976.

[55] Bronner and De Hoog 1984.

[56] Humphrey and Wisudha's 1979.

[57] Adapted from Bronner and De Hoog 1984.

[58] See Shaw 1979.

CHAPTER 8

ECONOMIC EXPECTATIONS AND INVESTMENT BEHAVIOR

8.1. Buying intentions

In Chapter 7, we endeavored to show that buying behavior is not always preceded by deliberate planning. This chapter will consider the relationship between the willingness to buy, buying intentions and buying behavior. This relationship should be placed between the decision making and the behavior nodes in Figure 2.5. An illustration of the lack of correspondence between intentions and behavior has been shown in Box 6.2.

Prediction of behavior in economic research appears to be very limited because of market imperfections, limited information processing by consumers,[1] all kinds of restrictions that may prevent buying intentions from being realized[2] and the possibility of purchase delays. Consideration will here be given to the role of intentions in explaining consumer behavior. *Intentions* can be defined as expectations regarding future purchases.

Theil and Kosobud studied data from the Quarterly Survey of Intentions (sampled by the U.S. Bureau of the Census) in the 1961–1966 period.[3] In part of the survey, the same households were questioned 12 months later. This makes it possible to relate buying intentions stated in a particular year to consumer behavior in the next year. Among many other questions put to them in the surveys the subjects were asked whether any member of the family expected to buy a car within the next 12 months. Response categories were "No", "Don't know", "Maybe", "Yes – probably" and "Yes – definitely" (the latter three categories being regarded as a declaration of intention). After 12 months, the same households were asked whether any member of the family owned a car and if so in what month and year the car was purchased. Using this information which was obtained from 19 samples each consisting of about 1000 families, it was possible to compile Table 8.1.

The proportion of people intending to buy a car was 8.3% and the proportion that actually purchased a car in the year following the survey was 10.0%. However, only 38.6% of the intenders and 7.4% of the non-intenders actually bought a car. Thus, although intentions explain purchases to some extent,

Table 8.1. Car buying intentions and purchases.

Intention	Behavior		
	No purchase	Purchase	Marginal
Don't intend	0.849	0.068	0.917
Intend	0.051	0.032	0.083
Marginal	0.900	0.100	1.000

From Theil and Kosobud (1968).

Table 8.2. Degree of fulfilment of purchase plans by purchase probability and by expenditure type.

Purchase probability	Durable goods	House services	Vacation	Education
0.1–0.4	9%	17%	0%	–
0.5	30%	20%*	50%*	0%*
0.6–1.0	33%	60%	62%	67%
All purchase plans	22%	49%	44%	64%

*Based on five reported plans or less.
From Ferber and Piskie (1965).

predictions are by no means perfect. The average correlation between buying intentions and behavior in 13 studies was 0.34; 42% of intenders realized their plans, whereas 88% of the non-intenders did not purchase.[4]

The impact of the certainty of the buying intention on the prediction of buying behavior has been studied.[5] A so-called 'plan-o-meter' regarding the purchase of a number of goods and services contained ten gradations of probability from zero to one. For example, a probability of one was associated with the response "Absolutely certain to buy", a probability of a half with the response "About even chances (50–50)" and a zero probability with "Absolutely no chance". The 250 households in a one-year panel in St. Louis stated that they intended to buy nine durables, three house services, a vacation and one type of education. For the durables, non-zero probabilities were reported by only 6% of the households, for house services it was 15%, vacation 47% and education 29%. In Table 8.2 the actual proportions of purchases are related to the probability of buying.

It appears from Table 8.2 that at higher levels of certainty regarding buying intentions, more plans are fulfilled, indicating additional explanatory power of graded purchase probabilities. However, several cells of Table 8.2 are based on very small numbers of observations. Partial correlations between consumer purchases and probabilities of buying are found to be in the 0.20–0.60 range for the four types of expenditure. These correlations are obtained with dichotomous probabilities (e.g. probability of zero or 0.1–0.9) as with the ten-point scales. It is concluded that the 'plan-o-meter' significantly explains purchases but the effect of graded probabilities is considered doubtful.

Purchase intentions comprise only part of economic expectations. General models of economic expectations will be considered in Section 8.2. Section 8.3 deals with the explanation of aggregate spending on a number of commodities from economic and psychological variables. Expectations regarding investments will be considered in Section 8.4. The psychology of ethical investments and initial public offerings will be considered in Sections 8.5 and 8.6, respectively.

Conclusion

Buying intentions are found to explain single purchases to some extent. Elaborated measures of intention, including graded probabilities, do not generally lead to more accurate predictions. The results are disappointing, although this could have been expected considering the lack of information processing and the casual planning of consumer purchases.[6]

8.2. Expectations

In economics, several theories on expectation formation exist, the most important ones being adaptive expectations and rational expectations.

Adaptive expectations theory assumes that expectations of future events are based on previous expectations about current events and on prediction errors evident from comparisons of previous expectations and current realizations. Alternatively, this amounts to the assumption that expectations are dependent on extrapolations from past realizations.[7] If no past realizations are known, expectations simply are equated to current outcomes. Adaptive expectations do not make use of a model or explanatory framework in forecasting events. The adaptive expectations model is considered less realistic for consumers since they are less likely to remember what they answered a couple of months ago and to compare this to realized outcomes.[8] In our opinion however, they may use such models in their investment behavior, especially because errors may become very costly here. As the theory of learning shows, reinforcements will facilitate learning.[9]

Rational expectations include structural models of the economy and generally have replaced adaptive expectations.[10] The rational expectations model (REM) includes the hypothesis that a 'true' economic model will be used in forming expectations, i.e. that all relevant and available information will be used.[11] This hypothesis has been investigated both by indirect tests, i.e. relating the model to investment data, and direct tests, i.e. by comparing REM with subjective information or with experimental outcomes. Here, we restrict ourselves to the latter type of test. Further assumptions of REM regard to the rationality in using the information:[12]

− unbiasedness, i.e. the forecast is an unbiased estimate of the realization;
− non-correlation of errors, i.e. previous forecasting errors will not affect current errors (since previous errors should be taken into account in making the forecast);
− efficiency, i.e. previously available information will not affect forecasting error (since it should have been taken into account when making the forecast);
− forecasting errors should diminish over time, due to learning.[13]

Although the latter assumption is not standard in finance, it has been recognized in the experimental approach to investment behavior. Tests of REM have been reviewed[14] and further investigated by a number of authors.[15] Generally, these tests have rejected REM, leading Anderson and Goldsmith to ". . . wonder whether the emperor wears no clothes."[16] From the psychological point of view, such a model is unlikely to hold in practice.

A hybrid model of expectation formation has been postulated, including adaptive expectations, rational expectations based on past experience and expectations based on new information.[17] Each of these possibilities may be given some weight in forming the resulting expectation. For example, if no information is available or if the environment is very turbulent, adaptive expectations may prevail. If there is no previous experience, adaptive expectations cannot be formed. Since expectations based on past experience seem to be sticky, in practice rational expectations should be given less weight than in it is assigned in REM. In new situations or in case of extraordinary events, both adaptive and rational expectations may be assigned low weight.

Conclusion

Adaptive and rational expectation models in economics are of limited value in explaining individual behavior. Lack of experience and limited cognitive capacities may hamper the use of rational models.

8.3. Consumer confidence

Family income in the twentieth century has steadily increased. There has been greater spending on commodities that are not strictly necessary for survival. This *discretionary* spending is not exclusively determined by the ability to buy (e.g. by income) but also by the *willingness to buy*.[18] Willingness to buy is an indicator of confidence, influenced by perceptions (subjective meaning) of income changes in the past and in the future (income expectations). Consumer studies showed that the timing of purchases and the possibility of delaying expenditure were becoming more important. Besides objective economic circumstances, the perception of conditions and optimistic or pessimistic economic expectations were becoming more important in explaining consumer demand.[19] Perceptions and expectations are assumed to be easily influenced by the media and by the occurrence of events.

Consumer perceptions and expectations have been measured directly in large scale consumer surveys.[20] This has resulted in the *Index of Consumer Sentiment* (ICS), based on the five questions presented in Table 8.3. The ICS can be obtained by adding the numbers associated with the answers and averaging over the survey sample. (As an alternative to the scores in Table 8.3, the two extreme categories "a lot better" and "a lot worse" can be scored $+2$ and -2 respectively.) Since these questions have been included in a number of consecutive surveys in a number of countries, ICS series can be constructed for different countries.

From inspection of these series, it appears that marked differences exist between consumers in different countries and at different times.

The ICS appears to be related to several economic variables, indicating the validity of the construct. The explained variance in ICS by the percentage of unemployed equals 17%.[21] The disposable personal income preceding the survey explains 6% of the variance and 51% can be ascribed to income increases relative to incomes six months earlier.

The ICS has frequently been used to explain expenditure on commodity groups. Aggregate non-discretionary expenditure – on food, shelter and other necessities – generally shows a steady increase over time, whereas discretionary expenditure fluctuate much more. Non-discretionary expenditure is assumed to relate substantially to the ability to buy (i.e. income) and to a much smaller extent to the willingness to buy (as expressed in the ICS). The effect of the ICS on discretionary expenditure is assumed to be substantial compared to the income effect.

Regression results regarding these hypotheses are presented in Table 8.4. The first four regressions in this table confirm the hypotheses. (The third and fourth relate to expenditures on durable goods.) The last regression includes the buying intention for durable goods, which obtains an insignificant coefficient and does not increase the explained variance in expenditure. As a conclusion, it appears that non-discretionary expenditure is mainly explained by income, discretionary expenditure by income and consumer sentiment; buying intentions do not explain discretionary expenditure in the presence of income and ICS.

Table 8.3. Questions regarding the Index of Consumer Sentiment in the Netherlands.

How do you think the general economic situation in the Netherlands has changed over the last 12 months?
got a lot better (+1)
got a little better (+1)
stayed the same (0)
got a little worse (−1)
got a lot worse (−1)
don't know (0)

How do you think the general economic situation in the Netherlands will develop over the next 12 months?
get a lot better (+1)
get a little better (+1)
will stay the same (0)
get a little worse (−1)
get a lot worse (−1)
don't know (0)

How does the financial situation in your household now compare with what it was 12 months ago?
got a lot better (+1)
got a little better (+1)
stayed the same (0)
got a little worse (−1)
got a lot worse (−1)
don't know (0)

How do you think the financial position of your household will change over the next 12 months?
get a lot better (+1)
get a little better (+1)
will stay the same (0)
get a little worse (−1)
get a lot worse (−1)
don't know (0)

Do you think it is a good time now to buy durable products?
it is a good time (+1)
it is neither a good nor a bad time (0)
it is a bad time (−1)
don't know (0)

From Van Raaij and Gianotten (1990).

Table 8.4. Regressions of non-durable and durable consumption on income and the Index of Consumer Sentiment.

	ND	ND	D	D	D
Constant	67.04	40.97	3.74	−48.00	−43.07
Y(−1)	0.24	0.27	0.13	0.18	0.17
ICS		0.20		0.40	0.34
BI					0.04*
R^2	0.79	0.87	0.29	0.76	0.75

*Not statistically significant.
Key: ND = consumption of non-durables; D = consumption of durables; Y(−1) = income lagged by one period; ICS = Index of Consumer Sentiment; BI = buying intention.
Adapted from Mueller (1963).

Similar results have been obtained regarding aggregate expenditure on durable goods.[22] Here, too, buying intentions were not significant if income and ICS were included. This caused the Survey Research Center at the University of Michigan to discontinue the Survey of Consumer Buying Expectations in 1973.[23]

Several critiques and extensions to the use of consumer perceptions and expectations in the explanation of consumer expenditures have emerged.[24]

Econometric issues in the use of the ICS pertain to multicollinearity among economic and psychological indicators and autocorrelation in the time series. Furthermore, the causality of effects has been questioned, i.e. the question of whether consumer confidence influences expenditure or expenditure generate confidence.

The structure of the ICS has been examined by using factor analyses. This technique allows different weights of the ICS questions and for different underlying dimensions of the ICS, e.g. willingness to buy and confidence. A number of alternative questions related for instance to the interest rate, inflation or unemployment might be included in the ICS. A particular interesting result is that an underlying dimension called 'the evaluation of the development of the household financial situation' appears to be significantly related to consumption and saving but a second dimension called 'evaluation of the general economic situation' does not appear significant in this respect.[25] However, they notice that the second dimension seems to be a 'leading' indicator for the first one. A different study also distinguishes a *sociotropic aspect of consumer confidence* (capturing the two questions on the general economic situation) from the personal aspect, albeit by a different method.[26]

An intriguing question is whether consumer sentiment can be explained from more general cultural trends in society, transmitted for instance via popular culture and mass media. The effects of pessimism, optimism and rumination on consumer sentiment, consumption expenditures and GNP growth have been studied.[27] Based on the concept of explanatory style[28] a pessimistic style is described as explaining bad events from causes that are stable ('lasting forever'), global ('affecting everything') and internal ('own fault'). An optimistic style is described as explaining bad events from causes that are unstable ('temporary'), specific ('affecting only this problem') and external ('due to the situation'). Pessimistic rumination refers to how frequently one is engaged in causal and non-action-oriented analyses of bad events. Explanatory style appears to be closely related to the type of attribution made in case of success or failure.[29]

The content of top 40 U.S. songs and cover captions of *Time* from 1955 to 1989 was analyzed with respect to explanatory style and pessimistic rumination.[30] For example, the 1969 Creedance Clearwater song 'Bad Moon Rising' scored high on pessimistic rumination ("I see the bad moon a-rising, I see trouble on the way. I see earthquakes and lightnin'. I see bad times today"). Optimistic explanations were found, for example, in the 1957 Everly Brothers song 'Wake Up Little Susie'. All of the information was aggregated on an annual basis. It was found that:

— change in GNP was predicted by change in aggregate personal consumption;
— change in consumption was explained by absolute level of consumer sentiment and change in ICS in the preceding year (change in GNP had no effect in the presence of the ICS variables);
— consumer confidence was explained by a two-year moving average of pessimistic rumination in songs in the preceding year and by rumination in *Time*;
— change in ICS was explained by the moving average of pessimistic rumination in songs;
— the moving average of pessimistic rumination in songs was explained from its own five years lagged value;
— rumination in *Time* was explained from the moving average of pessimistic rumination in songs in the preceding years.

Summarizing, cultural effects transmitted via songs and mass media affected consumer sentiment. Consumer sentiment affected consumption which in turn affected GNP. This study both supported and extended the theory of consumer expectations. Also, it comprises still another example of a *macro-psychological* theory of economic growth.[31]

How does society recover from pessimistic rumination? Since a negative autocorrelation of pessimistic rumination was found over a five-year lag, this indicates rumination cycles.[32] This may be due to:

- *homeostatic feedback* mechanisms, i.e. society automatically corrects deviations from the mean;
- age cohorts reared in different ways, e.g. those raised in the 50's may use a different explanatory style from those raised in the 60's, however generation cycles typically will be longer than five years;
- social learning of explanatory styles and defense mechanisms, e.g. the popular credo 'Don't Worry, Be Happy' frequently shown on buttons;
- current events, both political and economic.

When applying the ICS, a distinction might be made between regular (or heavy) buyers and irregular (or non-heavy) buyers of the commodities under scrutiny. For example, in explaining expenditure on cars (especially on new cars since car ownership typically starts with a used car), the perceptions and expectations of car owners might be much more important than those of non-owners. This points to the effect of habits next to attitudes on behavior.[33]

The ICS has been related to broad commodity groups. In marketing and consumer research, however, generic and specific consumer choice[34] has been of interest. To explain consumer behavior at a more specific level, certain conditions must be satisfied concerning the explanatory variables. These will be considered in Section 8.4. Section 8.3 will consider the prediction of behavior regarding saving and investment from attitudes and intentions.

Conclusion

Next to income, consumer confidence explains discretionary expenditure to a considerable extent. Buying intentions do not have a significant effect on discretionary expenditure next to income and consumer confidence. Despite the fact that several critiques and extensions of the ICS have emerged, the effect of economic expectations and perception on consumption cannot be denied. Optimistic and pessimistic cultural trends, possibly reflecting explanatory style regarding societal events, appear to influence economic expectations.

8.4. Expectations regarding investments

Investments are considered here as any item paying off utility at a later point in time. Several types of investment can be distinguished: investment in durable goods, such as houses, cars and household appliances (1), savings in bank accounts, government bonds and life assurance (2) and risky investments, such as stocks, non-government bonds, mutual funds and high yield notes, i.e. certificates of deposit or CD's (3). Yet a different class of investments is human resources, including education, skills, health etcetera. This shows that our concept of investment is not the same as in the theory of finance.

The portfolio aspect of investments should be stressed, i.e. they should be considered in connection.[35] The portfolio view comprises the idea of a multi-layered pyramid, consisting of money invested for security at the bottom layer, money invested for a chance at getting rich at the top layer, and in-between layers. This idea is consistent with the idea of a hierarchy of saving motives,[36] the most common of which is cash management, followed by security, goal saving and wealth management. Despite the portfolio aspects, most research has been dealt with one type of investment at a time.

Earlier the relation between economic expectations and the subjective discount rate was described.[37] It appeared that optimistic expectations are associated with a high subjective discount rate, inducing a low willingness to invest in the replacement of a durable good. Furthermore, significant effects of income and consumer sentiment on aggregate consumption of durables were found.[38]

Katona assumes that savings increase during a period of economic recession.[39] In an empirical survey, a significant effect of income and economic expectations on aggregate savings one year ahead was found.[40] So, it appears that economic expectations explain savings and investments in durables to some extent. Regarding the third, risky type of investment, attitudes and intentions might influence behavior in similar ways.

In several surveys (Gallup and Roper polls) the influence of attitudes and intentions on risky investments was assessed.[41] Questions concerning past, present and future personal financial situation, similar to those in Table 8.3, have been asked in a number of Gallup surveys. The percentage of people reporting a favorable financial situation has been correlated with the Dow-Jones Industrial Average (DJIA), a weighted price index of the stock market. The results shown in Table 8.5 indicate that the reported present and future financial situation is significantly correlated with the DJIA measured after the surveys, respectively. The reported present financial situation was also correlated with the DJIA measured before and during the surveys, respectively. Definite relationships appear to exist between financial attitudes and the DJIA.

The buying intentions regarding risky investments and savings have been assessed by asking investors the following question in the Roper polls (more than one option could be chosen):

"During the next few months do you think you are likely to put any money into public stocks, bonds, mutual funds, high yield investments (e.g. certificates of deposit or CD's), government bonds, savings, life assurance or other investments (e.g. gold, individual retirement accounts, collectibles)?"[42]

The percentage of affirmative answers have been correlated with the Stan-

Table 8.5. Correlations between attitudes, intentions and stock market indices.

| | | DJIA | | |
		Before survey	During survey	After survey
Reported	Past	n.s.	n.s.	n.s.
financial	Present	0.91	0.91	0.85
situation	Future	n.a.	n.a.	0.41
(Gallup)				

		S&P	DJIA
	Stocks Combined	n.s.	n.s.
Buying	Investments	0.55–0.62	0.47–0.52
intentions	Government bonds	−0.71 – −0.79	n.s.
(Roper)	Bank accounts	−0.58 – −0.63	n.s.
	Life insurance	n.s.	n.s.

Adapted from Lindauer (1987).

dard & Poor's (S&P) industrial stock average and with the DJIA. The correlations between stock buying intentions and the stock indices were not significant. The correlations with combined investments are significant, although with regard to the S&P this is entirely due to the buying intentions in respect of high yield notes and with regard to the DJIA it is due to mutual funds buying intentions. The savings intentions regarding government bonds and bank accounts correlate negatively with the S&P but not with the DJIA index.

It is concludes that the investor's intentions to buy stocks (or bonds) were unrelated to stock market activity, whereas reported present and future personal financial situation of the public yielded significant correlations. This result is consistent with that obtained with the prediction of durable consumption from attitudes and intentions.

Another type of research concerns the direct estimation of future stock prices.[43] Members of investment study clubs (non-professional investors, interested not only in profits but also in a deeper understanding of the stock market) were asked to estimate the expected stock price of the most important stock in their portfolio three months ahead. The estimated stock prices could be explained to some extent by an attitude model including opinions regarding among other things the price earnings ratio of the stock, the business volume and the cost level of the firm associated with the stock.

The research considered here and in the former section indicates that economic attitudes are better predictors of economic activity than intentions. This result is surprising since intentions are stated in direct agreement with the type of behavior to be predicted. Two explanations may be offered.

The first explanation is that attitudes are generally based on a number of attributes. The Index of Consumer Sentiment consists of five questions regarding different aspects of the economy. The factor analysis approach to economic attitudes also summarizes information about a number of attributes. In contrast, behavioral intentions are frequently assessed by only one survey question which is very specific. As a result, the attitude measures may be more reliable than the intentions and for this reason can be assumed to predict behavior more accurately. The attitude measures in Table 8.5, however, are also based on single survey questions and yet perform better than the intention measure.

The second explanation is the following.[44] Generally, two strategies of estimating future stock prices can be distinguished: *regressive prediction* is based on the belief that recent changes will reverse in the future and non-regressive prediction is based on the belief that changes will persist. The heuristic of representativeness may be applied to the estimation of future stock prices.[45] In an increasing (decreasing) series of stock prices, the most representative stock price is less (higher) than the final value and a price decrease (increase) will be predicted. In this case, the representative stock price is the intrinsic value of the stock, which tends to change only slowly over time. If the heuristic is applied to the price changes, however, the most representative price change (e.g. the average price increase) will result in an expected stock price increase. It depends on one's view of the world (represented by price realizations) which type of prediction will be made. In both cases, a prototype model of events (price realizations) is applied.

An experiment was conducted to assess the effect of news on the estimation of future stock prices.[46] The news in the experiment consisted of fictional news items, both good and bad. Fictional prices and recent price changes were presented and after this the subjects were prompted for their future price estimate. It was hypothesized that news in the media serves to provide plausible attributions of price changes. These attributions would support the persistence of price increases and impede regressive predictions. According to the hypothesis, people not exposed to the news are more likely to make regressive predictions than those exposed. The results confirmed the hypothesis, i.e. the inclusion of news led to behaviors suggesting less regressive predictions. The hypothesis of using a prototype model of future events or behavior implies that attitude models, reflecting the prototype model can be expected to predict behavior better than stated intentions.

Since news retrieval information systems are proliferating in organizations, the effects of information on the quality of MBA students' forecasts of stock earnings were investigated.[47] Information about earnings per share, net sales and stock prices in the first three quarters of a year of 15 firms was provided to all students in the experiment. The students then were asked to predict earnings per share in the fourth quarter and to indicate their confidence in the estimate on a nine-point scale. For each student, there were two replications of this procedure, the first of which included redundant information in addition to that stated above (e.g. "Sales increased 21% over the last 3 Qtrs."). The second included non-redundant information (e.g. "CEO reported record order levels. Results will be the best in our history.").

Although it was expected that redundant information would have no effect on the quality of forecasts and non-redundant information would improve them, the mean squared errors were higher in the two information conditions than in the baseline information condition. However, confidence of forecasting increased from baseline to baseline plus redundant to baseline plus non-redundant information conditions. The authors seem to explain the larger error in the information conditions by stating that non-diagnostic information may have diluting effects by weakening the effect of diagnostic information. In our view, the non-redundant information might have put too much emphasis on one of the three aspects of information, thus distracting the subjects from the complete picture. An alternative hypothesis concerning the non-redundant information might be that it had no effect on the *actual* earnings and thus gave the wrong information to the students. These alternative explanations are consistent with the idea of constructing a view on reality by providing information (in this case the wrong view).

Conclusion

Investment behavior can to some extent be explained from economic perceptions and expectations, whereas intentions to invest do not consistently explain behavior. The lack of effect of intentions on behavior may be explained from differences in reliability of the measures and from the lack of affinity with prototype models in making judgments regarding investments. Economic news and information tends to support the formation of economic expectations.

8.5. Ethical investments

Economic portfolio theory assumes that investments are made exclusively on the basis of expected return and risk.[48] However, an ethical investment information service was founded in London in 1983.[49] Clients of this service complete an 'Acceptable List Questionnaire' by indicating their personal criteria for investment. The service then compiles a list of companies meeting the criteria. Although the actual investment behavior of the clients is unkown, it may be assumed that they completed the list truthfully because they paid for it and selected a portfolio according to their preference criteria. The top 5 of the 14 criteria headings include companies dealing with South Africa, sales to military purchasers, tobacco, nuclear power and financial institutions (banks, insurance companies etcetera).

A sample of 125 completed lists were analyzed by means of principal components analysis in order to find underlying dimensions. Five factors were found, explaining 60% of the variance:

1. *post-industrial*, including nuclear power, animals, sales to military purchasers, political contributions and financial institutions;
2. *sinstock*, including alcohol, gambling and tobacco;
3. *mistrust*, including spread of overseas interests, proportion of business overseas and advertising;
4. *undue influence*, including size of company and newspaper production and television;
5. *human rights/pacifist*, including sales to military purchasers and South Africa.

The factors summarize reasons for not investing in the companies concerned, despite its eventual profitability. They seem to reflect societal concern as expressed for example by Greenpeace and Amnesty International.

Other ways of ethical investments include 'green funds' (investing in activities not harmful to the environment) and securities offered by scientific or charity organizations (giving less than average return). Green funds sometimes are stimulated by governments offering fiscal advantages.

Business ethics were studied by presenting several unethical cases from the Swedish financial world to MBA students and business executives.[50] It appeared that the students judged the cases as less unethical but more illegal than the executives. However, those who judged cases as illegal frequently judged them as unethical, too. Furthermore students judge the cases to occur more frequently in Sweden and in Western countries than the executives, thus expressing less confidence in the law.

Conclusion

Concern about the social consequences of economic behavior may influence investment decision making. The ethics of doing business appear somehow related to legal restrictions.

8.6. Initial public offerings

Since there is a clear trend of privatization in Europe, the government frequently sells company shares to the public which were not available on the market earlier. Private firms too may offer shares to the public that were owned previously privately. Since these shares were not publicly available earlier, they are named initial public offerings (IPO's). In this case, the psychology of investment is highly relevant since it is hard to form expectations of return on investment without a history of share prices and dividends.

This has initiated studies regarding the effects of investors' behavioral intentions and attitudes on applications for shares issued by the British Government.[51] Several IPO's were overscribed considerably, possibly due to wide knowledge and advertising of the issue and attractive terms. Frequently, profits can be gained by buying and immediately selling the shares. Also, small allocations of shares are made to large numbers of people, resulting in substantial commissions to dealers.

Three studies dealt with IPO's of twelve regional electricity supply companies in 1990, two electricity generating companies in 1991 and a second tranche of shares in British Telecom in 1991. In all three cases, surveys eliciting buying intentions, attitudes and several other issues were held between opening applications and three days before closing. As soon as the application closed, the same respondents were contacted again to ask whether they had applied. Intention to apply significantly explained behavior: of the 94 persons who intended to apply, 67% did; of the 136 persons who intended not to apply all but one did not apply.

Regressions on the intention variable were run using a variety of models. It appeared that the attitude regarding application, social norms, personal control and past experience with applications for IPO's explained 43–57% of the variance of application intention in the three studies. Personal control is a measure of the perception of how easy a desirable action can be performed. Unfortunately, no models were included explaining behavior from intentions and from the other variables simultaneously, so from this study the performance of intentions in the presence of attitudes cannot be judged. However, these studies may be considered as an application of a psychological model in the area of financial behavior.

Conclusion

The success of initial public offerings appears to be influenced by investors' attitudes. In addition to the large stakes involved, this makes IPO's attractive prospects for advertising agencies.

Summary

Behavioral intentions have been found to explain specific behavior only to a relatively small extent. Attempts at achieving better predictions with more accurate measures of intention have failed. Rational expectations do not appear to contribute much towards explaining economic decision making either.

It appears that economic perceptions and expectations, measured by the Index of Consumer Sentiment, next to income explain discretionary consumption and savings to a considerable extent. Adding behavioral intentions does not improve the predictions. Risky investments, too, are better explained from economic perceptions and expectations than from stated intentions. Possible explanations for the lack of predictive success with intentions are the relative unreliability of the measures and the correspondence of attitudes with prototype models of events, rendering attitudes more successful in explaining behavior.

Concern about the societal consequences of investments appears to influence investors' decision making to some extent. Psychological attitudes also appear in the evaluation of initial public offerings. Both observations give way to psychological research and application of psychological knowledge in the area of finance.

Notes

[1] See Chapter 7.

[2] See Chapter 6.

[3] Theil and Kosobud 1968.

[4] McQuarrie 1988.

[5] Ferber and Piskie 1965.

[6] See Section 7.1.

[7] See, for example, Van Witteloostuijn 1990.

[8] Wärneryd 1994.

[9] See Chapter 5.

[10] Van Witteloostuijn 1990.

[11] Muth 1961.

[12] See Anderson and Goldsmith 1994 for refinements.

[13] This assumption has been recognized by Blomqvist 1989 and included by Anderson and Goldsmith 1994.

[14] Lovell 1986.

[15] Blomqvist 1989, Peterson and Reilly 1991, Stanley 1994 and Anderson and Goldsmith 1994, among others.

[16] Anderson and Goldsmith 1994, p. 402.

[17] Wärneryd 1994.

[18] Katona 1975.

[19] See Table 3.5 in Section 3.6.

[20] See Mueller 1963.

[21] Mueller 1963.

[22] Adams 1964.

[23] McNeil 1974.

[24] Vanden Abeele 1983, Praet and Vuchelen, Stuart 1984, Van Raaij and Gianotten 1990.

[25] Van Raaij and Gianotten 1990.

[26] Bechtel et al. 1993.

[27] Zullow 1991.

[28] Abramson et al. 1978.

[29] See Section 11.3.

[30] Zullow 1991.

[31] Like McClelland's theory considered in Section 3.2.

[32] Zullow 1991.

[33] Bagozzi 1981.

[34] See Chapter 7.

[35] Shefrin and Statman 1994.

[36] Linqvist 1981.

[37] Section 3.6.

[38] Mueller 1963, see Section 8.2 and Van Raaij and Gianotten 1990.

[39] Katona 1974.

[40] Van Raaij and Gianotten 1990.

[41] Lindauer 1987.

[42] Lindauer 1987, p. 95.

[43] Antonides and Van der Sar 1990.

[44] Andreassen 1987.

[45] Andreassen 1987. See also Section 7.4.

[46] Andreassen 1987.

[47] Davis et al. 1994.

[48] Markowitz 1952.

[49] Anand and Cowton 1993.

[50] Wärneryd and Westlund 1993.

[51] East 1993.

CHAPTER 9

EMOTIONS

9.1. Introduction

In Chapter 3, several motivations and personality traits were dealt with. There is no doubt about the fact that emotions are strongly related to motivations. An emotion like hate may serve as a motivator to undertake a particular action, like revenge. Emotions may also accompany motivated actions. For example, sex is not only a powerful motive but a source of vivid emotional experience as well. The emotional experience itself may become a goal for which behavior is undertaken. Without a stake in the outcome of a transaction (motivation), no emotion will occur.[1]

Emotions can be expressed in numerous ways, as can be observed daily in the theater or the cinema. The way of expression may differ according to the type and the intensity of the emotion. Great joy will be expressed in a different way from mild gladness, for example. The facial expression frequently serves as a clue in detecting emotions. Ekman distinguished 7,000 facial expressions which could be matched correctly at least to some extent with emotions by members of quite different cultures.[2] Many other types of behavior can reveal emotional states, such as laughing, crying, clapping hands, using abusive language, etcetera.

A discussion in the *Psychological Bulletin*, however, shows that one should be careful in drawing conclusions regarding the universality of recognizing emotions from facial expressions. It seems that there is insufficient evidence to warrant the conclusion of perfect recognition.[3] Differences in culture exist regarding the accuracy of recognizing common emotions, such as happiness, surprise, sadness, fear, disgust and anger. Subjects differing in exposure to Western culture also show different accuracy of recognition. Furthermore, a number of methodological problems of research are mentioned in this area (presentation and selection of stimuli, response formats and contextual information). Ekman concludes that the debate essentially is about the definition of universality.[4] For him, universality deals with the issue of significant agreement across cultures regarding the interpretation of facial expressions of emotions, thus allowing some cultural variations. Universality should deal

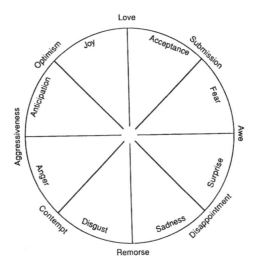

Figure 9.1. Plutchik's wheel of emotions. From Santrock (1988).

with the expression-feeling link, rather than with the correct verbal labeling of the emotions concerned.[5]

In English, more than 200 emotions are named and several attempts have been made to classify them.[6] Plutchik distinguishes four characteristics of emotions; they are:
– positive or negative;
– primary or mixed;
– polar opposites in many instances;
– of varying intensity.

In Figure 9.1, Plutchik's wheel of emotions is represented. It is assumed that opposing emotions, e.g. optimism and disappointment, cannot be experienced simultaneously. The inner circle of the wheel consists of primary emotions which can be mixed to produce emotions in the outer circle.

Emotions may be either positive (e.g. joy) or negative (e.g. sadness) and their intensity may vary according to the stimuli that produce them. For instance, winning a million dollars in a lottery is likely to produce intense happiness, whereas finding a dime on the street will only induce a slight experience of happiness.

A different approach in describing emotions has been based on the *Semantic Differential*.[7] The Semantic Differential is an instrument measuring three basic components of meaning of languages. The Semantic Differential requires people's ratings of words on a number of different adjectives, e.g. the word 'consumption' rated on 7-point adjective scales such as 'good-bad', 'active-inactive', 'influenced-influential'. Principal components analysis of the ratings typically reveals a three-dimensional structure, with dimensions identified as 'evaluation', 'activity' and 'potency' (in decreasing order of importance).

The Semantic Differential technique has been applied to words expressing affect (emotions) by Mehrabian and Russell.[8] A three-factor structure was found, the first two factors of which (pleasure and arousal) coincided with the Semantic Differential factors. The third factor (dominance) contributed considerably less towards explaining the variation of the scales. Evidence for a circular ordering of emotions in two-dimensional space has been found.[9] When people were asked to order eight emotions on a circle (pleasure, contentment, sleepiness, depression, misery, distress, arousal and excitement), 61% of the emotions were ordered clockwise as above. In 84% of the cases, the emotions were placed in adjacent categories and only 16% were placed in non-adjacent categories. The inexact ordering indicates the fuzziness of the boundaries between affect terms. For example, 'excitement' sometimes is placed instead of 'pleasure' and sometimes in place of 'arousal'. Actually, the fuzziness of the boundaries is the very reason why they are located on a circle. It appeared that many affective words find their place on the circle, the axes of which are defined as 'pleasure-displeasure' and 'arousal-sleepiness', respectively.

Plutchik's scheme has been shown to be partially inadequate.[10] In particular, positive correlations were found between 'anger' and 'fear' and between 'expectancy' and 'surprise', respectively. The two different schemes were investigated further by means of 149 descriptions of consumption stories, written by students, in the areas of esthetics, athletics, entertainment, dining, hobbies, fashion, religion and security. Different samples of students then rated all of the stories either according to Plutchik's categories or Mehrabian and Russell's (MR) three-factor paradigm. Three-dimensional spaces were estimated both according to the MR scheme and Plutchik's scheme. The latter lacked a clear interpretation of the second and third axes, however. Furthermore, the MR space explained the Plutchik space better than vice versa. Finally, the MR dimensions were more successful in explaining ratings of a fresh set of consumption stories than Plutchik's dimensions. The results suggest that the MR scheme is more useful in describing consumption experiences than Plutchik's. This is also evident from its use in evaluating advertisements.[11]

Next, several theories of emotions will be considered. The integration of emotions in utility functions will be dealt with in Section 9.3. Sections 9.3 deals with emotions in consumer choice behavior.

Conclusion

Several classification schemes for emotions exist. The scheme by Mehrabian and Russell appears to describe emotions best, particularly in the area of consumption experiences. Although the universality of emotions may be questioned, for research purposes the consistency of evaluating emotions is satisfactory.

9.2. Theories of emotion

Emotions are mostly accompanied by changes in the *autonomic nervous system*, such as adrenalin secretion, palpitations, nervous perspiration, etcetera. Fourteen physiological indicators accompanying experimentally induced anger or fear were examined.[12] Half of these indicators changed in the same direction or to the same degree in both types of emotions; the other half changed in different directions or to different degrees. The latter changes could thus be used as indicators of anger or fear, respectively. Other emotions, too, can frequently be classified unequivocally on the basis of physiological changes.[13] A general increase in activity of the autonomic nervous system often indicates a state of arousal. *Arousal* can be described as a general state of the organism involving excitation or a feeling of being stimulated.[14]

The assumed relationship between physiological changes and emotions has led to a discussion regarding the causal direction of the relationship. According to William James and Carl Lange,[15] stimuli in the environment trigger physiological states in the body and the activation of motor nerves. Next, the body's reactions are interpreted as an emotion. The *James–Lange theory of emotion* assumes that when you perceive a loss of your fortune following a stock market crash, you cry and then interpret the crying as feeling sad.

The James–Lange theory assumes the interpretation of physiological states as emotions, thus neglecting the cognitive interpretation of stimuli in the environment. A *cognitive theory of emotion* assumes that a state of arousal is produced by stimuli in the environment. Next, the individual looks at the external world for an explanation of the arousal. Having interpreted the world, the individual state is labeled as an emotion. For example, if you feel bad after you have done something wrong, you may label the feeling guilt.

A crucial experiment regarding the cognitive theory of emotion has been conducted by Schachter and Singer.[16] They injected subjects with epinephrine, a drug producing high arousal. Next, the subjects observed someone (a confederate of the experimenter) who behaved either in a euphoric way (e.g. firing bits of paper into a wastebasket) or in an angry way (e.g. stamping out of the room). When questioned, subjects who had not been told about the type of injection rated themselves as happy or as angry, depending on the behavior observed. Subjects who had been told about the true effects of the injection attributed their emotional state to the drug. The experiment indicates that in the absence of information individuals interpret the environment in order to label their emotions. The idea that both arousal and cognition are necessary to produce emotion is analogous to that of a juke box;[17] both a turntable (arousal) and a record (cognition) are needed to play the tune (specific feeling).

An intriguing study further supported the cognitive theory of emotion.[18] An attractive woman approached men while they were crossing the Capilano River Bridge in British Columbia. Only those without a female companion were approached. The woman asked the men to make up a brief story for a project she was doing on creativity. The men were assumed to be in a state of increased arousal, since the Capilano River Bridge sways precariously more than 200 feet above rapids and rocks. The female interviewer made the same request of other men crossing a much safer, lower bridge. The men on the Capilano River Bridge told more sexually oriented stories and rated the female interviewer more attractive than men on the lower, less frightening bridge. As hypothesized, the arousal of the men on the high bridge has been interpreted as sexual attraction for the female interviewer. States of arousal induced by preceding activities may be (mis-)attributed to emotional states, e.g. the increased arousal during a football match producing anger among supporters of the losing team.[19] Attribution theory[20] may provide explanations for the type of interpretations made in different circumstances.

In unexplained states of arousal, individuals may label their emotions on the basis of their own interpretation of the environment. This may impede rational decision making. For instance, imagine the bidding process in an auction. As the bids increase, states of high arousal are likely to occur. This may be interpreted by the bidder as eagerness to possess the item, eventually leading to unreasonably high bids. The stock market, too, frequently induces high arousal in the participants while the interpretation of the environment demands skilful analysis.

Several relations between arousal and experience and expressions of emotions exist.[21] On the one hand, experience may be caused by (mis)attributions of arousal. On the other, expressions may be caused by arousal and can be assessed by physiological measures. In addition, consistency of expression and experience is assumed, e.g. that crying causes sad feelings. Their view implies that emotions can be explained both from the cognitive and from the James–Lange theory of emotion.

Stress

Repeated instances of high arousal may lead to *stress*, described as the wear
and tear in the body due to the demands placed on it. Three factors inducing
stress are distinguished:[22] overload, conflict and frustration.

Overload refers to demands on an individual's adaptability on too many
instances or for too long a period. Many jobs, for example, place high demands
on employees, thus inducing stress. Information overload[23] may lead to stress,
such as students may experience in preparing for their exams.

Several types of *conflict*, too, may induce stress.[24] In *approach/approach
conflicts*, a choice has to be made between positively valued stimuli, e.g.
between different houses for sale. This is the less severe type of conflict,
since the outcome of choice is reasonably positive.

In *avoidance/avoidance conflicts*, a choice has to be made between
unattractive alternatives, e.g. selling stocks at a loss or taking the risk of
a further stock decline. These choices tend to be delayed until the last possible moment.

In *approach/avoidance conflicts*, a single alternative has both positive
and negative aspects. Entrepreneurs frequently face risky investments, which
could turn into a profit or into a serious loss. In these circumstances, deliber-
ations take place until decision time, at which the negative aspects frequently
become dominant.[25]

In *double approach/avoidance conflicts*, the choice is between two alternatives, each with both positive and negative consequences. For instance, the
decision to take a secure but relatively low-paying job or a high-paying job
based on a time contract.

Frustration refers to a situation in which a person cannot reach a desired
goal. Many of these situations are likely in practice, e.g. being delayed for an
important appointment by traffic, not being promoted at work, failing an exam,
dissatisfaction with a product, etcetera. Some of these frustrations concern
major life events, such as divorce or death, others are an accumulation of
daily hassles. Table 9.1 provides a rating scale for the degree of readjustment
associated with a number of life events.

A fourth factor leading to stress is *insecurity* and *uncertainty*. It is believed
that anxiety (which is closely connected to stress, see below) develops in
infancy, due to deprivation, neglect and loss of affection, leading to a general
fear of insecurity with other people.[26] More specifically, jealousy, the fear
of loss of affection to a rival, can be a stressful emotion based on insecurity.
Uncertain situations are also able to produce stress,[27] e.g. the uncertainty of
being pregnant or the uncertainty of dying in case of a serious disease.

Stress may be a relatively enduring experience, depending on the frequency of stressful events and on the type of person facing life's demands. A

Figure 9.2. Antecedents of stress.

personality trait, associated with a constant, undifferentiated, vague sense of fear is *anxiety*.[28] This fear might be connected with a lack of self-confidence, problems with adaptation to the society, insecurity felt with other people and coping with the strains of life. The terms stress and anxiety have been used interchangeably in the psychological literature.[29]

In general, stress is caused by situations including too many collative elements, leading to arousal.[30] See Figure 9.2.

The reactions of people to environmental stimuli frequently differs in the type and the intensity of the emotions associated with them. The more or less consistent way of reacting emotionally is characterized as *temperament*.

Frequently, emotions continue during a limited period of time. A relatively enduring emotional state is called a *mood*. Mood typically is less enduring than temperament: someone with a cheerful temperament at times may be in a sad mood. Temperament and mood may influence emotional reactions to events. Minor setbacks may be considered as amusing challenges if the person is in a good mood but induce anger if the person is in a bad mood.

Conclusion

In many instances, a large number of emotions can be distinguished and classified as opposite poles, as positive or negative and as primary or mixed. The expression of emotion depends on its type and intensity. Both the James–Lange theory of emotions and the cognitive theory take body changes as the starting point in explaining emotions. The essential difference is that the James–Lange theory assumes that different body reactions correspond directly with different emotions, whereas the cognitive theory assumes that cognitive interpretation of stimuli is necessary to attribute the general arousal to a specific type of emotion.

Repeated occurrence of arousal induces stress. Several factors are stress-inducing: overload, several types of conflict, frustration, insecurity and uncertainty.

Table 9.1. Social readjustment rating scale.

Rank	Life event	Mean value
1	Death of spouse	100
2	Divorce	73
3	Marital separation	65
4	Jail term	63
5	Death of close family member	63
6	Personal injury or illness	53
7	Marriage	50
8	Fired at work	47
9	Marital reconciliation	45
10	Retirement	45
11	Change in health of family member	44
12	Pregnancy	40
13	Sex difficulties	39
14	Gain of new family member	39
15	Business readjustment	39
16	Change in financial state	38
17	Death of close friend	37
18	Change to different line of work	36
19	Change in number of arguments with spouse	35
20	Mortgage over $10.000	31
21	Foreclosure of mortgage or loan	30
22	Change in responsibilities at work	29
23	Son or daughter leaving home	29
24	Trouble with in-laws	29
25	Outstanding personal achievement	28
26	Spouse begins or stops work	26
27	Begin or end school	26
28	Change in living condition	25
29	Revision of personal habits	24
30	Trouble with boss	23
31	Change in work hours of conditions	20
32	Change in residence	20
33	Change in schools	20
34	Change in recreation	19
35	Change in church activities	19
36	Change in social activities	18
37	Mortgage or loan less than $10.000	17
38	Change in sleeping habits	16
39	Change in number of family get-togethers	15
40	Change in eating habits	15
41	Vacation	13
42	Christmas	12
43	Minor violations of the law	11

How many of these events have you experienced in the last year? Add the numbers associated with each event. The sum is an index of how much life change related to stress you have experienced in this one year period. In their original study, Holmes and Rahe (1967) found that a score in the 200s was linked with about a 50 percent chance of illness and a score of 300 or above was associated with about an 80 percent chance of illness.

From Holmes, T.H. and R.H. Rahe, The social readjustment scale, *Journal of Psychosomatic Research* 11, 203–218. ©1967 Pergamon Press, Inc.

9.3. Emotions and the utility function

Since emotions are either positively or negatively valued, these might be considered as direct experiences of utility or satisfaction (respectively disutility and dissatisfaction). According to the axiom of greed, positive emotions will be pursued and negative emotions tend to be avoided. Due to differences in temperament and mood, people may react emotionally different to the same stimuli. This implies that the utility function of these stimuli is heterogeneous. Moreover, due to temporally different states of mood, the utility function will be unstable.

These arguments favor the inclusion of emotional states or their antecedents in the utility function. As emotions are accompanied by arousal and when superabundant by stress, the amount of stress might be included in the utility function.

An example of including stress in the utility function can be related to the approach/approach type of conflict.[31] Assume that an individual has to decide between commuting to her place of work (being accustomed to this for years) or purchasing a house near her job. The commuting is associated with a utility, $U(c)$, with c a vector of arguments, including expenditure and time but excluding stress. Living in a house near the job is associated with a different utility, $U(c')$. In addition, however, the purchase of the house induces an amount of stress, s, reducing the utility $U(c')$. Accounting for stress in the utility function amounts to including s in U. Choice in this situation depends on maximization of a utility function $U(c, s)$, subject to the appropriate constraints of income and time.

Another example relates to stress induced by the uncertainty of a situation.[32] A state of mind in which one does not know what is going to happen may be sufficiently unpleasant for sacrifices to be made to reduce it.[33] People are willing to take 30-fold higher immediate risks in order to avoid lower risks with delayed consequences.[34] Stress has been introduced in a utility function regarding hazardous jobs.[35] In the model, stress is assumed to be positively related to the probability, p, of an accident on the job: $s = f(p)$. Eventually, two states may occur: the healthy state 1 and the injured state 2. The market wage, adjusted for the probability of an accident on the job, is denoted by $w(p)$. The optimization problem of the worker amounts to selection of an optimal value of p from the market wage schedule as follows:

$$\text{Max}(1 - p)U_1(s, x) + pU_2(s, x)$$

$$\text{s.t. } s = f(p), \quad x \leq A + w(p)$$

where U_i is utility in state i, x is consumption and A is initial endowment. By choosing the optimal p (implied by the selected employment) the worker also accepts the level of stress associated with this employment. The wage function is shown to depend positively on p and is higher if stress is included in the utility function. By health and safety programs at the plant, risk reduction could be accomplished, leading to greater satisfaction on the part of the workers.

Another worked example concerns a two-period utility model of life and death, depending on wealth and stress.[36] Assuming a probability of death in the second period, p, the utility of life in the first period is assumed to depend on a 'stress function' $f(z, p)$, with z being the difference between utilities of life and death in the second period. If the utility of life in the second period increases (e.g. due to greater wealth), stress in the first period is assumed to increase. Dividing utilities evenly over the two periods, an individual in the latter case tends to transfer wealth from the second period to the first, thus compensating for the stress experienced in the first period.

Arousal is not always detrimental to human beings. For instance, job applicants are frequently more successful if they are moderately interested in a job than when they are very interested in it. This phenomenon has been experimentally investigated by Yerkes and Dodson with mice, chicks, kittens and men.[37] Motivation or arousal level, was manipulated by providing electric shocks of different intensities. The subjects were given a visual (brightness) discrimination task, varying in three levels of complexity. It was found that the easiest tasks were performed best at high levels of arousal (high levels of shock) and the most difficult tasks at low levels of arousal (weak shocks). The *Yerkes–Dodson law* states that tasks of moderate complexity are performed best at medium level of arousal (see Figure 9.3). For easy tasks, e.g. control tasks in a factory, high levels of arousal should be maintained to avoid lethargy. On the contrary, complex tasks, such as designing a new car, are executed preferably at low arousal levels. This might explain to some extent why managers, daily facing difficult decisions, frequently engage in stress prevention programs.

The effect of the Yerkes–Dodson law in combination with the tendency to seek an optimal level of arousal[38] might influence an individual's pattern of activity. It might be assumed that, in a state of high arousal, people are likely to look for activities that are easy to perform (e.g. mowing the lawn). In low arousal states, more difficult activities are likely to be performed (e.g. filling in a tax form).

The level of arousal and task complexity may also be related to the processing of information in consumer choice. Obviously, task complexity is increased by information overload. The level of arousal might be related to the degree of product involvement. These topics will be treated in the next section.

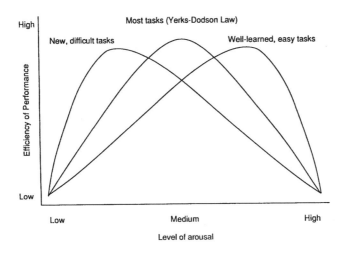

Figure 9.3. Visual presentation of the Yerkes–Dodson law. From John W. Santrock, Psychology: The science of mind and behavior, 3rd ed. Copyright ©1991 Wm. C. Brown Publishers, Dubuque, Iowa. All Rights Reserved. Reprinted by permission.

Conclusion

Economic behavior may be influenced by stress. This may be accounted for by including stress into the utility function. Since stress may be functionally related to particular circumstances and events, a stress function may be substituted for the stress factor in the utility function. According to the Yerkes–Dodson law the level of arousal appears to be related to the performance of several types of activity. Given the tendency to seek an optimum level of arousal, the Yerkes–Dodson law may explain the type of activity chosen.

9.4. Emotions and consumer choice

In Chapter 7, cognitive information processing has been dealt with in relation to consumer choice. This might be labeled the *information processing mode* (IPM) of choice. The consumer acquires information about brand attributes, forms evaluative criteria, judges the attributes in various brands and employs some judgment rule or heuristic to evaluate the brands in the choice set.

Affect for an object or brand can occur through other psychological processes, excluding cognitive algebra.[39] This is called the *affective choice mode* (ACM) and brand judgments resulting from this mode are called affective judgments.[40] Three characteristics of ACM will be considered next: holistic judgment, self-focus and the inexplicability of affective judgments.

Affective judgments are *holistic* and there exists a class of features ('preferanda') that form the affective reactions soon after perception has started.[41] For example, the style of a dress or a whiff of perfume might create an immediate holistic impression of a person, without one being aware of the attribute that caused it.

Affective judgments always relate to the *self* directly. The self is involved since the judgment is evaluative, rather than descriptive. "I like this car" is a direct personal judgment, whereas "This car has plenty of room" is a cognitive judgment. Frequently, in ACM, consumers judging a product project themselves as brand users, e.g. imagine the sight of the car in front of their own house.

Affective judgments are *difficult to verbalize or explicate*. Since the judgments are holistic, no reference is made to the characteristics that are responsible for them. Typically, if individuals are asked to explain their like or dislike of a product, they come up with statements such as "It seems that brand X suits me" or "Brand X does not appeal to me".

The concept of affective judgment has been challenged by cognitive theorists,[42] who state that objects are always perceived and that at least unconscious information processing precedes the affect. However, the *appraisal* (evaluation) of cognitive information has been added as a necessary and sufficient condition of emotion (affect).[43] Alternatively, cognition is allowed in the sense of sensation and object perception in ACM but excludes cognitive attention to individual features and their manipulation in cognitive algebra.[44]

A model has been developed, relating the choice modes (IPM and ACM, respectively) to the expressiveness of products and to the degree of involvement of consumers with the products.

The *expressiveness* of a product refers to its hedonic, symbolic or psycho-social consumption goals, rather than to its functional or utilitarian goals. For instance, the expressiveness of clothes serves psycho-social needs, whereas their protectiveness serves a functional goal. Expressiveness of products leads to imagery-construction, relating the product to one's private use of it. Notice that this process is non-verbal, related to one's self and holistic. The first hypothesis is that the more expressive the product, the more likely it is to be appraised via ACM.

The *involvement* with a product is known to mediate the cognitive effort made in information search and processing. A second hypothesis is that the higher the level of involvement, the greater the extent of information processing.

A third hypothesis deals with the exclusive use of a single choice mode. Since ACM is holistic and not explicated at the level of product attributes, it is hypothesized that the use of ACM will negatively influence IPM. These

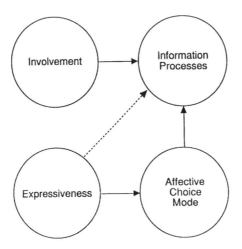

Figure 9.4. Relations between choice modes, involvement and expressiveness. From Mittal (1988).

three hypotheses are depicted in Figure 9.4.

The three hypotheses were tested in a study using 192 undergraduate and graduate students. Eleven products were selected, four of these being high involvement functional products (washing machine, alarm clock, shampoo, camera), four being high involvement expressive products (wristwatch, dress shirt, perfume, cologne) and three being low in involvement with no prior expectation on expressiveness (bulb, rubber band, pocket comb).

The students were asked to imagine that they had to live for one year in a city they did not know (London) and that they had to purchase one brand of a selected product while the brands were not familiar to them. Each student had to deal with one product, by answering a number of questions regarding its expressiveness, the degree of involvement and the choice mode used.

Questions regarding expressiveness referred to the desired level of prestige, expensiveness, fashion, sensual appeal, of the product, etcetera. The average scores regarding the expressive products mentioned above were all higher than for the other products in the study.

Questions regarding involvement referred to the importance of a right choice, concern about the outcome, care about the purchase, etcetera. The average scores regarding the high involvement products mentioned above were all higher than for the other products in the study.

Evidence for the use of the affective choice mode was gained from questions as to holistic or explicit descriptions of the product, weighting overall brand impressions or brand attributes and thinking about oneself as a user or about the product itself.

Use of the information processing mode has been detected by questions relating to the amount of information sought, the extensiveness of brand comparisons, the level of mental effort involved and the expected amount of time needed to make up one's mind.

Two dimensions of expressiveness have been found: one related to one's inner enjoyment and congruence of the product with one's self concept and one relating to one's public image in displaying the product. Both dimensions have been found to favor the use of the affective choice mode, as hypothesized. In addition, a small but negative coefficient has been estimated between the use of ACM and IPM, indicating the relative exclusiveness of the choice mode used. IPM is used extensively in the presence of high involvement. Although the measurement of the concepts of expressiveness and ACM might be improved, the results of the study are in agreement with the model presented in Figure 9.4.

The effect of involvement on information processing is consistent with the elaboration likelihood model.[45] The elaboration likelihood model (ELM) considers the factors that influence the likelihood of elaborated processing of information. The ELM states that in the absence of a motivation and the ability to process information, the attitude is likely to be based on peripheral cues, such as positive or negative affect, attractiveness or expertise of the information source, number of arguments, etcetera. Although ELM has emerged from the psychology of persuasion, expressiveness may be considered a peripheral cue in the development of an attitude toward a product.

The affective reaction to stimuli may not only be the result of judgment but may also guide the attention selection process in evaluating alternatives.[46] After perception of the object, a *primary affective reaction* determines whether *cognitive elaboration* of the object occurs. A positive primary reaction may cause selection of the alternative under low involvement or stimulate further cognitive processing under high involvement. A negative primary reaction is assumed to lead to rejection of the alternative. So affective reactions play a part in the early selection of possible choice alternatives.[47]

Another instance of emotions guiding decision making is in the estimation of probabilities and in risk taking. When either a happy or a depressed mood was experimentally induced, happy subjects tended to express higher probability estimates of positive future events (e.g. a vacation trip abroad) and lower estimates of negative future events (e.g. a nuclear power plant disaster) than the depressed subjects.[48] A similar result has been obtained by the finding that a depressed mood induces more worry about a number of possible causes of death and increased probability estimates that these causes would occur.[49]

Consumers and speculators in a good mood form more positive expectations about a product, a service or a stock.[50] Furthermore, they are willing to take more risk and thus tend to buy these particular goods more often than individuals in a bad mood. The index of consumer sentiment can be conceptualized as a measure of specific consequences of the consumers' mood at an aggregate level.[51] The result that positive (optimistic) expectations increase discretionary expenditure and decrease consumer saving[52] is consistent with this argument.

Recent economic experiences may affect consumer behavior.[53] The respondents in their survey were asked how positively or negatively the recent economic situation had affected them. Those who had negative experiences reported more comparison shopping, bargain hunting, energy consciousness and feelings of economic difficulty. This result could not be attributed to a lower income of these individuals, since the higher income group reported more negative effects of the recent economic situation than the lower income group.

Conclusion

The affective choice mode (ACM) can be distinguished from the information processing mode of choice (IPM). IPM appears to be facilitated by a high degree of involvement with the choice. ACM is facilitated by high expressiveness of the choice alternative. One theory precludes the simultaneous use of the two choice modes, whereas another theory assumes that IPM might be used if a choice alternative has been selected by ACM.

Summary

Several schemes for the classification of emotions have been described. The scheme by Russell and Mehrabian includes two dimensions: pleasure and arousal. The fuzzy boundaries between affect terms may be part of the lack of universality of emotions, among other things.

Two theories of emotions have been presented. The James–Lange theory of emotions considers physiological changes to be indicative of emotions. The cognitive theory of emotions is based on the interpretation of arousal by means of stimuli in the environment.

Stress is likely to occur after repeated states of high arousal caused by a number of events. Events can be associated with overload, conflict, frustration, insecurity and uncertainty, all of which are likely to produce increased arousal. This may eventually take the form of a personality trait, called anxiety. Mood is considered a relatively enduring emotional state and temperament is considered a relatively consistent way of emotional reaction to the environment.

A stress function refers to the functional relationship between increased levels of arousal and stressful events or situations. The stress function can be used as an argument in the utility function to obtain a better prediction of behavior.

The level of arousal is associated with the performance level of tasks with different degrees of difficulty. Medium levels of arousal are associated with optimal performance of most tasks, whereas high and low arousal is beneficial to easy and difficult tasks, respectively.

The information processing choice mode (IPM) in decision making appears to be applied in cases of high involvement with the choice alternative. The affective choice mode (ACM) appears to be used with high expressiveness of the choice alternative. Empirical research indicates that the use of one choice mode precludes the use of the other. Alternatively, the ACM may be used to select the alternatives in the choice set while the final choice is made using IPM.

BOX 9.1

EMOTIONS IN ADVERTISING

One of the most important elements of advertising is the emotional appeal of the ad. Product information provided in the ad will generate cognitive attitude formation but emotional appeal will trigger processes involved in the affective choice mode (cf. Section 9.3):

> "A benefit *claim*, whether stated verbally in an ad or implied visually, is a completely different stimulus from the benefit itself, objectively stated. A benefit lacks emotion; whereas a benefit claim *depends on* emotion."[54]

Numerous stimuli are available to support the benefit claims of products. In Table 9.2 a list of stimulus types is shown that can be used in ads presented either on radio or in print or via both media forms.

The creative part in advertising consists of selecting the appropriate stimuli to elicit those emotions which are favorably associated with a product. Depending on whether the goods are classified as informational or transformational[55] different emotions have to be elicited. Several informational and transformational motives associated with these types of goods are distinguished.[56] Typical emotional states that might be elicited in these cases are shown in Table 9.3.

Problem removal is generally portrayed by anger or annoyance with the problem, followed by relief offered by the brand (Example: detergents). *Prob-*

Table 9.2. Six types of emotional stimuli.

1.	Heard words and sound effects. Example: The convincing tone of Orson Welles' voice.
2.	Music. Example: The exciting music of the "Coke is *it*" theme.
3.	Seen words – which 'sound' in the mind but in *your* voice, not theirs. Examples: Filth, wonderful.
4.	Pictures. Example: The pitiful photographs of starving Third World children in UNESCO ads.
5.	Color. Example: The powerful and sophisticated black backgrounds used in Johnny Walker Black Label Scotch whiskey ads.
6.	Movement. Example: The excitement of a Mercedes-Benz tearing around a test track with consummate ease.

Taken from Rossiter and Percy (1987). *Advertising and Promotion Management.* Copyright 1987 by McGraw-Hill. Reproduced by permission of McGraw-Hill, Inc.

lem avoidance stimulates fear or an anticipated problem, followed by relaxation as you need not worry about the problem after using the brand (Example: deodorants).

Incomplete satisfaction generally begins with disappointment at what's available, followed by optimism as the new brand is suggested as being closer to the satisfaction ideal (Example: courier services). *Mixed approach-avoidance* often begins with guilt about indulging in a product with positive and negative features, followed by peace of mind when a brand is offered that promises to solve the conflict (Example: low calorie desserts). *Normal depletion* relies on the mild annoyance of running out of a product, followed by the convenience of easy replacement (Example: any regularly purchased product advertised by a local retailer).

The transformational motives *may* begin with the opposite of the positive end states shown in Table 9.3 or they may go straight to them. *Sensory gratification*, for instance, may focus solely on elation (Example: fizzy drinks) or on the dull-to-elation transition (Examples: spices and herbs). *Intellectual stimulation* plays on the excitement of something new and challenging (Example: personal computers). *Social approval* ends with brand usage that flatters the user (Example: fashion clothing, cars, vacation resorts).

The application of the cognitive theory of emotions to advertising is straightforward. Emotional stimuli produce states of arousal that are likely to be attributed according to the message in the ad. Obviously, the message is that positive emotional states are caused by the product involved.

Table 9.3. Typical emotions that might be used to portray each motivation.

Informational motives	Typical emotional state changes
Problem removal	Anger → relief
Problem avoidance	Fear → relaxation
Incomplete satisfaction	Disappointment → optimism
Mixed approach-avoidance	Guilt → peace of mind
Normal depletion	Mild annoyance → convenience
Transformational motives	
Sensory gratification	Dull → elated
Intellectual stimulation	Bored → excited
Social approval	Apprehensive → flattered

Taken from Rossiter and Percy (1987, p. 209). Advertising and Promotion Management. Copright 1987 by McGraw-Hill. Reproduced by permission of McGraw-Hill, Inc.

Notes

[1] Lazarus 1991.

[2] Ekman 1980.

[3] Russell 1994.

[4] Ekman 1994.

[5] Izard 1994.

[6] Schlosberg 1954, Plutchik 1980.

[7] Osgood et al. 1957.

[8] Mehrabian and Russell 1974 and Russell and Mehrabian 1977.

[9] Russell 1980.

[10] Havlena and Holbrook 1986.

[11] Batra and Ray 1986, Holbrook and O'Shaugnessy 1984, Holbrook and Batra 1987, Ray and Batra 1983.

[12] Ax 1953.

[13] Ekman et al. 1983.

[14] Saccuzo 1987.

[15] William James 1950 and Carl Lange 1922.

[16] Schachter and Singer 1962.

[17] Mandler 1962.

[18] Dutton and Aron 1974.

[19] Zillman 1978.

[20] See Chapter 11.

[21] Pieters and Van Raaij 1988.

[22] Santrock 1988.

[23] See Chapter 7.

[24] See Sacuzzo 1987.

[25] Miller 1959.

[26] Sullivan 1949.

[27] Shechter 1988.

[28] See Byrne 1966, for example.

[29] Spielberger 1976.

[30] See Section 3.4.

[31] See Section 9.2.

[32] Shechter 1988.

[33] Weinstein and Quinn 1983.

[34] Litai 1980.

[35] Viscusi 1979.

[36] Shechter 1988.

[37] Yerkes and Dodson, 1908.

[38] See Section 3.4.

[39] Zajonc 1980.

[40] Mittal 1988.

[41] Zajonc 1980.

[42] Lazarus 1984, Tsal 1985, Birnbaum 1981.

[43] Lazarus 1991.

[44] Mittal 1988.

[45] Petty and Cacioppo 1986.

[46] Van Raaij 1988.

[47] Contrary to Mittal 1988, Van Raaij 1984 does not assume a negative relationship between IPM and ACM but believes both choice modes support each other.

[48] Bower and Cohen 1982.

[49] Johnson and Tversky 1983.

[50] Pieters and Van Raaij 1988.

[51] Van Raaij 1989.

[52] See Chapter 8.

[53] Dholakia and Levy 1987.

[54] Rossiter and Percy 1987, p. 208.

[55] See Section 5.5.

[56] Rossiter and Percy 1987.

CHAPTER 10

WELL-BEING

10.1. Introduction

Well-being refers to a general sense of happiness or satisfaction with life. Well-being may exist on different levels of aggregation, i.e. on the individual level, the level of the family, the state or the entire country. Individual well-being might be considered as the outcome of an evaluation of experiences, activities, states and events in one's life and aggregate well- being might be considered as the average well-being of a group of individuals. Accordingly, well-being may be considered as an attitude toward one's life. Although well-being is associated with all possible conditions of life, its relation with the economy in particular has been of interest to economists and economic psychologists.

Since well-being covers such a large number of human conditions of life, several theories of well-being co-exist without an integrating framework. Several of these theories relate to preceding chapters and will be considered here. The theories are listed in Table 10.1.

Well-being might be related to the concepts considered in Chapter 9. Frequent experience of positive emotions and good moods make up a general positive evaluation of one's life, whereas unfavorable emotions and moods, stress and anxiety are assumed to affect individual well-being negatively. This constitutes the *bottom-up* theory of well-being. Emotions depend on personal reactions to life events and this will differ according to temperament, mood and personality. In the same vein, satisfaction with one's life as a whole may induce relatively positive evaluations in a specific life domain. This view is considered the *top-down* theory of well-being.[1]

Apart from individual differences in reactions, however, personal well-being might be described by the occurrence of events (e.g. finding a job according to one's expectations, death of the spouse, etcetera), the past and present state of affairs (e.g. socio-demographic states, financial situation, health status, etcetera) and the expected forecast for one's life (e.g. prospects of dying, future probabilities of obtaining a job). This view, for instance, has led economists to judge the welfare of an economy or an individual

Table 10.1. Theories on well-being.

Bottom-up	Well-being results from positive experiences.
Top-down	Well-being induces positive evaluations in specific life domains.
Objective	Well-being is judged from objective circumstances, e.g. income.
Teleological	Well-being depends on the attainment of terminal values.
Adaptation	Well-being depends on psychological adjustment to states of life.
Standards of judgment	Well-being depends on comparisons of life states with standards of reference, e.g. well-being of other people, own past well-being, aspiration level.
Endowment and contrast	Well-being depends both on the endowment and the contrast with previous experiences.

from measures of GNP or personal income respectively.[2] When subjective measures of well-being became available, however, it became clear that these only correlated to objective indicators of welfare to a small extent.

The determinants of well-being can be studied by Cantril's Self-Anchoring Striving Scale.[3] By this procedure, people are asked to state two anchoring points of their lives: their wishes and hopes – the realization of which constitutes their best possible lives – and their worries and fears – the realization of which constitutes the worst possible life they can imagine. Next, they indicate on a non-verbal ladder device (showing a scale from 1 to 10) where they stand on the ladder today, the top of the ladder representing the best life according to their own definition, the bottom representing their worst possible life. Besides a measurement of personal well-being, this procedure generates a number of hopes and fears on which the measure is based. Classification of reported hopes amounts to the general categories presented in Table 10.2. It appears that items in the category of economic hopes are mentioned most frequently, thus providing further support for the importance of economic items in everyday life[4] (this category consisting of items associated with 'a decent standard of living', 'housing', 'leisure time', 'an improved standard of living' and 'modern conveniences'). Other items have been mentioned frequently as well. This picture has consistently been found in a number of different countries.

The picture emerging from Table 10.2 appears to be more or less consistent with research into the explanation of well-being by objective indicators. This is illustrated by the belief that the happiest persons are those with the most advantages.[5] The happy person emerges as a young, healthy, well-educated, well-paid, religious, married person with high self-esteem, high job morale, modest aspirations, of either sex and of a wide range of intelligence.

A review of the literature ascertains that an overwhelming amount of

Table 10.2. Categories of personal hopes reported in the measurement of well-being.

Economic	65%
Health	48%
Family	47%
Personal values	20%
Keeping status quo	11%
Job or work situation	10%
International situation, world	10%
Social values	5%
Political	2%

From Easterlin (1974).

evidence exists for the positive relationship between subjective well-being within countries and income, satisfaction with income and the level of income relative to that of others.[6]

It appears from the literature that marriage and family satisfaction is the strongest predictor of subjective well-being in a number of studies. Furthermore, it has been found that previous divorce is not related to the happiness of persons who are remarried, thus ruling out the possibility of a selection factor of happier people getting or staying married. Self-esteem and internal locus of control[7] are found to be positively related to subjective well-being in a number of studies.[8] Health consistently appears to be positively related to subjective well-being in a number of studies. Employment positively relates to subjective well-being in several respects.[9]

Several studies show mixed results with respect to the relationship between well-being and social contacts, race, activities and extraversion. Age, gender, education and intelligence appear not to be consistently related to subjective well-being.[10]

Individual demographic variables together do not account for much more than 15% of the variance in subjective well-being.[11]

Cantril's measure of well-being[12] is based on two anchoring points, provided by the subject. In the absence of such a frame of reference, however, reports of well-being are likely to be influenced by accidental circumstances, affecting a person's emotional state or mood. It has been noticed that individuals construct their sense of well- being at the moment they are asked to report about it.[13] Thus, reports are likely to be unstable. For instance, greater happiness and satisfaction with their life as a whole has been reported by people who found a presumably lost dime on a copy machine than those who did not.

The above reported effect can be explained by the cognitive emotion theory.[14] People can be assumed to experience a general feeling, which may be good or bad at a particular moment. If asked to report on their well-being, a cognitive interpretation of the environment might induce positive or negative statements about life as a whole. This hypothesis is supported by observations regarding reported well-being on sunny and on rainy days.[15] Generally, more happiness with life as a whole has been reported on sunny than on rainy days. Directing the subject's attention to the weather before asking the well-being report, however, removed this effect. This result is the same as in the Schachter and Singer study with epinephrine.[16] By informing subjects about the effects of the drug, emotional differences due to the experimental conditions disappeared.

The instability of well-being reports is reflected in low test-retest correlation coefficients associated with the same type of questions asked at different moments in time. These coefficients typically are in the 0.30–0.50 range[17] and not exceeding 0.60 when the same question is asked twice during the same one-hour interview.[18] At the aggregate level, however, the instable effects of mood might disappear. Only very small changes were observed in the aggregate response to a happiness question asked in two surveys, taken within two weeks of each other.[19]

The cognitive interpretation process of emotions described above may be considered as a cognitive attribution.[20] Other cognitive interpretations might result from associating experiences with past events, stored in human memory. Present experiences may trigger memories that are congruent with one's emotional state. Given a memory network consisting of many positive experiences, the probability of associating events with positive memories is relatively high. This might increase the probability of positive reactions to life events. Affective conditioning[21] resists extinction, implying a good memory for these affects.[22] This process is consistent with the contention of rapid affective evaluation of stimuli (events).[23]

A memory network of positive experiences might be created by consciously reducing negative thoughts, increasing happiness[24] or by reciting positive statements in the morning, leading to a happier day.[25]

Along a different line of research, it might be assumed that satisfaction with life depends on the attainment of values.[26] Psychological end-states of life or *terminal values*,[27] include happiness, love, security, freedom, inner harmony, accomplishment and togetherness, among others.[28] Well-being might be associated with the extent to which an individual has attained these terminal values. Activities are to a certain extent *instrumental* in attaining the life values and well-being. A number of activities have been rated with respect to their importance for attaining life values.[29] This type of theory of well-being is considered as telic (or teleological), in that activities are specially planned to fulfil a purpose.[30]

In philosophy and theology, questions have been asked regarding telic theories of well-being. Should happiness be attained by satisfying one's desires or by suppressing them? Hedonists are inclined to believe in satisfaction of needs, although even then there might be more and less important desires as well as conflicting ones. Moreover, after the satisfaction of needs, it might be impossible to achieve great happiness. Ascetics favor the distraction from desires as leading to ultimate happiness.

An alternative view holds that happiness is derived from activities aimed at reaching a goal, rather than achievement of the goal itself.[31] For instance, the activity of climbing a mountain might cause greater happiness than reaching the summit.

An alternative theoretical view on well-being is related to the *standard of judgment*. Rather than stating well-being in absolute terms, people might judge their well-being relative to the well-being of other people or to their own past well-being. The aspiration level too[32] may function as a standard of well-being comparisons.

It has been found that downward comparisons with less fortunate persons and beliefs that others live in poor circumstances, can increase one's life satisfaction.[33] People's satisfaction with income depends on the income of others in their society.[34]

The *adaptation* theory of well-being predicts that positive (negative) events produce happiness (unhappiness) the more recently they have occurred.[35] Over time, the effect of the event on well-being is dampened by adaptation to the situation. After a while lottery winners are not happier and quadriplegics not less happy than normal controls. Cord-injury victims were extremely unhappy after their accidents but observed quick adjustments to this situation evident from increasing happiness as time went by.[36] Examining other handicapped groups, evidence was found indicating no less happiness as controls.[37] Using longitudinal data adaptation to new social roles was found after instances of unemployment.[38] However, well-being declined sharply during the first few weeks of unemployment and remained at a lower level after half a year. According to the adaptation theory of well-being, the events listed in the Social Readjustment Scale (Table 9.1) would only temporary affect well-being. Hence, stress would gradually disappear.

The theory on aspiration levels implies that well-being is a negative function of the difference between desires and the actual state of affairs. Cultures with high aspirations are relatively unhappy.[39] Cultures ignorant of modern consumption possibilities are relatively happy. Likewise, it had been expected that the Russian perestrojka and other rapidly changing political attitudes in

Table 10.3. Endowment effects and contrast effects in judgments of a current neutral situation. (The first figures relate to the stories, the figures in parentheses relate to the games.)

Previous event	Current neutral situation		
	Related	Unrelated	
Positive	6.8 (7.5)	7.1 (8.7)	Endowment effect
Negative	5.5 (7.3)	4.9 (6.4)	Endowment effect
	Contrast effect	Contrast effect	

Compiled from Tversky and Griffin (1991), in R.J. Zeckhauser (ed.), *Strategy and Choice*, Cambridge, MA: MIT Press.

Eastern Europe was breeding aspirations that could not (then) be met, leading to less well-being in these countries shortly after these changes.

Both the adaptation theory of well-being and the standards of judgment theory stress the differences between the present state and an adaptation level, formed by previous experiences and reference standards, respectively.[40] The adaptation level may be considered as an endowment, acquired by experience, social influences or aspirations. In addition to endowment effects, *contrast effects* have been considered in the judgment of well-being.[41] Students reading a negative story about a quiz in French before a neutral story, gave higher satisfaction judgments concerning the actor in the second story if the second story was related to the first (classes in Civics, Geometry and French) than if the second story was unrelated (a lunch with Susan). Conversely, a neutral story, preceded by a positive story yielded less satisfaction if the first story was related than if the first story was unrelated. Although in general positive first stories induced greater satisfaction with the second story than negative first stories (endowment effect), there was an additional effect working in the opposite direction (contrast effect). Similar effects were found for stories about planning a party and an Australian movie. The average judgments concerning the stories on a 10-point 'very happy – very unhappy' scale are shown in Table 10.3.

Similar results were found for judgments of a stock-market game earning $4, either preceded by the same game earning $2 in one condition (negative event) and $6 in another condition (positive event) or by a commodity-market game played under the same two conditions. Evaluations of earnings in this game are given in parentheses in Table 10.3. Unrelated events only produce the endowment effects; related events produce both the endowment and the contrast effects.

In a study regarding general and specific well-being, subjects spent an hour either in an extremely pleasant room or in an extremely unpleasant room.[42]

After the session, they rated both their general satisfaction and satisfaction regarding their current housing situation. For the general satisfaction, the endowment effect was found (higher satisfaction for those who were in the pleasant room than for the others). For the satisfaction with housing, the related event of staying in the room produced strong contrast effects (higher satisfaction for those who were in the unpleasant room than for the others).

Endowment and contrast effects are attributed to standards of judgments.[43] A different view on the evaluation of events includes the psychological effects occurring after withdrawal of a positive or negative stimulus. In the psychology of visual perception, it has been noticed that after being exposed to a bright red light for 30 seconds, subjects experience a green after-image.[44] The latter experience is just the opposite of that during stimulation. Solomon uses this example as an analogy for his *opponent-process theory* of acquired motivation.[45]

One of the characteristics of opponent-process theory of interest here, is that after affect-provoking stimulation a contrasting affect will take place. Examples of positive after-effects are parachutists experiencing exhilaration after the thrill (or terror) of jumping and sauna bathers experiencing exhilaration after the hot, exciting (or painful) sauna. Examples of negative after-effects are a junk's agony (or craving) after the contentment (or euphoria) during taking opiate and the loneliness or grief after losing a beloved one. Hence, Solomon speaks of the costs of pleasure and the benefits of pain. The relation with the above-mentioned endowment and contrast effects[46] is that positive (negative) after-effects may induce relatively positive (negative) judgments of consequent related neutral events. Solomon's theory in our view provides an alternative explanation of these effects.

Section 10.2 will describe research on well-being, using self-report measures. Section 10.3 will describe well-being in a specific life area (income). Poverty will be dealt with in Section 10.4. Further research on well-being applies to unemployment (Section 10.5) and consumer satisfaction (Section 10.6).

Conclusion

Several theories on well-being exist alongside one another. It appears that socio-demographic determinants of well-being provide only a modest explanation of the concept. Economic issues are prominent in the completion of subjective well-being reports. Top-down, bottom-up, objective and adaptation theories of well-being may be considered endowment theories. Teleological and standards of judgment theories of well-being may be considered contrast theories, in addition to the contrast effects of previous experiences on well-being.

10.2. Subjective well-being

Research on subjective well-being has generated a number of measuring instruments that can be considered indicators of well-being.[47] In this section, several scales and their properties will be described and the structure of well-being will be considered.

An important distinction regarding measures of well-being is whether the scale consists of only one item or multiple items. The Cantril-measure, considered in Section 10.1, is an example of a *one-item scale*.

Another frequently used one-item scale is the Delighted-Terrible scale.[48] The question asks: "How do you feel about your life as a whole?" Response categories are: "Delighted", "Pleased", "Mostly satisfied", "Mixed (about equally satisfied and dissatisfied)", "Mostly dissatisfied", "Unhappy", "Terrible".[49]

Others simply ask: "Taking all things together, how would you say things are these days?" There are three response choices: "Very happy", "Pretty happy" and "Not too happy".[50]

Fordyce's question is: "In general, how happy or unhappy do you usually feel?" Response choices are on an 11-point scale consisting of a series of mood adjectives, the top one being "Feeling extremely happy, ecstatic, joyous and fantastic".[51]

Fordyce also asks: "What percent of the time do you feel happy, what percent of the time do you feel unhappy and what percent of the time do you feel neutral?"[52] The subject is required to estimate these percentages such that they add up to 100%. The 'percent happy' is the well-being indicator.

The one-item scales, described above, generally show low (0.30–0.50) test-retest reliabilities, with the exception of the Fordyce scales.[53] This might indicate that these scales are affected by measurement error on the one hand and by different states of mood on the other hand. The popularity of these scales is probably due to their low costs as items in a survey.

Multiple-item scales consist of a number of questions tapping well-being by evaluating different domains of life, by using a number of different adjectives to evaluate life as a whole or by questioning the occurrence of different positive or negative events. For example, the Bradburn scale of positive affect relates to the number of five positive events experienced:[54]

"During the past few weeks did you ever feel:
– particularly excited or interested in something?
– proud because someone complimented you on something you had done?

- pleased about having accomplished something?
- on top of the world?
- that things were going your way?"

The positive affect score is the sum of positive answers to these five questions. The negative affect score is related to five negative events experienced:

"During the past few weeks did you ever feel:
- so restless that you couldn't sit long an a chair?
- very lonely or remote from other people?
- bored?
- depressed or very unhappy?
- upset because someone criticized you?"

Bradburn found that the positive and negative affect scales are independent from each other (although each of the scales was significantly correlated with a global measure of well-being) and that people compare these two affects in judging their well-being. The comparison is implied by the Affect Balance Scale, derived by subtracting the positive and negative affect scores of an individual.

The lack of correlation between positive and negative affect has been questioned.[55] For, intuitively, the more one experiences positive affect, the less negative affect will be expected, since both affects cannot exist simultaneously.[56] A solution is that the reported affect is a mean value, combining frequency and intensity of experiences. The frequency of positive and negative affect might be negatively related, whereas their respective intensities might be positively related. (In fact, a positive correlation of 0.70 has been found.) Since frequency and intensity of experiences are assumed to be independent, lack of correlation between positive and negative affect, measured on scales that combine frequency and intensity, is to be expected.

If frequency and intensity measures are available separately, a differentiated view of affective well-being emerges.[57] For example, someone who is:

- high in duration of positive affect and high in intensity will experience subjective well-being as an exuberant, enthusiastic and actively cheerful sort of happiness;
- high in duration of positive affect and low in intensity will experience subjective well-being as calm, untroubled and dispassionate contentment;
- low in duration of positive affect and low in intensity will experience a lack of subjective well-being as a chronic low level of unhappiness, a mild but persistent melancholy;
- low in duration of positive affect but high in intensity will experience a lack of subjective well-being as a more acute sort of depression accompanied

by a variety of strongly felt negative emotions such as embarrassment, guilt, grief and shame.

Generally, the multiple item scales of well-being are quite reliable, according to their estimated test-retest coefficients and internal consistency scores.

The scales described above are related to satisfaction with life as a whole. A number of evaluations of specific life concerns, such as housing, job, relations with other people, health and finances have been studied.[58] Survey questions typically are of the following type: "Now I would like you to indicate on this scale to what extent you are satisfied with your present situation in the following respects ......": "The house, flat or apartment where you live", "The income of you and your family", "Your present work – in your job or as a housewife", among other things.

Evaluations of different life domains were clustered on three dimensions.[59] The first dimension can be interpreted as how immediate or remote the life concerns are, psychologically. It appeared that evaluations concerning people's job, neighborhood, relations with other people, etcetera, clustered on the one end of this dimension, whereas evaluations regarding the larger society, national government, mass media, etcetera, clustered on the other end. The second dimension might be interpreted as a 'material-immaterial' dimension, in that evaluations of economic and physical concerns, housing, neighborhood, income, standard of living and transportation clustered at the 'material' end of this dimension and evaluations regarding health, relations with other people, leisure and the amount of time available clustered at the 'immaterial' end. The third dimension is more difficult to interpret. The structure found can be considered a 'cognitive map'[60] regarding well-being in different domains of life. It appears that roughly the same structure applies to nine Western societies (U.S. and eight West-European countries).

Multiple evaluations of four specific life domains were related to several evaluations of life as a whole.[61] Accounting for errors in the measurements, somewhat different correlations were found between evaluations of life domains and of life as a whole in both English-speaking and French-speaking samples of Canadians. (See Table 10.4.)

From this research, it appears that by using multiple measures of well-being and multiple evaluations of specific life domains measurement errors can be accounted for to a large extent and that well-being can be explained successfully by evaluations of one or two life domains. The life domains evaluated in the survey are among the most important items in the completion of subjective well-being reports (cf. Table 10.2). Although more research is needed, with more life domains and in different populations, the model estimated supports the bottom-up theory of well-being. The reverse causal relation, i.e. satisfaction with life as a whole explaining specific evaluations,

Table 10.4. Specific evaluations explaining well-being (Beta-coefficients).

Evaluations	Well-being English	Well-being French
Leisure	0.41	0.22
Health	0.31	0.30
House	0.16	0.12
Finance	0.20	0.37
Explained variance	67%	63%

From McKennell et al. (1978).

has not been tested, however.

Conclusion

Measures of subjective well-being can be classified according to the type of scale – one item or multiple items – and to the domain of evaluations – life as a whole or specific domains. Some empirical support for the bottom-up theory of well-being is obtained from research on the structure of well- being.

10.3. Well-being and income

In economics, utility is associated with the level of consumption of goods and services. The more goods and services can be purchased, the higher the level of utility is assumed to be. Since a higher income enables higher spending, the utility function of income is assumed to be increasing continuously. However, this view has been challenged by research relating aggregate measures of well-being to the level of GNP and to socio-economic status.[62]

Evidence has been shown for a positive relationship between income level and well-being within a country. At higher levels of income, the percentage of people in the U.S. claiming to be very happy[63] is consistently higher. In the period 1946–1970, the percentage of people reported as being not very happy is consistently higher for the poor and the lower income groups as compared with the wealthy and the higher income groups, respectively, in ten large scale surveys in the U.S. during this period. The same results have been found in seven surveys conducted in 1965 in Great Britain, West Germany, Thailand, Philippines, Malaysia, France and Italy. The Cantril measures of well-being were found to be consistently higher in upper than in lower socio-economic classes in 13 countries around 1960. Although the possibility that happy people are able to gain higher incomes has been mentioned, the data were

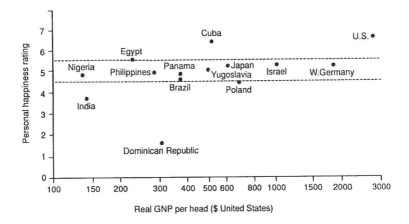

Figure 10.1. Cantril measures of happiness and GNP. From Easterlin (1974).

interpreted as primarily showing a causal connection running from income to happiness.[64]

In addition to comparing different income groups within a country, the aggregate differences in well-being between rich and poor countries have been studied. The results regarding the association between Cantril measures and GNP's per head of 14 countries around 1960 are presented in Figure 10.1. The data regarding Cuba and the Dominican Republic are considered somewhat suspect because of recent revolution and political turmoil in those countries.

It has been observed that India and the U.S. provide for a small positive correlation between GNP and happiness. However, the ratings for 10 of the 14 countries lie within a range of 1.1 points on the Cantril scale of well-being. The happiness scores of nine countries do not correlate substantially with their GNP's either. A strong association between GNP and aggregate well-being is lacking.

Another type of evidence regarding the association between income and well-being consists of national time series of happiness scores. Happiness did not increase consistently from 1946 to 1970 in the U.S., although the standard of living certainly increased dramatically in this period.

Summarizing the results, it appears that comparisons of well-being are much higher nationally than internationally and over time. The theory of *social comparison*[65] has been used to explain these results.[66] Within a country, people compare their situation with others. If many others are rich, you are unhappy. If you are more wealthy than most other people, you are very happy. Other people in a country serve as a reference standard of judgment in the evaluation of well-being.[67] Between countries, however, the reference

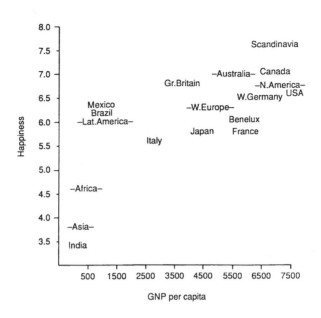

Figure 10.2. Happiness in several parts of the world by GNP per head in 1975. From Veenhoven (1984a).

standard is lacking, producing less striking differences in well-being.

The constancy of happiness over time might also be explained by a missing reference standard. Most people remember their former living standard, although the memory might fade over time. However, memories in a society gradually disappear because old people die and young people are born. Thus, in the aggregate, the reference standard of the past shifts over time. The constancy of happiness has been explained as the constant adaptation of aspiration levels.[68] Each fulfilment of a desire creates a new desire, thereby preventing an increase of happiness.

The results presented above have been criticized.[69] Figure 10.1 is considered selective because very poor countries are excluded. A new picture of happiness in seven parts of the world has been created, including the poorest parts. (See Figure 10.2.) From this picture, a clearly positive (marginally decreasing) relationship between happiness and GNP per head emerges.

Furthermore, economic changes in GNP tend to precede changes in happiness one year later.[70] It appears that the *satisfaction of needs*, rather than social comparison, explains happiness. In addition, changes in the economic tide rather than the level of affluence produce changes in happiness. We shall not elaborate on this debate here, since in Chapter 11 it will be argued that need satisfaction and social comparison are complementary rather than con-

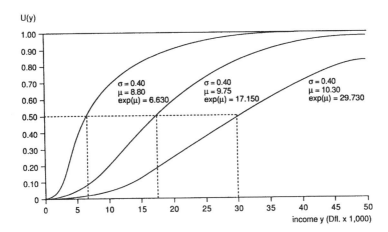

Figure 10.3. Lognormal utility functions of income with σ constant. From Kapteyn and Wansbeek (1985).

tradictory in evaluations of income. Next, a theory of income evaluation will be considered which deals directly with the utility of income.

Income can be considered the most general source of utility, at least in Western societies, since goods and services can be purchased with it (here disregarding financial assets). Utility from different goods and services can be aggregated to a utility function of the combined expenditure, such that these add to the total income. On the basis of theoretical considerations, not considered here, a lognormal *utility function of income* has been assumed.[71] Sketches of this utility function are presented in Figures 10.3 and 10.4.

The function is scaled on the $(0, 1)$ interval (the 0 and 1 bounds are chosen arbitrarily, since utility is determined up to a linear transformation) and shows the well-known S-shape of a cumulative distribution function. The lognormal distribution function is denoted by $\lambda(y; \mu, \sigma)$ and equals the cumulative normal distribution function of $\ln Y$, represented by $N(\ln Y; \mu, \sigma)$, with Y being income, μ and σ being location parameters of the distribution. It appears that the function is convex from below at small incomes and concave at higher incomes. So, at higher incomes, utility is marginally decreasing with income.

The parameters, μ and σ, of the distribution function are associated with the mean and variance of $\ln Y$ but can be given a psychological interpretation. In Figure 10.3, a few lognormal distribution functions have been drawn for different values of μ, holding σ constant. It appears that, with increasing μ, the utility function of income shifts to the right. Since 0.5 on the utility scale is associated with $\exp(\mu)$, the higher the value of μ is the greater the amount of income needed to evaluate it by 0.5; hence, μ can be seen as a *want* parameter.

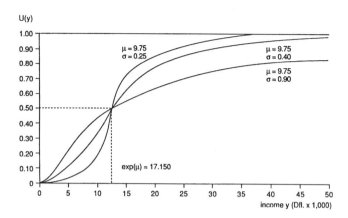

Figure 10.4. Lognormal utility functions of income with μ constant. From Kapteyn and Wansbeek (1985).

A hypothesis regarding μ has been that, at higher levels of income, μ would be higher since rich people are not as easily satisfied as poor people.

In Figure 10.4, a few lognormal distribution functions have been drawn with different values of σ, holding μ constant. It appears that a higher value of σ flattens the curve, indicating relatively small differences in utility with different incomes. At small values of σ, the function is steep, indicating greater *sensitivity* to income differences. The individual welfare function of income might be considered as the income distribution in a society, as perceived by the individual. If only a small part of the income distribution is perceived, e.g. incomes close to one's own income, the sensitivity to income differences will be large.

The lognormal welfare function of income (WFI) has frequently been measured in a number of surveys by means of the *Income Evaluation Question* (IEQ) presented in Table 10.5.[72] The typical pattern of income amounts, obtained in surveys, has been inserted in this table. The evaluative qualifications in the IEQ are associated with points on the (0,1) utility interval, such that the distance between each adjacent pair is equal. The parameters of the WFI are then estimated by ordinary least squares for each individual in the survey.

From the estimated WFI, one can derive a point estimate of well-being associated with a particular life domain (finances). In addition, the want parameter μ can be explained by several variables.

It has been found that one's own family income correlates positively with μ. Thus, the higher one's income, the less satisfaction is obtained from a particular income.[73] As a hypothesis, the effect of economic expectations

Table 10.5. The Income Evaluation Question.

Taking into account your own situation with respect to family and job you would call
your net-income (including fringe benefits and after subtraction of social security
premiums)*:

	week A	
per	month B	
	year C	

excellent	if it were above	Dfl. 45,000
good	if it were between	Dfl. 35,000 and Dfl.45,000
amply sufficient	if it were between	Dfl. 30,000 and Dfl.35,000
sufficient	if it were between	Dfl. 25,000 and Dfl.30,000
barely sufficient	if it were between	Dfl. 22,000 and Dfl.25,000
insufficient	if it were between	Dfl. 20,000 and Dfl.22,000
very insufficient	if it were between	Dfl. 17,000 and Dfl.20,000
bad	if it were between	Dfl. 12,000 and Dfl.17,000
very bad	if it were below	Dfl. 12,000

*Encircle your reference period.

From Kapteyn and Wansbeek (1985).

might be that optimistic expectations tend to decrease μ, leading to more
income satisfaction, whereas pessimistic expectations might increase μ. This
hypothesis remains to be tested, however.

A second result is that a larger family size, given the income, is related
to a higher level of wants. Thus, a larger family needs a greater amount of
income to be as satisfied as a smaller family.

Besides the family's own income, it appears that the relative position of the
income in one's *reference group* is associated with the want parameter, μ. The
reference group is assumed to consist of people in the same age, education,
work, and geographic categories. In fact, an income higher than the average
income in the reference group has a positive effect on μ, thus reducing the
utility of a particular income.[74] The income in the reference groups can also
be considered a perceptual standard[75] in the judgment of one's own income.

The depence of μ on income, family size and the reference group implies
that a change in these variables will induce a change in the welfare function of
income. This change can be considered an adaptation of economic well-being
to modified circumstances.

Conclusion

Two competing hypotheses on the determinants of well-being have been
investigated. Satisfaction of needs, a variant of the teleological theory on

well-being, assumes a positive relation between happiness and income. The theory of social comparison, based on the standards of judgment theory on well-being, assumes a positive relation between happiness and one's rank in the income distribution of society.

The theory of income evaluation includes both the satisfaction of needs and social comparisons in the economic well-being of an individual.

10.4. Poverty

Poverty can be considered the counterpart of well-being. So people reporting low levels of well-being would be considered poor. This raises the question of how poor is poor? The assessment of an exact subsistence level should answer this question. A social assistance policy applicable in many countries is based on financial support for people falling short of the subsistence level. This has resulted in several definitions of the poverty line, the level of income below which one is judged as poor.

A number of poverty line definitions are considered here.[76] The first poverty lines were based on the estimation of the cost of basic needs, such as food, housing and clothing. Methodological difficulties regarding this approach included distinguishing basic needs from other needs, defining the needs (e.g. which items should be included in the food category?) and establishing procedures for estimating the costs and the income associated with the poverty line.

Three other poverty line definitions are based on critical ratios of food and income (1), ratios of income and mean or median income in society (2) and on a percentage of the income distribution below which one is considered poor. The first definition assumes that the welfare of two households that spend the same proportion of their income on food is equal. The second and third definitions are based on the idea that poverty is a state of relative rather than absolute deprivation. The critical ratios and percentages in these definitions are frequently fixed by the administration or poverty researcher.

An official definition of the poverty line is based on political judgment regarding the income of the poor. In so far as official poverty lines reflect democratic decision making and are revised quickly in line with changing price levels and standards of living, their use may be defended.

Alternatively, the poverty line may be defined subjectively, i.e. an income level below which an individual does not believe that she can – in her circumstances – make ends meet. Since this poverty line is subjective, a direct measurement procedure has been developed for investigation. This amounts to the following survey question:[77]

"We would like you to tell us the absolute *minimum* income of money

Table 10.6. The average welfare level associated with the minimum income of one, two and four-person households in EC countries.

	Family size			Number of
	1	2	4	respondents
N. Ireland	0.56	0.56	0.56	48
Italy	0.53	0.59	0.64	115
Luxembourg	0.53	0.52	0.51	15
Ireland	0.49	0.49	0.54	120
United Kingdom	0.47	0.49	0.50	230
Belgium	0.41	0.45	0.48	157
France	0.40	0.44	0.48	264
Germany	0.38	0.40	0.42	410
Denmark	0.37	0.41	0.46	323
Netherlands	0.36	0.39	0.41	207

Adapted from Van Praag et al. (1980).

for a household such as yours – in other words, a sum below which you couldn't make ends meet.

For my household I would say that the absolute minimum money income necessary after tax would be:"

£ _____   per week   1
             per month 2   (ring appropriate number)
             per year   3

This survey question was posed in a survey of the European Community in 1976 which by then consisted of 10 countries.[78] The welfare question of income was also included in this survey.[79] The answers to the above question were related to the Welfare Function of Income to compute the level of welfare associated with the reported minimum income level. (See Table 10.6.)

Typically, the welfare associated with the minimum income of four-person households, on the $(0, 1)$ utility scale, ranged from 0.41 in the Netherlands to 0.64 in Italy. Adopting the assumption that the average welfare function of income is similar to the income distribution in a country, these figures suggest that a four-person family in the Netherlands is judged as poor if its income is below the 41% level of the income distribution, whereas in Italy this is below the 64% level of the income distribution. Generally, more persons in a family tend to increase the percentage below which a household is considered as poor. This is consistent with the idea that supporting a family is associated with less economic welfare than living on one's own or with a partner.

Conclusion

Poverty has been defined in several objective and subjective ways. Direct measurement of the poverty line is accomplished by the minimum income question. The welfare level associated with the minimum income can be found by using the individual welfare function.

10.5. Unemployment

Besides the decline in well-being after the loss of a job, already considered in Section 10.1, a number of psychological and economic factors are associated with paid work and unemployment. To the extent that these factors differ between employees and the unemployed, well-being might be affected.

In general, unemployment leads to a decrease in family income. According to the theory of income evaluation[80] an income decrease is associated with a lower utility level. The size of the decrease depends on the remaining family income, the possibilities of earning extra income and the social security benefits. Yet, there appear to be positive aspects in being unemployed. Using a sample of households with only one breadwinner, it was estimated that an unemployed individual with (on average) 9% less income is about equally satisfied with the income as an individual with a paid job. Several immaterial factors may account for this effect.[81]

A distinction has been made regarding the manifest and the latent consequences of work, the former being intended, the latter occurring as an unintended by-product of employment.[82] The latent consequences include a time structure on the available time, social contacts outside the family, goals and purposes transcending individual goals, status and identity and a certain level of activity. A number of manifest and latent consequences of work have been investigated in a sample of 500 households, one half consisting of employees and the other half consisting of unemployed individuals who are the only breadwinners in the households.[83]

It appears that the average perception of work characteristics (whether the work is dangerous, dirty, noisy, physically or mentally tiring, and close supervision on the job) does not differ between the two groups. (The average score was on the positive side of an 11-point scale, indicating that work was not very tiring.) A factor analysis of the perceived characteristics reveals that a physical and a mental fatigue factor can be distinguished, close supervision on the job forming a unique factor. These factors might indicate a particular aspect of well-being associated with the job.

Another aspect of well-being associated with a job is job morality, consisting of two components: job satisfaction (whether work is perceived as satisfying, boring and frustrating and whether one is personally involved and goes to work with pleasure) and work ethos (whether work should come first, is a duty to society and has to be done before enjoying life). (The average scores for job satisfaction and work ethos were on the positive side of an 11-point scale, indicating high job satisfaction and a firm work ethos.) It appears that job morality does not differ between the two groups.

The personal identity derived from the position in society differs significantly between employed and unemployed individuals. Unemployed individuals are less satisfied with their contribution to society, their contribution to other people, their personal development and their usage of capabilities. Finally, the frequency and satisfaction with social contacts with respect to their (former) colleagues is less for the unemployed than for the employed individuals.

All of the latent consequences considered above indicate that the unemployed should be less happy with their position than the employed individuals. The positive aspects of unemployment should therefore be sought in the availability of more leisure time (with which the unemployed actually are more satisfied than the employees) and the lack of need to work (although the unemployed do not consider work particularly inconvenient).

The manifest and latent consequences of work as operationalized above have been related to several variables associated with behavior on the job market. Both groups were asked to state the minimum income for which they would be willing to accept a job (the reservation income). The unemployed were asked to state the equitable income for an employee, otherwise in the same circumstances as themselves. The employees were asked to state the equitable income for an unemployed individual. Finally, the unemployed were asked to report job search behavior in the two weeks prior to the survey. Contrary to the expectations aroused by the suggested importance of the latent consequences of work, the explanation for some of the variance in the variables associated with job market behavior was found to lie mainly in financial and demographic variables. Regarding the latent consequences, it was found that personal identity has an expected positive effect on the reservation income, thus decreasing the probability of accepting a job at a certain income. Physical inconveniences of the former job negatively affect the intensity of job search behavior.

Conclusion

Unemployment appears to be associated with a number of unpleasant latent consequences. However, the utility of leisure and the lack of need to work induce a relatively positive net evaluation of unemployment, given the income and the circumstances of the household. Financial and demographic factors rather than latent consequences of unemployment appear to affect income judgments.

10.6. Consumer satisfaction

According to the bottom-up theory of well-being, pleasant experiences add to the global sense of well-being. Instead of dealing with global well-being, it might be relevant to focus directly on isolated economic experiences. Many of such experiences result from consumption of goods and services and have been studied by consumer researchers. Positive experiences are usually referred to as satisfaction with consumption and negative experiences as dissatisfaction.

In general, consumer researchers have adopted the idea that satisfaction and dissatisfaction are outcomes of a process including expectations prior to consumption and confirmation or disconfirmation of these expectations.[84] Expectations constitute a frame of reference about which one makes comparative judgments.[85] This is consistent with adaptation level theory[86] in which the standard of comparison is adapted according to perception of the stimulus itself, the context and psychological and physiological characteristics of the organism.[87] This implies that consumer expectations are influenced by:

— prior consumer experience with commodities and awareness of brand connotations;
— the context of communications, e.g. from ads, sales people or social referents;
— the personal way of perception and susceptibility to changes in one's opinions.

Two other theories based on comparison judgments should be mentioned.[88] In the comparison level theory, consumer judgment is based on comparisons of product performance and prior expectations on the attribute level. This may result in specific dissatisfaction with a product characteristic. The assimilation-contrast theory assumes that slight deviations of performance from expectations are ignored (assimilated), whereas deviations above a critical level induce strong effects of (dis)satisfaction. This assumption might be justified on two different grounds. From perception theory, it might be suggested that slight deviations of expectations are not perceived because they are below the perceptual difference threshold.[89] The theory of cognitive dissonance[90] might suggest that the purchase of a product is justified by finding plausible reasons for small product disorders or even by distorted perceptions of them.

Three subjective indicators of consumer dissatisfaction have been considered: complaints, problems and reported (dis)satisfaction.[91] Complaints can be considered unobtrusive measures of dissatisfaction. However, they are sub-jective because complaints depend on personal expectations and perceptions of a commodity. Furthermore, the decision to complain depends on whether or not the dissatisfaction is attributed to the manufacturer, whether the cause is perceived as stable or likely to persist and whether it could have been avoided according to the consumer. The latter factors refer to the kind of attributions made by the consumer.[92]

Consumer problems do not always result in complaints to sellers or con-sumer agencies. Frequently complaints are made to relatives and friends or consumers may stop buying a particular brand of product or service in a partic-ular store. This behavior is less readily observed by marketers and consumer researchers.

Satisfaction reports have been obtained by using survey questions similar to the well-being measures dealt with in Section 10.2. Examples are:

"Choose one of the following:
- I rarely or never use items in this category
- I am satisfied with items in this category
- I am somewhat dissatisfied with items in this category
- I am very dissatisfied with items in this category"[93]

"Was the purchase satisfactory, somewhat satisfactory, somewhat unsat-isfactory or unsatisfactory?"[94]

"How satisfied are you with the food products you buy?
- always satisfied
- almost always satisfied
- sometimes satisfied
- rarely satisfied
- never satisfied"[95]

"How do you feel about your car? I feel:
- delighted
- pleased
- mostly satisfied
- mixed (about equally satisfied and dissatisfied)
- mostly dissatisfied
- unhappy
- terrible"[96]

Since subjective indicators of satisfaction are influenced by the factors considered above, the use of objective indicators of consumer satisfaction is favored.[97] Examples of these indicators are: maintenance and running costs of appliances, scrutiny of warranties and standard contracts, content analyses of advertising and other sales promotion and other information available to consumers and the consumers' use of products (e.g. the food intake and its correspondence to nutritionists' norms).

Conclusion

Consumer satisfaction can be considered a specific aspect of well-being. The-ories on consumer satisfaction are mainly variants of the standard of judgment theory on well-being since they use expectations to a large extent. The mea-surement of consumer satisfaction proceeds very similarly to the measurement of subjective well-being. Dissatisfaction might result in complaints to sellers or consumer agencies; this depends partly on the causal attributions regarding the source of dissatisfaction.

Summary

Several theoretical views on well-being are distinguished. These are sum-marized briefly in Table 10.1. Socio-demographic variables do not explain well-being to any large extent. Several items are considered in the completion of subjective reports on well-being, notably economic issues, one's health and the family.

Measurements of subjective well-being comprise one-item and multiple-item scales. The reliability of the multiple-item scales is greater than that of the one-item scales, although the lack of reliability is not important in aggregate measures of well-being.

Measures of economic well-being are mainly based on the amount of in-come since income is instrumental in the satisfaction of needs. However, need satisfaction is not sufficient in explaining well-being, since aggregate well-being does not increase with increasing GNP's in a country. An alternative explanation for differences in well-being is social comparison in which well-being is explained from an individual's ranking in the income distribution in a country.

The idea that not the objective income distribution but rather its perception forms the basis for well-being is implied by the theory on the welfare function of income. In this theory, the individual welfare function of income is assumed to depend on the income level of the family, the family size and the social reference group. Thus, processes of need satisfaction and social comparison are both included in this theory.

Poverty can be considered a lack of welfare. The instruments of measuring well-being can be applied to the investigation of poverty. The poverty line has been investigated by direct questioning regarding the minimum income for a household. The level of welfare associated with the poverty line appears to be different across countries and across different family sizes.

Manifest consequences of employment include mainly the worker's income; latent consequences are unintended by-products of a job, such as a higher level of activity, status and identity, goals and purposes transcending individual goals, time structure and social contacts. The latent consequences diminish when an individual becomes unemployed. Yet the net utility of unemployment is relatively high, given the income and circumstances of the household, due to much leisure and a lack of need to work.

Consumer satisfaction deals with a very specific aspect of well-being. Consumer expectations serve as standards of judgment in theories of consumer satisfaction. Expectations can be adapted to prior consumer experiences, communications from social referents such as sales people and one's personal method of perception and susceptibility to changes in opinions. The measurements of consumer satisfaction are similar to those of well-being.

Notes

[1] Diener 1984.
[2] See Section 10.3.
[3] Cantril 1965.
[4] See Section 2.2.
[5] Wilson 1967.
[6] Diener 1984.
[7] See Chapter 3.
[8] Diener 1984.
[9] Warr 1984.
[10] Diener 1984.
[11] Andrews and Withey 1976.
[12] Cantril 1965.
[13] Schwartz and Strack 1987.
[14] See Chapter 9.
[15] Schwarz and Clore 1983.
[16] Schachter and Singer 1962.
[17] Campbell et al. 1976, Larsen et al. 1985.
[18] Glatzer 1984.
[19] Easterlin 1974.
[20] See also Chapter 11.
[21] See Chapter 5.
[22] Diener 1984.
[23] Zajonc 1980.
[24] Fordyce 1977.
[25] Kammann 1982.
[26] Rokeach 1973, Gärling et al. 1987.
[27] Rokeach 1973.
[28] These values are the seven most important for attaining life satisfaction in the study by

Gärling et al. 1987.

[29] Gärling et al. 1987. See also Chapter 2.

[30] Diener 1984.

[31] Scitovsky 1976.

[32] See Chapter 7.

[33] Wills 1981, Kearl 1981–1982.

[34] Easterlin 1974.

[35] Brickman et al. 1978.

[36] Wortman and Silver 1982.

[37] Cameron 1974 and Feinman 1978.

[38] Warr 1984.

[39] Easterlin 1974.

[40] In the sense described by Helson 1964, see Section 4.2.

[41] Tversky and Griffin 1991. The endowment described here should not be confused with the endowment effect described in Chapter 12.

[42] Schwartz et al. 1987, see Tversky and Griffin 1991.

[43] Tversky and Griffin 1991.

[44] Hurvich and Jameson 1974.

[45] Solomon 1980.

[46] Tversky and Griffin's 1991.

[47] An inventory of subjective well-being scales is presented in Diener 1984. Veenhoven 1984b has excerpted 150 empirical studies on happiness.

[48] Andrews and Withey 1976.

[49] See Andrews and McKennell 1980.

[50] Gurin et al. 1960.

[51] Fordyce 1978.

[52] Fordyce 1977.

[53] Larsen et al. 1985.

[54] Bradburn 1969.

[55] Diener 1984.

[56] This is a characteristic of emotional experiences – see Section 9.1.

[57] Larsen et al. 1985.

[58] Andrews and Inglehart 1979 and McKennell et al. 1978.

[59] Andrews and Inglehart 1979.

[60] See Chapter 5.

[61] McKennell et al. 1978.

[62] Easterlin 1974.

[63] In response to the Gurin et al. 1960 type of question.

[64] Easterlin (1974).

[65] See Section 11.4.

[66] Easterlin (1974).

[67] See Chapter 4.

[68] Easterlin 1974, see Chapter 7.

[69] Veenhoven 1984a, 1984b.

[70] Veenhoven 1987.

[71] Van Praag 1968.

[72] For an overview, see Kapteyn and Wansbeek 1985.

[73] Van Herwaarden et al. 1977.

[74] Van Praag et al. 1979.

[75] See Section 4.2.

[76] Hagenaars 1986.

[77] Goedhart et al. 1977, p. 510.

[78] Van Praag et al. 1980.

[79] See Section 10.3.

[80] See Section 10.3.

[81] Van Raaij and Antonides 1990.

[82] Jahoda 1981.

[83] Van Raaij and Antonides 1990.

[84] Oliver 1980.

[85] See Section 4.2.

[86] Helson 1959, 1964.

[87] See also Section 4.2.

[88] Poiesz and Von Grumbkow 1988.

[89] See Section 4.1.

[90] See Section 11.2.

[91] Ölander 1977.

[92] See Section 11.4.

[93] Day and Landon 1976.

[94] Best and Andreasen 1976.

[95] Handy and Pfaff 1975.

[96] Westbrook 1980.

[97] Ölander 1977.

PART II

INFORMATION PROCESSING IN A WIDER SENSE

CHAPTER 11

COGNITIVE CONSISTENCY

11.1. Introduction

An important psychological principle guiding human judgment, attitude formation, change and interpretation of the environment is cognitive consistency. We have positive attitudes toward persons and objects we treat in a favorable way; we like to change behavior or circumstances if we have a negative opinion about it and we like people who do things that are good for us. Cognitive consistency helps to organize our thoughts, experiences and behavior in a way totally different from the guiding principle of rationality in economics.[1] Examples of cognitive consistency in earlier chapters include perceptual judgment,[2] the functional theory of attitudes,[3] attitude-behavior consistency,[4] cognitive heuristics[5] and cognitive emotion theory.[6]

Cognitive consistency in relation to attitudes and behavior will be considered in Section 11.2, cognitive attributions regarding oneself and others in Section 11.3 and consistency in judgments and social comparisons in Section 11.4. In each section, an attempt will be made to relate cognitive consistency to economic phenomena. Firstly, however, the principle of cognitive consistency will be explained by presenting several early theories in this field.

A theory of *cognitive balance* has been developed,[7] which states that a positive or negative affect toward another person tends to be in a state of balance with an individual's affect toward an attitude object toward which the other person is also oriented. For example, if person A likes person B and if person B likes her own grocery store, C, balance theory predicts that person A will tend to hold a favorable attitude toward shopping in B's store. In this example, all of the three affective relationships between A, B and C are positive. If person A does not like person B, however, cognitive balance implies an unfavorable attitude toward shopping in C. (See Figure 11.1.)

A theory of *affective-cognitive consistency*[8] can be considered as a precursor of modern attitude theory.[9] The theory states that a strong positive affect toward a given object should be associated with beliefs that it leads to the attainment of a number of important values, whereas a negative affect should correspond with beliefs that it blocks the attainment of these values. The *cog-*

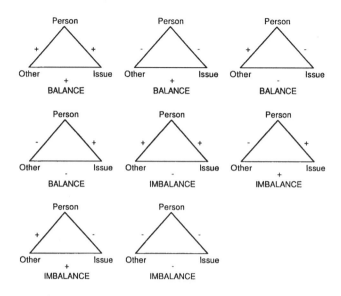

Figure 11.1. Cognitive balance with two persons and one issue.

nitive index, the weighted sum of the beliefs, is assumed to be consistent with
the affect toward the object. This consistency has been used in marketing
applications to predict purchase behavior from multi-attribute measures of
attitude.

Consistency also works in the reverse direction.[10] Eight subjects who favored the United States policy of giving economic aid to foreign nations were
placed under deep hypnosis and their positive feelings were reversed into negative ones. After this, the subjects (in contrast with a control group) expressed
negative beliefs and reduced importance to values associated with foreign aid.
For example, a subject believing that foreign aid would prevent economic depression before the hypnosis, believed that abandonment of foreign aid would
prevent economic depression after the treatment.

The theory of *cognitive dissonance*,[11] states that an inconsistency between
two or more cognitive elements in an individual's mind will motivate the individual to decrease the dissonance and avoid situations and information which
would be likely to increase the dissonance. The cognitive elements include
any knowledge, opinion or belief about the environment, about oneself or
about one's behavior. For example, a smoker believing that smoking is bad
for one's health will try to reduce the dissonance, e.g. by stopping smoking or by changing to a filter-tip brand. In addition, the smoker will seek
support from other smokers and point to the fact that many doctors smoke.
Finally, smokers may change their beliefs regarding health effects. It has been

found that non-smokers are more convinced about the relation between lung cancer and smoking than light smokers. Heavy smokers hardly believe in this relationship. The next section deals with cognitive dissonance in greater detail.

Whereas the theory of cognitive dissonance mainly deals with consistency after the act, the possibility of changing or choosing one's preferences may be considered, taking into account the possibility set of actions. For example, a person who is not in a financial position to invest because all of her money is needed for her present needs may develop aversive preferences toward investment behavior. She may state that renting a house is preferable to owning a house for many reasons or that saving money is useless because 'other people may take the profit', etcetera. Explaining saving behavior from attitudes toward saving[12] is not advised in this case. Rather, attitudes toward saving should be explained from the possibilities to save.

The idea of adaptive preferences has also been considered in explaining the overjustification effect.[13] A change in external rewards may induce a shift from internal to external motivation, implying a shift in preference. The mechanism of adaptive preferences may also play a part in the adaptation theory of well-being.[14]

Next, cognitive dissonance will be considered. The related theory of attribution will be dealt with in Section 11.3. The cognitive aspects of social comparisons will be dealt with in Section 11.4.

Conclusion

Cognitive consistency is a psychological principle explaining behavior from the human disposition to achieve and maintain correspondence between cognitions, feelings and acts. Theories explicitly dealing with consistency are the cognitive balance theory, the theory of affective-cognitive consistency, the theory of cognitive dissonance and the theory of adaptive preferences.

11.2. Cognitive dissonance

The effect of cognitive dissonance has been demonstrated in a classic experiment.[15] Psychology students were required to participate in the experiment as part of their psychology course. The first part of the experiment consisted of performing a very boring task, i.e. fill a tray with 12 spools, empty the tray, refill it with spools and so on. Next they were given a board with 48 pegs and required to turn each peg a quarter of a turn clockwise, start again when this had been completed and so on. In the second part of the experiment, subjects were told that they had been in a control condition and that in the experimental condition they would have met a confederate who had told them that the spool and peg tasks were fun, interesting and exciting. Then the subjects were told that the confederate was late and another experimental subject was in the waiting room. The subjects were asked to act as the confederate and were given either $1 or $20 for their cooperation.

Since the boring task was evaluated negatively by the students, telling other students that it was interesting created considerable cognitive dissonance. According to the theory, subjects would either refuse to cooperate (which they did not) or restore consistency by re-evaluating the task as enjoyable. In the $20 condition, however, it was assumed that the amount of money was sufficient to eliminate the dissonance because it gave the students a good reason to tell these lies. In actual practice the students behaved according to these hypotheses. The students in the $1 condition evaluated the task more positively and were more willing to participate in a similar experiment than students in the $20 condition. This has become known as the *compliance effect*.

The amount of cognitive dissonance can be illustrated by means of a ratio of elements dissonant with the behavior and elements consonant with the behavior. In the experiment described above these ratios would equal respectively:

Greater dissonance:

$$\frac{\text{Feeling that task is dull and trivial}}{\text{Pressure by experimenter} + \text{payment of \$1}}$$

Lesser dissonance:

$$\frac{\text{Feeling that task is dull and trivial}}{\text{Pressure by experimenter} + \text{payment of \$20}}$$

The effect of cognitive dissonance has frequently been found with subjects required to debate an issue from a standpoint opposite to their own. If the audience appears to be convinced by the debater (thus creating cognitive dissonance), a change in the former attitude can be observed. If the audience is not convinced, no attitude change takes place.[16]

Other experiments show the effect of cognitive dissonance on moral behavior. In one of these, children are told not to play with a very desirable toy. In one condition, they were threatened with severe punishment; in another condition with mild punishment for disobedience. Next the children were allowed to play with the toy for some time. After several weeks, the children who have been in the high punishment condition were more likely to play with the toy (without a threat of punishment) than children who had been in the mild punishment condition.[17] The mild punishment condition is assumed to create an internal justification for obedient behavior.

In a similar experiment, children participated in a contest to win a prize. Before and after the contest, attitudes toward cheating had been measured. Cheating behavior could be observed, although this was not apparent to the children. Those who had not cheated became more negative in their attitudes concerning cheating, whereas cheaters became more positive.[18]

These experiments are assumed to bear implications for the treatment of criminal behavior. From the point of view considered above mild punishment should be more effective in preventing crime than severe punishment. This is contrary to the economic price theory of crime[19] which states that upon increasing the cost of committing a crime, there will be fewer crimes.

Cognitive dissonance may have long lasting effects, as has been shown in an experiment.[20] Two groups of women engaged in two weight-reduction programs, both for four weeks, one involving much effort, the other involving little effort. Over the four weeks, both programs were equally effective in weight reduction. However, a year later the women in the high-effort program had an average weight loss of eight pounds, while those in the low-effort program lost nothing. The high-effort condition is assumed to create cognitive dissonance, in that internal justification is required for engagement in such difficult behavior. The internal justification has presumably been found in a changed attitude toward eating behavior. The mechanism at work in these programs may also strengthen the effect of precommitments[21] in which people engage in order to avoid bad consequences or to obtain greater benefits at a later period in their life.

The effect of *overjustification* has been related to the effect of cognitive dissonance. For example, students who were paid for solving jigsaw puzzles rated the task as less enjoyable than those who were not paid.[22] It appears that internal justification for the task performance (by means of a favorable attitude) is needed in the absence of external justification (the payment).

Cognitive dissonance effects have been observed in hazardous industries. Typically, some of the workers in these industries deny that they are working with dangerous substances and workers in a nuclear plant fail to wear safety badges that collect information on radiation exposure. This is explained by stating that those who believe the job is safe do not experience the unpleasant feeling of constant fear or doubts regarding their decision to take on such a dangerous job.[23]

Dissonance theory is assumed to be related to *consumer satisfaction* with a purchase.[24] After deliberate choice of a particular brand out of a number of alternatives, uncertainty regarding the choice might persist. (In the case of simple information processing[25] uncertainty might be even greater.) Dissonance reduction may be accomplished by forming more favorable attitudes toward the product that has been chosen and by a selective search for positive information on the product. In an experiment women were asked to rate the value of two appliances.[26] The women were then allowed to choose between the two appliances which were *wrapped* at that moment. A few minutes later with the appliances still wrapped the women were asked for a second evaluation. These evaluations systematically changed in favor of the appliance that had been chosen. This study may also be considered as an example of the endowment effect.[27] The function of advertising is mainly to give consumers some external justification for believing that what they have just bought meets their needs.[28]

The theory of cognitive dissonance is assumed to carry implications for persuasive communication and intended attitude change. Frequently, fear is communicated to induce changes in behavior. Since people tend to avoid information that increases cognitive dissonance, excessively high levels of induced fear are expected to be inefficient as a means of changing opinions. An early experiment shows this to be the case in dental hygiene behavior.[29]

Groups of high school students were given 15-minute lectures on oral hygiene practices, inducing differing levels of fear. Group I was given a strong fear appeal, emphasizing the painful consequences of tooth decay and diseased gums in that infections can spread throughout the body and cause arthritic paralysis, kidney damage or total blindness. Group II was given a milder and more factual description of the dangers. In group III, little mention was made of the consequences of tooth neglect. Several questionnaires were presented regarding dental hygiene and the lectures given. It appeared that students in group I were the most upset by the lectures, as compared with the other groups. The groups did not differ in the amount of factual information gained. However, the reported behavior changes one week after the lectures were the least frequent for group I as compared with the other groups. (See Table 11.1.)

The results considered above have been criticized in several ways. Much of the critique comes from attribution theory to be dealt with in the next section. For example, self-perception theory[30] states that the results in the boring task experiment1[31] can be explained from attributions regarding the actor's behavior. In the high reward condition, the subjects would deduce that their behavior was forced on them by the environment (an external attribution) and no change in attitudes would be necessary to retain their self-esteem. However, in the low reward condition subjects would deduce that their behavior was consistent with their attitudes since they engaged in the behavior by free will (internal attribution). Other experiments showed that the compliance effect only occurred if the subjects perceived duping and deceiving a fellow student as an aversive event that could have been avoided.[32]

Another phenomenon explained by self-perception theory if the so-called

Table 11.1. Effect of communications on dental hygiene behavior.

Type of change in behavior from precommunication to postcommunication	Control group to fear	Strong appeal to fear	Moderate appeal to fear	Minimal appeal
More like recommendations	22%	28%	44%	50%
Less like recommendations	22%	20%	22%	14%
No Change	56%	52%	34%	36%
Net Change in direction of recommendations	0%	8%	22%	36%

From Byrne (1966).

foot-in-the-door technique by which compliance with a request is brought about by a previous, smaller request.[33] Compliance with the small request induces a self-perception of giving in, thereby increasing the likelihood of compliance to a larger request. However, the first request should be large enough to bring about the self-perception of being a doer, otherwise compliance to the request will fail to induce compliance to the second request.[34] It was found that responding to 5 or 20 questions over the telephone (small first request) led to only 38%, respectively 35% of compliance with a request to answer 55 questions two days later (large second request). This was not significantly higher than the 31% compliance rate obtained without a first request. In this case, compliance with the first request occurred but self-perception of being a doer presumably did not. In contrast, responding to 30 or 45 questions (large first request) led to 74% compliance with the second request in both conditions. In the latter case first compliance presumably brought about the doer self-perception. Foot-in-the-door effects in general were found to be small in a meta-analysis including 120 experimental groups.[35]

A revised theory of cognitive dissonance[36] holds that *arousal* of cognitive dissonance only occurs if the actor perceives her behavior as an irrevocable aversive event. The interpretation of the state of arousal may result in taking responsibility for one's behavior, if its consequences were foreseeable. Taking responsibility implies the making of an internal attribution of behavior and a subsequent motivation to dissonance reduction. The making of an external attribution results in denying responsibility. In this case, dissonance reduction does not occur. This appears to be consistent with self-perception theory[37] although the state of arousal is not included.

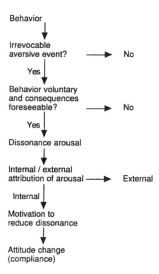

Figure 11.2. A revised theory of cognitive dissonance. Adapted from Cooper and Fazio (1984).

The revised theory of cognitive dissonance is consistent with the cognitive theory of emotion and several experiments have been conducted that obtained similar results with arousal of cognitive dissonance as with the arousal states considered in Section 9.1. Misattribution of dissonance arousal occurred if at the same time subjects were given a placebo that ostensibly produced, as a side effect, feelings of tension.[38] In this case no attitude change was evident. Likewise, external arousal induced by amphetamine[39] was misattributed to dissonance if the subjects were not informed about the drug. In this case, subjects changed their attitudes significantly. These results are consistent with experiments on the cognitive theory of emotions[40] and provide further support for this theory.

Evidence for the existence of dissonance arousal has been found by phys-iological measurements.[41] Also, experimentally induced dissonance arousal has been found to facilitate easy tasks and interfere with performance on more complex tasks.[42] This is according to the Yerkes-Dodson law.[43] The state of arousal is not implied by attribution theory and gives the revised theory of cognitive dissonance the status of a theory in itself. A summary of the revised theory of cognitive dissonance is shown in Figure 11.2.

Conclusion

Economic theory predicts a greater likelihood of highly rewarded behavior, whereas the theory of cognitive dissonance predicts a greater likelihood with a small reward. This results from an attitude change known as the compliance effect. Although attribution theory explains this effect from the attributions of internal causes, the revised theory of cognitive dissonance has shown that under several conditions arousal of cognitive dissonance is necessary to change the attitude.

11.3. Attribution theory

The preceding sections dealt with cognitive consistency in opinions, attitudes and judgments. Here, the process of interpreting events, other's behavior and one's own behavior will be considered. In this process, people follow some kind of logic, postulated in the theory of attribution. People are assumed to behave like 'naive scientists' in finding explanations for the occurrence of events and behavior and in their attempts to predict and control events in their own interest.[44] Several principles according to which people make sense of their environment have been formulated:

— People tend to attribute actions to *stable or enduring* causes, rather than to transitory or variable causes. For instance, an unfriendly treatment by one's boss is likely to be interpreted as being disliked by her, rather than attributed to a bad mood.

— Personal dispositions are more readily inferred from *intentional* than from unintentional behavior. For instance, if the boss does not have a better position to offer you, you don't blame her for that. If there are such possibilities, however, you will infer the boss's bad intent.

— The more a person is seen as causing an action the less the environment is considered as a cause and vice versa. Generally, in the above example either the boss or the circumstances will be seen as a cause.

— The *covariation principle* is fundamental to the attribution process. This means that events are attributed to causes if both occur repeatedly at the same time and if neither events nor causes occur in the absence of the other. Thus, if you think the boss likes you each time you are offered a better job, you attribute the boss's feeling as a cause of her behavior.

Regarding the attribution of intention and disposition, it is assumed that observers only make dispositional attributions on the basis of intentional behaviors.[45] Behavior is considered as intentional if observers believe both that the actor knew the behavior would produce the consequences observed and that the actor could have refrained from the action, i.e. that she had behavioral freedom. These are the same factors involved in the interpretation of dissonance arousal considered earlier.[46]

If the actor's behavior is judged to be intentional, certain conditions should hold to attribute a disposition. The observer is assumed to compare the act with other possible acts which may or may not produce the same consequences. If alternative acts could produce different (non-common) effects, the chosen act is more likely to be attributed to a disposition. A characteristic of this process is that inferred dispositions are congruent with the observed behavior, e.g. a kind personality is inferred from kind behavior. Hence, this is called the theory of *correspondent inference*.[47] An example of this is buying behavior, which is likely to be judged intentional since behavioral freedom is characteristic of this behavior. Furthermore, in sophisticated consumption cultures different purchases have different effects. Thus, consumption style is likely to be judged as a personal disposition. The cognitive heuristic of representativeness has been suggested as explaining correspondent inferences.[48]

It has been observed in a number of experiments that behavior is primarily judged as intentional, even if the actor is obviously constrained. For instance, individuals who have been required to state favorable opinions toward Castro are attributed pro-Castro attitudes more readily than individuals required to state anti-Castro opinions by the subjects in an experiment.[49] It appeared that the subjects hold the actors responsible for this behavior because the latter could have refused to do it. This general tendency to overestimate the importance of personal factor relative to environmental influences has been labeled the *fundamental attribution error*.[50]

The attribution theories described above relate to interpersonal perception. The theory developed by Kelly is more general in that it relates to events and to the perception of one's own and other's behavior.[51] He proposed the *configuration principle* of attribution including three criteria: consensus, distinctiveness and consistency.

— *Consensus* applies to the social agreement regarding an object, an event or a person. For instance, in judging the quality of a restaurant, it matters whether many people share the same opinion or whether they disagree with one another.

— *Distinctiveness* applies to the different opinions regarding different entities. For example, if different opinions are associated with different restaurants, distinctiveness is high.

— *Consistency* applies to the reliability of opinions. For example, is the quality of a restaurant always judged the same by the same person (consistency over time)? Are the judgments consistent with different choices from the menu (consistency over attributes)? Are the judgments consistent with perceptions from different senses (consistency over modality, i.e. vision, hearing, smell)?

Different patterns of attribution criteria are assumed to be associated with different types of attributions. For example, how is the favorable opinion of a target person regarding the quality of a particular restaurant to be attributed?

Table 11.2. Causal attributions with different configurations of criteria.

Consensus	Distinc- tiveness	Consis- tency	Dominant attribution
High	High	High	[Target]
High	High	Low	[Circumstance] × Target
High	Low	High	[Agent], Target or both
High	Low	Low	Circumstance [Ambiguous]
Low	High	High	[Agent × Target]
Low	High	Low	[Circumstance] × Agent × Target
Low	Low	High	[Agent]
Low	Low	Low	Agent × Circumstance [Ambiguous]

Adapted from Van Raaij (1986). The terms in brackets refer to the attributions presented in Fiske and Taylor (1984).

The combination of high consensus (many people like the restaurant), high distinctiveness (not each restaurant is liked by the target person) and high consistency (at each visit the target person likes the restaurant), *HHH*, is likely to produce an attribution to the restaurant's quality (a stimulus).

The combination of low consensus (disagreement with the target person), low distinctiveness (the target person likes most restaurants) and high consistency, *LLH*, is likely to produce an attribution to the target person's attitude.

The combination of low consensus, high distinctiveness and low consistency, *LHL*, is likely to produce an attribution to particular circumstances influencing the target person's judgment (e.g. a good mood). A summary of the most frequent attributions with different configurations of the criteria is shown in Table 11.2.[52] Different attributions result from different combinations of the criteria.[53]

If the target person in the above example is replaced by the person who makes the attribution herself, Kelly's theory applies to *self-perception*. For example, if I have a positive opinion regarding a restaurant, the *LLH* combination above induces me to think that I generally like restaurants more than most other people. The *LHL* combination induces me to think that I must be in a good mood to state such a favorable opinion regarding a restaurant that so many people dislike and which I did not enjoy in the past. This theoretical approach is in accordance with the theory of self-perception[54] stating that people, in the absence of internal cues regarding their feelings, infer their attitudes and emotions from their interpretation of the environment. Note how this relates closely to the *cognitive theory of emotions*.[55] However, dissonance arousal is not implied by self-perception theory.[56]

Kelly does not assume that people need all three criteria in making judgments.[57] In the absence of information regarding criteria, people are assumed to make use of preconceptions about what causes are associated with what effects. In the restaurant example above, the combinations of criteria are related to particular types of attributions. The combinations may function as *causal schemata* in human judgment, that can be used as shortcuts in information processing.

For example, an individual exclusively using the three causal schemata mentioned before, is frequently able to attribute a cause with limited information as follows:

— The scheme *HHH* is identified by the element of high consensus since this does not appear in the other two schemata. Thus, in the presence of high consensus information, the *HHH* scheme is applied and a stimulus attribution is likely to me made.

— The scheme *LLH* is identified by the element of low distinctiveness. Thus, if only low distinctiveness is perceived, the *LLH* scheme is applied and a person attribution is likely to be made.

— The scheme *LHL* is identified by the element of low consistency. Thus, awareness of low consistency leads to application of the *LHL* scheme and a circumstance attribution is likely to be made.

Obviously, schemata may differ across people, depending on their favorite combination of criteria. Application of these causal schemata can be regarded as using a set of *heuristics* in information processing.[58]

An extension of attribution theory is related to the causal inferences regarding success and failure in achievement tasks.[59] For example, in entrepreneurial behavior the success and failure of transactions might be attributed to *internal or external* and to *stable or unstable* causes. (See Table 11.3.) Success is frequently attributed to internal factors, such as ability or effort (depending on whether the entrepreneur is considered skilful or hard working). Failures, however, are frequently attributed to external causes, i.e. task-difficulty (a stable cause) and luck or chance (unstable). This idea shows that the fundamental attribution error, implying that causes are perceived as personal rather than situational, holds for observers but not for actors. The factor of stability in making causal attributions extends the idea that people are predisposed to making internal or external attributions.[60]

For example, consider a student going up for an exam. A failure may be attributed to the following causes:

— Stable-Internal cause: "I think I'm not clever enough to achieve high marks."

— Unstable-Internal cause: "I should have studied harder."

Table 11.3. Causal attribution of achievement behavior.

	Stable	Unstable
Internal	Ability	Effort
External	Task-difficulty	Luck, chance

From Weiner (1974).

- Stable-External cause: "They never allow more than 10% of the students to pass the exam."
- Unstable-External cause: "I had no chance to pass the exam since I got that terrible flu."

Furthermore, *self-handicapping strategies* frequently are used to avoid attributions damaging one's self-esteem.[61] For example, becoming drunk before doing an exam (or having very little sleep), provides an excuse for failure. Alternatively, passing the exam under these circumstances boosts one's self-image.

In addition to the two factors in Table 11.3, the intentionality of an actor's behavior may affect the type of attribution made.[62] A factor of controllability has been proposed to refer to the awareness of behavioral control. Although intentionality and controllability are correlated in practice, their difference is clear. For example, a suspect might not have had the intention to kill an old man (murder) but it may have occurred because of lack of control (manslaughter). Note that controllability implies both volitional behavior and foreseeable consequences.[63] The effect of the three factors on consumer reactions to product failure has been investigated.[64] It appears for instance that consumers demand refunds if the failure is attributed to stable causes under the control of the manufacturer or the store (e.g. misleading advertising). If the failure is attributed to stable causes not under the control of the manufacturer or the store (e.g. the company testing the product faked the test results) less refunds were demanded.

Outside observers, such as professors in the example above, are more likely to state dispositional causes, whereas actors (the students) are more ready to state external causes for their failures. So, judgment is dependent on the point of view of the judge. This process is referred to as the *actor-observer bias*.[65] The actor-observer bias may be explained by means of the availability heuristic.[66]

Another extension of attribution theory concerns the phenomenon of *learned helplessness*.[67] Learned helplessness refers to passive behavior resulting from exposure to uncontrollable events, i.e. a stay in prison. Frequently, in uncontrollable situations, learning that bad events cannot be changed generalizes to controllable situations, thus inducing depression. In an overview of attribution theoretical explanations of helplessness, it was found that stable, internal, global explanations of bad events, relatively often result in depression.[68] Interestingly, they distinguish global ("I am incapable") from specific explanations ("I am incapable of doing this"), in addition to the stability and Locus of Control factors. On the basis of the three factors distinguished, an Attributional Style Questionnaire (ASQ) was developed, measuring the type of attributions made in general.[69] The ASQ appeared to be correlated with depression.

The self-perception process where positive outcomes are attributed to internal causes and negative outcomes are attributed to external causes is referred to as the *self-serving bias*.[70] Other biases that might influence attributions are inter alia: involvement, preferences and believability.[71]

The self-serving bias may explain persistence in gambling by evaluating winners as reflecting one's skill or soundness of one's system and explaining away and discounting losses.[72] This led to the hypotheses that gamblers elaborate more on losses than on wins and that they react more to accidental circumstances (flukes) in the case of losses than in the case of wins. The first hypothesis was investigated by observing students' behavior after betting on sport events:

– they spent more time than expected in discussing losses than wins;
– they tended to play down the loss event (by stating that the outcome should have turned our differently) and to bolster the win event;
– they remembered their losses better than their wins.

The findings clearly indicate cognitive activity in order to restore consistency of mind and fact. The second hypothesis was tested by observing students' behavior after betting on a fluked basketball game in one condition, in which a player was bumped by an opponent and missed a relatively easy shot, with two minutes to play and four points in the lead. The other team came back and became champion. In the other condition, the game was the same but without the fluke. Those who lost:

– predicted victory of their original team more often in the fluke salient condition than in the other condition;
– placed higher bets on their original team in the next game in the fluke salient condition than in the original condition.

In a similar test of the second hypothesis, it was found that in the no fluke condition the students attributed the result more to ability of the teams than to luck. This was considerably less so for winners in the fluke condition; losers in the fluke condition even attributed the result more often to luck than to ability. The willingness to bet on the original team after a big loss in the fluke condition appeared considerably higher than after a smaller loss.

Concluding, it appeared that:

"This tendency to take wins at face value but to transform losses into 'near wins' can produce overly optimistic assessments of one's gambling skill and the chances of future success."[73]

Reflections on cognitive dissonance and attribution theory

Both the theory of cognitive dissonance and attribution theory deal with causal attributions. In some sense, attribution theory is more general because it deals with causal attributions of events, other's behavior and one's own behavior. The theory of cognitive dissonance deals exclusively with opinions, attitudes and judgments regarding one's own behavior and with self-perception. Yet attribution theory does not include the (revised) theory of cognitive dissonance, since it assumes neither cognitive arousal nor its conditions and effects.

The theory of attribution includes a number of principles and assumptions which are not structured within a coherent framework. In the literature, the principles of stable causes, intentionality and covariation,[74] the theory of correspondent inference, the configuration principle with its three criteria and the causal attribution of achievement behavior have been presented alongside one another. Given the present state of affairs, we suggest an integrated model based on the revised model of cognitive dissonance[75] combined with the configuration principle regarding the attributions.

A first step in the attribution process is a judgment as to whether a behavior is voluntary or whether the consequences of behavior or an event are foreseeable. This implies the principle of intentionality[76] and the condition of controllability.[77] If behavior is judged as involuntary or the results of a behavior or event are judged as uncontrollable or not foreseeable, external attributions are made. Otherwise, the attribution process proceeds.

The second step involves the application of the configuration principle, including its three conditions of consensus, distinctiveness and consistency. The criterion of consistency has been differentiated so as to include consistency over time, which implies the stability of causes and covariation over time. The criterion of distinctiveness refers to the covariation of particular events or behaviors and particular causes.

If attribution theory is applied to one's own behavior or cognitions, dissonance arousal is assumed according to the revised theory of cognitive dissonance. If it is applied to events or another person's behavior, the conditions of judgment have not yet been stated. It could be the case that attributions differ according to the degree of involvement of the judge, her own experience with the behavior, the heuristics applied if background information is lacking or the legal provisions of judgment in court.

Conclusion

Important factors in making cognitive inferences are the principle of covariation, the tendency to attribute stable causes and the perception of behavior as intentional. The configuration principle deals with the consensus, distinctiveness and consistency of opinions. The combinations of these three criteria yield different likelihoods of attributions to a person, a target and circumstances. The cognitive attribution of achievements is assumed to depend on the internal/external factor and stability and controllability of causes. An attempt at integration of attribution theory and the theory of cognitive dissonance yields a two step model in which the intentionality of behavior and the foreseeability of consequences are considered first. In the second step, the configuration principle is applied in making the attribution.

11.4. Social judgment

In Chapter 10, judgments of well-being have been related to need satisfaction and to social comparison, the latter by using other people as a reference standard of judgment. Here, income judgments will be related to both factors at the same time. First, however, several distributive principles regarding income will be considered.[78]

The simplest principle amounts to an *equal* income for everyone in a particular environment. This principle is very unlikely to be adopted in practice since people may have different needs (e.g. some people have to take care of children, others do not) or employ different amounts of efforts and abilities (e.g. work or unemployment). Deviations from an equal income distribution will be considered as undesirable according to this principle.

A second distributive principle amounts to an income distribution based on people's different needs. By the *need principle*, a distribution of income is considered as undesirable if different people's needs are not fulfilled to the same extent. The type of needs can be quite variable, e.g. physiological, safety, social and psychological needs may be considered. The need principle is frequently applied in practice, e.g. by social benefits and subsidies to groups with particular needs (the elderly, the handicapped, etcetera). To the extent that needs are not fulfilled, the need principle would predict dissatisfaction with income.

The last principle we shall deal with is *equity*.[79] According to this principle, people compare the outputs of an action with the inputs. A particular ratio of outputs and inputs is judged as fair in a normative sense. In the equity principle, for example, income is considered a compensation for efforts and abilities. A formal statement of the equity relationship is:

$$\frac{O_a}{I_a} = \frac{O_b}{I_b}$$

where O denotes individual outputs (e.g. income) and I individual inputs. In judging the equity of an output, individual a relates the own output to the own input and compares this ratio with the ratio of another individual, b (b might also be considered as a representative of a group of individuals, e.g. the reference group). If the ratios are not equal, inequity is perceived.

Inequity produces cognitive inconsistencies which can be solved in various ways. Overpaid piece-rate workers, for example, tend to reduce their production rate but would try to improve the quality of the product (restoring equity by reducing their O/I ratio). Overpaid hourly-rate workers would increase their production rate (restoring equity by increasing their inputs).[80]

In an experiment on a proofreading task,[81] subjects who were told that they were unqualified but being paid the same rate as qualified subjects found more proofreading errors in a text than subjects who were told either that they were qualified or being paid the same rate as unqualified subjects.

Lower unemployment rates were observed for occupations with higher pay and for workers with greater education and skill.[82] This was attributed to the greater difficulty of monitoring skilled work than unskilled work. Unskilled workers would easily detect inequity and because of this, underpaid workers relatively often would reside in unemployment.

In a survey regarding tipping behavior, it was found that tipping was positively related to bill size, patronage frequency and perceived quality of service but not to the interaction of frequency and quality (the latter indicates that regular customers are not buying future services with their tips).[83] The result is consistent with customers buying social approval because regular customers should value their server's social approval more than irregular customers. Additional evidence shows that for irregular customers only 33% of the variance in tip amount could be explained by bill size, whereas for regular customers this was 70%. Furthermore, the result is consistent with equitable relationships, i.e. tipping in exchange for good service.

Cognitive inconsistencies might also be reduced by changing opinions.[84] For instance, if people perceive themselves overpaid, they might convince themselves that they deserve it.[85] Alternatively, they may assign a lower value to pay than those with less pay and otherwise in the same circumstances.[86] The latter result suggests that payment may be a restrictive operationalization of the equity relationship.

Research regarding incomes as outputs in the equity relationship has included direct questioning regarding equitable incomes of other persons.[87] In

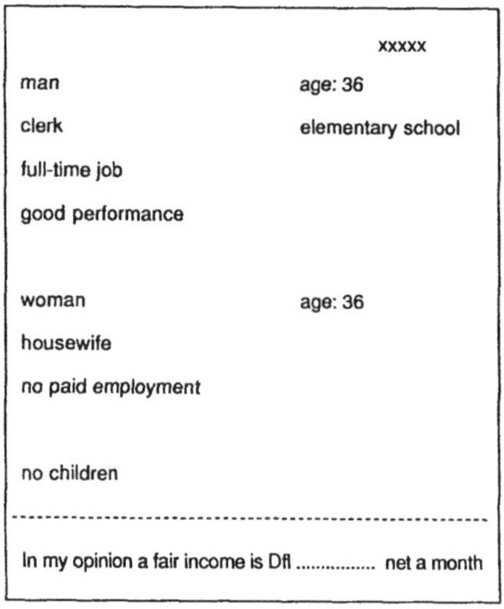

```
┌─────────────────────────────────────────────┐
│                                         xxxxx │
│  man                          age: 36         │
│  clerk                        elementary school│
│  full-time job                                │
│  good performance                             │
│                                               │
│                                               │
│  woman                        age: 36         │
│  housewife                                    │
│  no paid employment                           │
│                                               │
│                                               │
│  no children                                  │
│  - - - - - - - - - - - - - - - - - - - - - - -│
│  In my opinion a fair income is Dfl .......... net a month│
└─────────────────────────────────────────────┘
```

Figure 11.3. A vignette used in equity research on incomes. From Hermkens and Boerman (1989).

this research, subjects are presented a *vignette* describing several characteristics of a particular type of employee. (See Figure 11.3.) Subjects are then asked to state the equitable amount of income for the particular individual. It appeared that equitable income was explained to some extent by occupational prestige, the number of paid jobs performed by the household, the quality of job performance and household size.[88]

Merit criteria of effort, seniority, qualification and position were used in vignettes including two workers at the same time.[89] Students' parents were asked to distribute a bonus between the two workers. If the two workers had the same salary, the bonus distribution was highly influenced by both effort expended and seniority. Since a senior usually earns more than a trainee, the larger bonus assigned to the senior presumably was given to compensate her relatively low income. With unequal incomes in favor of the senior, the bonus was influenced by effort but not by educational level. Finally, it was found that a bonus assignment to two salesmen, one superior in talent (because of his charm) and the other superior in effort, favored the effort. In all three cases, effort tended to be highly rewarding.

Equity is assumed to imply cognitive comparisons with other individuals. However, the need principle may incorporated in the equity relationship.[90] This is accomplished by considering the utility of income as the output in the equity relationship instead of the income itself. To be consistent, utility of inputs (i.e. the subjective value of activities) should be substituted, too. The utility function is assumed to indicate to what extent needs are satisfied. The equity relationship for an individual a in this case can be stated as:

$$\frac{U_a(Y_a)}{V_a(I_a)} = \frac{V_a(Y_b)}{V_a(I_b)}$$

where $U(\cdot)$ denotes the utility function of income,[91] $V(\cdot)$ a value function of inputs, Y the income and I the amount of inputs. Since utilities and values are subjective, the other's utilities of output and input cannot be included in the equation. Instead it is assumed that the other's outputs and inputs are evaluated by the utility and value functions of individual a.

This idea has been applied to income judgments of employed and unemployed individuals. In this case, a clear difference in the utility of input activities can be assumed. So, in the hypothetical case of equal incomes of a working individual a and an unemployed individual b (otherwise in the same circumstances as a), the equity relationship is not equal. With individuals in different circumstances, however, the equity relationship might be equal. For example, if a single individual with a paid job compares herself with the unemployed head of an incomplete family with four children, the income utility in the latter case will be less, possibly compensating for the lower value of the inputs. So, even in the case of equal incomes, the income utility in the incomplete family might form an equitable ratio to the value of the inputs.

This hypothesis has been tested by relating the income utility of breadwinners to the family size and the employment level (whether or not working), holding the income level constant. It appears that the income utility of employed people, given the income, on average is lower for employed breadwinners and those with larger families than for unemployed breadwinners and those with smaller families.

Another result from this study is related to direct questions regarding the equitable income of an individual used for comparison.[92] This question reads:

> "Which net monthly family income would you consider as equitable for an unemployed individual, otherwise in the same circumstances as you are?"

It appears that the (log-) difference between own income and the reported equitable unemployment income is related to the utility of the own income, thus implying the need principle in equity judgments of income. Similar results have been obtained with information from the unemployed when asked analogous questions regarding the equitable income of employed individuals. As a conclusion, it appears that the need principle (satisfaction of needs) supports the equity principle (social comparisons) in judgments of income.

Equity and fairness

Fairness refers to honesty, sincerity, propriety or manners. The term has been frequently used by economists to explain anomalous behavior, which is not explained by economic theory.[93] For example, an economically efficient way to allocate scarce resources is the price mechanism. However, people consider it unfair to auction tickets for games or to increase the price of snow shovels after a snow storm.[94] They prefer inefficient mechanisms such as lotteries and queueing. Deviations from game theoretic predictions of behavior[95] also are frequently explained by referring to fairness. Although several rules for fairness have been developed, the psychological mechanism of fairness has only recently been investigated.

A relationship is suggested between fairness and equity as follows.[96] The larger an individual's input into obtaining some valuable item, the more equitable is it to keep a large share of the benefits derived, according to the equity relation. An individual's input creates a psychological entitlement or 'right' to the benefits. Without entitlements, the propensity to share the benefits in general will increase. Psychological entitlement will be less if property rights are undefined (e.g. beachcombing), defined by luck (e.g. gains in a casino) or by gift (e.g. money given to subjects in an experiment). For example, experimental subjects asked to allocate money between themselves and another subject, kept more money for themselves if they had earned the right to allocate than if they were given the right by chance.[97] Increasing the price of snow shovels after a snow storm is considered unfair because the psychological entitlement of the sellers is considered exactly the same as before the snowstorm. Thus, a price increase disturbs the equity relationship.[98]

Communication may activate the underlying norms of fairness.[99] Sharing benefits with unknown individuals is found less likely than with those engaged with in a social relationship. Thus, identification tends to increase cooperation in social dilemmas.[100]

Conclusion

Three principles of social judgment are the equality rule, the need principle and the equity rule. It appears that substituting utilities of outcomes and inputs in the equity relation results in a combination of social comparison and and the need principle in making judgments.

By considering entitlements as inputs in the equity relationship, fairness effects regarding the allocation of resources (outputs) may be explained.

Summary

Cognitive consistency plays a part in several psychological mechanism, e.g. perceptual judgment, cognitive heuristics, emotions and attitudes. The theories of cognitive balance, affective-cognitive consistency, cognitive dissonance and attribution deal with cognitive consistency in an explicit way.

The early theory of cognitive dissonance explained the attitude change under conditions of low reward from the human disposition to reduce cognitive inconsistency. The revised theory of cognitive dissonance included the arousal of cognitive dissonance under conditions of irrevocable aversive events. Depending on the making of internal attributions regarding these events, the motivation to reduce the dissonance induces the attitude change (compliance effect).

The theory of cognitive dissonance bears implications for the theory of crime, persuasive communications and voluntary commitment to programs directed at changing undesirable behavior. Also, it explains the phenomenon of overjustification.

Attribution theory deals with causal explanations people make regarding events, the behavior of others and their own behavior. Inferences regarding the own behavior influence the individual's self-perception. In the attribution process, several principle are assumed to be at work. The disposition to attribute actions to stable causes and to the actor's intentions leads to corresponding inferences regarding the personality of the actor.

The principle of covariation implies the attribution of events to causes that are frequently associated with them. The configuration principle assumes that attributions are made on the basis of consensus, distinctiveness and consistency of behavior and opinions. Different configurations are associated with different dominant attributions. A subset of configurations (schemata) may be selected by means of which it is possible to make attributions more quickly, without considering all of the three criteria.

The attribution of achievements, such as success or failure, is assumed to be based on the internal/external factor, the stability of causal factors and controllability of the behavior. Judgments regarding one's own behavior are influenced by the self-serving bias. Furthermore, biased judgment results from whether or not behavior is considered from one's own position or from that of others (the actor-observer bias).

A provisional integrative theory, combining attribution theory and the theory of cognitive dissonance, consists of two steps. In the first step, the intentionality of behavior and the foreseeability of consequences are considered. The second step deals with the configuration principle in making the attributions.

Another instance of cognitive consistency is implied by the equity relation

which holds a correspondence between one's own and another's ratio of outputs and inputs. Inequity may be restored by changes in one's own outputs
and inputs and in the perception of one's own and the other's outputs and
inputs. A different specification of the equity relation, including utilities of
outcomes and inputs, comprises a combination of the need and the equity
rules in social judgments. Fairness may be explained by applying the equity
relationship to entitlements and the allocation of resources.

BOX 11.1

ATTRIBUTION OF POLITICAL MESSAGES

Biased attributions can easily be observed in public speeches of politicians.
The speeches of Gerald Ford and Jimmy Carter on the occasion of their 1976
presidential nominations for their respective parties have been used in an
experiment.[101]

First of all, the actor-observer bias can be observed from their speeches.
The incumbent president Ford blamed the congressional opposition for the
country's ills (an external attribution) whereas the presidential contender
Carter blamed president Ford for the same ills. This section will deal with the
attributions of listeners to the speeches regarding their message.

Two six-minutes videotaped excerpts of the speeches regarding the current
(1976) state of the country and its lack of progress since 1974 were shown
to 200 undergraduates of the University of Connecticut. Each student was
shown only one of the tapes. Prior to viewing, the students had indicated their
preferred candidate and their involvement in the 1976 presidential election.

After viewing the tapes, the students estimated the percentage of people
that agreed with the message; they indicated the perceived knowledge and
expertise of both politicians and their opinion about whether the speakers
had blamed the congressional opposition or the president merely to get themselves elected (i.e. a personal attribution for the content of the speech). The
knowledge and expertise of the speakers can be considered a factor in the
influence of the speech on other people, i.e. the extent to which the outcomes
of their behavior can be controlled. In addition, the students indicated how
extreme they thought the speech was.

The subjects who were less involved in the elections did not differ on the
variables mentioned above. The results regarding the highly involved subjects
are presented in Figure 11.4. It appears that the message of the preferred candidate was perceived as less extreme than that of the non-preferred candidate.
Furthermore, the estimated consensus and the perceived knowledge and ex-

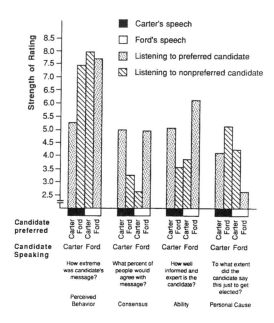

Figure 11.4. Perceived factors in political messages. From Lowe and Kassin (1978). In: D. Krech et al.: Elements of Psychology. Copyright ©1982 by Alfred A. Knopf. Reproduced by permission of Mc-Graw-Hill, Inc.

pertise were higher for students who listened to their preferred candidate than for those who listened to their non-preferred candidate. So both perceived consensus and perceived controllability seem to be biased by the preferences of the students.

Both perceived consensus and perceived controllability might have influenced the biased inference regarding the message. Those who listened to their non-preferred candidate to a greater extent inferred that the candidate spoke the way she did just to get elected than those who listened to their preferred candidate.

In conclusion, the attribution process does not consist solely of making cognitive judgments according to a set of objective criteria and deducing the right cause. Rather, judgment appears to biased (again) by subjective factors such as preferences and involvement.

Notes

[1] See Chapter 12.
[2] See Section 4.2.
[3] See Section 6.1.
[4] See Section 6.3.
[5] See Section 7.4.
[6] See Section 9.1.
[7] Heider 1958.
[8] Rosenberg 1960a.
[9] See Chapter 6.
[10] Rosenberg 1960b.
[11] Festinger 1957.
[12] See Chapter 8.
[13] See Section 3.1.
[14] See Section 10.1.
[15] Festinger and Carlsmith 1959.
[16] Scott 1957.
[17] Freedman 1965.
[18] Mills 1958.
[19] Tullock 1974.
[20] Axsom and Cooper 1980.
[21] See Section 12.6.
[22] Calder and Staw 1975.
[23] Akerlof and Dickens 1982.
[24] See Section 10.5.
[25] See Chapter 7.
[26] Brehm 1956.
[27] See Chapter 12.
[28] Akerlof and Dickens 1982.
[29] Janis and Feshbach 1953.
[30] Bem 1972.
[31] Festinger and Carlsmith 1959.
[32] See Cooper 1971 and Cooper and Worchel 1970.
[33] Freedman and Fraser 1966.
[34] Seligman et al. 1976.
[35] Beaman et al. 1983.
[36] Cooper and Fazio 1984.
[37] Bem 1972.
[38] Zanna and Cooper 1974.
[39] Cooper et al. 1978.
[40] Schachter and Singer 1962.
[41] Croyle and Cooper 1983.
[42] See Cooper and Fazio 1984.
[43] See Section 9.3.
[44] Heider 1958.
[45] Jones and Davis 1965.
[46] Cooper and Fazio 1984, see Section 11.2.
[47] Ross and Fletcher 1985.

[48] See Section 7.3.
[49] Jones and Harris 1967.
[50] Ross 1977.
[51] Kelly 1967.
[52] See also McArthur 1972; a different table is constructed by Fiske and Taylor 1984.
[53] Kelly and Michela 1980.
[54] Bem 1972.
[55] See Section 9.1.
[56] See Section 11.2.
[57] Kelly 1972.
[58] See Section 7.3.
[59] Weiner 1974.
[60] Rotter 1966, see Section 3.3.
[61] Jones and Berglas 1978.
[62] Weiner 1985.
[63] See Section 11.2.
[64] Folkes 1984.
[65] Jones and Nisbett 1971.
[66] See Section 7.3.
[67] Maier and Seligman 1976.
[68] Peterson and Seligman 1984.
[69] Peterson et al. 1982.
[70] Zuckerman 1979.
[71] See also Box 11.1.
[72] Gilovich 1983.
[73] Gilovich 1983, p. 1122.
[74] Heider 1958.
[75] Cooper and Fazio 1984.
[76] Heider 1958.
[77] Weiner 1985.
[78] Arts et al. 1991, Deutsch 1975.
[79] Adams 1965, Walster and Walster 1975, Cook and Hegtvedt 1983.
[80] See Adams 1963.
[81] Adams and Jacobson 1964.
[82] Akerlof and Yellen 1990.
[83] Lynn and Grassman 1990.
[84] See Section 11.2.
[85] Lea et al. 1987.
[86] Haberfeld 1992.
[87] Jasso and Rossi 1977, Hermkens 1986.
[88] Hermkens and Boerman 1989.
[89] Overlaet 1991.
[90] Antonides and Van Raaij 1989.
[91] For example, the Welfare Function of Income, considered in Chapter 10.
[92] Antonides and Van Raaij 1989.
[93] Kahneman et al. 1986a, 1986b, Camerer and Thaler 1995.
[94] Kahneman et al. 1986a, 1986b.
[95] See Chapter 14.

[96] Frey and Bohnet 1995.

[97] Hoffman et al. 1992.

[98] See the concept of 'fair' pricing in Section 4.3.

[99] Frey and Bohnet 1995.

[100] See Chapter 14.

[101] Lowe and Kassin 1978.

CHAPTER 12

RATIONALITY

12.1. Introduction

The economic assumption of rationality has been the subject of much debate in economics as well as in economic psychology. Economics is based on the assumption of rational behavior, in the sense that it can be understood by asking how well-informed individuals would act to secure their best advantages.[1] It is assumed that individuals have utility functions or preference orderings that enable them to rank order all possible states of the world in terms of the satisfaction provided for them. Furthermore, individuals are assumed to be able, on the basis of their financial and psychological possibilities, to determine which states of the world are attainable for them. From these states, individuals choose the ones yielding the highest utility.[2]

The conception of rationality described above actually is a normative assumption according to which the results of choice are obtained. A useful distinction of rationality has been made between the rationality in the *process of human thought* and the rationality as the *product of thought*.[3] Theory of rationality associated with the results of thought can be seriously misleading by providing 'solutions' to economic problems that are without operational significance. For example, economic theory predicts choice by maximization of utility subject to constraints. However, the use of cognitive heuristics might lead to quite different predictions.[4] On the other hand, perfectly rational procedures might lead to non-optimal outcomes if the wrong information is used (e.g. as a result of perceptual errors). It has been noticed that economics generally uses data from which after the fact explanations are derived.[5] This points to the lack of psychological realism in economic models, too.

In the preceding chapters, psychological theories have been presented that offer more realistic explanations of human behavior. Simplified information processing has been considered, dealing with the questions of process rationality and constraints on information handling.[6] The results of these theories make clear that individuals are unable to arrange in perfect order all possible states of the world according to their preference, as the assumption of rationality requires.

Mental images of economic relationships[7] obviously appears to vary for different groups of people, implying possibly different behavior even with equal preferences and constraints.

Other theories dealing with process rationality are theories of perception,[8] expectations,[9] emotions[10] and cognitive consistency.[11]

The economic assumption of rationality is associated with several *axioms* that will be considered in Section 12.2. These axioms deal with preference orderings and utility functions. With certain arguments excluded from the utility function, behavior frequently appears to be irrational. For instance, with stress left out of the utility function, the outcome of the maximization process is different from the outcome based on preferences including stress.[12] The same applies to excluding motivations and personality characteristics[13] from the utility function.

Economics took as its starting-point the stable preferences of the so-called *representative consumer*.[14] This implies that the utility function does not change over time and that individual differences in the utility function are not considered. However, learning behavior,[15] emotions[16] and changing aspiration levels[17] frequently produce instable preferences, thus yielding irrational behavior from the economic point of view.

Psychological variables may enrich the utility function in a number of ways. This has implications for the testing of hypotheses derived from such enriched theories since much information is required, usually not available in economic and social statistics. Even if the information were available, however, there are two reasons why it is at least doubtful that it would be used by economists.

The first reason is that detailed information regarding psychological variables is not necessary to make the predictions usually made in economics.[18] In many instances economics may suffice with aggregate predictions that hold more or less true in practice. This reason refers to the negligibility assumption[19] according to which it makes little difference to predictions if heterogenous preferences are neglected. This argument should be rejected, however, in the light of the many cases in which economic predictions have proved to be false.

The second reason is that for aggregate predictions, heterogeneous preferences and for relatively long-term predictions unstable preferences do not matter because these differences cancel out in the aggregate and over time. Nevertheless, individual differences might improve aggregate predictions. For example, imagine the prediction of the proportion of home-ownership in a country. Most likely, home owners have preferences systematically different from tenants and both groups might influence the proportion in a different way. Thus, better predictions might be possible if the preferences of these groups are taken into account separately. The instability of preferences should be taken into account to the extent that fluctuations over time are not random. However, many preference changes are not random as is evident for example from the determinants of aspiration levels.[20] Since systematic differences in utility do not cancel out, economics should take these into account.

Two other simplifying assumptions of economic theory have been distinguished.[21] Domain assumptions refer to application of the theory to situations (domains) where complicating factors are known to be absent. For instance, the theory of supply and demand relevant without state interventions. It is obvious that no economic theory can be applied to domains where psychological factors are not present. Heuristic assumptions refer to the use of simplifying heuristics with the objective of approximating reality successively. After developing fairly satisfactory models of reality, the simplifying assumptions should gradually be relaxed. Note that heuristic assumptions explicitly state that certain variables are left out for the moment. In this respect, economic psychology can be considered an attempt to replace the simplifying assumptions in economic models by more realistic ones. Ideally, a theory should explain both the process and the outcomes of decision making.

Several axioms regarding preferences for certain and uncertain outcomes are considered in the literature.[22] Decision making regarding uncertainty will be dealt with in Chapter 13.

Section 12.2 deals with several axioms of economic choice. Section 12.3 deals with the value function which is used to explain a number of economic anomalies, including the endowment effect (Section 12.4), mental accounting (Section 12.5), status quo bias (Section 12.6) and sunk costs (Section 12.7). Self-control, important in dynamic choice, is considered in Section 12.8.

Conclusion

Rationality can be distinguished according to the process and the outcomes of thought. Although process rationality may lead to outcome rationality, this is by no means obvious. Thus, outcome rationality may often not give a realistic view of economic behavior. Economists may state that psychological variables may be neglected in economic models, that economic models are only valid in specific domains or that heuristic assumptions are warranted awaiting more complex models.

12.2. Axioms of economic choice

The theory of economic choice is based on several axioms which are known to be violated frequently in practice.[23] Here, we shall concentrate on the most controversial axioms.

The *axiom of completeness* states that for any two states of the world (e.g. two outcomes of choice, two commodity bundles, etcetera) A and B, under every possible condition, the consumer either prefers A to B or prefers B to A or is indifferent. This axiom is frequently violated because of the instability of the preference function. Because of different mood states, for example, an individual might prefer apples to oranges on one day and oranges to apples on the other day. A solution might be to make preferences *stochastic*, implying that there is a certain probability that A is preferred over B. However, besides random fluctuations there are systematic effects in preference changes, depending on the context of judgment, that are not fully captured by stochastic preferences.[24]

The *axiom of greed* states that if A contains more of one good than B and at least as much as B of all other goods, A will be preferred to B. Two objections to this axiom have been noticed: *satiation and altruism*.[25]

Unsatiable greed implies that stimuli satisfying needs[26] retain their function even when needs have been satisfied to a certain extent. However, it can be shown experimentally that upon satisfaction of particular needs other needs become prominent and stimuli satisfying the first need lose their reinforcing value.

It is observed that rats being allowed both to run a wheel and to drink water spend about 2.5 times as much time drinking as they spend on running.[27] If the rats are required to spend three times as much time on running than on drinking, the rats run more but drink less than normally. Under this condition, drinking rewards running but running punishes drinking. If the rats are required to spend nine times as much time on drinking than on running, they run less and drink more than normally. Under this condition, running rewards drinking but drinking punishes running. It appears that both drinking and running are positive reinforcers up to a certain point, beyond which these activities become negative reinforcers. Similar results have been obtained by varying the motivational states of the rats.[28] If rats were deprived of water for some time, water functioned as a positive reinforcer for running. If the rats were deprived of exercise for some time (by blocking the wheel), running functioned as a positive reinforcer for drinking.

It appears that primates have a need for sensation and excitement for which activities are performed without external reward.[29] The *Premack principle*[30] may also operate on a student who, after sitting in the lecture-room listening to her professor for one hour, becomes satiated and starts playing tennis which satisfies her deprived need for exercise. Although the economic concept of marginal utility predicts that, after consuming commodity X for a while, the deprivation of a commodity Y may increase the marginal of utility of commodity Y relative to commodity X, it does not predict that the marginal utility of commodity X becomes negative. Since Premack's experiments include mutually exclusive activities, it would be interesting to observe behavior with both X and Y freely available, after consumption of X for some time. Any consumption of X under these circumstances would violate the satiation assumption.

Altruism[31] is inconsistent with the axiom of greed, since it is incompatible with the wish to increase one's own utility. In Becker's theory of altruism,[32] this problem is modeled such that the goods and services provided to the beneficiary appear in the utility function of the altruist. In this way, altruism is not an argument against the axiom of greed.

The *axiom of transitivity* states that if A is preferred to B and B is preferred to C, then A is preferred to C. Anyone failing to satisfy this axiom can be exploited as a *money pump*. For example, since a wristwatch is preferred to a wallet by a particular individual, you might change a wallet for the individual's wristwatch plus some money. Next, since the individual is known to prefer a tie-pin to a wallet, you might change a tie-pin for the wallet plus some money. Next, since the individual prefers the wristwatch to the tie-pin (intransitivity), you might change the wristwatch for the tie-pin plus some money. This could be repeated until the money pump ran dry or until the individual realizes the intransitivity of her preferences. Intransitivity is also incompatible with the principle of cognitive consistency.

In an early experimental demonstration of intransitivity 62 students were asked to make pairwise choices between three hypothetical marriage partners; 17 chose intransitively.[33] A possible solution to account for intransitivity in economic models is to model preferences as stochastic implying probabilities of choice instead of deterministic choice. This solution causes some troubles, however, since intransitivity can hardly be distinguished from incompleteness in this case. In fact, the above experiment was repeated with verbal descriptions of marriage partners, such as a "pretty, average charm, well-to-do woman" and a "plain, very charming, wealthy woman".[34] The experiment was conducted twice with one week between the two tests. It was found that 22.8% of all pairwise choices were reversed on the second test, which indicates moderately stochastic preferences. In such cases one can hardly tell whether preferences are transitive or stochastic, however.

Conclusion

Several axioms of economic theory are frequently violated in research, notably the axioms of completeness, greed and transitivity of preferences. Stochastic preferences are expedient to some extent, although not in case of the axiom of greed.

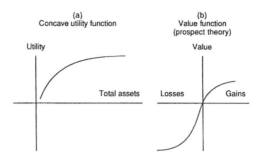

Figure 12.1. Examples of a hypothetical utility function and a value function.

12.3. The shape of the value function

Economics frequently assumes a utility function that is marginally decreasing.[35] Furthermore, the same utility function is applied to capture the pleasure of a gain and the pain of a loss. However, people's preferences as revealed from their choices have been observed to be inconsistent with this assumption regarding the shape of the utility function. This inconsistency has been noticed in *prospect theory*[36] dealing with choice under uncertainty. Since prospect theory will be dealt with in Chapter 13, uncertainty will not be considered here.

Consider a lady who has purchased a coat for $200. After this, she is not willing to sell it for $250. How is this result to be explained? (Shopping costs are assumed to be negligible.) In Figure 12.1a, a utility function of income has been sketched concave from below. With the purchase of the coat, the income is diminished by $200 (disregarding the durability of the coat, possibly exceeding the income period). The utility of the income decline is $U(Y) - U(Y - 200)$ which approximately equals the subjective value of the coat, V. After the purchase, the value of the coat appears to be greater than $U(Y + 250) - U(Y - 200)$. With the utility function of Figure 12.1a, this effect cannot be explained. A possible explanation is provided by assuming different value functions for gains and for losses. The assumption made in prospect theory includes a different shape of the *value function* with the following characteristics:[37]

- It is defined over gains and losses with respect to some natural reference point. Changes in the reference point can alter choices.
- It is concave for gains and convex for losses.
- It is steeper for losses than for gains.

A hypothetical value function has been sketched in Figure 12.1b. The purchase of the coat is associated with out-of-pocket costs which are considered as a loss and the value of the purchase price can be inferred from the value function for losses. The sale is associated with opportunity costs which are considered as a gain and the value of the selling price can be inferred from the value function for gains. The result now can be explained by the shape of the value function.

Evidence for the shape of the value function has been found in concave psychophysical functions for gains and convex functions for losses.[38] The exponents of the power functions were on average 0.45 for monetary gains and 0.55 for losses, supporting the relative steepness for losses.

Several phenomena studied in behavioral economics may be explained by using the value function. Next, we will consider the endowment effect, status quo bias, mental accounting and sunk costs.

Conclusion

The value function in prospect theory has been suggested as an alternative to the utility function. The value function is assumed to be concave for gains and convex for losses. Furthermore, losses loom larger than commensurate gains.

12.4. Endowment effect

The behavior of the lady in the situation described in the former section is an example of the so-called *endowment effect*, examples of which are the following:[39]

> "Mr. R bought a case of good wine in the late '50's for about $5 a bottle. A few years later his wine merchant offered to buy the wine back for $100 a bottle. He refused, although he has never paid more than $35 for a bottle of wine."

> "Mr. H mows his own lawn. His neighbor's son would mow it for $8. He wouldn't mow his neighbor's same-sized lawn for $20."[40]

Prospect theory explains the above-mentioned examples as follows. Keeping the wine is preferred to selling for $100 and buying at $35, i.e. the value of the wine exceeds $U(100) - U(-35)$. Likewise, the subjective value of mowing one's own lawn exceeds $U(20) - U(-8)$. This is explained from the steepness of the value function for losses. Thaler (1980) argues that keeping the wine is associated with *opportunity costs*, that is when keeping the wine the opportunity of using $100 is foregone. Saving the opportunity costs is viewed as a gain. In contrast, purchasing a bottle is associated with *out-of-pocket costs*, i.e. a straight loss. Since losses are weighted heavier than gains, Mr. H is not willing to sell his wine.

A policy of some film processing companies is to process and print any photographs, no matter how badly exposed they are. Customers can ask for refunds for any pictures they do not want. The endowment effect helps explain why they are not besieged by refund requests.

Another policy in retailing is the case of a two week trial period with a money back guarantee. At the time of the purchase, the costs are not considered as out-of-pocket costs since the transaction can still be canceled. Two weeks later, however, the endowment effect has been at work and the costs of keeping the article are seen as opportunity costs. This makes the transaction more likely[41] (see also Box 12.1).

When trading-in a car, people do care more about obtaining a high price for their used car than about paying a high price for the new car.[42] This preference is consistent with the endowment effect. Fund raising techniques of non-profit museums in preventing paintings from being purchased by foreigners and leaving the country are based on the endowment effect, since probably less funds would have been raised for acquiring these paintings.[43] The *willingness to accept* the price to prevent the loss of the painting (WTA) usually is much higher than the *willingness to pay* for them (WTP). In a number of different surveys and experiments, the ratio of WTA and WTP varies from 1.4 to 1.6.[44] In a number of market experiments, the median reservation prices of sellers and buyers, expressed by their bids, have a ratio exceeding 1.5.[45]

The endowment effect was also obtained by asking half of a sample of government employees their (marginal) *reservation prices* for increasing their monthly labor time from 160 to 162 hours (WTA).[46] The other half of the sample was asked how much wage reduction they would accept to reduce their labor time from 162 to 160 hours per month (WTP). The ratio of WTA and WTP was 10.8 in the investigation. Further evidence came from questions asked to students, school teachers and bank employees. The difference with the employee sample was, that the two questions were asked to the same sample, albeit with at least three hours in between. It was found that:

— students' reservation prices for changing an express train ticket for a ticket for a slower train (WTA) was higher then the willingness to pay (WTP) for exchanging their normal ticket for an express train ticket in 80% of the cases;

— teachers' reservation prices for a one-hour increase in their monthly labor time (WTA) was higher than the wage reduction accepted for a one-hour reduction of their teaching load (WTP) in 89% of the cases;

— a similar question for bank employees yielded a WTA exceeding the WTP in 91% of the cases.

Conclusion

The endowment effect is considered an anomaly of behavior according to economic theory. Prospect theory explains the effect by using different values for gains and losses, i.e. the pain of giving up an item is assumed larger than the pleasure of acquiring that item. This idea is frequently applied in marketing.

12.5. Mental accounting

The value function[47] has been used in mental arithmetic concerning the combined value of objects or events. Standard economic theory, for example, would predict that obtaining $20 once or $10 twice results in the same amount of satisfaction. This appears not to be the case in practice, however.

Individuals, households and firms are assumed to have explicit and/or implicit accounting systems that are kept separate from each other. Several examples may illustrate this fact (Reprinted by permission of R. Thaler, Mental accounting and consumer choice, Marketing Science, Volume 4, No. 3, Summer 1985, ©1985, The Institute of Management Sciences):

> "Mr. and Mrs. L and Mr. and Mrs. H went on a fishing trip in the northwest and caught some salmon. They packed the fish and sent it home on an airline but the fish were lost in transit. They received $300 from the airline. The couples take the money, go out to dinner and spend $225. They had never spent that much at a restaurant before."[48]

This example violates the principle of *fungibility*. Had the money been obtained by a salary increase of $150 a year for each couple, the extravagant dinner would not have occurred. Now, the extra income has been put in a 'windfall' account, separate from the regular income account.[49]

> "Mr. X is up $50 in a monthly poker game. He has a queen high flush and calls a $10 bet. Mr. Y owns 100 shares of IBM which went up 1/2 today and is even in the poker game. He has a king high flush but he folds. When X wins, Y thinks to himself, "If I had been up $50 I would have called too.""[50]

This example shows that the money won or lost in a poker game is separated from the stocks account. Both Mr. Y and Mr. X could afford a bet of $10 out of a comparable increase in wealth of $50. However, Mr. X put both amounts into the same account, while Mr. Y puts them into different accounts. Each account is assumed to be evaluated separately.

> "Mr. and Mrs. J have saved $15,000 toward their dream vacation home. They hope to buy the home in five years. The money earns 10% in a

money market account. They just bought a new car for $11,000 which they financed with a three-year car loan at 15%."[51]

In this example, actually two separate accounts have been used, probably to be sure that the vacation account remained unaffected by the purchase of the car. This mental accounting appears to be based on a lack of *self-control* in managing the savings account.[52]

"Mr. S admires a $125 cashmere sweater at the department store. He declines to buy it, feeling that it is too extravagant. Later that month he receives the same sweater from his wife for a birthday present. He is very happy. Mr. and Mrs. S have only a joint bank account."[53]

Here, the money for the sweater came from the 'gift' account instead of coming from the 'clothing' account. Contrary to predictions from economic theory, the gift item has been chosen outside the set of normally preferred items.

The examples above show that money values frequently are not cleared within the same mental (or even physical) account. This implies psychological rather than economic mechanisms to evaluate the balance of different accounts. This psychological mechanism has been called *mental arithmetic*.[54] In mental arithmetic, use is made of the value function considered earlier,[55] since different mental accounts might contain debits or credits, being valued as gains and losses, respectively.

The joint value of two outcomes, x and y, evaluated in one account has been denoted by $v(x + y)$. In this case the outcomes are *integrated*. The evaluation of two different accounts with outcomes x and y, respectively, has been denoted by $v(x) + v(y)$. In this case the outcomes are *segregated*. It has to be considered which of the two evaluations produces greater utility. In fact four possibilities exist: both outcomes are positive, both outcomes are negative, mixed outcomes with positive balance and mixed outcomes with negative balance.

Both outcomes are positive

Since the value function is concave, it is assumed that $v(x) + v(y) > v(x+y)$, so segregation is preferred. The moral of this is not to wrap all Christmas presents together.

This assumption has been tested empirically with 87 students who were presented with the following instructions:

"Below you will find four pairs of scenarios. In each case two events occur in Mr. A's life and one event occurs in Mr. B's life. You are asked to judge whether Mr. A or Mr. B is happier. Would most people rather be A or B? If you think the two scenarios are emotionally equivalent, check "no difference". In all cases the events are intended to be financially equivalent."[56]

The first scenario dealt with two positive outcomes:

> "Mr. A was given tickets to lotteries involving the World Series. He won $50 in one lottery and $25 in the other. Mr. B was given a ticket to a single, larger World Series lottery. He won $75. Who was happier?"

Answers: (A) 56, (B) 16, (no difference) 15.[57]

In advertising, segregate gains are used in the presentation of products. Each of a multitude of the product's uses is evaluated separately. In addition, extra bonuses are included, such as "if you call right now".

Both outcomes are negative

Since the value function for losses is convex, it is assumed that $v(-x) + v(-y) < v(-x-y)$, so integration of losses is preferred. An empirical test of this assumption has been conducted by means of the second scenario:

> "Mr. A received a letter from the IRS saying that he made a minor mistake on his tax return and owed $100. He received a similar letter the same day from his state income tax authority saying he owed $50. There were no repercussions from either mistake.
> Mr. B received a letter from the IRS saying that he made a minor arithmetical mistake on his tax return and owed $150. There were no other repercussions from this mistake.
> Who was more upset?"

Answers: (A) 66, (B) 14, (no difference) 7.[58]

Sellers should be aware of the integration effect regarding losses. Additional options to a car or a house are sold easily since their costs are integrated with the high purchase price. Credit cards pool many small losses into one larger loss and in so doing reduce the total value lost.[59] Travelling agencies and hotels make use of the integration effect by charging the total costs of their services, rather than charging each night's stay and each meal separately.

The value function for losses also explains the perception of price differences at different price levels.[60] A $5 difference at a price of $25 is perceived differently from a price difference of $5 at a price of $500. In the former case the value of the price difference is $v(-25) - v(20)$ which is greater than the price difference in the latter case, $v(-500) - v(495)$, because of the convexity of the value function for losses. So mental accounting gives an alternative explanation for the consumer's sensitivity to price differences.

Mixed outcomes with positive balance

Consider the outcome $(x, -y)$ where $x > y$ so there is a net gain and $v(x - y)$ is positive. From the value function, it appears that $v(x) + v(-y) < v(x - y)$, so integration is preferred. An empirical test of this effect has been conducted by the third scenario:

> "Mr. A bought his first New York State lottery ticket and won $100. Also, in a freak accident, he damaged the rug in his apartment and had to pay the landlord $80. Mr. B bought his first New York State lottery ticket and won $20.
>
> Who was happier?"

Answers: (A) 22, (B) 61, (no difference) 4.[61]

It has been noticed that, since the integrated value is positive, the negative value is canceled by the positive one. A trivial application of this effect is in voluntary trade, where the benefits of goods are higher than the costs. This also argues against delayed delivery of goods by the seller and delayed payment by the buyer. A further application is the withdrawal of income taxes and premiums from the payment of the loan, rather than the collection of these separately in the next year. Health insurance payments are also frequently deducted from the payment of the loan.

Mixed outcomes with negative balance

Consider the outcome $(x, -y)$ where $x < y$, a net loss. In this case $v(x) + v(-y) < v(x - y)$ and it cannot be told without more information as to which side of the inequality is greater. If x is small relative to a large outcome y, it is more likely that $v(x) + v(-y) > v(x - y)$ and segregation is preferred. (See Figure 12.2a.) This has been called the '*silver lining*' principle, in which the pain caused by bad news is mitigated by a little bit of pleasure from good news. With x more or less equal to y (but still less), it is more likely that $v(x) + v(-y) < v(x - y)$ and integration is preferred (see Figure 12.2b) as in the mixed case with positive balance. In fact, these two cases melt into each other. The 'silver lining' effect has been tested empirically by means of the fourth scenario:

> "Mr. A's car was damaged in a parking lot. He had to spend $200 to repair the damage. The same day the car was damaged, he won $25 in the office football pool. Mr. B's car was damaged in a parking lot. He had to spend $175 to repair the damage.
>
> Who was more upset?"

Answers: (A) 19, (B) 63, (no difference) 5.[62]

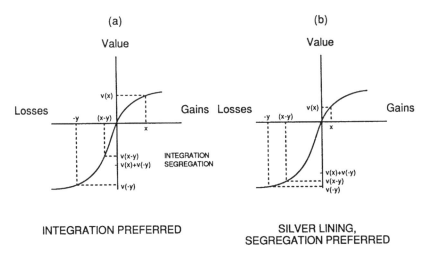

Figure 12.2. Application of the value function to mixed outcomes.

The 'silver lining' effect is used in rebates as a form of price promotion. The rebate generally is worth only a small portion of the purchase price and is used to mitigate the pain of spending. Rebates for small items have the additional feature that not all consumers collect the rebate.

Conclusion

The value function has been applied in mental arithmetic, dealing with decisions taken in different domains of spending and with the most preferred way of being confronted with gains, losses and mixed outcomes. The results appear to be relevant in explaining economic behavior in everyday life and in marketing.

12.6. Status quo bias

The *status quo bias* has been defined as:

"Doing nothing or maintaining one's current or previous position."[63]

Evidence of the status quo bias has been obtained from questionnaires including hypothetical situations.[64] For example, people are told a story in which they have inherited a large sum of money from their great uncle, invested in a particular way (the status quo). They are asked to select one out of four investment opportunities to invest their inheritance (one of which was the status quo). A strong bias toward the status quo alternative was found in general.

A different survey split consumers into several groups, according to the number of electricity outages they had experienced per year.[65] Each group was shown several alternatives, including different frequencies of electricity outages associated with different bills, higher (lower) bills were associated with less (more) outages. In the group, characterized by 3 outages per year, 60.2% preferred the status quo to the alternative combinations; in the group, characterized by 15 outages per year, 58.3% preferred the status quo. Although the reliability of electric currency was quite different in the two groups, both preferred the situation they were accustomed to. Hence, the status quo may also be indicated as a habit effect.

Drivers' preferences for car insurances were investigated in a natural *quasi-experiment*.[66] In New Jersey, the default option of car insurance is coverage, excluding the right to sue, which may be purchase additionally. In Pennsylvania, the default option is coverage including the right to sue, which may be redeemed. In New Jersey, 20% acquired the full right to sue, whereas in Pennsylvania, 75% retained the full right to sue. Thus, the economic impact of the status quo may be considerable.

The status quo bias is related to prospect theory, since giving up the status quo incurs a loss, whereas adopting an alternative constitutes a gain. From the shape of the value function, we know that losses are weighted heavier than gains, resulting in maintaining the status quo relatively often.

Conclusion

The status quo bias may be considered a habit effect insofar as the status quo refers to what is usual or conventional. Regarding new choice alternatives, the status quo refers to the alternative which is *presented* as the status quo.

12.7. Sunk costs

Economic theory implies that historical costs are irrelevant for present decision making and only incremental costs and benefits should be taken into account. In everyday life, however, this implication of economic theory is frequently neglected thus forming another instance of irrational behavior. Two examples of *sunk costs* are the following:

> "A family pays $40 for tickets to a baseball game to be played 60 miles from their home. On the day of the game there is a snowstorm. They decide to go anyway but note in passing that had the tickets been given to them, they would have stayed home."

> "A man joins a tennis club and pays a $300 yearly membership fee. After

two weeks of playing he develops a tennis elbow. He continues to play (in pain) saying "I don't want to waste the $300!""[67]

A possible explanation of the sunk costs effect has been given by means of a mental accounting system.[68] Let the value of the game in the above example be $v(g)$ where $g > 0$ since seeing the game produces pleasure. The value of the payment for the tickets is $v(-40)$, which is evaluated as a loss. Going through the snow produces pain and is denoted by $v(-c)$, the value of the loss function for costs c. With free tickets, it is a matter of indifference to the family whether they stay at home (which equals a zero value) or go to the game, which equals $v(g) + v(-c)$, so $v(g) = -v(-c)$. Going to the game implies $v(g) + v(-c - 40) > v(-40)$, which is explained from the convexity of the loss function. (This is evident from substitution of $-v(-c)$ for $v(g)$, which follows from the indifference relation above.)

The sunk costs effect is related to the effect of *cognitive dissonance*.[69] Upon engaging in behavior associated with costs, attitude changes make the behavior more likely in the future. The sunk costs are held to produce a negative value that has to be compensated by a positive value, produced by the attitude change. Other determinants of the sunk cost effect are social commitment to the investment and the size of the money at stake among other things.[70]

The effect of sunk costs has been illustrated by an experiment in which customers at an all-you-can-eat pizza restaurant were randomly given free lunches. They, in fact, ate less than the control group who paid the $2.50 normal bill. Investors tend to keep their stocks too long when prices are falling, indicating another deviation from economic theory concerning sunk costs.[71] Furthermore, the sunk cost effect has been applied to business investment decision making.[72]

Conclusion

The sunk cost effect is not explained by economic theory although is frequent in reality. Again, the value function explains the effect. An alternative explanation has been given by the theory of cognitive dissonance.

12.8. Self-control

We have considered time preference as a motivation to allocate resources available for consumption toward or away from the present.[73] However, under some circumstances individuals may change their minds and change the allocation. For example, pregnant women who had decided against delivery under anaesthesia were tempted to change their minds when delivery became imminent.[74] This is an example of *time-inconsistent preferences* due to a lack of self-control. Before discussing strategies to enhance self-control, an explanation of this phenomenon will be given.

A shift of the value function may explain time-inconsistent preferences.[75] Similar to a shift of the value function due to the endowment effect,[76] a shift of the reference point may cause the inconsistency. In the example above, long before delivery anaesthesia was evaluated at V_1, considered from reference point 1, which value is not high enough to decide for it. Just before delivery, the reference point has shifted to the right and not having anaesthesia is considered as a loss, considered from reference point 2, which is evaluated at $V_2(-V_2 > V_1$ since the value function is steeper for losses than for gains). This causes the increased temptation to have anaesthesia. After delivery without anaesthesia, the value function will shift to its original position (reference point 1), however and the mother will be happy not having given in to her temporary desire. The same factors affecting the change in reference point causing the endowment effect will operate in causing the time-inconsistent preferences.

The problem of *self-control* has been dealt with in economic problems.[77] A planner and a doer may be distinguished in the human mind.[78] The doer is myopic and completely selfish and tries to maximize utility temporarily. The planner derives utility from the consumption of the doers but is not myopic and maximizes total lifetime utility. This is similar to the idea of a utility function that flip-flops from one preference state (myopic) to the other (long-term).[79] Analogously, desire and willpower may be considered as opposite forces operating on the human mind.[80] The planner has control over the doer by using two main techniques:
— the doer can be given *discretion* by either changing her preferences or her incentives;
— the doer may be *constrained* by imposing rules of behavior.

Discretion

The doer can be given discretion in several ways:
— The doer's preferences can be changed directly. For example, physical exercise may be given intrinsic value. In this case, a selfish myopic doer guarantees the benefits of doers later in time.
— Time binding, i.e. thinking of the positive benefits of delay, may be effective in changing the doer's preferences, too. This seems particularly effective with externally imposed constraints.[81]
— Regret and guilt may be effective in changing the doer's preferences by imposing psychic costs.

– Monitoring of inputs to a saving or dieting plan may be imposed. Calculating the economic costs and keeping track of one's savings or calorie
intake acts as a tax on any behavior which the planner views as deviant.
– Incentives (reinforcements) can be explicitly altered. By taking the drug
Antabuse, alcoholics avoid negative reinforcement by not drinking alcohol.
By putting a large money amount in the dieting club's account, the negative
reinforcement of losing the money is avoided by a fixed weight reduction
before a date set in advance.

Rules

Frequently, people appear to restrict their own behavior in order to protect
themselves against future negative consequences. People save part of their
money to protect themselves against later poverty. People engage in dieting
plans and exercise to have a satisfactory life later. A famous example is from
the Odyssey in which Ulysses had to protect himself against the temptation
of the singing Sirens. He put wax in the ears of his crew and had himself tied
hard and fast to the mast of his ship. The crew was told to tie him even tighter,
should he beg to be released. Ulysses' problem has been interpreted as one
of changing tastes, the solution of which is referred to as *precommitment*.[82]
Several conditions for a definition of precommitment have been stated.[83]
Precommitment is a solution to problems of control over one's changing
preferences. The lack of self-control in credit card users has already been
mentioned.[84] About three-quarters of American credit card users are incurring
high finance charges at any moment in time due to expiration of the grace
period. It is suggested that many users do not intend to borrow on their
credit card, yet find themselves doing so anyway due to lack of self-control.
Anecdotal evidence for precommitment involves consumers who put their
credit cards in trays of water and place them in a freezer in order to prevent
impulsive purchases.

Restrictions may eliminate all doers' discretion. For example, people pay
to go to 'fat farms' which essentially are resorts that promise not to feed their
customers (cf. the Odyssey). Less extreme restrictions might be imposed
which limit the range of doer discretion. For example, the debt ethic is a
norm, putting a ban on borrowing, that is used to limit spending to the
budget constraint. An appeal to higher authority may also be considered a
rule limiting the doer's discretion. A higher authority may be represented by
higher-order principles or a religious doctrine, violations of which would be
in disagreement with one's constellation of beliefs and values.

A weaker rule is to prohibit borrowing except for specific purchases, like
housing and automobiles. A variant of this is a prohibition on dissaving

combined with limits on borrowing. This happens in the case of Mr. and Mrs. J who financed a car and did not use their savings for the vacation house.[85] Voluntary restrictions of this kind have been referred to as *self-imposed constraints*.[86] Rules can be imposed on a specific class of decisions, as in the case of a smoker who buys cigarettes by the pack instead of the carton, thus, hopefully, rationing herself to one pack a day.

Bundling of costs refers to the idea of considering violation of a rule not as an isolated event but rather as a possible series of violations. Bundling could imply that eating an ice-cream is not considered as a 'cost' of 250 calories but as an extra 250 calories a day, with obesity as the inevitable outcome.[87]

Some evidence for the effect of precommitment on saving behavior exists.[88] Consider an individual who is saving a proportion S of an income, Y. Now the individual is given a mandatory pension plan that forces her to save a proportion $P < S$. Economic theory would predict that total savings remain equal. However, the psychic costs involved in the pension plan are lower (the planner has to limit the doer to a smaller extent) and total savings are expected to go up. This would also be the case in Katona's theory of discretionary savings,[89] which says that individuals save a proportion of discretionary income, instead of total income. If this proportion equals S, the pension plan increases savings by $(1 - S)PY$. In in each case total savings were found to be higher with the pension than without the pension.[90]

For reasons of self-control, an individual, earning $12,000 per year in 12 monthly instalments of $1,000, will save less than an (identical) individual, who receives a salary of $10,000 per year paid in monthly instalments plus a guaranteed bonus of $2,000 paid in March each year.[91]

The marginal propensity to consume from different mental accounts has been studied.[92] Three main accounts are distinguished: current spendable income, current assets and future income. The temptation to spend is highest in the current income account, followed by temptation to spend from the current assets account and then from the future income.

It is assumed that savings plans including pension payments, mortgage payments etcetera, are based on regular income. With a lower regular income, these payments will be executed and yet the individual will prefer not to borrow or dissave (because of the debt ethic). The bonus of $2,000 will be used for savings, especially through the purchase of durable goods.

Some evidence for this effect comes from Japan, where the saving rate is high, combined with common bonus schemes. A frequently used technique of self-control is used by taxpayers who claim too few exemptions in order to assure a tax refund. It has been noticed that some self-deception is necessary in these self-control techniques but doers apparently can easily be deceived.[93] Self-deception commonly occurs in setting one's watch a few minutes ahead

Table 12.1. Strategies in maintaining self-control.

Reducing desire	Increasing willpower
Avoidance	Discretion
Postponement	Preference change
Distraction	Time binding
Substitution	Regret, guilt
	Monitoring, cost assessment
	Altering incentives
	Rules
	Precommitment
	Self-imposed constraints
	Norms, authority
	Bundling of costs

in order to get to places on time.

So far, we have concentrated on the control of the planner over the doer. In addition, several strategies of desire reduction are considered:[94]
- avoidance, which is simply an escape from tempting situations;
- postponement of a decision, e.g. by first consulting one's partner;
- distraction, e.g. by doing something else;
- substitution, e.g. by consuming light beer instead of malt beer.

A summary of strategies involved in maintaining self-control is shown in Table 12.1.

Conclusion

A theory of self-control has been postulated to deal with precommitments in economic behavior. A dual economic personality is assumed comprising a doer and a planner. The doer acts in the interest of short-run utility (myopic) whereas the planner maximizes long-term utility. Precommitment is considered a restriction of the doer imposed by the planner. From the outside this is observed as a self-imposed constraint.

Summary

Frequent economic assumptions are perfect information, stable preferences and a representative consumer. Such assumptions can imply that the effects of imperfect information, instability and heterogeneity of preferences can be neglected, that the theory can be applied only to a specific domain or that the theory is considered an approximation to reality awaiting further improvement. The economic assumption of rationality refers to the assumption that economic agents make the best choice given the restrictions in spite of the process of decision making. An assumption regarding process rationality implies that decision making proceeds in the best possible way in spite of the outcomes achieved. Ideally, a theory should explain both the process and the outcomes of decision making.

Economic theory is based on several axioms regarding preferences that are frequently violated in practice. A solution commonly applied in empirical research is to make preferences stochastic. This may leave the axioms of completeness and transitivity indistinguishable from each other, however. The axiom of greed is violated because different states of motivation produce different effective reinforcers.

Several anomalies in economic behavior are difficult to explain by means of the usual utility functions. A value function has been proposed in prospect theory that is concave for gains and convex for losses. In addition, it is steeper for losses than for gains. Furthermore, what is considered a gain or a loss depends on the choice of a reference point. The value function explains the endowment effect, the status quo bias and the sunk cost effect and plays an important part in mental accounting.

The endowment effect refers to the relatively high valuation of a loss as compared with a commensurate gain. This is explained by the shape of the value function in prospect theory. In a sense, the status quo bias is a variant of the endowment effect, since people are unwilling to give up a special endowment: the status quo. The sunk cost effect is explained too by the relative steepness of the value function for losses. Several psychological factors also contribute to this effect.

Mental accounting refers to the psychological process of evaluating gains and losses that are segregated or integrated. It appears from the application of the value function that segregation of two gains is preferred over integration whereas integration of two losses is preferred over segregation. In case of a gain that is greater than a loss, integration is preferred. If the loss is much greater than the gain, segregation is preferred (silver lining). If the loss is slightly greater than the gain, integration is preferred.

Precommitment refers to self-imposed constraints on behavior. This can be explained by assuming a dual personality including a planner and a doer. The planner maximizes long-term utility, whereas the planner deals with utility in the short run. The doer can be given discretion under several conditions. Elimination of doer's discretion is accomplished by imposing rules for the doer's behavior. The identification of a planner and a doer might be a problem in empirical research.

BOX 12.1

A THOUGHT EXPERIMENT ON THE ENDOWMENT EFFECT

The following exercise has been taken from Thaler.[95]

"Suppose your neighbors are going to have a garage sale. They offer to sell any of your household goods for you at one half of the original purchase price. You must only tell them which goods to sell and they will take care of everything else, including returning any unsold items. Try to imagine which goods you would decide to sell and which goods you would decide to keep. Write down five items you are willing to sell and five items that you would prefer to keep.

Now imagine that some of the goods you decided to keep are stolen and that your insurance will pay you half of the original price. If you could also replace them at half price how many would you replace? (Assume identical quantity.)

Many people say that there would be some items which they would not sell in the first case and wouldn't buy in the second case, even though transaction costs have been made very low in this example."[96]

A class-room experiment (conducted by the author at Erasmus University, Rotterdam, The Netherlands with about 250 undergraduate students) in which each student imagined only one item to sell or to keep, respectively, yielded a large majority of students who would not sell at a fancy fair and would not buy a similar item at half price. This also confirms the endowment effect to some extent.

Notes

[1] Lea et al. 1987, p. 103.
[2] MacFadyen 1986.
[3] Simon 1978.
[4] See Section 7.3.
[5] See Chapter 2.
[6] See Chapter 7.
[7] See Chapter 2.
[8] See Chapter 4.
[9] See Chapter 8.

[10] See Chapter 9.

[11] See Chapter 11.

[12] See Chapter 9.

[13] See Chapter 3.

[14] Deaton and Muellbauer 1980.

[15] See Chapter 5.

[16] See Chapter 9.

[17] See Chapters 8 and 10.

[18] Friedman 1953.

[19] Musgrave 1981.

[20] See Chapter 8.

[21] Musgrave 1981.

[22] See, for example, Schoemaker 1982.

[23] See Lea et al. 1987.

[24] See Section 12.3.

[25] Lea et al. (1987).

[26] Reinforcers, see Chapter 5.

[27] Mazur 1975.

[28] Premack 1965, 1971.

[29] Scitovsky 1976.

[30] Lea et al. 1987, pp. 110–111.

[31] See Section 3.5.

[32] Becker 1965.

[33] May 1954.

[34] Davis 1958.

[35] Deaton and Muellbauer 1980.

[36] Kahneman and Tversky 1979.

[37] Thaler 1980.

[38] Galanter 1990.

[39] This endowment effect should not be confused with the endowment effect considered in Section 10.1.

[40] Thaler 1980, p. 43.

[41] Thaler 1980.

[42] Purohit 1995.

[43] Frey and Eichenberger 1994.

[44] Kahneman et al. 1990.

[45] Tietz 1992, Kahneman et al. 1990.

[46] Ortona and Scacciati 1992.

[47] See Section 12.3.

[48] Thaler 1985, p. 199.

[49] See also Section 12.8.

[50] Thaler 1985, p.199.

[51] Thaler 1985, p. 199.

[52] See also Section 12.6.

[53] Thaler 1985, p. 199.

[54] Thaler 1985.

[55] See Section 12.3.

[56] Thaler 1985, p. 202.

[57] Thaler 1985, p. 203.

[58] Thaler 1985, p. 203.
[59] See Ausubel 1991.
[60] See Section 4.3.
[61] Thaler 1985, p. 204.
[62] Thaler 1985, p. 204.
[63] Samuelson and Zeckhauser 1988, p. 8.
[64] Samuelson and Zeckhauser 1988.
[65] Hartman et al. 1991.
[66] Johnson et al. 1993.
[67] Thaler 1980, p. 47.
[68] See Section 12.4.
[69] See Section 11.2.
[70] Antonides 1995.
[71] Shefrin and Statman 1985.
[72] Arkes and Blumer 1985 and Statman and Caldwell 1987.
[73] See Section 3.6.
[74] Christensen-Szalanski 1984, Jungermann 1988.
[75] Hoch and Loewenstein 1991.
[76] See Section 12.3.
[77] Thaler 1980 and Hoch and Loewenstein 1991.
[78] Thaler 1980.
[79] Winston 1980.
[80] Hoch and Loewenstein 1991.
[81] Hoch and Loewenstein 1991.
[82] Strotz 1955/1956.
[83] Elster 1979.
[84] Ausubel 1991.
[85] See Section 12.4.
[86] See Section 6.3.
[87] Hoch and Loewenstein 1991.
[88] Thaler 1980.
[89] Katona 1975, see Section 8.2.
[90] Cagan 1965, Katona 1965 and Munnell 1974.
[91] Thaler 1980.
[92] Shefrin and Thaler 1988.
[93] Thaler 1980.
[94] Hoch and Loewenstein 1991.
[95] Thaler 1980.
[96] Thaler 1980, p. 46.

CHAPTER 13

CHOICE UNDER UNCERTAINTY

13.1. Expected utility

In the preceding chapter, rationality regarding sure prospects has been discussed. Frequently, outcomes of behavior and states of the world are uncertain. In this case, decision making is assumed to imply the evaluation of possible outcomes, taking into account the probability of their realization. This evaluation may take place in different ways. Facing uncertain outcomes, economic theory has predicted choice from the theory of expected utility, several variants of which are distinguished.[1] A generalized version of the expected utility model is that people maximize

$$\sum_{i=1}^{n} F(p_i)U(x_i)$$

where n equals the number of possible outcomes, p the objective probability of an outcome (the sum of n probabilities equals one) and x a vector of outcome elements. The outcomes are evaluated according to a value function, $U(\cdot)$ and the objective probabilities are weighted by a function $F(\cdot)$. In the sequel, for ease of presentation a prospect to be evaluated will often consist of only two outcomes, so n equals 2.

Formally, a distinction between uncertainty and risk should be made. *Risk* refers to situations where probabilities are known or at least knowable whereas *uncertainty* refers to situations where probabilities are unknown or even cannot be defined.[2] The general model of expected utility above allows for subjective probabilities that can be based either on known objective probabilities (i.e. perceived probabilities) or on estimated probabilities of uncertain situations. In this chapter, the function $F(p)$ refers either to perceived risk or to estimated probability.

The simplest variant of the model is the expected monetary value (EV), implying the objective values of the outcomes to be weighted by their respective objective probabilities, i.e. $\Sigma p_i x_i$. Let the outcome of tossing a coin be a gain of $1 for heads and a loss of $1 for tails. In this case, the outcomes are

+1 and −1 and the objective probabilities are 0.5 for each outcome. The EV model assumes an *expected value* of zero in this case, which equals the value of not playing the game. If the outcomes of the game had been +10, 000 and −10, 000 respectively, the expected value would still have been zero, although most people would prefer not to play this game. From this example, it will be clear that the EV model does not correctly explain preferences. The individual willingness to gamble may vary across people, however. The sensation seeking scale may be related to this type of behavior.[3]

The EV model implies that the value of an outcome increases proportionally to an increase in its objective size, e.g. $20 is valued twice as high as $10. In solving the *St. Petersburg paradox* (see Box 13.1), a marginally decreasing utility function has been assumed, such that value increments are less than proportional to increasing objective outcomes.[4] The theory of *expected utility* assumes that a prospect is evaluated such that the utilities of the outcomes are weighted by their respective objective probabilities. In this case, the general function for two outcomes, x and y and a probability p, associated with the occurrence of x, is: $pU(x) + (1-p)U(y)$. Since the utility function is assumed to be concave, $U\{px + (1-p)y\} > pU(x) + (1-p)U(y)$, for outcomes x and y and probability p. (See Figure 13.1.) From this inequality, it follows directly that not playing the coin tossing game is preferred, since the utility of zero (not playing) is greater than the expected utility of playing. The theory of expected utility is assumed to account more adequately for the preferences regarding uncertain prospects than expected value theory.

Risk aversion bears implications for insurance behavior. The monetary expected value $rx^0 + (1-r)x^1$ in Figure 13.1 is evaluated higher than would be expected on the basis of a linear (or convex) utility function. This implies that people are willing to pay more than the difference between x and the monetary expected value to avoid the risk of losing $(x^1 - x^0)$. Obviously, this phenomenon is the basis for the insurance market.

The concavity of the utility function implies that the utility of a sure prospect equal to the expected value of a gamble is greater than the utility of the gamble. It is said that the concavity of the utility function is equivalent to risk aversion.

Another characteristic of expected utility theory is the evaluation of outcomes as final states. The final states include the assets held before the gambling decision and the gains and losses from the gamble. For example, with assets (wealth) w, the utilities of the outcomes in the tossing game are $U(w)$ for not playing the game, $U(w + 1)$ for heads and $U(w - 1)$ for tails.

The assumptions of expected utility theory have been challenged in a series of experiments using stated preferences for lotteries.[5] The main issues in this research are subjective probabilities involved in a gamble (*certainty effect*,

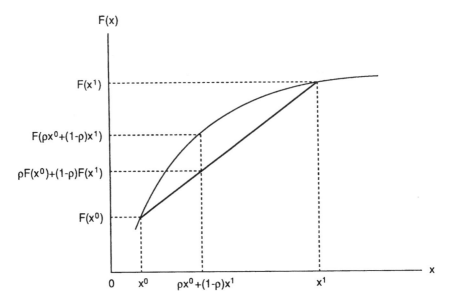

Figure 13.1. A concave function of a variable. From Odink, J.G. and J.L. Schoorl, 1984. Inleiding tot de micro-economie. Groningen: Wolters Noordhof.

see Section 13.2), risk seeking for unfavorable prospects (*reflection effect*, see Section 13.3) and the evaluation of outcomes in relation to different points of reference (*framing effect*, see Section 13.4). Cognitive simplification of risky choice will be considered in the Section 13.5.

Conclusion

Several specific models can be derived from the general version of the expected utility model. Objective probabilities and outcomes yield the expected value model. Objective probabilities with utilities of outcomes yield the expected utility model. A concave utility function in this model accounts for risk aversion. The expected utility model typically deals with final outcomes (i.e. with zero as the reference point).

13.2. The certainty effect

The certainty effect refers to the tendency to overweight outcomes that are considered certain, relative to outcomes which are merely probable. In the following, let (x, p) denote a prospect in which an outcome x will occur with a probability p. The prospect (x) denotes a sure outcome x. A number of subjects are asked to state their preference for prospect A or B:

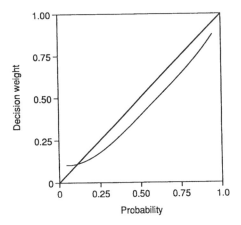

Figure 13.2. A weighting function of probabilities. From "The Psychology of Preferences," by Daniel Kahneman and Amos Tversky. Copyright ©1982 by Scientific American, Inc. All rights reserved.

Problem 1	Answers
A: (4,000, 0.80)	20%
B: (3,000)	80%[6]

Although the expected value of prospect A is greater than that of B, the sure prospect is preferred by most respondents. Since the answers differ to some extent, the risk aversion effect is not as strong for each respondent. Now consider the following problem:

Problem 2	Answers
C: (4,000, 0.20)	65%
D: (3,000, 0.25)	35%[7]

Both C and D imply a certain degree of risk. According to expected utility theory, the modal answer to the first problem implies $U(3,000)/U(4,000) > 0.80$ (because $U(3,000) \times 1.0 > U(4,000) \times 0.8$), while in the second problem the inequality is reversed. Apparently, reducing the probability of winning from 1.0 to 0.25 (respectively in B and D) has a greater effect than the reduction from 0.80 to 0.20 (respectively in A and C). This has been attributed to the certainty effect, which has been confirmed in a number of alternative problems as well.

  A solution to this apparent inconsistency of stated preferences is the assumption of a weighting function $F(\cdot)$ of probabilities. The weighting function in Figure 13.2 was derived from a number of different lottery problems. With respect to the above inconsistency, it appears from inspection of the weighting function that $F(0.20)/F(0.25) > F(0.80)/F(1.0)$. It is assumed that $F(0.0) = 0.0$ and $F(1.0) = 1.0$, so it appears from the shape of the weighting function that it changes dramatically near its two end points. These changes contribute to the certainty effect.

The certainty effect has been found in a number of alternative problems, including non-monetary outcomes. Consider the following example:

Problem 3		*Answers*
A:	50% chance to win a three-week tour of England, France and Italy	22%
B:	A one-week tour of England, with certainty	78%[8]

The results indicate risk aversion with non-monetary outcomes. Next, consider a lottery with two uncertain outcomes:

Problem 4		*Answers*
C:	5% chance to win a three-week tour of England, France and Italy	67%
D:	10% chance to win a one-week tour of England	33%[9]

As in the example with monetary outcomes, the weighting function might explain the certainty effect here. In the absence of a sure outcome, the effect of the weighting function is prominent under some conditions. Consider the following problem:

Problem 5		*Answers*
A:	(6,000, 0.45)	14%
B:	(3,000, 0.90)	86%[10]

Although B is not a sure outcome in this case, it appears to be preferred by most of the subjects. Now consider a prospect with low probabilities:

Problem 6   *Answers*
C: $(6{,}000, 0.001)$ 73%
D: $(3{,}000, 0.002)$ 27%[11]

Although the ratios of the probabilities are equal in these two prospects, the preference change is attributed to the *possibility* of winning in the second prospect. Alternatively, one might state that the small probabilities are below the absolute threshold of sensation. In a situation where winning is possible but not probable, most people choose the prospect that offers the larger gain.

A test of weighted probability

The assumption of a weighting function of probabilities has been examined by means of survey data concerning an income gamble. The following survey question was presented to about 400 main breadwinners in Dutch households (the average reported gains are shown in the column "Answers"):

> "Somebody proposes a game to you. Chances on winning and losing are even. If you lose, your net family income falls by 5%. If you win, it increases. What increase is equivalent to a 5% loss in order that you will accept the game?"

		Answers
	A loss of 5%	A gain of 13%
Similarly:	A loss of 10%	A gain of 23%
Similarly:	A loss of 20%	A gain of 37%
Similarly:	A loss of 30%	A gain of 53%[12]

The welfare function of income[13] has been employed to obtain the utility of incomes in the four states of gains and losses.[14] The survey question implies four instances in which the individual is indifferent to the current sure income Y and a gamble of the form $\{(1 - q)Y, 0.5; (1 + r)Y, 0.5)\}$, with q the percentage in the question and r the percentage stated in the answer. The utility of each prospect is found by applying the generalized version of the expected utility model.[15] Indifference between the gamble and the sure prospect implies:

$$F(0.5)U\{(1 - q_j)Y\} + F(0.5)U\{(1 + r_j)Y\} = U(Y)$$

for each question j. Application of the indifference relation to the four questions yields an estimate of $F(0.5)$ for each individual. With the lognormal utility function of income, the average estimate is 0.472 (standard deviation of the mean equals 0.001) and 0.447 (0.002) if a log-linear utility function is employed. As a conclusion, it appears that the weighting function corresponding to a probability of 0.5 is significantly less than this value. This is in agreement with the shape of the weighting function in Figure 13.2.

Conclusion

The certainty effect can be explained by a weighting function of probabilities. Typically, the weighted value of small probabilities is higher than their objective value. The weighted value of intermediate probabilities is lower than their objective value. This applies both to numerical and non-numerical outcomes. A test of weighted probability has been conducted by means of the estimated empirical welfare function of income. The result of this test is according to prospect theory.

13.3. The reflection effect

Section 13.2 dealt with positive prospects, i.e. prospects that involve no losses. Problems 1, 2, 5 and 6 above have been presented with reversed signs of the outcomes, so gains have been replaced by losses of the same size. Prospects with a negative outcome x are denoted by $(-x, p)$. A comparison of the original with the reverse problems is presented in Table 13.1. It appears that in each problem the preference between negative prospects is the mirror image of the preference between positive prospects. Thus, the reflection of prospects around 0 reverses the preference order. This has been labeled the reflection effect.

The results regarding problem 1 in Table 13.1 imply that the reflection effect changes risk aversion in the positive domain into *risk seeking* in the negative domain. Risk seeking for losses implies that a gamble is preferred to a sure loss, even if its expected value is less than the certain outcome. As in the positive domain, the certainty effect is evident from problems 1 and 2 in the negative domain. In the negative domain, the certainty effect leads to a risk seeking preference for a loss that is merely probable over a smaller loss that is certain. The same psychological principle, the overweighting of certainty, favors risk aversion in the domain of gains and risk seeking in the domain of losses.

The model of the reflection effect includes the value function.[16] The convexity of the value function for losses accounts for the risk seeking in the domain of negative prospects.

With the coin tossing game, mentioned in Section 13.1, it has been observed that the aversion to playing this game increases with the size of

Table 13.1. Preferences between positive and negative prospects.

Positive prospects		Negative prospects	
Problem	*Answers*	*Problem*	*Answers*
1 (4,000, 0.80)	20%	(–4,000, 0.80)	92%
(3,000)	80%	(–3,000)	8%
2 (4,000, 0.20)	65%	(–4,000, 0.20)	42%
(3,000, 0.25)	35%	(–3,000, 0.25)	58%
5 (3,000, 0.90)	86%	(–3,000, 0.90)	8%
(6,000, 0.45)	14%	(–6,000, 0.45)	92%
6 (3,000, 0.002)	27%	(–3,000, 0.002)	70%
(6,000, 0.001)	73%	(–6,000, 0.001)	30%

From Kahneman and Tversky (1979, p. 268).

the stake. That is, if $x > y \geq 0$, then $(y, 0.50; -y, 0.50)$ is preferred to $(x, 0.50; -x, 0.50)$. With $v(\cdot)$ being the value of the function for a particular outcome, there holds:

$$v(y) + v(-y) > v(x) + v(-x) \quad \text{and} \quad v(-y) - v(-x) > v(x) - v(y)$$

Setting $y = 0$ yields $v(x) < -v(-x)$, so the value of a gain is smaller than the value of a loss with the same size. Letting y approach x, the second part of the above inequality can be stated in differential form: $v'(x) < v'(-x)$, with v' the first derivative of v. This shows that the value function for losses is convex and steeper than the value function for gains.

Conclusion

The reflection effect in risky prospects can be explained by means of the value function which is concave for gains and convex for losses. Hence, risk aversion applies to gains and risk seeking applies to losses. In addition, as in sure prospects, it appears that the value function is steeper for losses than for gains.

13.4. The framing effect

The previous sections dealt with gains and losses relative to the status quo or one's current assets. However, the interpretation of an outcome depends on the choice of a *reference point*. For instance, an unexpected tax withdrawal from a monthly pay check is experienced as a loss, not as a reduced gain. A shift in the reference point can easily be induced by altering the description of outcomes. The preference reversals in these cases are called framing effects. Framing effects arise when the same objective alternatives are evaluated in relation to different points of reference. The reference point can be considered a perceptual standard[17] in the evaluation of a prospect.

A well-known example of framing is the Asian disease problem presented to a large number of physicians:

Problem 7

"Imagine that the U.S. is preparing for the outbreak of a rare Asian disease, which is expected to kill 600 people. Two alternative programs to combat the disease have been proposed. Assume that the exact scientific estimates of the consequences of the programs are as follows:

If Program *A* is adopted, 200 people will be saved.
If Program *B* is adopted, there is a one-third probability that 600 people will be saved and a two-thirds probability that no people will be saved.
Which of the two programs would you favor?"[18]

With this formulation of the problem, 72% of the subjects stated a risk-averse preference for Program *A* over Program *B*. A second group of subjects were presented with the same problem but a different formulation of the programs:

Problem 8

"If Program *C* is adopted, 400 people will die.
If Program *D* is adopted, there is a one-third probability that nobody will die and a two-thirds probability that 600 people will die."[19]

With this formulation of the problem, 78% of the subjects stated a risk-seeking preference for Program *D* over Program *C*. The two versions of the problem describe identical outcomes, however, in problem 7 the death of 600 people is the normal reference point and the outcomes are evaluated as gains, whereas in problem 8 no deaths is the normal reference point and the outcomes are evaluated in terms of lives lost. (See Figure 13.3.) Because of the *S*-shaped value function and the overweighting of certainty, the two frames elicit different preferences.

The Asian disease problem has been stated in terms of employees laid off or saved in case plants need to be closed and the vice-president has to explore alternative ways to avoid this crisis.[20] This shows the relevance of the framing concept to organizational behavior.

Two issues regarding the framing effect are questioned here: the generalizability and the stability of the effect. The framing effect has been examined with a number of choice problems in real life, e.g. loss of human lives in a nuclear and a chemical waste accident, loss of time in boring lectures, loss of time in traveling, loss of dairy cows and seals.[21] In general, the results show

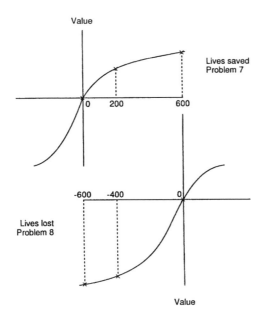

Figure 13.3. Shift of the reference point in the Asian disease problem.

the reflection effect, however less pronounced than in the case of the Asian disease problem. In problems of everyday life (loss of time, jobs, etcetera) the results fail to confirm the risk-seeking tendency in the negative domain.

The perceived importance of the problem appears to affect the risk attitude. Two samples of Dorset farmers responded to 'Asian disease' variants involving their dairy cattle, one version with and one without insurance cover. The perceived importance was assumed to be lower with the insurance cover. The choice of a certain loss was 53% with insurance cover and 38% without it.

Two student samples responded to problems concerning the loss of human lives in a nuclear disaster and the loss of seals in case of a contagious disease. This resulted in 22% and 47% of preferred certain losses, respectively (51% and 70% of preferred certain gains, respectively). Obviously, human lives are perceived as more important than seals.

Irrespective of the way the problem is framed, respondents are more risk-averse if the problem is less important. This suggests different value functions for different decision domains.

The framing effect has been shown by presenting differently framed questions to different samples of individuals. The stability of the effect has been studied using different frames of the same problem presented to the same subjects.[22] A sample of 60 students were asked to state their preference

Table 13.2. Three different frames of the same gamble.

Positive	Negative	Mixed
15% Chance of winning $150, $20 investment	Amount to be won: $150, 85% chance of losing, $20 investment	15% Chance of winning $150, 85% chance of losing, $20 investment

From Levin et al. (1987, p. 45).

(yes/no) for investment of $20 to obtain 15% chance of winning $150. Table 13.2 contains the framing conditions.

Eighteen different gambles were constructed by varying the amount of investment ($10 and $20), the probability of winning (5%, 10% and 15%) and the amount to be won ($100, $150 and $200). One-third of the subjects were presented with the positively framed gambles first, one-third with the negative gambles and one-third with the mixed gambles. After working through the 18 gambles in the first condition, each subject also answered the problems in the two other conditions.

The framing effects were considered in the usual way by comparing the answers between subjects in the condition presented first. The reflection effect was evident with the effect of the mixed condition falling in between the effects of the two other conditions.

The stability of the framing effect has been considered by within-subject comparisons of the condition presented first with the other conditions. The average responses to the positive problems were nearly the same as the average responses to the negative problems, whichever was presented first. It is concluded that this demonstrates the strength and the persistence of the framing effect. Once information is presented in a particular frame, it is difficult to reverse preferences by presenting the same information differently.

Conclusion

The shape of the value function is different above and below the reference point. The location of the reference point is influenced by the framing of a prospect, leading to different results with different contexts of a problem. Although the framing effect is evident with two different groups of subjects, an experiment using the same group of subjects indicates that the reference point associated with the first presented frame is still used in a subsequent different framing of the problem.

13.5. Simplification in risky choice

Although induced changes in the point of reference are a powerful instrument to influence preferences, these attempts fail under some conditions. One of these conditions is the possibility of simplifying the choice problem. This includes satisficing behavior.[23]

The isolation effect

A cognitive simplification of particular games will alter the outcome preferences.[24] Consider the following game in which the answers had been given before the game started:

Problem 9
First stage:
75% chance to end the game without winning anything;
25% chance to reach the second stage.

Second stage:	*Answers*
(4,000, 0.80)	22%
(3,000)	78%[25]

The preferences for the outcomes closely resemble those of problem 1, which is exactly the second stage gamble. It appears that people ignore the first stage of the problem, which reduces the expected outcomes of the second stage to 25%. Stated in final outcomes, the game is (3,000, 0.25) and (4,000, 0.20), which exactly equals problem 2. It is said that the gamble in the second stage has been isolated from the first stage. The effect of this is that the event 'not winning 3,000' is included in the event 'not winning 4,000', whereas these events are independent in terms of final outcomes. Using the terminology of Chapter 12, the two stages of the game are put into different mental accounts. A real life situation in which this *isolation effect* is likely is the investment in a risky venture (stage 1). If the venture fails, the investment is lost. If the venture succeeds, one can choose between a fixed return and a percentage of earnings (stage 2). The isolation effect predicts that the choice of fixed returns is more likely in this case.

A second example of the isolation effect consists of the following problems:

Problem 10
In addition to whatever you own, you have been given 1,000.
You are now asked to choose between:

Answers

A: (1,000, 0.50)   16%
B: (500)   84%[26]

Problem 11

In addition to whatever you own, you have been given 2,000.
You are now asked to choose between:

Answers

C: (−1,000, 0.50)   69%
D: (−500)   31%[27]

The choice between A and B and between C and D appears to be isolated from the bonus that has been given before the start of the game. Evaluation of the problems with the bonuses integrated with the prospects amounts to equal final expected outcomes: $A = C = (1,000, 0.50)$ and $B = D = (1,500)$.

It is of interest to consider the situation of a hypothetical loss before presenting a subject with the prospect.[28] In this case, the sunk cost effect might appear.[29] If a loss of 1,000 is presented before the prospect in Problem 10, alternative A might be preferred because it provides the opportunity of avoiding the loss. This situation is evident in losing projects of many firms.[30] After termination of these projects, returns on the stock of the terminating companies frequently show a marked increase. Investors, too frequently keep their losing stocks too long.[31] This might also be explained from the sunk cost effect. It seems that the isolation effect does not appear in the case of sunk costs.

Aspiration level

The reference point appears to be related to the level of aspiration in some sense. In risky decisions regarding investments, for example, the aspiration level may be a target return level.[32] In this case, failures to obtain these returns will be considered losses. Similarly, return may be related to above target probabilities and consequences, in which case returns will be considered gains.

Decomposition of the choice problem

The Fishbein model of attitude[33] includes cognitive beliefs concerning the probability that an object possesses some attribute. The weight components in this attitude model are similar to the utility level provided by the attribute. In this sense, the Fishbein model is an expected utility model which assumes the processing of information regarding all relevant attributes. In Chapter 7, alternative non-compensatory models have been considered.

Under several conditions, not all aspects of the choice problem will be taken into account. Investment decisions are often eliminated from consideration because the probability of ruin exceeds some critical level.[34] Here, a conjunctive rejection rule might be in effect.

Individuals tend to compare probabilities first.[35] If the difference is sufficiently large, a choice is made on this basis alone. If not, dollar dimensions are considered. This behavior might result from a lexicographic choice rule. Simplified decision rules are assumed to be used more frequently in complex choice problems.

A striking example of the neglect of small probabilities is given with regard to insurance behavior.[36] Subjects in a management game were presented with five insurances with a constant premium of $500. Each of the insurances covered the same expected loss of $495. However, the probabilities associated with the loss events were different: 0.002, 0.01, 0.05, 0.10 and 0.25, respectively (the sizes of the losses varied accordingly). The fractions of subjects choosing insurance were 33%, 45%, 52%, 49% and 73%, respectively. It appeared that low probabilities tended to be ignored, despite the severity of the loss in these cases. This result was used to explain the non-use of seat belts, since the probability of an accident is extremely low and consequently will be ignored.[37] Analogous to the absolute threshold for physical stimuli,[38] it seems as if there exists an absolute threshold for probabilities, too.

Heuristics

The heuristics considered in Chapter 7 may be used in the evaluation of choice problems under uncertainty. In judging the probability of a particular outcome, the heuristics of representativeness and availability may be applied. These heuristics might affect the weighting function of probabilities.[39]

Conclusion

The simplification of risky prospects includes the isolation of problem parts, the use of an aspiration level as a reference point, the reliance on probabilities only (neglect of the outcomes) and the use of cognitive heuristics in assessing probabilities.

Summary

The generalized expected utility model contains a class of models including the expected value model, the expected utility model and prospect theory.

The expected value model does not account for risk aversion. The expected utility model deals with risk aversion since the utility function is concave. The expected utility model is based on utilities of final outcomes instead of gains and losses with regard to a certain reference point.

Prospect theory explains several effects, not explained by the expected utility model: the certainty effect, the reflection effect and the framing effect. This is accomplished by the assumption of a value function as dealt with in Chapter 12 (explaining the reflection effect and the framing effect) and a weighting function of probabilities (explaining the certainty effect). Although the framing effect can be shown with different groups of subjects, using the same group of subjects with different frames indicates that the first presented frame is persistent in judgments made with respect to subsequent frames.

Risky choice can be simplified in different ways. The isolation effect states that problems consisting of different parts are split. The preferred choice may be based on an isolated part of the problem.

Aspiration levels in risky decision making may serve as reference points of the value function. According to whether outcomes are above or below the reference point, outcomes are considered as gains or losses.

The choice problem may be simplified by only considering the probabilities associated with different prospects and neglecting the outcomes. This may occur, for instance, if the probabilities are very different. Finally, cognitive heuristics may be applied to the weighting of probabilities.

BOX 13.1

THE ST. PETERSBURG PARADOX

The *St. Petersburg paradox* concerns a gamble that has been considered by Bernoulli in a scientific journal published in St. Petersburg.[40] The game proceeds as follows:

A fair coin is tossed until it falls heads. If this occurs on the first trial, 2 ducats is paid. If it is on the second trial, 4 ducats is paid, on the third 8 ducats and so on with $16, 32, 64, \ldots$ In general, 2^n ducats will be paid if heads falls on the n-th trial. How much is this game worth?

Given the right to play the game, many people are willing to sell this right for less than 20 ducats. Mathematically, however, it can be shown that its expected value is infinite:

$$EV = \sum_{n=1}^{\infty} p^n 2^n = \sum_{n=1}^{\infty} (0.5)^n 2^n = 1 + 1 + 1 + \cdots = \infty$$

These facts constitute the paradox. Why is an infinite expected payoff judged to be worth less than 20 ducats?

Bernoulli suggested that the evaluation of the game was based on expected utility instead of expected value. If utility were a negatively accelerated function function of value, each equal monetary increase of fortune would give decreasing satisfaction to the player of the game. For example, with a logarithmic utility function of the payoffs, i.e. $U(2^n) = \ln(2^n)$, the game's utility is $2 \ln 2$ (by the same procedure applied in Note 1), which is finite indeed. A number of possible explanations for the paradox have been offered.[41]

The assumption of expected utility may solve the St. Petersburg paradox but modified paradoxes can be created based on the utility function assumed. In the above example, a new game can be devised with payoffs:

$$V = 2^{2^n} \quad and\ utility \quad U = \log_2 V = 2^n$$

The expected value of the new game is:

$$EV = \sum_{n=1}^{\infty} p^n 2^{2^n} = \sum_{n=1}^{\infty} (0.5)^n 2^{2^n} = 2 + 2 + 2 + \cdots = \infty$$

The expected utility of the game with the modified payoffs is: $(0.5)2 + (0.5)^2 2^2 + (0.5)^3 2^3 + \cdots = 1 + 1 + 1 + \cdots = \infty$ and a new paradox is there, although its value will be judged somewhat higher than in the standard game.[42]

The paradox may be solved in a different way.[43] An information processing heuristic has been assumed, since the computation of expected values is considered not realistic. The assumed heuristic involves computation of the expected number of trials first and the payoff on this trial in the second place. The expected number of trials m is:[1]

$$m = \sum_{n=1}^{\infty} n(0.5)^n = 2$$

So the expected return given by the heuristic is $2^m = 4$ ducats, which is considerably less than infinity. It is not assumed that people sum the series

---

[1] m is the mathematical expectation of a random variable X with probability density function $(0.5)^n$, $n = 1, 2, 3, \ldots$ and zero elsewhere. The moment-generating function of this p.d.f. (see Hogg and Craig 1970) is:

$$M(t) = \sum_{n=1}^{\infty} e^{tn}(0.5)^n = \sum_{n=0}^{\infty} (e^t/2)^n - 1 = 1/(1 - e^t/2) - 1 = e^t/(2 - e^t)$$

The first moment of the distribution is $M'(0) = 2$, which is the required expectation. Its variance is $M''(0) - \{M'(0)\}^2 = 2$.

above to find m but they may estimate the expected number of trials from past experience. The heuristic can be successfully applied to several other games.[44]

Notes

[1] Schoemaker 1982.

[2] Deaton and Muellbauer 1980.

[3] See Section 3.4.

[4] Bernoulli 1738.

[5] Kahneman and Tversky 1979.

[6] Kahneman and Tversky 1979, p. 266.

[7] Kahneman and Tversky 1979, p. 266.

[8] Kahneman and Tversky 1979, p. 267.

[9] Kahneman and Tversky 1979, p. 267.

[10] Kahneman and Tversky 1979, p. 267.

[11] Kahneman and Tversky 1979, p. 267.

[12] Van de Stadt et al. 1984, p. 24.

[13] See Section 10.3.

[14] These are final states as described in Section 13.1.

[15] See Section 13.1.

[16] Kahneman and Tversky 1979, see Section 12.3.

[17] See Section 4.2.

[18] Kahneman and Tversky 1980, p. 343.

[19] Kahneman and Tversky 1980, p. 343.

[20] Bazerman 1984.

[21] Van der Pligt and Van Schie 1990.

[22] Levin et al. 1987.

[23] See Section 7.3.

[24] Kahneman and Tversky 1979.

[25] Kahneman and Tversky 1979, p. 271.

[26] Kahneman and Tversky 1979, p. 273.

[27] Kahneman and Tversky 1979, p. 273.

[28] Statman and Caldwell 1987.

[29] See Section 12.5.

[30] Statman and Caldwell 1987.

[31] Shefrin and Statman 1985.

[32] Schoemaker 1982.

[33] See Chapter 6.

[34] Schoemaker 1982.

[35] Payne and Braunstein 1971.

[36] Slovic et al. 1977.

[37] Slovic et al. 1978.

[38] See Section 4.1.

[39] See Section 13.2.

[40] Bernoulli 1738/1954.
[41] Vlek and Wagenaar 1979.
[42] Savage 1954.
[43] Treisman 1988.
[44] Treisman 1988.

CHAPTER 14

GAME THEORY

14.1. The Prisoner's Dilemma game

- The inhabitants of Dirty City have been asked to fight littering and put their waste in trashcans. Apparently, the request was not successful.
- The inhabitants of the cities around Lake Chemistry have been asked to reduce the consumption of drinking-water since the water-company is not able to supply sufficient quantities from the heavily polluted lake. However, each day at noon the water runs out.
- Each year, the population of fish in the North Sea decreases and the average size of the fish caught is reduced.

The situations described above are examples of a common social dilemma described in "The Tragedy of the Commons".[1] Anyone of the old New England villages could graze his cows freely on the Commons or public grassland. Since the Commons is a 'free good', it pays to increase the number of one's cattle. However, if everyone does so, the grass gets scarcer until finally it is destroyed entirely. So, in the end, everyone is worse off than before, since no cattle can be grazed any more. The dilemma is caused by the fact that the individual gain of grazing one extra cow on the Commons is greater than the additional overgrazing created by one more animal.

The Commons dilemma can be considered as an extension of the well-known *Prisoner's Dilemma* involving only two participants. Two prisoners are suspected of being involved in some crime, which they did not confess. The District Attorney talks to them separately. If they both confess, they get the standard sentence for their crime, being three years in prison. If neither of them talks, they get only one year in prison. However, if one of them talks and the other does not, the first one goes free, while the other gets ten years in prison. Communication between the prisoners is not allowed. Each prisoner will realize that talking results in a less severe sentence, regardless of the behavior of the other prisoner. If both of them think this way, both will confess in the end. Obviously, this is the purpose of the District Attorney.

ᵥThe situations, described above, are analyzed formally in *game theory*. The game theoretical representation of the Prisoner's Dilemma has been

		Prisoner II	
		deny	confess
Prisoner I	deny	(-1, -1)	(-10, 0)
	confess	(0, -10)	(-3, -3)

Figure 14.1. The payoff matrix of a Prisoner's Dilemma.

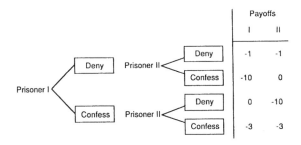

Figure 14.2. Extensive form representation of the Prisoner's Dilemma.

given in Figure 14.1. Each prisoner might adopt the *strategy* of denying or confessing. Depending on the strategy adopted by the other prisoner, this leads to particular outcomes or *payoffs*, for each prisoner. By convention, the payoffs of Prisoner I (II) are given in the left (right) part of each cell in the *payoff matrix*. Since the outcomes are numbers of years in prison, which are evaluated negatively, the sign of the payoffs is negative.

Inspection of the payoffs of Prisoner I shows that denying leads to one or ten years in prison, depending on the other prisoner's behavior. Confessing by Prisoner I leads to release or three years in prison, respectively. It appears that both of the payoffs of Prisoner I are higher with confession than with denial. The *rational strategy* for Prisoner I is confession. Inspection of the payoffs of Prisoner II leads to exactly the same result. For both prisoners, the rational strategy is confession, leading to the non-optimal outcome of three years in prison each. This outcome is a *stable equilibrium* since neither of the prisoners is willing to change his strategy unilaterally.

Figure 14.1 depicts the so-called *strategic form representation* of the Prisoner's Dilemma (PD) game. It is assumed that both players of the game move simultaneously, such that neither player knows the decision of the other player before making his own decision. This lack of knowledge of the other's move is called *imperfect information*. Suppose that the rules of the game are changed, such that the decision of Player I is known to Player II in making his decision. What decision will Player I make in this game? This situation is depicted in the *extensive form representation* of the PD in Figure 14.2, in which Player II decides after Player I. Player I will recognize that Player II is rational in that Player II will maximize his payoffs. If Player I chooses to deny, it is to be expected that Player II, knowing that Player I has denied, will confess, leading to the worst outcome for Player I. Also, if Player II knows that Player I has confessed, it can be expected that he will confess, too. In this case, too, it is rational for Player I to confess. So perfect information for Player II does not alter the results of the PD game. Suppose that Player II is represented by his lawyer in the conversation with the District Attorney. What instruction will Player II give to his lawyer? In this case, Player II imagines the possible decisions to be taken by Player I. The instruction to the lawyer will be: "Tell the District Attorney that I am willing to confess", regardless of the other's decision. This example shows that a strategy can be delegated to an agent, since it is a plan of action.

The equilibrium of the PD game results from the individually rational strategy of both players. However, the equilibrium is inefficient, since a better outcome is available for both players. *Cooperation* of the players by both denying will make each of them better off. Collectively, the cooperative strategy could be considered rational. The deviation from cooperative choice therefore has been called *defective choice*. The characteristics of the PD game are that the payoffs of a defective choice are greater than those of a cooperative choice respectively and that the payoffs in the equilibrium are smaller than with mutual cooperation.

Many other games exist next to the PD, with different payoff matrices and with or without equilibrium.[2] Analysis of these games proceeds along the same lines as with the PD, considered in this chapter. Several other games will be considered in Section 14.5.

The PD game is frequently played by more than two people, as indicated by the Commons example. In the next section, the representation of the *N*-persons PD will be considered. Section 14.3 will deal with psychological effects on choice in PD games. Dynamic choice in PD games will be considered in Section 14.4. Section 14.5 deals with several other experimental games.

Conclusion

Social dilemmas involve situations where the outcomes of one's own choice are dependent on the choices made by other people. The Prisoner's Dilemma, according to game theory, results in a stable inefficient equilibrium because each player pursues his own benefits instead of maximizing joint benefits. It appears that imperfect information leads to the same choices as perfect information, according to game theory.

Table 14.1. Payoffs of contributing to a fixed
public good.

Number of contributors	Costs per contributor	Net benefits per contributor
20	$6.00	$114.00
19	$6.32	$113.68
15	$8.00	$112.00
10	$12.00	$108.00
5	$24.00	$96.00
1	$120.00	$0.00
0	$0.00	$0.00

14.2. The N-persons Prisoner's Dilemma

The occupants in an apartment building want to instal safety equipment at the main entrance. They make a collection to finance the purchase. How many of the occupants will pay the appropriate contribution?

The situation described above will be considered in more detail. Suppose that the building includes 20 apartments and the safety equipment costs $120. One of the occupants asks all the others whether they will contribute to finance the purchase. (This person is also involved in a second dilemma, since if nobody takes this initiative, no money will be collected and taking the initiative can be considered a cooperative act; the volunteer in some sense is exploited by the other occupants.) If all of the occupants cooperate, the costs are $6 per apartment. The benefits of the equipment for each of the occupants will be worth at least $120. This amounts to a net benefit of at least $114. If no one cooperates, the equipment will not be installed and each of the occupants misses the opportunity to enjoy the net benefits of cooperation. With 10 contributors, the costs are doubled for each of them. However, the net benefits of the occupants are different in this case. Each 'cooperator' has a net benefit of $120 − $12 = $108, whereas each 'defector' has $120 because the contribution is nil. If only one person is willing to contribute her net benefits are nil. Table 14.1 shows the costs, benefits and net benefits (payoffs) with different numbers of contributors.

The figures in Table 14.1 are graphically depicted in Figure 14.3a. The payoffs of the defectors are constant, given the contribution of at least one individual. The payoffs of the contributors increase with their total number. These results are characteristic for the natural provision of a public good. In this case, the purchase of the public good is relatively likely, since the payoffs increase substantially with only a few contributors. Those who make

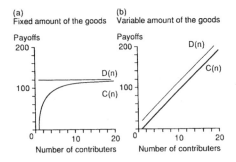

Figure 14.3. Individual payoffs of a public good.

Table 14.2. Payoffs of contributing to a variable public good.

Number of contributors	Total costs	Net benefits per contributor
20	$200	$190
19	$190	$180
15	$150	$140
10	$100	$ 90
5	$50	$40
1	$10	$0
0	$0	$0

no contribution to the public good are called *free riders*. According to game theory, the defective choice of a free rider is rational since the individual payoff is always higher than the payoff of a contributor.

The shape of the payoff curve may vary with the payoff structure of the game. In the example above, let the contribution be a fixed amount, e.g. $10 by agreement. On the safety market, a variety of equipment is available at different prices. In the price range $10–$200, for each extra $10, more or better equipment can be purchased. For example, a solid bolt costs $10, a reinforced glass panel costs $60 and efficient measures cost $200. In this case, the payoffs are presented in Table 14.2.

Total benefits per individual increase with the number of contributors since increasing amounts of equipment can be purchased. Note that this applies to the contributors as well as to the free riders (in contrast to the payoffs of free riders in Table 14.1). The net benefits of the occupants increases linearly with the number of contributors. The net benefits per individual are depicted graphically in Figure 14.3b. The difference between the defector's and the contributor's payoff is positive and constant. In this case, it is likely that the

Table 14.3. Payoffs for the 'Take Some' and
the 'Give Some' games.

(a) The 'Take Some' game

Number of cooperators	Payoffs to defectors	Payoffs to cooperators
3	–	$1
2	$2	$0
1	$1	–$1
0	$0	–

(b) The 'Give Some' game

Number of cooperators	Payoffs to defectors	Payoffs to cooperators
5	–	$12
4	$20	$9
3	$17	$6
2	$14	$3
1	$11	$0
0	$8	–

From Dawes (1980). Reproduced, with permission, from the Annual Review of Psychology, Vol. 31, ©1980 by Annual Reviews Inc.

probability of a defective choice does not depend on the number of cooperative choices.

In Figure 14.3a, the difference between $D(n)$ and $C(n)$ decreases with an increasing number of cooperative choices. In this case, it may be assumed that the probability of a defective choice is reduced if more people contribute already. However, in both cases, the rational choice is defective.

Numerous instances of N-persons PD games exist in reality, several of which are listed in Table 14.4.

The N-persons PD has frequently been investigated in experimental research. In the experimental 'Take Some' game,[3] each of three players simultaneously holds up a red or blue poker chip (the game being easily extended to more than three players). Each player who holds up a red chip receives $3 in payoff but all of the players are fined $1 for that choice. Each player who holds up a blue chip receives $1 with no resultant fine. The payoffs for this game are presented in Table 14.3a. By holding up the red chip, a player's net benefit is $2, which is equivalent to the sum of the fines of the other players.

Table 14.4. Examples of N-persons Prisoner's Dilemmas.

Dilemma	Defective choice
Tax paying	Tax evasion
Arms race	Any further armament
Overfishing	Exceeding fishing quota
Pricing	Price under competitor's price
Queuing	Any attempt to precede a queue
Advertising	Any increase of the advertising budget

Table 14.5. A public step good game with three players. (See text for explanation.)

Number of cooperators	Payoffs to defectors	Payoffs to cooperators
3	$3	$2
2	$2	$1
1	$0	–$1
0	$0	–$1

In this game, one can *take some* from others. This game is analogous to that involved in the examples of littering, drinking-water and fishing at the start of this chapter.

In the 'Give Some' game, each of five players may keep $8 from the experimenter for herself or give $3 from the experimenter to each of the other players. If all give, each player gets $12 (4 × $3), while if all keep, each player gets her $8 from the experimenter. Of course, the game can be played with any number of players. The payoffs for this game are presented in Table 14.3b. This game is analogous to that of contributing to a public good, considered above. Both the 'Take Some' and the 'Give Some' game can be represented graphically as in Figure 14.3. The $D(n)$ line would be located above and parallel to the $C(n)$ line.

A variant of the above mentioned games is the *public step good* or common resource pool game.[4] In this variant, each of the players may contribute a certain amount. Only if the total contributions exceed a certain threshold, the sum of the contributions is magnified and distributed equally among the players, otherwise the contributions are lost. For example, three players each owning $1 which may either or not be contributed. If total contributions are less than $2, they will be lost, otherwise they are tripled and distributed evenly among the players. Table 14.5 shows the net payoffs of defectors and cooperators (payoffs minus contributions).

Conclusion

The Prisoner's Dilemma game with two players can easily be extended to N players if the payoff matrix is the same for each player. A graphical representation of the game shows the payoff curves for cooperative and defective choices according to the number of cooperative players. A number of economic choices are subject to N-persons PD games, the defective choices being made by free riders. 'Take some', 'Give some' and public good games are used to study N-persons PD games experimentally.

14.3. Psychological variables in the Prisoner's Dilemma

In the experimental application of PD games, substantial deviations from the game theoretic rational strategy have been observed. Moreover, as everyone knows from own experience, people contribute voluntarily to public goods and are able to make agreements to avoid 'Commons tragedies'. How is this behavior to be explained?

The explanation of 'irrational' behavior is that the payoffs are evaluated in terms of utilities. If the utility function is defined over the payoffs exclusively, this explanation can be cast in the game theoretic representation of Section 14.1. Only a transformation of payoffs into utilities is needed and the analysis of games proceeds as usual. Even the results of the PD game are unaltered, since by the transformation of a monotonic increasing utility function the characteristics of the PD game are preserved. (The rank order of utilities and payoffs is the same.)

However, as has been argued in the previous chapters, a number of variables may influence the utility of the outcomes of behavior. The transformation of payoffs into utilities offers the opportunity to include psychological variables in the utility function, changing the characteristics of the game. Several psychological variables are considered here that offer different explanations of behavior in game situations.[5]

Altruism

Few of us would accept $500 with nothing for our friend in lieu of $498 for each of us. This example shows that people are not insatiably greedy[6] and can behave in an altruistic way. Altruistic behavior may occur for different reasons:

An individual may have an altruistic (cooperative) disposition,[7] which renders cooperative choice more likely.

An individual may behave in an altruistic way because of tactical reasons.[8] This implies the expectation that upon one's own behavior, other people feel obliged to cooperative behavior, too. However, in many large scale social dilemmas, social interaction is limited and *tactical altruism* is not assumed to be an important determinant of behavior.

The *sociobiological argument* for altruistic behavior is that selfish behavior is less likely to survive in the process of natural genetic selection since its outcomes are less successful. Analogously, a 'social evolution' toward altruistic and cooperative norms and morals may take place. Altruistic behavior may be selectively directed to members of a social group being on good terms with each other, e.g. relatives, friends, club or tribe members, etcetera. This may influence the type of choice in dilemmas taking place inside or outside these social groups.

Conscience and norms

Norms and conscience may influence the utility of payoffs. For example, different norms regarding the division of resources may differentially affect the utility of the results of division.[9] Also, as a result of different types of learning,[10] a defective choice might induce feelings of guilt.

In a public step good experiment the initial endowments of four subjects in each of six groups was varied pairwise.[11] That is, two members of each group obtained 40 Austrian schillings (low endowment) and the other two obtained 80 schillings (high endowment). It was assumed that social norms would induce equitable contributions from the players, i.e. those with low endowment should contribute less than those with high endowment. Elicitation of what contribution was expected from the different players and what contribution was considered fair was consistent with the hypothesis. However, the average actual contributions, made in private, were not significantly different between those with low endowment and those with high endowment. Expression of norms and actual behavior appeared to be different in this study.

Communication

In experiments with 'Give Some' games, high degrees of cooperative choices have been observed (up to 94%) when communication between the participants was allowed. However, several aspects of communication might be responsible for this effect. A hierarchy of three aspects is assumed.[12] First, the subjects get to know each other as human beings (humanization); second, they get to discuss the dilemma with which they are faced (discussion); third, they have the opportunity to make commitments about their own behavior and to attempt to elicit such commitments from others (commitment). Commitment entails discussion and discussion in turn entails humanization.

Four conditions of a 'Take Some' game were compared, one involving no communication at all, one allowing 10 minutes communication about an irrelevant topic, one allowing discussion of the game (but no commitments) and one requiring commitments. The four conditions yielded cooperation rates of 30%, 32%, 72% and 71%, respectively. It appears that humanization does not increase the cooperation rate. Discussion significantly increases but does not guarantee cooperation. Forced commitment does not increase cooperation (actually, every subject promised to cooperate), although the authors admit that the commitment did not arise spontaneously from the group process.[13]

The information from the social group was varied in the public step good game mentioned above.[14] Each of the four subjects in a group was required either or not to write down how large a contribution was expected from each of the other players. Then, they were asked to make their contribution in private. It appeared that the average actual contributions in six groups did not differ significantly across the two conditions. Considering the information provided as an attempt at social commitment, it appears that this attempt has failed, in agreement with the results obtained in the communication experiment.[15]

Group size

Generally, it has been found that group size varies inversely with cooperation rate in dilemma games. The group size effect has been attributed to the perceived effectiveness and noticeability of group members' behavior.[16] In several experiments, however, the results could have been attributed to different payoff structures. More specifically, the harm from defection should be diffused among more people. This effect could result from the game depicted in Figure 14.3a, where the $D(n)$ and the $C(n)$ curves approach each other with increasing cooperation rate. Decreasing cooperation was found in a comparison of three-, six- and nine-person games with equal slopes of $D(n)$ and $C(n)$ lines, respectively.[17] This shows a group size effect, independent of the payoff structure of the game.

Noticeability

The public disclosure and identifiability of choices has been found to increase the rate of cooperation relative to anonymous choices. If the other players know which players make defective choices, group sanctions can be taken, e.g. by threats or hostile behavior. Comments on defectors were common such as "If you defect on the rest of us, you're going to live with it the rest of your life".[18] They observed that the defectors remained after the experiment until all the cooperators were presumably long gone.

Furthermore, noticeability might induce cooperators to model the behavior of defectors.[19]

Expectations

The expectations regarding whether the other players would cooperate or defect might affect one's own choice. If the other players are expected to cooperate, the temptation to defect might increase. Also, if the other players are expected to make defective choices, one might avoid being a sucker by making a defective choice, too. Generally, strong positive correlations have been found between expectations of the group's cooperativeness and one's own cooperative choice. It has also been found that defectors are more accurate at predicting cooperation rates than cooperators. However, in general the subjects are poor at predicting who would and who would not cooperate. In a study of Prisoner's Dilemma games, subject's expectations regarding the choices of the other player were used to explain behavior.[20] It was found that expectations significantly explain behavior, although their effects are influenced by the values and the signs of the payoffs.

Moralizing

In one study, the experimenters moralized at the subjects by delivering a 938 word sermon about group benefit, exploitation, ethics and so on.[21] The sermon worked very effectively by producing cooperation rates comparable to those found in the discussion and commitment groups of the earlier experiment.[22]

   The psychological factors, considered in this section, are assumed to affect the utility of the payoffs. The utility is assumed a compensatory function of the objective payoffs and the psychological factors involved.[23] This is illustrated with the following dialogue:

   "He: Lady, would you sleep with me for 100,000 pounds?
   She: Why, yes. Of course.
   He: Would you sleep with me for 10 shillings?
   She: (angrily) What do you think I am, a prostitute?
   He: We have already established that fact madam. What we are haggling about is the price."[24]

Conclusion

In practice, it appears that many cooperative choices are made in PD games. This results from the utility of cooperative and defective choices which usually differs from the objective value of the payoffs. As noticed in earlier chapters, psychological variables may play a part in the utility function. Regarding game theory, altruism, conscience and norms, communication, group size, noticeability, expectations and moralizing may influence the utility of the payoffs.

14.4. Dynamic games

The previous sections dealt with one-shot games, finished when all of the players have moved only once. However, many games are played repetitively, either with a known or an unknown number of trials. These are *dynamic games* that offer the players the opportunity of learning. Also, the players can be assumed to maximize their long-run payoffs which might lead to behavior different from the maximization of short-run payoffs.

First, consider the dynamic PD game with a fixed number of trials. The last trial of this game would be most similar to the one-shot game, since the players can move only once. Even the information from the preceding trials would not change the character of the last trial, since each player knows that other players know that the game will be finished after their next move. In this case, the individually rational (defective) choice is predicted. On the last trial but one, the players can expect that, on the next trial, the defective choice will be prevailing and each of the players will assume that the others know this, too. So the choices in the last trial are not influenced by the choices in the last trial but one. Apparently, the last trial but one has the same character as the last trial and defective choice is predicted. This argument applies to the last trial but two and so on. In the dynamic PD game with a fixed known number of trials, each trial (including the first one) is assumed to elicit the same type of choices.

If the number of trials is not fixed or unknown, the above argument does not apply and it will be rational to make a cooperative choice, taking the risk of being exploited. In this case, the long-term payoffs from cooperative choice may carry greater weight than one (higher) short-run payoff from exploiting the other player(s) once. Theoretically, ignorance of the number of trials or an infinite game, may result in cooperative choice. A game with a large known number of trials, however, may be perceived as an infinite game.

In experimental multiplay PD games, cooperation appeared as a U-shaped function of time elapsed.[25] Initially, cooperation declines but after 30 to 60 trials, it begins to rise. This finding reflects a shift from short-range to long-range thinking.[26] The multiplay game may consist of two stages. The initial stage involves defensive and/or exploitative motives (resulting in defective choices). These different motives cannot be distinguished from each other and frequently defensive motives (not to be exploited by the other player) are interpreted as exploitative motives. This might induce non-cooperative

Table 14.6. Payoff matrix of the multiplay
PD computer tournament.

		Player II	
		cooperate	effect
		---	---
	cooperate	(3,3)	(0.5)
Player I			
	defect	(5,0)	(1,1)

behavior, which in turn might be interpreted as exploitative. The result is the familiar self-fulfilling prophecy, which often underlies persistent mutual non-cooperation. After having experienced mutual non-cooperation, the subjects may realize that the equilibrium is inefficient and try to cooperate.

In several experiments, the confederate fails to cooperate initially and then begins to cooperate. This '*reformed sinner*' strategy proves to be very effective in that the subjects usually become very cooperative after the confederate's reform. Also, it has been found that subjects are more cooperative when they have observed two other people engage in a non-cooperative exchange than when they have observed cooperative or exploitative exchange. The experience of non-cooperation triggers the onset of cooperative behavior.[27]

The multiplay strategy can be modeled in a number of ways. For example, the effect of the non-cooperation experience on a player's strategy can be summarized as: "After 20 trials of mutual defective choice, choose cooperatively and see what happens. If the other player chooses defectively on her next trial, return to the strategy of defective choice". This example probably is too defensive, since it provides the other player a very limited opportunity to try cooperative choice. A model of multiplay strategy can easily be written as a computer program and different programs can play against one another to reveal the most effective strategy in the iterative PD game.

At the University of Michigan, a computer tournament was conducted with a number of computer programs performing multiplay PD game strategies.[28] Fourteen programs were devised by economists, mathematicians, political scientists, psychologists and a sociologist. Each program played against one another program, against itself and against a program generating choices in a random way. Each game consisted of 200 trials with the payoff matrix given in Table 14.6. The tournament was conducted five times to obtain more stable results.

The winner of the tournament was TIT FOR TAT, submitted by Anatol Rapoport. TIT FOR TAT starts with a cooperative choice and thereafter does what the other player did on the previous move. The TIT FOR TAT computer program is extremely simple (four lines in Fortran) and has been effective when played with humans.[29] Although TIT FOR TAT obtained the highest average score against the other programs, the other programs obtained equal or higher scores against TIT FOR TAT. Especially against the RANDOM program, TIT FOR TAT appears to be too generous.

Two properties of the programs appeared to be responsible for success: niceness and forgiveness.

A decision rule is nice if it will not be the first to defect or if at least it will not be the first to defect before the last few moves (say before move 199). The top eight programs were all nice and none of the remaining programs was nice.

Forgiveness of a decision rule is its propensity to cooperate in the moves after the other player has defected. TIT FOR TAT is very forgiving, since it does not remember a defective move for more than one trial. It appeared that the rules which were not nice were not very forgiving either.

A second tournament with 62 entries from six countries,[30] including TIT FOR TAT, resulted in a second victory for this program. Considering the question of whether TIT FOR TAT is the best decision rule, this depends on the population of other rules (the environment). Had only the top half programs of the second tournament been included, TIT FOR TAT would have came in fourth after the ones which actually came in 25th, 16th and 8th. Although TIT FOR TAT appears to be very robust against a large population of programs, it is not necessarily the best in a smaller sample.

TIT FOR TAT (and its variations) is the most effective program (among those studied) to elicit cooperative choices from human beings.[31] This may be so because the individual realizes that the strategist will not tolerate being exploited, which should lead to attempts to achieve the next best outcome, mutual cooperation. It has been found that TIT FOR TAT induces considerably more cooperation than the consistently cooperative strategy. Furthermore, the individual may develop the expectation that the strategist is willing to cooperate. In a study of negotiation,[32] TIT FOR TAT elicited more concessions than when the strategist made concessions in each trial. The latter strategy was, in turn, more effective than never making a concession.

Consider the following example:

Suppose you want to sell your house. A potential buyer offers you less than the asking price but her offer is fair. Would you reduce the asking price? If yes, by how much? TIT FOR TAT would amount to a fair reduction of the asking price, thus eliciting further concessions from the potential buyer. After an only slightly increased offer, the seller should reply with no concession, acting as a strong negotiator, not allowing exploitation.

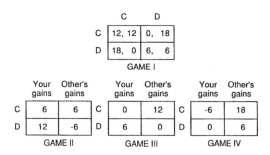

Figure 14.4. Decompositions of a Prisoner's Dilemma game. From Pruitt and Kimmel (1977). Reproduced, with permission, from the Annual Review of Psychology, Vol. 28, ©1977 by Annual Reviews Inc.

The decomposed Prisoner's Dilemma

In the PD games considered above, the payoffs have been stated as resulting from simultaneous choice in each trial. In the decomposed PD game, the payoffs consist of the summed outcomes of one's own and of the other's choice. In this way, the same PD game can be decomposed in an infinite number of ways. In Figure 14.4, three decompositions (game II, III and IV) of a PD (I) are presented. The total payoff for an individual ("You" in this case) is computed by summing "Your gains" resulting from one's own choice and "Other's gains" resulting from the other's choice. If both choose cooperatively in game III, "Your gains" equals 0 (resulting from one's own choice) + 12 (resulting from the other's choice) = 12, which is equal to the left hand figure in the northwest cell of the payoff matrix in game I.

An example of a decomposed PD game in practice is two workmen who have a series of opportunities to help each other. Here, the move of Player I may be followed after considerable time by a move of Player II. The average degrees of cooperation over 20 trials with games I–IV are presented in Figure 14.5. It appears from this figure, that the subjects' behavior in the games differs in the short-run as well as in the long-run. In the same decomposed games, subjects were asked for their motives for playing cooperatively or defectively.[33]

Game II elicits the least cooperative behavior. Subjects playing cooperatively in this game give as a reason that they want to obtain a fair division by this choice. Subjects playing defective give as a reason that they achieve a mutual defective outcome. Obviously, the latter subjects like the high payoff for themselves *plus* a fair division of payoffs.

Game III elicits the highest cooperation rate from the start. The reported reason for this behavior is "Getting the other to play *C*". The reported reason for defective choice was "Achieving payoff resulting from playing *D*".

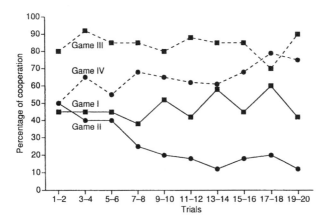

Figure 14.5. Degree of cooperation in decomposed Prisoner's Dilemma games. From Pruitt, D.G. "Motivational processes in the decomposed prisoner's dilemma game." Journal of Personality and Social Psychology 14, 227–238. Copyright (1970) by the American Psychological Association. Reprinted by permission.

Game IV starts with moderate cooperation rates, which gradually increase. The reported motive for playing C was "Getting the other to play C". The reported reason for playing D was "Avoiding payoff resulting from playing C".

The reasons for cooperative behavior, stated in Games III and IV indicate tactical altruism.[34] In game II, the main reason is obtaining a fair division, which indicates equity considerations. The defective choices in the games seem to be inspired mainly by greedy motives.

The decomposed games in Figure 14.4 recall the framing effect.[35] The games result in the same payoffs but are presented in a different way, eliciting different behavior. In particular, in the simultaneous PD the payoffs are integrated, whereas in the decomposed PD they are segregated.[36] Moreover, some decompositions are framed with positive outcomes for oneself, others with negative outcomes. This might induce different evaluations resulting from the shape of the value function.[37] Evidence was found for segregation rather than integration of the payoffs in subjects' behavior in decomposed games.[38] Furthermore, segregation in this experiment was consistent with the use of a value function.

Conclusion

Dynamic games are distinguished according to whether the number of occasions to play the game is fixed, unknown or infinite. A fixed number of trials results in the same behavior at each trial, according to game theory. With an unknown or infinite number of trials, the behavior depends on the individual time preference and on the experience with the game. A simple strategy eliciting cooperative choices and yielding high payoffs in dynamic games is TIT FOR TAT. The decomposition of PD games may influence the perception of the payoffs. Decomposed games showing a large difference between the own and the other's payoffs are influenced by tactical altruism; a small difference between these payoffs elicits greedy motives or equity considerations.

14.5. Other experimental games

A great variety of experimental games exist, the psychological aspects of which are of increasing concern to experimental economists, since game theoretic solutions generally are violated by subjects' behaviors. This includes behavior at problems of logic, auctions, international markets, stock markets, distribution markets, and coalition formation, among many other games.[39] Here, we will consider the Chicken game, the Trust game, the Dictator game and the Ultimatum Bargaining game because of their economic implications and frequency of study.

Chicken game

The Chicken game represents a social dilemma, frequently encountered in traffic congestions[40] and in *brinkmanship*.[41] Traffic congestions may occur for instance if on a sunny day many people decide to go to the beach by car, which in this case may be called the defective choice and refraining from visiting the beach may be called the cooperative choice. The N-person graphic representation of the game in Figure 14.6 shows that taking the car to the beach offers advantages to abstaining from this up to a certain point. If too many people go, it becomes a disadvantage because of traffic congestion.

The application to brinkmanship may be shown by analogy with the following game. Suppose two speedboats are approaching each other at high speed. Diverging from the chosen course indicates lack of courage (being a chicken). So they go ahead and what will happen? Not giving in has some advantage *if* the other boat changes its course (left part of Figure 14.6). However, if both hold on, the consequences may be dramatic (right part of Figure 14.6). Similar situations may occur during brinkmanship. One way to induce the other party to give in, is to pretend that one is forced to act this way (e.g. by throwing away the steering-weel in the analogy above).

Experimental Chicken games may be set up and analyzed the same way as the Prisoner's Dilemma game considered before.

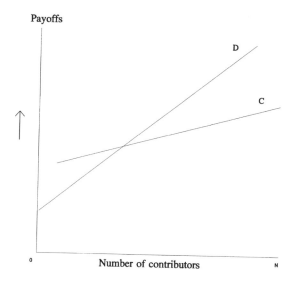

Figure 14.6. *N*-person Chicken game.

Trust game

The Trust game is assumed to hold in situations of hoarding and business establishments. When food supply is normal, there are some disadvantages in maintaining a stock of food (left part of Figure 14.7). However, when people are hoarding, for example because of an expected price increase, at some point it becomes advantageous to hoard as there may not be any food left otherwise (right part of Figure 14.7). This situation can also be observed at parties where food is scarce. In business establishments, it may be advantageous when a number of firms are located in the same area. However, when some firms are starting to disappear, at some point it becomes a disadvantage to stay.[42]

Both in the chicken and in the trust game, the payoff lines cross, unlike the payoff lines regarding the PD game. More defecting strategy choices in *N*-person PD games were found than in *N*-person chicken and trust games, the latter of which yielded the smallest proportion of defecting choices.[43]

Ultimatum Bargaining game

The Ultimatum Bargaining game has some history in experimental economics and economic psychology.[44] The game is played by two persons, one of which, the Proposer, is asked to distribute a sum of money between herself and the other, the Responder. The Responder then is asked to accept or to reject the distribution. If the Responder accepts, both will be payed according to the

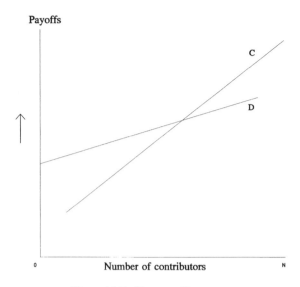

Figure 14.7. *N*-person Trust game.

proposal. If the Responder rejects the distribution, both obtain nothing. This game is played, for example, in seller-buyer, employer-union and bilateral monopoly contexts.[45] The game theoretic predictions of the game are that Proposers offer a very small sum to the Responder, thus keeping most of the sum for themselves. The Responders are assumed to accept any non-zero offer. However, in practice Proposers frequently offer a 50–50 or 60–40 split and Responders frequently reject low offers, such as 80–20 or 90–10. Why?

The Why-question has kept experimental economists busy for some time because they could not explain such 'irrational' behavior by normative theory.

Social influence might be a reason, so they took steps to guarantee anonymity to the players by preventing Proposers and Responders from seeing each other, by using sealed envelopes containing the proposals and responses and by making payment in sealed envelopes so that even the experimenters did not know the identities of the players. Although the offers were a bit more extreme, the game theoretic predictions still did not predict behavior.[46]

Although experimental economists usually provide money in order to elicit incentive compatible behavior, the payoffs might have been too small to observe the behavior predicted by game theory. Dividing a sum of $5 is one thing but how about dividing a sum of $100,000? However, even with stakes as high as $100, the distributions were no different from those with $10 and even offers of $30 were rejected in some cases.[47]

Fairness or equity has been proposed as a motive to deviate from purely self-interested behavior. The need level of the players was varied by revealing whether they were students from the former Soviet Union (high need level) or students from western countries (low need level).[48] Proposers were asked to divide 300 Austrian schillings (about $25). They did not find any differences in proposals and responses in this respect, however. On average, Proposers offered 112.5 Ös and Respondents rejected offers below 77.5 Ös. This result is consistent with that obtained with respect to the public step good game.[49]

Another variation in the experiment was that the Respondents had to share their offer with a third person. They either received 90%, 50% or 10% of the offer. Under these circumstances, Proposers on average offered 144.1 Ös and Respondents rejected offers below 91.5 Ös. So, a high need level *as part of the game structure* induced more generosity in the Proposers and more demand in the Responders.

If fairness is to explain behavior in Ultimatum Bargaining games, information about the payoffs may be an issue. In a recent experiment Proposers were given 100 chips for distribution.[50] However, in one condition the Proposers were told that the chip value was 30 cents to them and only 10 cents to the Responders, whereas the Responders were told that all chips were worth the same. In this condition, offers are close to 50% of the chips, implying a 75–25 distribution of real value which is inequitable. It appears that the Proposer's behavior is apparently but not really equitable. A disadvantage of this experiment is that Proposers may think that it is okay to cheat because the experimenter provides asymmetric information.

Personality characteristics may affect behavior in Ultimatum Bargaining games. Altruism may play a part here, although this cannot explain rejected offers.[51] The effect of Machiavellism on acceptance behavior of Respondents in a hypothetical Ultimatum Bargaining game was studied.[52] Machiavellism was measured by a social-psychological scale.[53] High scores on the scale were associated with opportunistic items such as 'Flatter important people', 'It's O.K. to cut corners', 'People only work hard if forced'. Low scores were associated with high morale such as 'Honesty is the best policy' and 'Most people are basically good'. People with high scores tended to accept 70–30 and 80–20 offers more often then those with low scores on the Machiavellism scale.

As a conclusion, manners rather than altruism seem to explain behavior in bargaining games.[54]

Dictator game

An Ultimatum Bargaining game without opportunity for beneficiaries to respond has been called a Dictator game. The Proposer knows that the offer made cannot be rejected. Obviously, the game theoretic prediction is that

Proposer takes all. However, offers tend to converge to 50–50, despite the lack of any sanction on the Proposer taking everything. Tipping may be considered an example of a dictator game, although the tip is likely to be given in exchange for good service.[55] The offers may shrink if the Proposer feels that she has earned the right to the sum allotted or if the relationship with the beneficiaries is made less personal.[56]

Conclusion

Experimental games provide opportunities to study economic behavior in a social context. Psychological factors appear to influence behavior in these games. Although economists tend to refer to fairness when explaining the allocation of resources, equity theory provides a richer explanation of this behavior. It predicts an equal distribution in dictator and ultimatum bargaining games and explains several observed deviations from the equal distribution.

Summary

In social dilemmas, individual choices are influenced by the choices made by other people. A particular type of social dilemma, the Prisoner's Dilemma (PD), is characterized by individually rational choices that lead to stable, jointly inefficient outcomes. The strategies in PD games are cooperative or defective, depending on whether equal choices of the players lead to an unstable, jointly beneficial outcome or an inefficient equilibrium, respectively. The PD game can be represented in strategic form or in extensive form. Analysis of the extensive form representation shows that imperfect information does not alter the strategy of a player who moves before the opponent.

The N-persons PD is an extension of the PD game with two players. If the payoffs for the strategies are the same for each person in the game, a graphical representation shows the payoff curves (or lines) of cooperative and defective choices as a function of the number of cooperative players. Typically, the payoffs of free riders are higher than the payoffs of cooperative players. This situation frequently occurs in practice and can be shown experimentally by using 'Take some', 'Give some' and public good games.

The cooperative choice in PD games, not predicted by game theory, frequently occurs in experiments and in practice. This results from the utility of payoffs that may be different for cooperative and defective choices. The utilities may be influenced by psychological variables, such as altruism, conscience and norms, communication, group size, noticeability, expectations and moralizing.

The number of occasions on which a PD can be played is found to influence the strategies of the players. A fixed number of trials leads to the same (defective) strategy at each trial, according to game theory. An unknown or infinite number of trials may lead to cooperative choice if the time preference of the players is sufficiently low and if the players have experience with the game. Experience may result from actually playing the game or from observation of other players. The 'reformed sinner' strategy, changing to a cooperative strategy after a number of defective choices, often induces the opponent to play cooperatively as well. A successful strategy in PD games is TIT FOR TAT, which plays cooperatively once and thereafter imitates the opponent's moves.

The decomposed Prisoner's Dilemma consists of a game played in two stages separated by some time period. The payoffs in each stage can be varied infinitely, such that each variation yields the same payoff matrix of the original PD game. Some decomposed games show great differences between one's own and the opponents outcomes. These games elicit strategies of tactical altruism in experiments, resulting in many cooperative moves. Other decomposed games show small differences between the outcomes of the players. These games elicit greedy motives or equity considerations, resulting in less cooperative moves. Decomposed PD games may present the players with differently framed payoff structures that may be explained by applying the value function regarding gains and losses considered in Chapter 12.

Several experimental games have been used to test economic rationality of behavior. Contrary to expectations, people frequently do not behave exclusively in their own interest, in general. Under normal circumstances, cooperativeness and fairness prevail, as predicted by equity theory.

Notes

[1] Hardin 1968.

[2] See Colman 1982, Hamburger 1977, Harris 1972 and Rapoport and Guyer 1966, among others.

[3] Dawes 1980.

[4] Offerman et al. (forthcoming), Van Dijk and Grodzka 1992.

[5] See Dawes 1980.

[6] See Section 12.2.

[7] See Section 3.5.

[8] See also Section 14.4.

[9] See the distributive principles in Section 11.3.

[10] See Chapter 5.

[11] Van Dijk and Grodzka 1992.

[12] Dawes et al. 1977.

[13] Similar results were found by Frey and Bohnet 1995.

[14] Van Dijk and Grodzka 1992.

[15] Dawes et al. 1977.

[16] Olson 1965, see also Stroebe and Frey 1982.

17 Bonacich et al. 1976.
18 Dawes et al. 1977.
19 Buchanan 1965.
20 Antonides 1992.
21 Dawes 1980.
22 Dawes et al. 1977.
23 Dawes 1980, see also Section 6.3.
24 Dawes 1980, p. 191.
25 Rapoport and Chammah 1965.
26 Pruitt and Kimmel 1977.
27 Pruitt and Kimmel 1977.
28 The tournament is reported in Axelrod 1980a.
29 Oskamp 1971.
30 Axelrod 1980b.
31 Pruitt and Kimmel 1977.
32 Komorita and Esser 1975.
33 Pruitt 1970.
34 See Section 14.2.
35 See Section 13.4.
36 See Section 12.5 on mental accounting.
37 See Section 12.3.
38 Antonides 1994.
39 Overviews of this research are given in Hamburger 1979, Colman 1982, Liebrand et al. 1992 and Kagel and Roth 1995 among others.
40 Hamburger 1979.
41 Rapoport and Chammah 1966.
42 Hamburger 1979.
43 Liebrand et al. 1986.
44 See, for example, Güth et al. 1982, Thaler 1988 and Güth and Tietz, 1990.
45 See Meyer 1992.
46 See Hoffman et al. 1994, Bolton and Zwick 1993.
47 See Hoffman et al., forthcoming.
48 Oppewal and Tougariova 1992.
49 Van Dijk and Grotzka 1992.
50 Kagel et al. (in press).
51 Camerer and Thaler 1995.
52 Meyer 1992.
53 Christie and Geis 1970.
54 Camerer and Thaler 1995.
55 See Section 11.4.
56 Camerer and Thaler 1995.

CHAPTER 15

NEGOTIATION

15.1. Introduction

The games considered in Chapter 14 are abstractions from a complex reality. In reality, we are never facing a situation presented as a payoff matrix including well-defined choices. Rather, we find ourselves involved in a buyer-seller relationship haggling over the price of some item; we try to obtain the best settlement for the alimony in case of a divorce; we try to find the best business partner in a joint venture. What do these situations have in common? How do we go about in these situations? Which factors are blocking the way to the best solution? Are there general rules or guidelines to obtain the best result?

To some extent, game theory provides a means to structure the situations, to analyze the choice alternatives and to find the strategy that maximizes our payoffs. For example, when filing our tax return, game theory may be helpful in our understanding of the consequences of concealing extra income (tax evasion) or declaring all income (tax compliance). It may help in classifying the situation as a Prisoner's Dilemma and in considering people as free riders if they conceal any income. However, the value of game theory in bargaining problems is limited because:

- it does not provide information of how to interpret and to classify the situation (who are the players in the game, what are their possible strategies?);
- it does not provide feedback regarding the correctness of our perceptions of the situation (does strategy X really obtain outcome Y?);
- it does not transform objective data (e.g. gains and losses) into our personal values or utilities (what is my personal value of an extra $1000, how do I value the effort of working during a weekend?);
- in many instances, it requires computations beyond our cognitive capacities.

One may argue that these limitations are similar to those associated with using the learning, attitude or expectation models considered in earlier chapters. However, in bargaining situations, it appears to be much less likely that people behave according to game theoretic predictions because of the greater complexity of the decision situation, in addition to the failure of game theory

Table 15.1. A structure of bargaining situations.

	One issue	Two or more issues
Two parties	Distributive bargaining	Integrative bargaining
More than two parties	Division and coalition bargaining	

to describe behavior in simple situations.[1] For this reason, a different theoretic framework is needed to describe human behavior in bargaining situations.

In general, negotiation is considered as a wider concept than bargaining.[2] *Negotiation* includes all kinds of activities to resolve social problems, whereas *bargaining* is considered the part of negotiation that aims at agreement. Here, we use the two terms interchangeably. The literature on negotiation (except for game theory) hardly uses any formal models but concentrates on the context of bargaining situations, the social processes involved and the outcomes obtained. Furthermore, it provides several guidelines to obtain the best outcomes, to avoid traps or to act as a third party in an effective way. In Section 15.2, the structure of negotiations will be explained to help understand bargaining problems. Section 15.3 considers the strategies and tactics of negotiation and Section 15.4 deals with psychological factors in negotiation behavior. Section 15.5 deals with negotiations in market contexts.

15.2. The structure of negotiations

Bargaining may be distinguished according to the number of participants and the number of issues involved. Two parties negotiating one issue are usually engaged in *distributive bargaining*.[3] This applies for instance to price negotiations by buyers and sellers and wage negotiations by employers and unions. Theoretically, these are the least complex situations. Frequently, however, distributive bargaining may be changed into *integrative bargaining* by adding an aspect of different interest to the parties. When two or more issues are involved, integrative bargaining becomes possible, in which the value of one issue may be traded off against another. For example, a higher price may be negotiated at the expense of a delay in payment. Frequently, mediators are looking for new aspects that may overcome impasse and make integrative bargaining possible. When more than two parties are involved, coalition formation and the division of payoffs within the coalition become relevant. (See Table 15.1.)

The distributive bargaining case may be used to introduce some terminology to clarify the negotiations. Consider the situation of a seller and a buyer

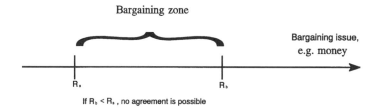

Figure 15.1. Display of a distributive bargaining situation.

of a second-hand car at the informal market. The only possible outcomes are
a contract, in which the car is exchanged for money, and no contract. An
important concept is the *reservation price*, marking the borderline of the two
outcomes.[4] The buyer's reservation price, R_b is the highest price the buyer
is willing to pay; a higher price implies no contract. The seller's reservation
price, R_s is the lowest price the seller is willing to accept; a lower price
implies no contract. Obviously, if $R_b < R_s$ no agreement is possible. With
$R_b \geq R_s$, the bargaining zone (or agreement zone) equals $R_b - R_s$. In this
case, the bargaining zone contains the profit margin of the two parties.

Any profit of the buyer (the buyer's surplus) will be obtained at the expense
of the seller's profit (the seller's surplus). Hence, distributive bargaining is
also called a zero-sum game. (See Figure 15.1.) In a distributive bargaining
situation, the only alternative to a negotiated agreement is 'no contract'. In
general, a negotiator should determine the 'Best Alternative To a Negotiated
Agreement' (*BATNA*[5]). If the value of the *BATNA* is higher than that of an
agreement, the agreement should be canceled. Thus, one's reservation price
should equal the value of the BATNA at least.

The distributive bargaining game can be played in innumerable different
ways. Either the buyer or the seller may start negotiations by making an
opening bid. The other may either accept, quit or counter-offer, etcetera.
The sequence of offers and counter-offers is often called the *negotiation
dance*. This process is rather elusive and difficult to formalize. Frequently,
it is stated that a concession by one participant elicits a concession by the
other participant because of equity in social exchange, i.e. the other party feels
obliged to make a concession because of fairness considerations.[6] Negotiation
may include many different tactics, several of which will be considered in
Section 15.4. With both reservation prices known to each of the players,
agreements usually occur at the midpoint of the bargaining zone.[7]

Restrictive forms of the distributive bargaining game are the Ultimatum
Bargaining game and the Dictator game.[8] In these games, the bargaining
zone is exactly known to both players and there is no room for negotiation. In

Table 15.2. Three parts of the bargaining situation.

Social context	Bargaining process	Bargaining outcomes
Negotiator attributes	Negotiator interests	Contract
Negotiator resources	Negotiator expectations	Payoffs
Bargaining orientations	Bargaining tactics	Distribution of payoffs
Bargaining history		Utility of payoffs
		Market position

Adapted from *Journal of Marraige and the Family*, "A Conceptual Approach to Explicit Marital Negotiation", John Scanzoni, Karen Polenko; 42:1, 31–44 using Figure page 33.

these games, frequently an uneven distribution of the bargaining zone occurs, possibly due to the different roles allocated to the players by the experimenter.

A model of negotiation in marriage is adapted here to be applied in general.[9] Basically, it consists of three parts, each of which includes several elements shown in Table 15.2.

The social context refers to the elements that are given to the bargaining situation:

— The element of negotiator attributes includes variables such as gender, age, location, type of affiliation (e.g. firm, shop, household), legal status, employment status, etcetera. Frequently, the attributes determine the type of negotiation, for example worker-employer, producer-distributor or shop-household negotiation.

— Resources include education and knowledge, budgets of time and money, the social network, bargaining skills and decision authority. In general, resources generate power to be employed in the negotiation process. For example, the likelihood of making concessions may be greater for one who is in a hurry than for one who has time. Bargaining skills will be considered in more detail in Section 15.3.

— Bargaining orientations include the negotiator's self-esteem (this may be important in losing one's face), sex-role preferences (pre-eminently in the household) and nature of the issue under negotiation. For example, a European firm aiming at a foreign market such as China may appraise a joint venture with a local firm in China higher than a joint venture with another European firm.

— The past behavior in bargaining may affect one's orientations, especially in dynamic negotiations. Past behavior may indicate whether one can trust the other party and whether the other party communicates well and acts cooperatively. Furthermore, past behavior may include misunderstanding and resentment. This element may heavily affect one's behavior in future negotiations.

— The market position influences the power to be exerted in the negotiation process. The market position may include the number of buyers relative to the number of sellers and the availability of unique expertise or facilities.

The bargaining process includes the communication and tactics employed in the 'negotiation dance' and allows modifications of one's bargaining position. For example, the reservation prices may be changed during the negotiation process. The outcomes of the bargaining process may be considered in different ways. A very simple way is to observe whether or not the parties reach agreement. In the Ultimatum Bargaining game, the Respondents are observed to accept or reject the proposals made. Other outcomes include the absolute and relative payoffs to the parties. The absolute payoff may be worthwhile as such but may be highly inequitable when it is considered relative to the payoffs of other parties. Here, too the Ultimatum Bargaining game provides an example of this crucial distinction. Finally, the utilities of the payoffs may be considered. The poor man may be better off with an equal distribution than the rich man. A firm urgent in need of cash may be unwilling to accept a deal with delayed payoffs.

The next section will describe a number of strategies and tactics used in the bargaining process.

Conclusion

Bargaining situations may be characterized by the parties' reservation outcomes. The negotiated outcome may become more valuable by integrative bargaining, i.e. enlarging the pie. The negotiation outcomes may be considered in various ways, affecting the likelihood of agreement. Even profitable outcomes may be neglected if the equity conditions are not met.

15.3. Strategies and tactics of negotiation

Two different types of negotiation have been distinguished.[10] The first type has been called *positional negotiation* and takes the bargaining positions of the parties as given. Tough negotiations of this type include *inter alia* seeing the other party as opponent, striving for victory and demanding concessions, and threating and exerting pressure. Any deviation from one's position will be considered as a loss. Soft negotiations of this type include *inter alia* seeing the other party as a friend, aiming at agreement and making concessions for the sake of friendship, making offers and avoiding pressure. Positional negotiation may also be called win-lose negotiation since the other party's gain is perceived as one's own loss. Frequently, this results in distributive bargaining.

The second type has been called *principled negotiation* and is based on the principles underlying one's position. For this reason, a positional change may occur in the interest of one's principles. The parties see each other as problem solvers, striving for a sensible solution, creating possibilities of mutual interest, investigating opportunities and respecting each other's principles. This type may also be called win-win negotiation and frequently results in integrative bargaining. Objective criteria are decisive and the negotiation problem is separated from the human aspect. Since the principles of the negotiating parties may differ, the parties may value different aspects of an agreement. In fact, some aspects may be traded off against other aspects. The example of the deep-sea mining industry has been mentioned.[11] Typically, the industry wants to avoid extreme losses, whereas the nations want the profit of the activity. In this situation, risk may be traded off against profit. For example, the mining companies may pay a low tariff until the break-even point. Above the break-even point, they may pay a much higher tariff.

Another 'trick' concerns the strictness of an agreement.[12] Several aspects of an agreement may be weakened to increase the likelihood of a deal. Agreements may be procedural versus substantial, temporary versus permanent, partial or comprehensive, in principle or definitive, eventual or unconditional, without engagement or binding, secondary or primary. For example, if two parties disagree about the terms of a payment (substantial), they may agree about what to do in this situation, e.g. reside in arbitration (procedure). Principled negotiation is similar to *firm flexibility*,[13] involving unwillingness to compromise on ends (firm), yet being open-minded and innovative with respect to means to these ends (flexibility).

Although the above-mentioned types of negotiation constitute different approaches, the behaviors associated with each type may be manifold.[14] Four groups of negotiator tactics have been distinguished, each of which involves a different concern for one's own and the other party's outcomes.[15] The dual concern model is shown in Figure 15.2.

Problem solving (integrative bargaining or firm flexibility) occurs if there is concern for both one's own and the other party's outcomes. Both contending and yielding belong to positional bargaining, implying exclusive concern either for one's own or for the other party's outcome, respectively. Inaction results from lack of concern for any outcome. Costs of negotiation and time pressure may prevent one using this type of strategy. The groups shown in Figure 15.2 include a number of different tactics. Table 15.3 shows the tactics[16] classified according to the positional and principled types of negotiation.

Emotional behavior includes manipulation, humor, seductive behavior, threats, violence, cynicism and ridicule and primarily belongs to the positional type of negotiation because it is not linked directly to certain princi-

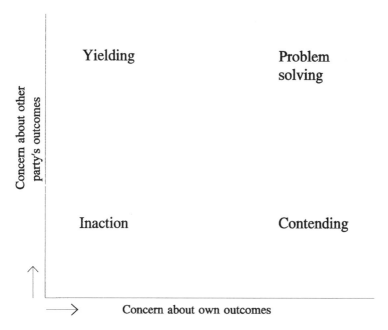

Figure 15.2. The dual concern model. From D.G. Pruitt, *American Behavioral Scientist*, 27(2), pp. 167–194, ©1983 by Sage Publications, Inc. Reprinted by permission of Sage Publications, Inc.

ples. However, in principled negotiation, arguments may be presented in an emotional way to communicate the importance of one's principles.

Force includes physical force by acting helpless or ill, crying and agression. Other types of force include stating a time limit or an ultimatum. Leaving the scene includes resigning, yielding, talking about other topics, physically leaving the scene, delaying and breaking off negotiations. Force, insisting and leaving the scene typically belong to the positional type of negotiation.

Offering services and other resources is used as rewards, whereas withdrawing resources is used as punishment rather than as parts of an agreement. For this reason these tactics are classified as positional negotiation.

Commitment to one's position includes convincing the negotiation partner of the fact that one is incapable to change one's strategy. This may be helpful in brinkmanship.[17]

The contending strategies, discussed above, may be used if the other party is weak, if the issue is of great importance and the closer one moves to one's reservation outcome. Yielding is somehow the opposite of contending and may occur for altruistic reasons of different variety,[18] positive mood and concern for future negotiations. Furthermore, yielding is more likely if the issues are unimportant and time pressure is high.[19]

Table 15.3. Classification of negotiation tactics.

Positional negotiation	Principled negotiation
Emotional behavior	
Force	
Insisting and leaving the scene	
Offering and withdrawing resources and services	
Commitment to one's position	
Yielding (giving in)	
Coalition	
Distort information	Overt information
Yielding according to roles	Deciding according to roles
	Trade-offs and compensation
	Cost cutting
	Integrative bargaining and bridging
	Reasoning

Adapted from *American Behavioral Scientist* 27, D.G. Pruitt "Strategic choice in negotiation," 167–194 (1983), ©1983 by Sage Publications, Inc. and from *Journal of Economic Psychology* 14, E. Kirchler "Spouses' joint purchase decisions: Determinants of influence tactics for muddling through the process," 405–438 (1993) with kind permission of Elsevier Science – NL, Sara Burgerhartstraat 25, 1055 KV Amsterdam, The Netherlands.

Yielding is considered less likely when negotiating as a representative of constituents. Indirect coalition includes referring to constituents, reminding the partner of children's needs or referring to neighbors. Since this tactic is based on social pressure, it has been classified as positional negotiation. Alternatively, children's needs may also be used in principled negotiation. Direct coalition includes talking in the presence of others and clearly has nothing to do with principled negotiation.

Distorting information includes lying and mispresenting information. Since principled negotiation implies being honest about one's principles, distorting information has been classified as positional negotiation, although even in principled negotiation one's true position may be disguised strategically, e.g. by making an offer very much deviating from one's reservation price. Overt information includes talking openly about one's interest, e.g. claiming a need for a product. This tactic has been classified as principled negotiation assuming that the information concerns one's principles. However, giving away one's reservation price obviously does not belong to principled negotiation.

Yielding according to roles may occur because the partner is responsible for the products at stake (e.g. dinner). Although roles may have been assigned on the basis of principles, yielding of this kind has been classified as positional. For the principle regarding the product at stake may be very different than the principle of role assignment. In contrast, deciding according to roles has been classified as principled negotiation, assuming that the roles are directly related to one's principles or norms.

Trade-offs include offers of trade-offs, bookkeeping and reminding the other of past favors. Although this tactic is not directly related to principles, the principles may include the procedure of trade-offs as a kind of equity norm. For this reason, it has been classified as principled negotiation. Compensation includes rewarding the other party for cooperative or yielding behavior. A related strategy is cost cutting, including ways to reduce the other party's costs in exchange for a concession. Integrative bargaining, including expanding the pie, clearly belongs to principled negotiation. Bridging includes the development of a totally new option, satisfying both parties' aims. An example is the exchange of orchestration and implementation power.[20] Orchestration power refers to the power to make the important and infrequent decisions, whereas implementation power refers to the unimportant, time-consuming decisions within the limitations set by the partner who has the orchestration power. A possible solution to the division of power in a joint enterprise, for example, is that one firm is allowed to control the activities of a managing director whereas the other firm chooses the person to occupy this position. Reasoning includes talking in an emotionally neutral way about product alternatives and logical argumentation. Since reasoning excludes emotions, it has been classified as principled negotiation. However, as mentioned above, principled negotiation may include the emotional presentation of arguments.

One tactic, buying without the partner's consent, has been excluded from Table 15.3 because it neglects negotiation. Although physical force and coalition (for social pressure) are unlikely to be used in business, the other tactics may be applied in a variety of contexts. The next section deals with psychological factors influencing the bargaining process and the evaluation of the outcomes.

Conclusion

The distinction between positional and principled negotiation serves to classify a number of different negotiation tactics. Tactics may not only influence one's share of the cake but may also determine its size. In this respect, principled negotiation or 'firm flexibility' may prove helpful.

Table 15.4. Classification of variables influencing the process of negotiation.

	Individual psychological variables	Social-psychological variables
Perception	Quality of objects Magnitude of probabilities	Liking Group-size Noticeability Expectations
Evaluation	Money (relative value) Time (discounting) Gains and losses	Altruism Power Norms
Information processing	Heuristics (aspirations, reservation outcomes) Cognitive dissonance	Communication Third party Market position

From Antonides (1991).

15.4. Psychological factors in negotiation behavior

Behavior in negotiations may be affected by a number of psychological processes. These processes may directly or indirectly affect the utilities of the outcomes of the negotiations. We may distinguish individual psychological and social-psychological factors on the one hand and perception, evaluation and information processing on the other hand. This is shown in Table 15.4.

Individual psychological variables

Perceptual processes transform objective into subjective entities.[21] Perceptual thresholds and biased estimation operate on the perception of objective stimuli. Judgments regarding office space or sales volume may be subject to this type of distortions. Furthermore, low probabilities are likely to be neglected.[22] These factors may affect negotiations, for instance concerning an insurance contract.

The evaluation of income is likely to occur according to the welfare function of income.[23] Similar ideas may apply to the evaluation of wealth.[24] The evaluation of expenses may occur according to the value function for losses.[25] Mental accounting may play a part too. For example, $100 is likely to be perceived as an expense from one's purse but may go almost unnoticed as part of the total bill to one's credit card.[26] Postponement and delay of payment or spending may be evaluated according to the time preferences of the negotiation parties.[27] These factors may be taken into account when negotiations include payment or spending, as is frequently the case. Furthermore, it makes a difference whether a payment occurs to compensate a loss (e.g. a division sold by a firm in financial trouble) or for a different reason (e.g. a state-owned firm sold in the course of privatisation). Likewise, it matters whether expenditures come from a positive financial position (e.g. investments made from profits earned) or from a debt position.

Information processing includes the use of cognitive heuristics which may lead to inefficient outcomes. Satisficing implies the acceptance of an offer meeting one's aspiration level which may differ from the optimal solution.[28] Knowing the other party's aspiration level and hiding one's own may be useful in negotiations.

In this respect, framing effects, anchoring and adjustment, availability and overconfidence have been considered *inter alia*.[29] Framing effects may occur for example in negotiations between management and the union. If the union demands a rise in salary to $12 per hour and management is not willing to pay more than $10 per hour, any agreement between $10 and $12 will be considered as a loss by both parties. The parties are likely to behave risk-seeking by declaring impasse and invoking arbitration. However, if the problem is reframed such that the union considers any rise above $10 as a gain and management considers any rise below $12 as a gain, the parties are likely to behave risk-averse and settle for an agreement.[30]

The effect of anchoring and incomplete adjustment in salary negotiations has already been mentioned.[31] The availability of information is likely to affect behavior in negotiations. Out-of-pocket costs usually are much more concrete than opportunity costs[32] and information presented in a vivid manner is usually more salient than objective information. This may affect the evaluation of alternatives during negotiation. Overconfidence may lead a party to believe in a favorable outcome during negotiations and to make few concessions. In the example above, an overconfident union or management may invoke arbitration rather than settle for an agreement, even if arbitration is likely to result in a rise to $11.

Cognitive dissonance may be used in negotiations as well. For example, a temporary deal is likely to last beyond the set time because the parties may adjust their opinions to the actual situation. Also, cognitive dissonance may increase the utility of the outcomes by diminishing eventual dissatisfaction.

Social-psychological variables

The personal relationships in negotiation are important. Angry parties are less likely to make concessions and to engage in integrative bargaining. Personal relationships may affect sociobiological altruism in the sense that parties on good terms become more altruistic to one another.[33] Personal relationships may be improved by gift giving.[34]

Group size, noticeability and expectations may affect the likelihood and the maintenance of agreements between parties. For example, in large cartels such as OPEC, control of production arrangements is difficult and thus they are difficult to maintain.[35] Moreover, the greater the number of parties, the greater the variety of opinions and the more time is needed to reach agreements.

Altruism may affect concession making and cooperation during negotiations. Empathy may reduce greediness and selective altruism may facilitate cooperation with similar parties.

Power may stem from different sources and may be used in negotiations. Power may depend on the market position, authority, age, education, skills, etcetera.[36] High power may result in a larger share of the negotiated agreement. Earlier, a distinction has been made between orchestration and implementation power.[37]

Conscience and norms may affect negotiations in the same way as they operate in social dilemmas.[38] Norms regarding equal or fair divisions may affect the type of agreement and conscience may prevent non-cooperative behavior by avoiding guilt.

Since it is essential to obtain information regarding the other party's needs and objectives, communication is necessary. Several possible strategies have been considered,[39] three of which pertain to communication:

— building trust and sharing information that is not essential to one's bargaining position, e.g. discussing the distribution rule before negotiating an agreement;

— asking questions, for example: "How much are you paying annually to replace your car fleet?";

— strategically giving away non-essential information, for example: "Our stockholders would appreciate investments in real estate." Frequently, such behavior is reciprocated in negotiation.[40]

Third parties in negotiations are assumed to mediate conflict resolution in various stages of negotiation. In the early stage, mediators will clarify issues and identify the zone of agreement as far as possible. In later stages, they attempt to stimulate integrative bargaining by generating or helping to generate solutions with joint gains to the parties.[41] Third parties tend to be more effective if both negotiation parties agree with their mediation and if the pressure to reach a solution is high.[42] Ineffective tactics include making procedural arrangements and reducing emotional tensions. Effective tactics by mediators include:[43]

— acting as a communication link between the parties;

— intervening with their constituents;

— emphasizing the need to make concessions;

— separating multiple issues to reach partial agreement rather than aiming at package deals;

— occasionally threatening to stop mediation.

The market position may influence one's perception of the market. For example, supply and demand may influence a buyer's perceived probability that a seller on the second-hand market will accept a bid.[44] Likewise, supply and demand may influence a home owner's perception that a buyer will accept an offer.[45] The perceptions concerned may change in the light of new information, third party effects and time pressure. The perceptions of both parties will determine the likelihood and the type of the deal. In this respect, the matching efficiency of firms and job applicants in experimental job markets has been studied.[46]

Conclusion

A number of psychological factors may influence negotiations, including cognitive, affective and social factors. In a sense, this section applies to negotiation a number of psychological theories dealt with in earlier chapters.

15.5. Negotiation in market contexts

Much literature and examples in negotiation pertain to two or more parties. A market context is different because it includes many parties or an unknown number of parties. In this case, the parties may negotiate inefficient agreements or they may use heuristics in deciding about agreements.

Unknown number of parties

Most markets include an unknown or (practically) unlimited number of parties, e.g. job markets, second-hand markets and home production markets. Since it is impossible to negotiate with all parties on the market, a search will be undertaken for the best agreement available. Since search time is costly, the search will be terminated after some time. Although search models exist in economics[47] and in operations research[48] these models rely on probability distributions of events that are frequently unknown. In such complex situations, people resort to heuristics. Satisficing amounts to searching the market until an alternative exceeding the aspiration level has been found.[49]

In the context of negotiation, the situation is even more complex, since the problem is not only to find a negotiation partner but also to obtain a satisfactory agreement. Although the reservation outcomes of the parties are

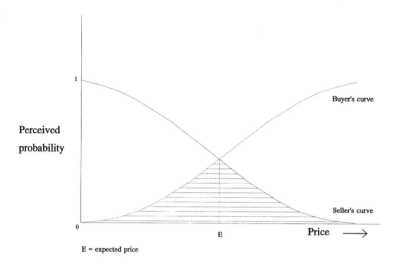

Figure 15.3. Buyer's and seller's perceived probabilities that a price is acceptable to the other party. From Stroeker (1995).

unknown to a particular agent, it is conceivable that the agent has a certain idea of what outcomes will be acceptable to the other parties. This situation has been investigated with respect to the housing market.[50]

A Dutch sample of 134 buyers and sellers of a house provided information on the perceived probability that offers respectively bids were acceptable to another party. Sellers were asked to state their original asking price, the average price one would pay for the house and their reservation price. For each of these prices, the percentage probability that the house could be sold for this price was elicited. Similar questions were asked of buyers of a house. From this information, for each individual a perceived lognormal probability distribution was estimated. The perceived distribution functions of a buyer and a seller are shown in Figure 15.3. The intersection of the two curves indicates the maximum joint probability of agreement at the price concerned. The zone of agreement is indicated by the shaded area in Figure 15.3. In the survey, the result of negotiations on average was as expected from these perception functions. In addition, the location of the perception function varied according to whether the party was represented by a real estate agent, how many options were rejected and the duration of the negotiations.

A similar investigation was conducted regarding negotiations on the Dutch second-hand market.[51] Here too, perceived probability functions were estimated from survey information. It appeared that the buyers' functions in general differed according to the age and the new price of the second-hand items concerned. The sellers' functions in general did not vary according to these characteristics. The realized agreements on second-hand markets deviated considerably from the predictions based on the perceived probability distributions for most second-hand goods in the survey. A problem in this type of research is the trouble in finding matched pairs of sellers and buyers, i.e. pairs of negotiators concerning the same item. Neither the housing study nor the second-hand market study included both the seller and the buyer of the same item, however. This has been left to future research.

Many parties

Although markets frequently exist of (practically) unlimited numbers of participants, their numbers in experimental job markets have been limited.[52] The subjects in the experiments were assigned either the role of job candidate or the role of recruiter. In each of six runs, there were 16 candidates and 8 recruiters. Each candidate was given a desired ordering of firms indicated by their dollar equivalent in salary (more preferred firms being worth more money). Similarly, each recruiter was given a desired ordering of candidates indicated by their dollar equivalent in salary. Candidates were required to negotiate a salary higher than $40,000 and recruiters were required to negotiate a salary lower than $50,000. Each recruiter could hire a maximum of two candidates. Negotiations took place in ten rounds. Recruiters' scores were obtained by calculating the amount of salary below $50,000 and the hired candidates' dollar equivalents. Candidates' scores were obtained by calculating the amount of salary exceeding $40,000 and the firm's dollar equivalent.

Finally, it was observed how many inefficient matches had occurred, that is recruiters that could have hired more preferred candidates while these candidates also preferred the firm represented by this particular recruiter. The average number of candidates in the six runs that could successfully 'jump ship' was 6.5, the average number of firms that could successfully replace one candidate was 2.5 and the average number of firms that could replace two candidates was 1.5. It appeared that the matching solutions found in these experimental markets were by no means perfect.

Conclusions

Market contexts are characterized by a number of participants. Here, in addition to negotiating the best outcome, the problem is to find the best match in the market. Without knowledge of the number of parties available, negotiators may use probability distributions to estimate the probability of agreement. A large but limited number of parties may appeal to one's cognitive and social capacities, possibly inducing cognitive heuristics.

Summary

Game theory may be useful to structure and classify negotiation situations. However, negotiation behavior includes a number of different psychological aspects, not considered by game theory.

Basically, four types of negotiation situations may be distinguished with respect to the number of issues and the number of parties involved. In distributive bargaining, the reservation outcomes directly show the possibility or impossibility of agreement. In integrative bargaining, the negotiation issue may be enlarged to such an extent that an agreement becomes more profitable to all of the parties involved.

The bargaining situation includes the social context, the bargaining process and the negotiation outcomes. Bargaining outcomes include the utility and equitability of payoffs which are likely to be affected by psychological factors. The relevant factors may be individual psychological or social-psychological; they may play a part in the perception and evaluation of issues and in the processing of information during negotiations.

A basic distinction of negotiation tactics is between positional and principled negotiation. Positional tactics do not change the bargaining positions whereas principled negotiation tactics may do. Several bargaining positions may possibly be related to the same interest of a party. However, principled tactics do not change but investigate the parties' interests underlying the bargaining positions.

In a market context, negotiation appeals to one's information processing capacity. In the absence of market information, negotiators may use probability distributions regarding the acceptability of offers. With many parties, inefficiencies of negotiated outcomes are likely to occur.

BOX 15.1

A NEGOTIATION CASE

Salary negotiations are like many other distributive bargaining situations, including the sale of a house, a second-hand good, household task divisions, etcetera. In the following example, an MBA job candidate applies her principled negotiation skills to a salary negotiation with a recruiting publishing firm using a positional strategy. She has passed all the necessary tests and this situation occurs in the final stage of the procedure.

Recruiter

Good morning Mrs. Smith, let's see if you are willing to accept our terms of the contract. Would you like some coffee?

Candidate

Good morning Mr. Jones, what makes you think that our contract will include your terms only? Yes, I would like some coffee, thank you.

Well, I am the employer and there were a hundred of candidates, so I am afraid you don't have much choice. How about $2,500 a month?

Mr. Jones, my reason for choosing your firm was to replace the late Mr. Goodenough because of my special knowledge of the chemistry book market. How did you come by $2,500?

We always offer $2,500, that is our standard policy.

Aha, please tell me about the standard candidate and I will summarize my vita once more.

Let's cut this short. We know about your chemistry knowledge and I may offer you $300 extra.

Sir, I am not asking for $300 extra but I want the salary I am entitled to. Did you take into account my three years of experience in marketing? Marketing jobs are well-paid as you certainly know.

Yes, I know but the company has cut salaries for new MBA's and $500 extra is the best offer I can make and nothing more.

Well, it depends, how about gratifications?

Gratifications are given only in extraordinary cases.

Mr. Jones, in the marketing department, I hit the sales top-10 several times. Isn't that extraordinary? I think a small percentage of the sales is reasonable.

Mrs. Smith, you are like an iron lady. Do you think I can offer bonuses to candidates without further ado?

Mr. Jones, I only ask you whether it is reasonable to pay extra for good performance. The authors also obtain a percentage, don't they?

Are you insisting on this? In that case, I have to put it to the board meeting. Anyhow, what percentage are you thinking of?

What do you think about the firm's profit percentage applied to my annual salary? Of course, only if this is above zero.

Yes, you are funny. In case the board agrees, could you start next month? You get 24 days vacation per annum.

Yes, I think so but please tell me about the firm's policy of paying overwork.

Overwork has been accounted for in the salary.

Also for holidays?

Don't you take holidays?

Yes but I don't know I will take 24 days. Will you pay salary on the remaining days?

It is not our policy but I shall see what I can do for you.

Don't you think it is reasonable?

Yes, it sounds reasonable but we have our policy.

My policy is to be reasonable. Are you going to put this to the board as well?

Three days later Mrs. Smith received a contract including $3,000 salary with 10% bonus if the firm's profit would allow this and payment of unused vacation days.

Notice the positional negotiation strategy used by the firm: creating a friendly atmosphere, using threat and standard policy. The principled negotiation strategy stresses equity and reasoning.

Notes

[1] See Chapter 14.
[2] Stroeker 1995.
[3] Raiffa 1982.
[4] This concept is similar to the concept of the reservation income, considered in Section 10.5.
[5] Fisher et al., 1983.
[6] Cialdini 1985.
[7] Raiffa 1982.
[8] See Chapter 14.

[9] Scanzoni and Polonko 1980, see also Antonides and Hagenaars 1989.

[10] Fisher et al. 1983.

[11] Fisher et al. 1983.

[12] Fisher et al. 1983.

[13] Pruitt 1983.

[14] An overview of different behavioral tactics has been provided by Pruitt 1983 and by Kirchler 1993, 1995 with respect to negotiation within the household.

[15] Pruitt 1983.

[16] Pruitt 1983 and Kirchler 1993.

[17] See Section 14.5.

[18] See Sections 3.5 and 14.3.

[19] See Pruitt 1983.

[20] Safilios-Rothschild 1976.

[21] See Chapter 4.

[22] See Section 13.5.

[23] See Section 10.3.

[24] See Antonides and Van der Sar 1990.

[25] See Chapter 12.

[26] See Section 12.5.

[27] See Section 3.6.

[28] Raiffa 1982.

[29] Neale and Bazerman 1991.

[30] Neale and Bazerman 1991, p. 45.

[31] See Section 7.3.

[32] Neale and Bazerman 1991, see also Section 12.3.

[33] See Section 14.3.

[34] Isen and Levin 1972, see also Section 4.5.

[35] See Section 14.3.

[36] See Walster et al. 1973 and Gray-Little and Burks 1983.

[37] See Section 15.3.

[38] See Section 14.3.

[39] Bazerman 1994.

[40] Cialdini 1985.

[41] Raiffa 1982.

[42] Hiltrop 1988.

[43] Hiltrop 1988.

[44] Stroeker 1995.

[45] Antonides 1992.

[46] Sondak and Bazerman 1989, see also Section 15.5.

[47] Stigler 1961.

[48] Wagner 1969.

[49] See Section 7.4.

[50] Antonides 1992.

[51] Stroeker 1995.

[52] Sondak and Bazerman 1989.

CHAPTER 16

ECONOMIC PSYCHOLOGICAL METHODS

16.1. A classification of studies

In the preceding chapters, a number of economic psychological studies have been reported. Obviously, each study was designed with a different objective and aimed at a different target. In addition, a variety of methods were used. However, the studies can be classified according to several criteria. This chapter will consider the objective of a study, the unit of observation and the method used. Since economic psychological studies are pre-eminently empirical, no distinction will be made between empirical and theoretical studies.

Research objective

A first criterion is the objective of a study. Many research institutes have been founded by the government or other types of administration to investigate particular problems of society, e.g. concerning health, income, education, economy, etcetera. Furthermore, many industries have their own departments of research and development and many of them use marketing and opinion bureaus to investigate specific problems. This is called *applied research* from which theories in specific areas have been developed, such as theories on unemployment, taxation, environmental economics and marketing.

Although much effort and money is available for applied research, scientific endeavors aimed at understanding our world and the human being are also being made. At universities and scientific institutes, theories are being developed and tested in order to acquire a basic understanding of the principles and mechanisms that are common to a number of different problems. This is called *pure research* and from this general theories have been developed, such as the economic theory of demand, the theories of perception, learning, evaluation and decision making, etcetera. The contents of the preceding chapters reflect a classification of economic psychological studies according to the general theories developed in pure research. Here, the studies will be classified according to two other criteria: the unit of observation and the method used.

Unit of observation

Economics used to be concerned with the behavior of society or markets as a whole and with the larger areas, such as oligopolies, (bigger) firms and administration. Psychology typically has been concerned with individual behavior and with social groups, including the organization. Gradually, however, economics has become interested in individual behavior and psychology has extended its interest to larger groups (e.g. the unemployed, the elderly). Even so, a classification of studies according to the unit of observation might be useful.

Many studies reported in preceding chapters are aimed at understanding individual economic behavior. Therefore, typically samples of individuals are studied. This is characteristic of the *micro* study of economic behavior.

Several studies relate to the behavior of social groups and organizations. Sometimes, the behavior of a single group is studied, sometimes a sample of groups (firms) is taken. This is characteristic of the study of economic behavior at the *meso* level.

Several studies are concerned with the behavior of large groups, such as whole nations. A number of conditions are related to the development of nations and the differences between them. This constitutes the study of economic behavior at the *macro* level.

Method

A useful distinction between research methods can be made by classifying them as naturalistic *observations* or as *experiments*.

In naturalistic observations, conditions and events are recorded, frequently supplemented with individual reports. The recordings of conditions and events are used to generate *statistics*, such as GNP, price index, number of residents, etcetera. Many statistics are drawn up regularly, forming a *time series* of observations. Frequently, however, unique recordings are made, which are explained from individual reports or from other recordings. For example, recordings of buying behavior are explained by incomes and attitudes. Strictly, in this type of research, explanations cannot be used to form predictions of events. The results at best show a *statistical* relationship between several variables, frequently interpreted as a *causal* relationship. For instance, from the statistical relationship regarding buying behavior, it cannot be concluded in general that positive attitudes predict future consumption, since consumption might predict attitudes as well.[1]

Table 16.1. Classification of economic psychological studies.

	Experiments	Naturalistic observations
Micro	Animal studies	Interviews
	Physiological studies	Surveys
	Choice experiments	$N = 1$ studies
	$N = 1$ studies	
Meso	Market simulations	Market studies
	Test markets	Organizational studies
	Token economies	Participation
Macro	Government policy	Time series studies
	Revolutions	Comparative studies
		Primitive societies

In experimental studies, conditions are manipulated intentionally to induce changes in behavior. To the extent that uncontrolled variables are not *confounded* with the behavior, different outcomes can be attributed to the conditions manipulated. This attribution is a causal explanation of the behavior studied in the experiment.

In Table 16.1, a number of economic psychological studies are classified according to the unit of observation and to their use of naturalistic observations or experiments. These methods will be dealt with in more detail in Section 16.2.

Section 16.3 discusses several experimental designs. Section 16.4 deals with economic psychological methods of measurement and Section 16.5 with the reliability and validity of observations. Section 16.6 considers a number of interrogatory techniques used in research.

Conclusion

Economic psychological studies can be classified according to their research objectives, the unit of observation and the type of method used. A classification according to the theories involved in the studies has already been made in the preceding chapters.

16.2. Economic psychological methods

Micro level experiments

Animal experiments have been conducted mainly to study the principles of reinforcement.[2] Since the utility function is a cornerstone of economic theory, knowledge of reinforcement principles is highly relevant. This type of research is relatively cheap, since the experimental data can be gathered easily. Also, it can be controlled very effectively, since the manipulation of conditions, e.g. motivational states and the reinforcement, can be very precise. Furthermore, it offers the opportunity of studying a large range of conditions and behaviors, e.g. very high or low deprivation, very high and low rates of reinforcement. Obviously, animals cannot replace human beings in building economic psychological theories but these experiments might suggest hypotheses to be tested in other ways.

Physiological experiments have been conducted mainly in the study of emotions.[3] It is assumed that physiological measures are reliable in that the instruments cannot 'lie'. Many *experimenter biases*, such as experimenter liking, social desirability, response tendencies (e.g. answering "Yes" more frequently than "No"), are avoided by taking physiological measurements. In studies of highly subjective response, objective measures may be preferred to or at least support subjective measurements.

In choice experiments, individuals are required to make either an actual or a hypothetical choice. In these experiments, the behavior of subjects approximates or at least bears some implications for real life behavior. Typically, in these studies, conditions are *varied purposefully*, so that different groups of subjects face different conditions. For instance, electric shocks of different intensities have been used to induce different levels of arousal.[4] Task performance has been compared between different conditions of shock intensity. In an observational study, the *spontaneous* level of arousal would have been measured by using physiological techniques. Task performance would have been compared between groups with high levels of arousal and groups with low levels. As far as economic psychology is concerned, the experimental methods regarding choice have been applied in studies of perception, information processing, attitude, emotion, consistency and rationality, uncertainty and social dilemmas.

A few studies have been conducted with only one subject who put himself in different conditions[5] and observed his own behavior. These studies are exceptional, although contemporary computer technology could enable individuals to study their own behavior in response to stimuli that are 'controlled' by the computer (e.g. in choosing at random from a limited stimulus set).

Meso level experiments

Market simulation studies involve playing a game of real life under controlled conditions. For instance, a simulation of the housing market would involve groups of buyers and sellers, negotiating to obtain target outcomes according to certain rules (both set by the experimenter). Another simulation example is the allocation of limited resources (e.g. money) to the members of an organization (e.g. a firm). Coalition behavior in a market (e.g. oligopoly) can also be experimentally investigated. Besides having relatively low costs and high control, these experiments have the advantage[6] of studying conditions that have never occurred in practice (or under very unfavorable conditions) and of minimizing self-selection biases (a selection effect resulting from the fact that the economic agents were allowed their own choice of institution in which to participate).

Test markets can be considered as a meso level experiment, since the effect of introducing of a new product (by a firm) or new policy measures (by an administration) can be compared with the effect of the status quo. Since experimental control is minimal in this case, the results are highly relevant in practice. However, the choice of the test market and the timing of the test are critical, since minor events or deviations may influence the results.

Token economies[7] in hospitals, prisons or classrooms can be considered as experiments since the conditions are more or less under control of the staff. Token economies are intermediate regarding the control of simulations and test markets. However, their relevance as experiments may be questioned since their purpose is not to test scientific theories but to solve specific problems. The results of token economies are still valuable as observations, of course.

Macro level experiments

Policy measures at the macro level can be considered experiments since these are under the control of the administration. Frequently, economic policy is inspired by economic theory. Hence, the results of the measures can be viewed as a test of economic theory and eventually lead to theoretical adjustments. Usually, policy aims at small economic changes that are predictable to some extent. However, transforming whole nations from communism to capitalism can hardly be called an experiment since control is almost absent.

From the previous chapters, it appears that economic psychological experiments have mainly been conducted at the micro level. At the meso and macro levels, psychology is certainly involved in economic experiments. However, psychological theory does not yet provide clear hypotheses to be tested at these levels.

Micro level observations

The most obvious way to extend one's knowledge of people is to ask them questions. This is exactly what happens in a personal interview. Questions may be asked regarding the reasons for their behavior, regarding their attitudes, expectations, emotions, education, etcetera. The answers are elicited by *introspection*, i.e. looking into one's own thoughts and feelings to discover the reasons and motives for behavior. In fact, this is the oldest method in psychology and William Wundt in 1879 made extensive use of it. First, however, his subjects were trained in the method of introspection and had to participate in a minimum of 10,000 practice observations. Later, it has been noticed that subjective reports are vulnerable to a number of distortions, errors and biases. Besides interviewer bias (cf. experimenter biases), lack of memory, etcetera, the method of introspection has been criticized because the nature of one's thoughts and feelings could be changed by the method itself. The cognitive theory of emotions[8] and the theory of cognitive consistency[9] support this view. Yet, the personal interview has survived and is applied by many marketing research organizations. Its greatest value is probably in explorative research and in problems demanding divergent solutions, such as in creative thinking and product innovations. Usually, interviews are held with small samples of subjects, sometimes being highly selective (e.g. business managers, top economists, people well below the poverty line, etcetera). Usually, the responses in a personal interview are recorded carefully, transcribed and interpreted by trained judges.

The survey is a large scale investigation of people's behavior, conditions and opinions, usually with rather simple questions and with precoded answers. The survey is used if the researcher already knows which questions to ask and which answers are to be expected, e.g. in hypothesis testing and in time series construction. Frequently, the answers are transformed into numerical values, which are stored in computers. This offers the possibility of using statistical techniques to examine the relationships between the variables in the survey. Short versions of psychological tests of personality and motivation[10] can easily be included in survey questionnaires.

Several types of surveys can be distinguished, e.g. the structured personal interview in which a number of questions are asked and the responses are scored (coded) by the interviewer, the structured interview by telephone, the mail survey in which the respondent completes a questionnaire by himself and the computer assisted interview in which the questions appear on a computer monitor and the answers are typed on the keyboard. The survey types have different advantages and costs. In surveys, special attention has to given to the sample selection and to the handling of non-response.

Observations of only one person are usually made if the person possesses outstanding qualities or experiences extreme conditions. Biographies and autobiographies form rich sources of material for scientific analysis.[11] Individuals with brain injuries or other functional disturbances are frequently observed since their experiences can be considered as rare experiments of nature, that cannot be conducted by human researchers. A single case study is sometimes able to refute a scientific hypothesis, although it can never be used as evidence in favor of a hypothesis.

Meso level observations

Market studies are observational investigations of a particular (type of) market. In contrast to marketing studies (which involve micro level observations, e.g. opinions regarding a product), market studies examine the behavior and the conditions of a market as a whole, e.g. a market's turnover, structure (leaders/followers), barriers (goodwill/ advertising), employment, etcetera. Types of markets may be studied irrespective of the commodities exchanged, e.g. auctions, second-hand markets, department-stores, etcetera. Economic psychological studies might involve *inter alia* the psychological conditions, e.g. the flow of information in a market (the fashion market, the stock exchange), the image of economic agents,[12] indicators of expectations in a market and the interaction of market agents.[13] The methods used in this type of research are data sampling (e.g. figures of sales, employment, stocks), expert interviews and opinion research.

Organizational studies involve the analysis of the structure and functioning of organizations, such as industries, firms, public and commercial services. These studies are usually not conducted within the area of economic psychology.

A participating observation usually involves the observation of a group of people with special characteristics or activities while the observer temporarily becomes a member of the group. A well-known example is Günter Wallraff,[14] who participated in a community of Turkish immigrants. The study by LaPiere[15] is another example of this approach. These studies frequently signal a particular state or process going on and provide suggestions for explanation and solution of the problems involved. Usually, these studies are not taken as evidence for certain hypotheses but may refute established ideas (e.g. attitudes predict behavior).

Macro level observations

Economic studies on the macro level use national accounts of different aspects of a society. Besides economic statistics, a number of indicators of social phenomena exist.[16] For instance, mortality rate and life expectancy are indicators of health. Many of these statistics are kept on an annual or quarterly basis, which allows the analysis of time series. In time series, aggregate data at different points in time are used as the observations in research. Economic psychological examples of this approach have been considered with respect to expectations.[17]

Aggregate statistics are also used in cross-sectional studies where different countries are compared. For instance, the effect of the tax burden on GNP might be considered by statistical analyses of these variables with the countries as units of observation. Economic psychological examples of comparative studies are considered in the area of well-being.[18] A special type of study concerns the achievement level judged from national prose material.[19]

The study of primitive societies can be considered as case studies of natural experiments. In these societies, conditions are totally different from those in the Western world today. As such, these provide unique opportunities to test the generality of economic psychological theories and might suggest adaptation of the theories.

It appears that economic psychology has been involved in observational studies on the meso and macro levels to a greater extent than in experimental studies at these levels. On the micro level, the effort involved is more or less even. We would here point out that experimental studies on the micro level may be accompanied by observations that may provide additional tests of the hypotheses involved in the study.

Conclusions

It appears that economic studies have mainly used naturalistic observations whereas economic psychological studies made use of both experiments and naturalistic observations. Furthermore, economic studies have mainly been performed on the meso and macro level of observation. Economic psychological studies have mainly been performed on the micro level of observation. However, the two disciplines are extending their interests in that economists become involved in micro-level experiments and psychologists in meso-level experiments and observations.

16.3. The validity of experiments

Consider a firm, producing a detergent on a national scale, confronted with decreasing sales in some parts of the country. A small survey indicates that an unfavorable image of the firm[20] might be responsible for this. The firm decides to investigate whether a promotional campaign would be able to improve its image. A test of the campaign is conducted in a city in the East of the country where the image appears to be most unfavorable. The campaign includes the provision of free samples of the detergent together with an accompanying letter enumerating its benefits and an example of a calculation of the favorable price per unit of weight. During the campaign,

Table 16.2. Results of an image improving campaign.

	National	City of campaign
Image before campaign	3.1	1.5
Image after campaign		3.5
Number of respondents	5000	500
Response rate	50%	30%

the firm suffers from negative information in the media regarding the use of the detergent. After the campaign, the survey is conducted again (this time with a detailed questionnaire) using the same people who had been involved in the first survey in the city. To reduce the costs, the firm's employees serve as interviewers in the survey. The results of the survey are summarized in Table 16.2.

From Table 16.2, one might conclude that the campaign has been effective, since it has improved the image substantially (slightly above the national level) even in a city with an unfavorable image of the firm and despite the negative opinion regarding detergent in the media. The general sales manager of the firm has decided thereafter to conduct the campaign on a national scale. Is this a wise decision?

To evaluate the results of the campaign, one must first show that the obtained effect can be attributed confidently to the *independent* variable that was manipulated by the experimenter.[21] Then it is necessary to investigate whether the campaign or some other variable produced the image change and whether the image change occurred because of people's revised opinions with respect to the firm. This concerns the question of *internal validity* of the campaign as an experiment.[22] A number of objections to the internal validity of the campaign experiment can be raised.

Maturation

Since the survey was only repeated in the city where the campaign was conducted, the effect of the campaign cannot be distinguished from the effect of a spontaneous improvement of the firm's image. In other words, would the image change have occurred without the campaign? Maybe the second survey only picked up a nationwide tendency to evaluate firms more positively than before. At least a second survey should have been conducted in other parts of the country to recognize this effect. This would have served as a *control group* for comparison with the experimental group.

Maturation can only affect results if the data are obtained at different points in time. This is typically the case in experimental research with measurements before and after some kind of manipulation. Maturation involves spontaneous changes not only over days or weeks but also over smaller time periods. In experimental sessions of one hour, for example, subjects may become bored, tired or hungry, which might affect the measurements accordingly.

Testing

In the second survey, after the campaign, the respondents might perform better than in the first survey, since they have become familiar with the questions. This may affect the results in a variety of ways. The familiarity with the questions may produce more complete answers to the questionnaire, thus reducing *partial non-response*. (It might also reduce the number of "Don't know" answers.) In the second survey, the questions might be better understood, producing answers different from the first survey. For example, the tendency to answer "Yes" more often than "No"[23] might be reduced in a second survey. The testing effect can be established by presenting the questionnaire to a fresh sample at the same time as the second survey.

Instrumentation

The second survey included a longer questionnaire than the first one. This implies a change in the measurement device, possibly influencing the results. Since the sample in the 'campaign condition' is much smaller than in the national survey, the costs of asking a number of additional questions are relatively low. This may provide an economic justification to extend the questionnaire but changes in the response might be the result.

Instrumentation may arise from a great many seemingly futile changes, such as altering the order of the questions,[24] changing instructions to the respondent for clarity reasons, changing the answer categories or response scales or improved observation by the interviewer in the repeated measurements.

Selection

The selection of the city for the campaign strongly influenced the results. The subjects were not *selected at random* from the national population as there were no equal chances of being included in the survey. For this reason, one is not allowed to compare the results of the second survey with the national results of the first survey.

Regression

The city of the campaign was chosen because of its extremely unfavorable image toward the firm. However, considering the small sample and volatility of image measurements, the unfavorable image might result from temporary conditions or from conditions determined by chance. In this case, statistical regression might explain the results. Statistical regression refers to the fact that the extreme scores in a particular distribution will tend to move toward the mean of the distribution as a function of repeated testing. The results should at least have been compared with a *matched control group* with the same unfavorable attitude toward the firm.

Mortality

It appears that the number of respondents dropping out of the repeated survey was higher than in the first cross-section. Obviously, it is easier to have subjects participating only once than on two successive occasions. With an average response of 50% in the first survey, a response of about 25% in the second survey was to be expected. If the non-response is systematic, however, this is called differential mortality, which may present problems in the interpretation of the results. During the campaign, people with unfavorable attitudes toward the firm are more likely to drop out, thus contributing to a more favorable image estimate of the firm in the city.

History

During the campaign, the detergent was given negative attention in the media, which might have influenced the image in the city. In this case, the effect of the campaign might have been even greater than without the attention in the media. Other events, e.g. approval of the firm's detergent by a consumer organization, might have contributed to a positive image change. Anyway, the effect of history may be confused by the experimental manipulations.

Experimenter bias

To reduce the costs of the survey, the firm's employees interviewed the sample of respondents in the city. This might have contributed to the positive results in a number of ways. The employees might have been aware of the unfavorable image in the city. This might have biased their observations in the first survey in a negative way. In addition, since the employees are likely to have a positive attitude toward the firm and its promotional campaign, they will want the campaign to be successful and themselves to be part of the success. This might have biased their observations in the second survey in a positive way. These instances of experimenter bias may induce a self-fulfilling prophecy, which is detrimental to the internal validity of the campaign test.

The effect of experimenter bias may appear far-fetched to those not acquainted with experiments. However, consider the following experiment:[25]

Undergraduate students served as experimenters in a simple maze problem with rats as subjects.[26] Half of the students (randomly selected) were told that their rats were bright and therefore learned quickly. The remaining students were told that their rats were dull and would show 'little evidence of learning'. Actually, the rats were drawn randomly from a relatively homogeneous population. After the experiment, the students working with the presumably 'bright' rats presented data suggesting that their rats performed approximately 50% better than the rats presumed to be 'dull'.

If experimenter bias can be shown in experiments with rats, then experiments with human beings are probably much more vulnerable to this effect. Experimenter bias can show up in a number of ways.[27] The experimenter may unintentionally provide cues for expected-desired behavior of the subjects, for example:

— paralinguistic cues, e.g. variations in the tone of voice;

— kinesic cues, e.g. by changes in posture or facial expression;

— verbal cues, e.g. humming.

In addition, the experimenter may unintentionally misjudge or misrecord the subject's responses. Another example of experimenter bias is the Halo effect. The *Halo effect* is based on a generalization of an isolated judgment to an overall person evaluation, e.g. a positive person evaluation from the appreciation of her nice blue eyes.

Possible reductions of the experimenter effect can be accomplished by running the experiment with experimenters or data collectors who are unaware of the hypothesis being tested. In this case, the experimenters are called *blind*, since they don't know which results are to be expected. A further reduction can be obtained by minimizing the contact between experimenter and subject, e.g. by written or tape-recorded instructions or automated data collection procedures. Monitoring of experimenters also tends to reduce experimenter bias. Many market research organizations screen their survey data for the existence of interviewer effects.

Even if an experiment appears to be internally valid in that all of the above factors are under control, the experimental effect can be attributed to a number of causes inherent in the manipulated variables. In the example above, it can be assumed that an image change results from changed beliefs regarding the firm or its products or from changed importance weights in the attitude.[28] Alternative explanations are possible, however. The free samples

of the detergent and the visits by the interviewers (social attention) might have
induced favorable attitudes by various mechanisms, e.g. by social modeling,
positive reinforcement[29] or by the process of cognitive dissonance.[30]

The evaluation of the internal validity of experiments considered above can
be supplemented by evaluations of *external validity*. This refers to the question
to what extent the experimental results can be generalized to the population.
Because the campaign experiment is internally invalid for a number of reasons,
one is not allowed to generalize the results. However, there may be reasons
for which the results of an internally valid experiment may not be generalized
to the population.

The experimental setting produces a number of unintended, frequently
unavoidable effects. The experience of being in the experiment and being
measured may induce people to behave differently. These *reactive effects*
appear to be present in the so-called 'Hawthorne effect'. The 'Hawthorne
effect' refers to the effect of attention given to workers at the Hawthorne
plant of the Western Electric Company. Every condition applied with a view
to increasing working output appeared to have a positive effect. This result
could be attributed to one factor common to all conditions: attention paid to
the workers. The 'Hawthorne effect' may be present in experimental research.

Experimental subjects are frequently clever in ascertaining the purpose of
the experiment. Their reactions are in accordance with their hypotheses concerning the experiment. This points to the role behavior of subjects as elicited
by the *demand characteristics* of the situation. This has been shown, for example, in a sensory deprivation experiment.[31] Two groups of subjects were
randomly assigned to one of two conditions. In the experimental condition,
the subjects faced an experimenter with a white coat, a medical history was
taken and a tray of drugs and medical instruments, labeled the 'emergency
tray', was in full view. During the instructions, they were told to report any
unusual experience. Finally, they were shown a red button marked 'Emergency alarm' which they could press if they could not stand the situation any
longer. The demand characteristics in this condition were such that reports of
bizarre experiences could be expected. In the control condition, the subjects
were told that they were a control group for a sensory deprivation experiment
and were not exposed to the medical environment. All subjects spent three
hours in an isolation room. The demand characteristic group showed more
symptoms of sensory deprivation than the controls, e.g. reports such as that
"the walls of the room are starting to waver".

The techniques used in the measurement of attitudes have been
questioned.[32] It is generally assumed that individuals are motivated and able
to report their true attitude and that the measurement technique has no influence on the attitude and the behavior. The biases considered above indicate

that these assumptions are frequently violated.

Several add-on techniques have been employed to deal with these problems. The bogus pipeline technique[33] is based on the researcher's claim to be able to detect any false answer of a subject. It is assumed that this technique increases the subject's motivation to reveal her true attitude. The credibility of the claim can be increased by using a technical device (e.g. a lie detector) that will warn the researcher in case of false answers. Also, the researcher may claim that she has already obtained (or will obtain) the relevant information.

Another method of dealing with unwillingness to respond is the *randomized response* technique, based on confusing the answer with a random variable.[34] For example, a question as to whether a person has ever stolen anything is likely to be answered negatively, even if the person has actually ever stolen something. Now, let the subject toss a coin (in private so that the researcher does not know the result) and ask her to respond in the following way:

– If heads appears: answer "Yes" to the question.
– If tails appears: answer the question truthfully.

This procedure is likely to reduce false answers since the individual behavior cannot be detected. However, repeating this procedure with a number of subjects enables the researcher to study the distribution of the answers, which should be 50–50% if nobody has stolen. If 55% of the subjects gives an affirmative answer, the researcher infers that on average 10% of the subjects has stolen something. (50% of affirmative answers were given because heads appeared and 50% times 10% because heads appeared *and* the subject has stolen in the past.)

Several types of randomized response methods exist. A special type of data obtains if some unobserved process is confused with a judgment. For example, if tax authorities make judgments regarding taxpayers' files, this may result in judgments to the advantage of the administration, judgments to the advantage of the taxpayer and neutral judgments. The second type of judgment is likely to be the result of a taxpayer's error. However, the first type of judgment may result from either error or attempted tax evasion or both. In the latter case, two processes are confused and have to be disentangled by means of statistical techniques. This technique may also be applied to find the determinants of the unobserved process generating randomized response data.[35]

Interaction of selection and treatment

The campaign might have affected the participants in a special way, differently from the way the national population would have been affected. This might raise a number of alternative reasons for the effect of the campaign. For example, the inhabitants of the city in the East of the country might be more easily persuaded than people in the rest of the country because their culture, in contrast to the rest of the country, values trust in other people. Alternatively, the city's inhabitants might be less intelligent than their countrymen, thereby accounting for the effect of the campaign. Because of the interactive selection effect, the results cannot be generalized to the population.

Interaction of testing and treatment

The first survey might have made the inhabitants of the city more aware of the effects expected from the campaign. These reactivity effects include the wish to help the experimenter, develop personal defenses against the experimental treatment (e.g. selective attention to instructions or exaggeration of one's own opinion). To generalize the results to people that will not be involved in the experiment (i.e. conducting the campaign without the preceding survey) may result in failure of the campaign.

Conclusion

An experiment may be invalid for a number of reasons, some of which could have been avoided or at least could have been detected. Even if an experiment is internally valid, external invalidity may not allow generalization of the results. Reactive affects and demand characteristics of the situation may prevent subjects from giving valid answers. Several add-on techniques may help to elicit true answers, if there are reasons to doubt the subjects' statements.

16.4. Experimental designs

The design of an experiment may determine its vulnerability to internal and external invalidity effects. A number of different experimental designs exist, differentially affecting internal and/or external validity.[36] Here, three designs are considered that produce internally valid experiments. Important characteristics of these designs are the use of controls next to experimental subjects and random assignment of subjects to these groups.

The pretest-posttest control group design

In order to attribute the results of experimental treatment unequivocally to the manipulation of experimental variables, a control group is necessary for comparison with the experimental group. Since frequently it is not known which

$$\begin{array}{ccccc} R & O_1 & X & O_2 \\ R & O_3 & & O_4 \end{array}$$

Figure 16.1. The pretest-posttest control group design.

personal characteristics might influence a person's reaction to an experiment, assignment of subjects to the experimental and the control group should be random. *Randomization* is achieved by giving each subject an equal chance of being assigned to the experimental or the control condition, for example by tossing a coin or by using a random number generator in a computer. A *pretest* and a *posttest* should be included in this design for both conditions.

By convention, the randomization is denoted by R, observation or testing of the subjects by O and experimental treatment by X. The design is depicted in Figure 16.1.

By using a control group, the effects of testing and maturation have been accounted for, since both groups are tested twice.

History would produce equal differences between posttest and pretest in both groups to the extent that historical events are general. The design calls for simultaneous tests of experimental and control groups in the same environment. Frequently this is not the case in practice, since observations are taken at different times, in different rooms, by different experimenters, etcetera. This may differentially affect the *intrasession history* of the subjects (e.g. the experimenter's introductory remarks, the fire across the street, the picture on the wall, etcetera). At least, the sources creating possibly different histories should be randomized over the two conditions.

Instrumentation is controlled by the design if the intrasession history is under control. With standardized instructions and printed questionnaires, a great deal of control is achieved. If there are many opportunities for experimenters to influence the response, they should at least be kept blind with respect to the condition to which the subjects are assigned.

The effects of regression and selection are accounted for by the proper randomization procedure at the start of the experiment.

Obviously, the experimenter should take measures against drop-out of subjects (e.g. by making the subject's payment contingent on the completion of the experiment, by personally reminding the subjects to take the experimental treatment and the second test, etcetera). At least, the design detects differential mortality in the experimental and control conditions.

Because of the pretest included in the design, the interaction effect of

$$
\begin{array}{llll}
R & O_1 & X & O_2 \\
R & O_3 &   & O_4 \\
R &   & X & O_5 \\
R &   &   & O_6
\end{array}
$$

Figure 16.2. The Solomon four-group design.

testing and experimental treatment is possible. If this effect is considered likely, other designs should be taken into consideration. An example of this situation is a study of the effects of a movie showing the benefits of free enterprise on attitudes toward entrepreneurs. In this case, a pretest on these attitudes is likely to sensitize the subjects and this might affect their feelings on viewing the movie. One may not conclude that, without the pretest, the movie would have the same effect on the posttest.

Although the subjects are randomly assigned to the conditions, the total group of subjects might be a selective sample of the population. This is the more likely as more difficulties in getting subjects for the experiment have occurred.

The reactive effects and demand characteristics of the measurements are not controlled by the design but have to be minimized by the measures considered above.

The Solomon four-group design

Solomon devised a design that controls both the main effect of testing and the interaction of testing and experimental treatment.[37] It is depicted in Figure 16.2.

The effect of testing can be detected by comparing O_4 with O_6 and the interaction effect by comparing O_2 with O_5. In addition, the effect of experimental treatment is replicated in four different ways: $O_2 > O_1$, $O_2 > O_4$, $O_5 > O_6$ and $O_5 > O_3$. The design has the same advantages regarding internal validity as the pretest-posttest control group design (in fact, the first two conditions are similar) but has greater opportunities for generalization.

The posttest-only control group design

Although a pretest includes a check on the similarity of experimental and control groups, the randomization procedure in principle is sufficient to assure

$$R \quad X \quad O_1$$
$$R \qquad\quad O_2$$

Figure 16.3. The posttest-only control group design.

this. Omitting the pretest results in an extremely simple design, depicted in Figure 16.3.

The design is similar to the last two conditions of the Solomon four-group design. It controls both for the main effect of testing and for the interaction effect, although it does not measure these effects. The design has the additional advantage of reducing the costs involved in the two other designs above.

Conclusion

Experimental invalidity can be controlled to some extent by the experimental design. Desirable aspects of an experimental design are the randomization of subjects, the use of a control group and a pretest. Omitting the pretest reduces the costs of an experiment while retaining experimental validity.

16.5. Validity and reliability of observations

Obviously, we want the naturalistic and experimental observations to be valid and reliable indicators of the phenomenon under scrutiny. For example, if we ask a survey question: "In general, how happy or unhappy do you usually feel?", we expect the answer to be an accurate indicator of well-being. Here, the concepts of validity and reliability will be considered in more detail.

Validity will be defined as the extent to which an observation is a measure of what it is supposed to measure. Several types of validity are distinguished: content validity, criterion validity and construct validity.

Content validity refers to the correspondence between the observation and the content of what is measured. Regarding the question on well-being it is assumed that happiness covers the content of the well-being concept to a certain degree. This will not always be the case, however. Satisfaction with life as a whole may tap just another part of the content of well-being. Furthermore, the content of well-being implies happiness in a number of life domains. The content validity will be higher if the observations refer to economic well-being, social well-being, physical well-being, etcetera. The concept of content validity is somehow related to the concept of face validity.

Face validity refers to the plausibility that an observation measures a certain phenomenon. Plausibility implies that laymen can easily see the connection between the observation and the concept to which it refers. Content validity frequently implies face validity but the reverse may not be true.

Criterion validity refers to the performance of observations in predicting a criterion. For example, survey observations regarding the individual time preference would predict subsequent saving behavior. To measure criterion validity, correlations or regression coefficients will be computed regarding the observation and the criterion. If the correlation is high, it indicates predictive validity. The choice of a criterion is crucial in judging validity. The correlations between time preference measures and health related behaviors were not high.[38] These correlations would indicate low criterion validity. However, the survey observations dealt with preferences for sums of money at different points in time whereas the criterion is not monetary. This points to the necessity of a correspondence between the content of observations and the content of the criterion. This point has also been raised with respect to behavior to be predicted by attitudes.[39] It appears that criterion validity decreases as content validity is lacking.

Construct validity refers to the connection between observations and related concepts. This type of validity is applied if the concept indicated by the observations is essentially abstract, so that validity cannot be assessed by content or prediction. For example, locus of control is an abstract motivation and the validity of observations regarding this motivation can only be assessed by relating them to other constructs (such as field dependence/ independence or personality variables like introversion/ extraversion) or behaviors (such as entrepreneurial behavior or information seeking). Construct validity can be judged on the basis of theoretical relations (the nomological network) between the construct of interest and other constructs or behaviors.

A methodology to assess the validity of observations has been developed,[40] including the judgment of validity from a correlation matrix of observations regarding different constructs measured by different methods. The structure of such a multitrait-multimethod matrix is shown in Figure 16.4 for two constructs and two methods.

The northwest triangles in the matrix represent the correlations between observations of the same concept (or trait) measured by different methods. For example, r_{21} is the correlation between two measures (numbered 1 and 2) of the first concept. To the extent that different measures of the same concept are correlated this indicates *convergent validity* of the observations. The use of very different methods to assess convergent validity is recommended.[41] If convergent validity is high the observations can be confidently attributed to the concept under investigation.

	$T_1 M_1$	$T_1 M_2$	$T_2 M_1$	$T_2 M_2$
$T_1 M_1$	r_{11}			
$T_1 M_2$	r_{21}	r_{22}		
$T_2 M_1$	r_{31}	r_{32}	r_{33}	
$T_2 M_2$	r_{41}	r_{42}	r_{43}	r_{44}

Figure 16.4. A multitrait-multimethod correlation matrix of observations.

The southwest part of the matrix consists of a square matrix. The northwest–southeast diagonal of this submatrix contain correlations with respect to the same methods measuring different concepts. For example, r_{42} refers to the correlation between two concepts (numbered 1 and 2) measured by the second method. To the extent that different concepts measured by the same method are not correlated this indicates *discriminant validity* of the observations. The use of unrelated concepts to assess discriminant validity is recommended.[42] If discriminant validity is high with unrelated concepts, the observations are not influenced by the method of observation and can be attributed to their respective concepts.

Validity of observations is an issue with some tradition in psychology since measuring the unobservable is prevailing in this science. In economic psychology, many concepts are unobservable so the validity of subjective indicators has to be investigated. In economics, it seems as if the validity of observations is always perfect but nothing is less true. Many economic phenomena are measured by proxy variables that at best can be seen as objective indicators. Examples of proxies are measured income (as a proxy of permanent income), years of schooling (proxy of years of education) and unemployment registration (proxy for unemployment). The validity of proxy variables in economics can be judged according to the validity criteria considered above.

Although the validity of observation might be the first issue to be considered, the reliability of observation is an important concern. *Reliability* can be defined as the accuracy and consistency of observation. For example, unemployment figures should exactly reflect the level of unemployment in a population (accuracy) and should show the same picture in two randomly split halves of the population. Several indicators of reliability are distinguished.

Test-retest correlations refer to the correspondence between two observations of the same phenomenon made at different points in time. For example, well-being measures[43] fluctuate due to different states of mood even within the same interview session. This is not preferred in practice. By using an IQ-test in accepting a job candidate it is assumed that the IQ measured before acceptance is still present when the candidate starts work. Generally, test-retest reliability decreases the longer the period between the two measures.

Reliability can also be assessed by correlating *parallel forms* of observations. For example, if two different versions of the Sensation Seeking Scale[44] are highly correlated, each version is known to measure sensation seeking in a reliable way.

A procedure which is familiar to the method of parallel forms is the computation of a *split-half* reliability coefficient. This procedure can only be applied to multiple item observations since a split of the items (e.g. a random split or a split of odd and even numbered items) is required. The correlation between the two test-halves indicates the reliability of the test with respect to its *internal consistency*.

Obviously, a number of items can be split in numerous ways. A summary measure of reliability resulting from correlations of all possible splits is the Kuder–Richardson formula; another internal consistency measure is Cronbach's α.[45]

Finally, *inter-rater* reliability provides a measure of accuracy of observations. This reliability coefficient refers to the correlation between observations made by two different judges. For example, the Thematic Apperception Test[46] scored by two different judges yields a measure of agreement between the scores that is considered a reliability coefficient.

Generally, the effect of lengthening a set of observations regarding a concept is an increase in reliability. The Spearman-Brown formula[47] states the effect of lengthening a set of observations n times on reliability as a function of the reliability of the original set as follows:

$$r_n = \frac{nr_1}{1 + (n - 1)r_1}$$

For instance, extending a one-item measure of well-being to a four-item scale will increase its original average reliability of (say) 0.40 to 0.73. The Spearman-Brown formula is graphically depicted for $n = 2$ in Figure 16.5.

Since reliability coefficients refer to observations of a particular concept by a particular method, they can be substituted into the diagonal of the correlation matrix shown in Figure 16.4. For example, r_{33} in the matrix refers to the reliability of observing the second concept by the first method. It appears that the validity coefficient of an observation can never exceed its reliability. If the original measurement is not accurate, it cannot be validly related to anything. If it is highly accurate, it may or may not be validly related to some

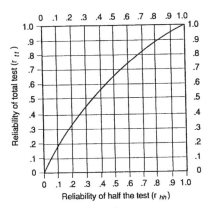

Figure 16.5. The effect on reliability of increasing a set of observations two times. Taken from Guilford (1965, p. 459). Fundamental Statistics in Psychology & Education. Copyright ©1965 by McGraw-Hill. Reproduced by permission of McGraw-Hill, Inc.

criterion.

In general, reliability is unlikely to approach 100%. This implies that validity coefficients are attenuated due to unreliability of the measurements. If the reliability of the measurements is known, a correction for *attenuation* is:[48]

$$r_{12}^* = \frac{r_{12}}{\sqrt{r_{11}r_{22}}}$$

with r^* the disattenuated validity coefficient, r_{12} the attenuated validity coefficient regarding measures 1 and 2, r_{11} and r_{22} reliability coefficients regarding the measurements. The disattenuated coefficient shows the validity as if the measurements were 100% reliable.

Conclusion

Validity and reliability of measurements is an issue both in experimental and in naturalistic observations. Validity refers to whether a measurement indicates what is intended to be measured, reliability refers to the accuracy and consistency of the measurement. Both validity and reliability can be assessed in different ways.

16.6. Questioning techniques

The research described in the previous chapters frequently includes empirical data, obtained by means of surveys, interviews and experiments. Usually, the data consist of respondents' answers to questions. Obviously, different types of questions may obtain different answers.

The first issue of concern in designing a question is the measurement level. Four measurement levels of variables are distinguished:[49]

— A *nominal level* refers to categories, e.g. male/female, brands, shops. Categories may be indicated by numbers, which have no arithmetical meaning, however.

— An *ordinal level* refers to a rank order of magnitudes, e.g. brand preference, socio-economic status. A rank order may be indicated by numbers on which any order preserving transformation is allowed, e.g. adding or subtracting a number does not change the rank order.

— An *interval level* (cardinal level) refers to equal intervals between adjacent categories, e.g. temperature, some attitude scales. Intervals may be numbered, although any linear transformation retains the cardinal level, e.g. the transformation of Celcius grades into Fahrenheit grades.

— A *ratio level* refers to a true zero point in addition to equal intervals, e.g. income, costs, age, probability. Only multiplication by a positive constant retains the ratio level, e.g. multiplication of a centimeter scale by 100 results in a meter scale.

Each level above includes the preceding level, i.e. an interval level includes an ordinal level but the reverse is not true. The measurement level may be different from the level of the underlying variable to be measured. For example, 'masculinity' may be considered an ordinal variable (present in females to some extent) but usually is measured at the nominal level. Temperature in physics is a ratio variable but is usually measured on Celcius or Fahrenheit interval scales.

The level of measurement determines the type of statistical operations allowed. For example, the mean and standard deviation only have meaning for interval and ratio levels measurements but not for category and ordinal level measurements. For this reason it may be advantageous to obtain interval level data in research. Sometimes, the assumption of interval level measurement is made, although strictly an ordinal level applies.

Questioning techniques are applied to obtain data at one of the levels mentioned above. Questions may be asked in open (unlimited number of answering alternatives) or closed form (limited number of alternatives). Open questions are appropriate if the answer can be anything (e.g. "Please tell me what you think now") or if the answer is very precise, for example income, age, probability or percentage. Closed questions are appropriate if the answer falls in one of a few categories (e.g. gender, civil status) or if the answer is imprecise or not exactly known (e.g. income brackets, opinions and attitudes). Often, precise information (e.g. age) is elicited by asking closed questions (e.g. asking for age brackets) for reasons of speed or ease. To maximize the information value of the answers, the brackets should be so constructed that all of them contain the same number of answers.

Except for eliciting socio-demographic information, closed questions are frequently applied in measuring intentions, opinions, evaluations and attitudes. As a general rule, the number of answering categories should not exceed nine because of people's limited information capacities. Frequently, 5-point and 7-point scales are applied.[50] Next, a number of closed form questioning techniques will be summarized.

Category scale

At the nominal level, questions may be asked in the form of category scales, for example:

"Which party will you vote for?"   * Democrat
                                     * Republican

thus forcing a party choice. Frequently, forced choice is avoided by including a 'Don't know' category.

Ordered category scale

At the ordinal level, the categories may be rank ordered, for example:

"Taking all things together, how would you say things are these days?"
                                     * Very happy
                                     * Pretty happy
                                     * Not too happy

Here, the order is fixed, unlike the simple category scale.

Comparison scales

Frequently, researchers are interested in rankings of alternatives, e.g. political parties, policy objectives, brands, shops, etcetera. Besides asking respondents to rank order the alternatives, paired comparisons or constant-sum scales may be used. Paired comparisons may include simple comparisons like the voting intention question above or comparisons between three or four alternatives. From paired comparisons between A and B, C and D, B and C, etcetera, the rank order of A, B, C and D may be derived indirectly.

Constant-sum scales require the respondent to divide points or money among a limited number of alternatives, for example:

"Please divide 100 points among the following attributes of a pencil such that the points reflect the relative importance of the attributes in choosing a pencil."

Color	_____
Ease of handling	_____
Writing performance	_____ +
Sum	100

Constant-sum scales imply psychological trade-offs between alternatives and provide information on the size of the difference between alternatives.

Semantic Differential scale

The Semantic Differential scale requires the evaluation of an alternative on a bipolar scale defined with contrasting adjectives, for example:[51]

"Buying a color television set with an expected lifetime of 10 years is:"

Good ___ ___ ___ ___ ___ ___ ___ Bad
       3   2   1   0   1   2   3

The numbers suggest that the scale is at the interval level of measurement, although the unit number does not always have the same psychological meaning, i.e. a difference between 2 and 3 may be psychologically different than a difference between 1 and 2. Frequently, the numbers are omitted since the equal spacing of the answer bars serves the same purpose. A number of different Semantic Differential scales may be described by a limited number of dimensions.[52]

Likert scale

Likert scales[53] require respondents to approve or disapprove a certain statement, frequently reflecting an attitude or norm, for example:

"Buying a color television set with an expected lifetime of 10 years is good."

* Strongly approve
* Approve
* Undecided
* Disapprove
* Strongly disapprove

Thurstone scale

A Thurstone scale[54] is constructed in two steps. In the first step, a large number of different attitude statements are elicited from a relatively small sample, for example: "Democratic policy increases the welfare of the country." In the second step, a large sample is asked to sort the statements into categories that are seemingly equally spaced, for example:

Favorable ___ ___ ___ ___ ___ ___ ___ Unfavorable
         A   B   C   D   E   F   G

From each category, a statement is included in a separate ordered battery of items. The items are selected on the basis of agreement that they belong to certain categories, according to the sample and on the basis of equal spacing along the continuum. The value of an item roughly coincides with the rank order of the category from which it was selected. Administering the scale is very simple: a respondent simply chooses the item that fits her attitude best. Her score equals the value of the item selected.

Magnitude estimation

Most of the scales above are category scales. A respondent's sensitivity of judgment by means of category scales differs over the range of stimuli, i.e. discrimination is relatively better at one end of the stimulus continuum than at the other.[55] For example, estimating the lengths of bars using an 11-point scale results in overestimations at the medium stimulus range. With magnitude estimation (prompting for exact length estimates in *cm*'s) respondents are uniformly sensitive over the stimulus range in general.

An alternative type of magnitude estimation, frequently applied in computerized questionnaires, is magnitude estimation by drawing a line. The length of the line should correspond with the perceived magnitude of the stimulus. Magnitude estimation should result in better estimates than category scales.[56]

Conclusion

Questions may be asked at different measurement levels, allowing different statistical techniques. Frequently, however, assumptions should be made regarding the measurement level of a scale, for example interval level of measurement regarding a Likert scale.

Summary

Economic and psychological studies have been classified according to their research objective, their unit of observation, the methods used and the theories to which they are related. The preceding chapters represent a classification of studies according to the theories involved. The research objectives distinguished are pure and applied research. The preceding chapters deal mainly with pure research. The distinguished units of observation are the individual (micro level), the group or organization (meso level) and large groups or whole nations (macro level). The research methods are distinguished according to whether they make use of experiments or naturalistic observations. Experiments are especially designed to study causal relationships whereas naturalistic observations are mainly used to study statistical relationships.

The methods considered have different advantages and disadvantages. Many experimental biases are absent in physiological measurements. In meso level experiments, conditions that do not occur in practice can be varied and are cheap compared to real life experiments on this level. Micro level observations may have their pitfalls and may be expensive but may yield information that cannot be obtained in other ways. Meso level observations are cheap and very useful in obtaining information regarding new or unknown processes. Macro level observations pertain to complete information regarding aspects of a population rather than a sample or a subpopulation, e.g. the costs of health care in a country or GNP.

The internal validity of experiments is influenced by a number of factors. Maturation refers to spontaneous, unintended changes in the subjects whereas history refers to the particular uncontrolled events occurring in the experimental sessions. Testing refers to the effects of repeated testing with the same measurement device whereas instrumentation is due to changes in the method of measurement. Selection refers to the unequal probability of subjects of being included in the experiment whereas differential mortality relates to the unequal probability of subjects dropping out of the experiment. Regression refers to the tendency of extreme scores to move toward the average score. Experimenter biases may affect an experiment because experimenters may provide cues to the subjects or may misjudge the subjects' responses. To some extent, experimenter bias may be reduced by running the experiment 'blind'. Several designs avoid the internal experimental invalidity by randomization of the subjects, the use of a control group and the inclusion of a pretest and a posttest.

The external validity of experiments is influenced by reactive effects and demand characteristics and interactions between experimental treatment with selection and testing. Add-on techniques, such as the bogus pipeline and the randomized choice, may be used to reduce the bias in the answers of the subjects.

Validity and reliability are important issues in experimental and naturalistic observations. Validity refers to the extent that the measurements relate to the concept that is measured. Content validity, criterion validity and construct validity are distinguished. The convergent and discriminant validity of measurements can be assessed by a multitrait-multimethod matrix. Reliability refers to the accuracy and the consistency of the measurements. Reliability can be assessed by test-retest correlations, parallel forms of observations, split-half reliability coefficients and inter-rater correlations. The larger the number of items in a measurement the more reliable the observation of a concept will be; this relationship is captured by the Spearman–Brown formula. The validity of an observation can never exceed its reliability. Validity coefficients can be corrected for unreliability of the measurements, however.

A number of questioning techniques are used in research. The type of question is directly related to the measurement level, which in turn determines the allowable statistical techniques.

Notes

[1] This is indicated by the want theory regarding well-being in Section 10.3.
[2] See Chapter 5.
[3] See Chapter 9.
[4] See Section 9.3.
[5] See Section 7.2.
[6] See Cox and Isaac 1986.
[7] See Box 5.1.
[8] See Section 9.1.
[9] See Chapter 11.
[10] See Chapter 3.
[11] See Box 3.1.
[12] See Section 6.4.
[13] See Chapter 14.
[14] Wallraff 1985.
[15] See Box 8.1.
[16] See OECD 1982.
[17] See Chapter 8.
[18] See Chapter 10.
[19] McClelland et al. 1953, see Section 3.2.
[20] See Section 6.4.
[21] Campbell and Stanley 1963.
[22] Neale and Liebert 1973.
[23] Messick 1967.
[24] Turner 1978.
[25] Rosenthal and Fode 1963.
[26] See Section 5.3.
[27] Barber and Silver 1968.

[28] See Chapter 6.

[29] See Chapter 5.

[30] See Section 11.2.

[31] Orne and Scheibe 1964, see also Section 3.4.

[32] Pieters 1988.

[33] Jones and Sigall 1971.

[34] See Dawes and Smith 1985, pp. 550–555.

[35] See Antonides and Robben, 1995.

[36] Campbell and Stanley 1963.

[37] Solomon 1949.

[38] See Section 3.6.

[39] See Section 8.3.

[40] Campbell and Fiske 1959.

[41] Campbell and Fiske 1959.

[42] Campbell and Fiske 1959.

[43] See Chapter 10.

[44] See Section 3.4.

[45] Cronbach 1984.

[46] See Section 3.2.

[47] See Cronbach 1984.

[48] Bohrnstedt 1970, Nunnally 1978.

[49] See Siegel 1956.

[50] See Section 7.2.

[51] Heise 1970.

[52] See Section 9.1.

[53] Likert 1970.

[54] Thurstone 1970.

[55] Stevens and Galanter 1957.

[56] Stevens and Galanter 1957.

CHAPTER 17

CONCLUSIONS

The first part of this book was devoted to theories dealing with particular aspects of behavior. The second part dealt with more general principles transcending these aspects. Here, we shall review these issues and try to state some general conclusions reflecting the personal opinions of the author.

First of all, we remind the increasing integration of economics and psychology on the subjects of interest.[1] Furthermore, the overlap of research at the micro, meso and macro levels is increasing.[2] This is also evident from the joint meetings of the International Association for Research in Economic Psychology (IAREP) and the Society for the Advancement of Behavioral Economics (SABE) in 1986 at Shefayim, Israel and in 1994 at Rotterdam, The Netherlands and IAREP and the Society for the Advancement of Socio-Economics (SASE) in 1991 at Stockholm, Sweden.

An important contribution of economic psychology to the field of economics is the extension of the concepts of utility and restrictions. On the one hand, these concepts might be extended so as to explain every possible behavior, which reduces the usefulness of this approach. On the other hand, many psychological concepts are available and many psychological theories do exist that can be integrated meaningfully into an economic psychological approach. In economics, several innovative concepts have been introduced to make the theory more realistic ("New home economics", search theory, reference groups, individual welfare concepts, etcetera). Also, critical arguments have been raised regarding the present state of economic theory, such as bounded rationality,[3] the intrinsic pleasure of stimulation[4] and ideas on preference selection and multiple selves.[5] Given these trends, we favor the alternative of integrating economic and psychological concepts and ideas. This appears to be consistent with the developments and critiques mentioned above.

The extension of economic concepts may include intrinsic motivations.[6] Usually, utility is associated with the manifest consequences of behavior[7] which serve as extrinsic motivators in obtaining reinforcements.[8] Latent or

357

immaterial consequences are associated with intrinsic motivations, e.g. status and prestige are associated with the need for achievement.[9]

Since in our opinion the introduction of psychological variables serves to provide better explanations of economic behavior, the indirect method of measurement in economics needs to be supplemented by direct measurements. Although subjective variables can be investigated by unobtrusive measures,[10] in many instances it is more convenient and cheaper to use direct measurements such as interviews and surveys. Examples of large-scale direct measurements are Katona's Index of Consumer Sentiment[11] and the well-being measures.[12]

An intriguing issue is whether the concept of utility or value is sufficient to explain behavior in the long run. Utility is defined over a very large set of commodities and (in prospect theory) value is defined over gains and losses. Commodities and changes in assets play an important part in theories of well-being, next to adaptation, social reference and needs. In most of these theories, well-being can be assessed by investigating the current (relative) value of accomplishments. However, utility and value may be totally irrelevant if well-being depends on the approximation of psychological end-states of life.[13] According to Buddhism, these end-states should even be reached by detachment from values. The relation between utility, value, well-being and the attainment of terminal values no doubt needs further research.

The inclusion of terminal values, latent consequences of behavior and intrinsic motivators in the utility function implies a different view on rationality. For instance, it might explain the collective rationality shown in social dilemmas.[14] Rationality also is affected by the principle of cognitive consistency. For example, even poor people may prefer an equitable income distribution to an equal distribution, although they might be better off in the latter case. Cognitive consistency affects rationality in an indirect way, too. Several cognitive heuristics based on cognitive consistency[15] may induce deviations from rational behavior. A very basic assumption affecting rationality is the shape of the value (or utility) function.[16]

The assumption of a differently shaped value function for gains and losses is incompatible with traditional utility theory. Firstly, it includes the possibility of ever increasing losses, as might be the case with debts or bad health (pain), whereas in traditional utility theory a zero utility is associated with the lack of any assets and the utility function does not take negative values. Secondly, it assumes a reference point from which outcomes are considered. The reference point may differ across people and may shift upon adaptation to a new situation. Traditional utility theory does not assume a reference point other than the baseline level associated with zero utility. Thirdly, a convex value function for losses accounts for risk seeking in case of a loss, whereas the traditional concave utility function implies risk aversion everywhere. Finally, the value function is assumed to be steeper for losses than for gains; this explains the endowment effect and several other economic anomalies.

A problem with the value function is the assessment of the reference point. With experimental lotteries, it seems natural to consider the reference point as the outcome of not playing the game. However, someone visiting the fair may decide to spend \$10.00 irrespective of the risk associated with the lottery. Here, the reference point is minus \$10.00 and not playing may be associated with a loss. Risky investments seem to lack a stable reference point as well, since not investing might incur a loss by inflation. The returns from securities such as government bonds or bank accounts may serve as reference points here. A problem occurs if there is no sure prospect, for example in choosing a job after finishing education (not choosing in this case being associated with even more uncertainty).

The welfare function of income[17] has a different shape at different income ranges. It is convex for low incomes and concave for higher incomes. Although it does not deal with income changes, prospect theory might explain why the lognormal utility function performs so well in this case. Since low incomes might be perceived as losses, the convex part of the function correctly describes the income evaluations here. Higher incomes might be perceived as gains, the evaluations of which are better described by the concave part of the function. Since on average the own income is evaluated above 0.5 on the (0,1) utility scale, it may be hypothesized that the reference point for income evaluation is lower than the own income on average. This could be explained by steady income increases in the past, creating the experience of income gains. Obviously, income decreases would be perceived as losses. This could mean that someone who has experienced an income decrease has a greater marginal income utility than someone who has experienced an income increase, even if the actual income level is the same. These hypotheses remain to be tested.

The idea of a reference point in judgment also plays a part in perception.[18] The price level in the past is used as a reference point for the judgment of inflation (although the reference prices may differ across people). One's own age and one's own level of schooling serve as perceptual standards in judging another person's age or schooling.[19] The aspiration level[20] can also be used as a reference point for judgment, e.g. in judging the degree of one's success or in judging the acceptability of a proposal. The importance of reference points, gains and losses supports the idea that differences are more important psychologically than absolute magnitudes or quantities. The pervasiveness of changes is reflected in the common need to revise one's expectations, aspirations and evaluations. Frequently, changes (or events) induce stress.[21]

The reference point for judgment frequently is located in one's own circumstances, e.g. the household income, the personal level of education, the personal need for achievement, etcetera. Factors more directly associated with these reference points will influence behavior more directly than remote factors, such as the national economy, the national education system or the entrepreneurial opportunities in a country.[22] The consequences of remote factors on one's circumstances are usually mitigated, at least in one's own perception.

The conflict model of buying behavior[23] explains the buying impulse from the net response strength, being the difference between the strengths of approach and escape behavior. This idea can be elaborated in the light of recent studies of mixed outcomes.[24] It appears that integration of gains (commodities) and losses (expenditures) is preferred to segregation if the net outcome is positive, so payment and delivery should occur at the same time. If the net outcome is negative, segregation is preferred, so payment and delivery should not occur at the same time ("Buy now, pay later"). From the distinction between primary and avoidance commodities (providing positive reinforcement and avoiding negative reinforcement, respectively), it might be suggested that the value of these commodities is different. Avoidance commodities (e.g. aspirin) might be valued higher (in the presence of negative reinforcement) than primary commodities because the value function for losses is steeper than for gains.

One reason why the value function should be steeper for losses than for gains can be explained by attribution theory.[25] People tend to attribute success (a gain) to their own abilities and effort, whereas a failure (a loss) is attributed to situational circumstances. Besides the negative value of a loss, one does not have the (positive) feeling of responsibility for one's own behavior. Presumably, the pain of attributing a negative outcome is greater than the pleasure of taking responsibility for a positive outcome.[26]

Future research

From the above, we conclude that situational changes may affect mental processes to a large extent. The study of these dynamic processes seems to be important in economic psychology and can be accomplished in several ways. The experimental technique pre-eminently appears to be suitable for investigating the effect of changes on mental processes and behavior.[27] However, many real life events cannot be manipulated in the laboratory (fortunately). These events might be studied by means of naturalistic observations. This can be accomplished by life history analysis in cross-sectional surveys, e.g. by using the social readjustment scale.[28] Preferably, however, panel studies should be conducted to analyze the effect of events at one time upon mental processes and behavior at a later time.

The processes to be analyzed in this research can be manifold: adaptation, cognitive consistency, reference points, expectations, aspirations and well-being all can be studied as consequences of changes in the environment and as determinants of behavior. This research is not only important from a scientific point of view but might also be more useful to the policy of agents in society who want to change the opinions, well-being and behavior of society.

The stress on studies of dynamic behavior does not mean that other types of research should be neglected. As argued before, much effort is needed to integrate psychological variables and theories into economic concepts in order to make them more realistic and more efficient in predicting behavior.

Notes

[1] See Section 2.1.
[2] See Section 16.1.
[3] Simon 1978.
[4] Scitovsky 1976.
[5] Elster 1986.
[6] See Section 3.1.
[7] See Section 10.4.
[8] See Chapter 5.
[9] See Section 3.2.
[10] See Webb et al. 1966.
[11] See Section 8.2.
[12] See Section 10.2.
[13] Terminal values, see Rokeach 1973.
[14] See Chapter 14.
[15] Classified as prototypes in Section 7.3.
[16] See Section 12.3.
[17] See Section 10.3.
[18] See Chapter 4.
[19] See Section 4.2.
[20] See Section 7.4.
[21] See Section 9.1.
[22] See Section 8.2.
[23] See Section 5.4.
[24] See Section 12.5.
[25] See Section 11.3.
[26] Van Raaij 1986.
[27] See Chapters 14 and 16.
[28] Table 9.1.

QUESTIONS

Chapter 2.

1. In psychology, preferences are:
    a) directly measured
    b) assumed to be stable
    c) assumed to be homogeneous
    d) inferred from behavior

2. The structural paradigm in economic psychology differs from the basic paradigm:
    a) because it can be applied to macro-phenomena
    b) by distinction of objective and subjective determinants of behavior
    c) by distinction of an objective and a subjective structure
    d) by a greater correspondence with the mental structure of the economy

3. The overjustification effect implies, among other things, that after payment of voluntary work:
    a) the demand for this work will decrease
    b) labor supply for this work will increase
    c) this work will no longer be performed voluntarily
    d) the reward will be experienced as just

Chapter 3.

4. A positive time preference causes:
    a) better health
    b) worse health
    c) a lower implicit discount rate
    d) a higher implicit discount rate

5. Field independence as an aspect of cognitive style will contribute to:
    a) expressiveness
    b) information processing
    c) affective choice mode
    d) involvement

6. The individual risk attitude depends upon:
    a) the motivation to take risks

b) the perception of risks
c) both motivation and perception
d) neither motivation, nor perception

Chapter 4.

7. It is assumed that inflation is perceived if:
   I. the size of new coins is under-estimated.
   II. the size of old coins is over-estimated.
   a) I is true, II is not true
   b) II is true, I is not true
   c) both I and II are true
   d) neither I, nor II is true

8. The difference threshold in perception indicates a defective:
   a) learning motivation
   b) stimulus generalization
   c) stimulus discrimination
   d) absolute threshold

9. Human sensitivity regarding the increase of wealth can best be described by:
   a) Weber's law
   b) Fechner's law
   c) Stevens' law
   d) a Cobb–Douglas utility function

Chapter 5.

10. Alhadeff's conflict model of consumption can best be considered an:
    a) approach-approach conflict
    b) avoidance-avoidance conflict
    c) approach-avoidance conflict
    d) information overload

11. The drawing of government securities can be considered a reinforcement with:
    a) fixed ratio schedule
    b) variable ratio schedule
    c) fixed interval schedule
    d) variable interval schedule

12. According to Alhadeff's conflict model, consumption is:

a) socially learned behavior
b) biologically determined behavior
c) cognitively learned behavior
d) conditioned behavior

Chapter 6.
13. In the hedonic price method:
   a) attributes are stepwise selected
   b) the implicit price of consumption is estimated
   c) the marginal attribute prices are estimated
   d) the "beliefs" are input in the price regression

14. The image profile of a shop is based upon:
   a) the satisfaction of purchases made in the shop
   b) price, promotion, place and products of the shop
   c) modal salient attributes of the shop
   d) an objective comparison of shop attributes with those of other shops

15. The Fishbein attitude model regarding products:
   a) is non-compensatory
   b) concerns objective attributes
   c) concerns opinions regarding attributes
   d) concerns a fixed number of attributes

Chapter 7.
16. 'Satisficing' concerns:
   a) an attitude regarding an information display
   b) a heuristic in information processing
   c) a simple choice of the best alternative
   d) a linear model with attribute cutoffs

17. The aspiration level regarding the purchase of durable goods:
   I. decreases with the progress in the life cycle of the household.
   II. decreases with pessimistic economic expectations of the household.
   a) I is true, II is not true
   b) II is true, I is not true
   c) both I and II are true
   d) neither I, nor II is true

18. Miller's magical number SEVEN concerns:
   I. the channel capacity for single stimuli.

II. the number of information units ("chunks") that can be processed.
a) I is true, II is not true
b) II is true, I is not true
c) both I and II are true
d) neither I, nor II is true

Chapter 8.
19. Expenditures on durable goods can best be explained by:
a) income
b) income and buying intentions
c) income and the Index of Consumer Sentiment (ICS)
d) income, buying intentions and the ICS

20. According to Fishbein and Ajzen, voting behavior can be explained by an attitude, corresponding with behavior regarding:
a) target
b) action
c) context
d) time

21. I. Multiple acts (Fishbein and Ajzen) can be explained by attitudes corresponding with respect to target.
II. Single acts can be explained by attitudes corresponding with respect to target.
a) I is true, II is not true
b) II is true, I is not true
c) both I and II are true
d) neither I, nor II is true

Chapter 9.
22. According to Mittal, the more expressive a product is:
a) the more information processing will dominate
b) the more affective choice mode will dominate
c) the more information processing will precede the affective choice mode
d) the more the affective choice mode will precede information processing

23. Affective judgments are not:
a) holistic
b) expressive
c) self-oriented

d) difficult to verbalize

24. You walk in the city and you want something. You decide that actually you want a new coat.
    This is a typical example of:
    a) the affective choice mode
    b) the cognitive theory of emotions
    c) Plutchik's combination of emotions
    d) the James-Lange theory of emotions (based on physiological indicators)

Chapter 10.
25. In the telic (or teleological) theory of well-being the following activities play a part:
    a) ascetic activities
    b) hedonic activities
    c) instrumental activities
    d) neither of these activities

26. Subjective well-being depends upon:
    a) socio-demographic factors
    b) the absolute level of income
    c) the relative level of prosperity within a group
    d) the relative level of prosperity and absolute income

27. That the lognormal welfare function differs according to income and family size has to do with:
    a) perceptual standards
    b) the sensitivity regarding income differences
    c) perfect distinction of money amounts
    d) the concavity of this welfare function

Chapter 11.
28. The largest cognitive dissonance is found in the performance of:
    a) a dull task for a high reward
    b) a dull task for a minor reward
    c) an interesting task for a high reward
    d) an interesting task for a minor reward

29. The tendency to consider the failure of an exam as bad luck implies an attribution with an:
    a) internal stable cause

b) internal instable cause
c) external stable cause
d) external instable cause

30. Let X+Y represent a positive relation between two objects and X-Y a negative relation. According to Heider, a cognitive balance between objects I, II and III exists if:
a) I+II, II+III, I–III
b) I–II, II+III, I+III
c) I+II, II–III, I–III
d) I–II, II–III, I–III

Chapter 12.
31. The axiom of greed is often invalid because of:
a) the operation of the money pump
b) the Premack principle
c) reversible preferences
d) stochastic preferences

32. In mental accounting:
a) the balance of gains and losses is computed
b) heuristics are applied to the computation of gains and losses
c) losses are evaluated different from gains
d) the balance of gains and losses is evaluated

33. The endowment effect is based upon:
  I. concavity of the value function for out-of-pocket costs.
  II. convexity of the value function for opportunity costs.
a) I is true, II is not true
b) II is true, I is not true
c) both I and II are true
d) neither I, nor II is true

Chapter 13.
34. The expected value of uncertain outcomes is a function of:
a) weighted probabilities and utilities of outcomes
b) objective probabilities and utilities of outcomes
c) weighted probabilities and objective outcomes
d) objective probabilities and objective outcomes

35. Concavity of the utility function implies:
    I. risk aversion.
    II. a certainty effect.
    a) I is true, II is not true
    b) II is true, I is not true
    c) both I and II are true
    d) neither I, nor II is true

36. The expected utility theory:
    I. evaluates end-states of expected gains and losses.
    II. assumes risk-seeking behavior under uncertainty.
    a) I is true, II is not true
    b) II is true, I is not true
    c) both I and II are true
    d) neither I, nor II is true

Chapter 14.
37. In Prisoners Dilemmas, choice is often cooperative. This occurs especially:
    a) in large groups
    b) if the choice is visible
    c) in order not to be exploited oneself
    d) because of the assumption of rationality

38. The inefficient equilibrium as a result of a Prisoner's Dilemma is based upon:
    I. individual rationality.
    II. collective rationality.
    a) I is true, II is not true
    b) II is true, I is not true
    c) both I and II are true
    d) neither I, nor II is true

39. If more players in an N-persons Prisoner's Dilemma choose cooperatively, the payoffs of free-riders:
    a) become larger
    b) become smaller
    c) remain the same
    d) depend upon the PD-structure

Chapter 15.

40. The bargaining situation consists of three parts:
    a) social context, bargaining tactics and negotiated contracts
    b) bargaining history, negotiator expectations and payoff distribution
    c) social context, bargaining process and bargaining outcomes
    d) bargaining history, negotiator interests and utility of payoffs

41. I. Principled negotiation pertains to the principle to hold firm to one's
        bargaining position.
     II. Firm flexibility pertains to the principle to hold firm to one's bargaining
         interests.
    a) I is true, II is not true
    b) II is true, I is not true
    c) both I and II are true
    d) neither I, nor II is true

42. Dividing orchestration and implementation power in negotiation is a
    negotiation tactic regarding:
    a) commitment to one's position
    b) coalition
    c) bridging
    d) force

Chapter 16.

43. Market-studies especially are:
    a) experimental on the micro-level
    b) experimental on the meso-level
    c) observational on the micro-level
    d) observational on the meso-level

44. The following experimental design is especially vulnerable to:

     ‾‾‾‾‾‾‾‾‾‾‾

    X   O

          O

     ‾‾‾‾‾‾‾‾‾‾‾

    a) testing
    b) selection
    c) regression
    d) instrumentation

45. The reliability of a test can be derived from the:
   a) social desirability of the answers
   b) internal consistency
   c) internal validity
   d) test length

GLOSSARY

Absolute threshold. The stimulus intensity at which the stimulus is perceived in 50% of the cases and not perceived in the other 50%.

Action orientation. Tendency to convert intentions or plans into actual behavior.

Actor-observer bias. Outside observers are more likely to state dispositional causes for behavior, whereas the actor is more inclined to state external causes.

Adaptation level. Average stimulus intensities and background stimuli subjects are accustomed to.

Adaptation theory of well-being. This theory predicts that events affect happiness the more recently their occurrence.

Adaptive expectations. Expectations that are formed on the basis of previous expectations and their differences with realized outcomes.

Adequacy-importance model of attitude. The idea that an attitude is composed of a set of evaluations concerning the satisfying attributes of an object or behavior and a set of importance weights associated with the attributes.

Affective choice mode (ACM). Affective judgment which occurs through psychological processes, excluding cognitive information processing.

Affective-cognitive consistency. A strong positive affect toward a given object should be associated with the belief that it leads to the attainment of a number of important values, whereas a negative affect should correspond with the belief that it blocks the attainment of these values.

Altruism. Unselfish concern for the welfare of others.

Anchoring. Cognitive heuristics by which judgments are made on the basis of irrelevant frames of reference.

Anxiety. A personality trait associated with a constant, undifferentiated, vague sense of fear.

Applied research. Research of institutes and industries conducted in order to solve specific problems.

Approach behavior. Behavior shown to have positively reinforcing consequences.

Approach/approach conflict. Conflict we experience when we have to choose between two attractive stimuli.

Approach/avoidance conflict. Conflict we experience when a single choice situation includes both positive and negative aspects.

Arousal. A general state of the organism involving excitation or a sense of being stimulated.

Aspiration level. A fairly immediate goal, i.e. something almost within reach.

Asymptotic value of information transmission. With an increase from a medium to a large amount of input information, the amount of transmitted information will finally level off and reach a maximum value.

Attenuation. Reduction of the size of an effect due to measurement error or unreliability.

Attitude. Individual predisposition to evaluate an object or an aspect of the world in a favorable or unfavorable manner.

Attribution theory. A theory about the human motivation to discover the underlying causes of behavior as part of our interest in making sense out of the environment.

Autonomic nervous system. The part of the peripheral nervous system that takes messages to and from the body's internal organs.

Availability. Cognitive heuristic by which judgments are made on the basis of the ease with which relevant information (e.g. related instances and events) can be brought to mind.

Avoidance commodity. A commodity which is capable of avoiding a negative reinforcer, e.g. an aspirin.

Avoidance response. Behavior shown to avoid a stimulus because of related unpleasant experiences.

Avoidance/avoidance conflict. Conflict we experience when we have to choose between two unattractive stimuli.

Axiom of completeness. For any two states of the world A and B, under every possible condition, the individual either prefers A to B or prefers B to A or is indifferent to both.

Axiom of greed. If A contains more of a good than B and at least as much as B of all other goods, A will be preferred to B.

Axiom of transitivity. If A is preferred to B and B is preferred to C then A will be preferred to C.

Bargaining. The part of negotiation that aims at agreement.

Bargaining position. The composite of context, principles, interests and restrictions of a negotiating party.

Bargaining zone. The zone of agreement, consisting of acceptable outcomes, i.e. the profit margin of the negotiation parties.

Basic economic psychological paradigm. This paradigm has been presented by Katona (1964). It is assumed that the objective environment influences subjective well-being, including economic attitudes and expectations. Attitudes and expectations regarding the personal situation and the economy as a whole influence economic behavior.

BATNA. Best Alternative To a Negotiated Agreement, in many situations the BATNA amounts to the status quo.

Biofeedback. Providing the individual with information about bodily processes so that the individual can keep track of those processes.

Biological mechanisms. Bodily processes, e.g. physiological maturation. These processes are assumed to play a part in the development of the central nervous system enabling learning in early childhood.

Bit (binary digit). A unit of information.

Black Box. In theories of classical and operant conditioning the organism is referred to as the black box because the mental activities of the organism cannot be seen and therefore must be inferred.

Blind experimenters. Experimenters who are unaware of the hypothesis being tested.

Bogus pipeline. Experimental technique to increase the truthfulness of the subject's response by claiming that false responses can be detected by the experimenter.

Bottom-up theory of well-being. Frequent experience of positive emotions and good moods make up a general positive evaluation of one's life, whereas unfavorable emotions and moods, stress and anxiety are assumed to affect individual well-being negatively.

Brinkmanship. Negotiating at the risk of a catastrophe.

Bundling of costs. Perception of costs as accumulating over time.

Buying intentions. Expectations regarding future purchases.

Cantril's measure of well-being. Subjective indicator of well-being obtained by first asking individuals about their best and worst possible lives. They then indicate their present life as somewhere in between.

Category scale. Psychological measurement scale including a limited number of labeled choice alternatives.

Causal schemata. Connected beliefs regarding the causes of events and behaviors formed in the past.

Certainty effect. The certainty effect refers to the tendency to overweight outcomes that are considered certain, relative to outcomes which are merely probable.

Channel capacity. The maximum amount of transmitted information of a communication system.

Characteristics approach Lancaster (1966). defines a utility function on the basis of the amounts of characteristics contained in goods and services.

Chicken game. Experimental game in which defective choice results in a higher payoff than cooperative choice, until the number of defectors becomes critical. If the number of defectors becomes too high, cooperative choice results in a higher payoff than defective choice.

Choice axioms. The essential properties that must be true of individual choices. The theory of economic choice is based on several axioms.

Classical conditioning. A process – initially discovered by Pavlov – in which a previously neutral stimulus acquires the ability to elicit a response by repeated association with a stimulus that naturally produces a similar response.

Cognitive balance theory. A positive or negative affect toward another person tends to be in a state of balance with an individual's affect toward an attitude object toward which the other person is also oriented (Heider 1958).

Cognitive consistency. A psychological principle guiding human judgment, attitude formation and change and interpretation of the environment while retaining consistency of opinions and beliefs.

Cognitive dissonance. A kind of tension or uneasiness we feel when our behavior is inconsistent with our attitudes. Festinger (1957) stated that we try to reduce this tension by cognitively justifying things that are unpleasant.

Cognitive dissonance theory. An inconsistency between two or more cognitive elements in an individual's mind will induce the individual to decrease the dissonance and avoid situations and information which would be likely to increase the dissonance.

Cognitive elaboration. Processing of new information and relating this to the existing knowledge stored in memory.

Cognitive index. The weighted sum of beliefs.

Cognitive learning. In cognitive learning, behavior changes may occur as a result of insight.

Cognitive styles. Individual differences in the ability to differentiate the environment and integrate information.

Cognitive theory of emotion. This theory assumes that a state of arousal is produced by stimuli in the environment. The arousal is then explained by a cognitive interpretation of the environment.

Collative properties. Properties that depend on comparison of information from different sources, e.g. comparison of a stimulus with accompanying stimuli or with stimuli encountered in the past. These include novelty, change, surprisingness, ambiguity, incongruity, blurredness and power to induce uncertainty.

Comparison scale. Psychological measurement scale asking for judgment or preference of an alternative in comparison with at least one other alternative. (See constant-sum scale.)

Compliance effect. A change in opinion or attitude to be consistent with emitted behavior.

Conditioned response (CR). A response that is produced by a conditioned stimulus; a classical conditioning term.

Conditioned stimulus (CS). An initially neutral stimulus that produces a conditioned response after repeated association with an unconditioned stimulus; a classical conditioning term.

Configuration principle. The principle of making causal attributions according to a combination of judgments regarding consensus, distinctiveness and consistency.

Conflict. An experience we have when we must decide between two or more incompatible stimuli.

Conjunctive attitude model. This model assumes that all of the salient attributes of an object exceed minimum levels in order to be evaluated positively.

Consensus. Criterion in the process of attribution, referring to the social agreement regarding an object, an event or a person.

Consistency. Criterion in the process of attribution, referring to the reliability of opinions.

Constant-sum scale. Psychological measurement scale requiring the division of points or money between a limited number of alternatives, reflecting the judgment or preferences regarding the alternatives.

Construct validity. Validity of observations regarding a construct assessed by its correlations with related concepts.

Consumption services. Functions of commodities that directly produce consumer satisfaction. Several characteristics may combine to form a service.

Content validity. Validity referring to the correspondence between observations and the content of what they measure.

Control group. A group of subjects in an experiment who are not exposed to the experimental manipulations and who serve as a standard for judgment of the experimental results.

Convergent validity. Validity referring to the extent that different measures of the same concept are correlated.

Correspondent inference. An inference about a person's disposition that corresponds to that person's behavior.

Covariation principle. Causes are attributed to events if both occur at the same time and if neither causes nor events occur in the absence of each other.

Criterion validity. Validity referring to the performance of observations in predicting a criterion.

Crowding out. A decrease of internal motivation due to an increase of external motivation. (See overjustification.)

Cultural invariance. The relative constancy of psychological processes or results across different cultures (e.g. different countries).

Cutoffs. Minimum levels in a conjunctive attitude model.

Defective choice. Choice in a social dilemma which maximizes the own payoffs regardless of choices made by others involved in the dilemma.

Delay of gratification. Behavior indicating an ability to defer immediate reward for more desirable future gratification.

Descriptive models of behavior. Models that give a realistic account of behavioral processes, without assuming rationality.

Dictator game. Experimental game in which subjects allocate resources to themselves and other persons. The other persons cannot influence or sanction the allocation result.

Discretionary expenditures. Expenditures on commodities that are not necessary for survival.

Discriminant validity. Validity referring to the extent that different concepts measured by the same method are not correlated.

Disjunctive attitude model. This model assumes that objects are valued because of one or more outstanding attribute.

Distinctiveness. Criterion in the process of attribution, implying different opinions regarding different entities.

Distributive bargaining. Bargaining concerning the allocation of negotiated outcome shares to the parties.

Double approach/avoidance conflict. Conflict we experience when we have to choose between two alternatives, each with both positive and negative consequences.

Dynamic games. Games that are played repetitively, with either a known or an unknown number of trials.

Economic behavior. The behavior of consumers/citizens that involves economic decisions and the determinants and consequences of economic decisions.

Ego-defensive function of attitudes. To keep one's self-perception in agreement with reality.

Elimination by aspects model (EBA). This attitude model assumes that objects are compared on successive attributes. All alternatives below the cutoff value of an attribute are eliminated from the choice set in the sequence of comparisons.

Embedded Figure Test (EFT). A test to measure cognitive differentiation by asking subjects to locate a simple geometric figure within a more complex one.

Endowment effect. After acquisition of a good, it becomes more valuable to the owner.

Equity principle of distribution. The individual outcomes of a distribution (e.g. of income, goods, etc.) are compared with the individual inputs. Equity requires the ratios of outputs to inputs to be equal.

Evaluation Question Approach. Questioning technique in which respondents are prompted for stimulus magnitudes corresponding with psychological judgments, usually presented as labeled (evaluative) categories.

Event matching. A cognitive heuristic assuming that subjects choose their behavior according to the proportion of rewarded trials.

Expected utility model. A model assuming that a prospect is evaluated such that the utilities of the outcomes are weighted by their respective objective probabilities.

Expected value model. A model assuming that the objective values of the outcomes are weighted by their respective objective probabilities.

Experiment. A carefully regulated setting in which one or more of the factors believed to influence the behavior being studied are manipulated and all others are held constant.

Experimenter bias. Bias in observations due to unintentional cues provided by the experimenter, misjudgment or inaccurate scoring of responses.

Expressiveness of a product. The hedonic, symbolic or psycho-social consumption goals of a product, rather than its functional or utilitarian goals.

External cause. Belief that a person's achievements are caused by task conditions, luck or chance.

External locus of control. The belief that the outcomes one obtains (rewards and punishments) come from powerful others or are the result of luck and circumstance.

External validity. Validity referring to the question to what extent the experimental results can be generalized to the population.

Extinction. The reduced likelihood of a conditioned response after a series of unreinforced presentations of the conditioned stimulus.

Face validity. Validity referring to the intuitive plausibility that an observation measures a certain phenomenon.

Fechner's law. Fechner related the perceived difference to the objective difference by equating the just noticeable difference to the unit of sensation.

Field-dependence. The extent to which a subject is influenced by the environment in the perception of stimuli and in the processing of information.

Figure Drawing Test. A measure of cognitive differentiation whereby subjects are asked to draw a male and a female figure.

Final states. Final states combine the assets held before an act (e.g. a gambling decision) and the gains and losses resulting from the act.

Fishbein model of attitude. The idea that an attitude is composed of a set of beliefs regarding the consequences of behavior regarding an object and a set of evaluations regarding the consequences.

Fixed interval schedule. On this schedule, reinforcement follows the first response emitted after a fixed time period.

Fixed ratio schedule. On this schedule, reinforcement occurs after a fixed number of responses.

Foot-in-the-door technique. Compliance with a request is brought about by a previous, smaller request.

Framing effect. The different evaluation of prospects according to a different description of the outcomes.

Free riders. Those who make no contribution to a public good.

Frustration. An experience resulting from a situation in which a person cannot reach a desired goal.

Functional theory of attitude. Katz's theory (1960) pointing to the instrumental or utilitarian, the ego-defensive, the value-expressive and the knowledge function of attitudes.

Fundamental attribution error. The tendency to overestimate the importance of personal factors relative to environmental influences on a person's behavior.

Fungibility. An accounting principle according to which the balance of different accounts is not influenced by the type of accounts. This principle is violated in mental arithmetic.

Game theory. A theory which predicts optimal choice if the outcomes depend on others' choices.

Generalized reinforcer. A type of secondary reinforcer that is not specifically related to any single need state, e.g. money or praise.

Halo effect. The tendency to rate an individual inappropriately on a wide range of traits because of prior information on only one or a few of these traits.

Hedonic price method. An application of the characteristics model, in which the prices of commodities are related to their objective characteristics. This method yields implicit marginal prices of characteristics as a result.

Heuristics. Strategies or rules of thumb that suggest a solution to a problem but do not ensure that it will work.

Homeostatic feedback. Information about a system's position of balance, usually inducing the system to return to its natural or average state.

Image. A public attitude toward an object or agent in society.

Imperfect information. The lack of knowledge of the other's move in a dilemma game before one's own move.

Implicit interest rate. Interest rate inferred from a subject's revealed time preference or from his answers to questions regarding the future allocation of resources.

Importance weights. Weights attached to attribute values in multiattribute models of attitude.

Incentive compatible behavior. Behavior that is a truthful response to incentives offered.

Income Evaluation Question (IEQ). People's evaluation of their net-income, taking into account their own living circumstances (i.e. family and job).

Independent variable. The manipulated or influential factor in an experiment; can be changed independently of other factors.

Index of Consumer Sentiment (ICS). A quantitative index of people's confidence in the economy.

Information chunk. Translation of two or more bits of information into one chunk by grouping, organizing or coding them into something that can be treated as a whole.

Information display. A structured display of information by product attributes and by brands.

Information overload. A situation in which stimuli overload our adaptability.

Information processing choice mode (IPM). Cognitive judgment based on conscious perception and integration of information.

Informational commodities. Commodities converting negative feelings into neutral feelings.

Instrumental function of attitude. The function of an attitude in guiding behavior that leads to positively valued consequences.

Integrative bargaining. Bargaining concerning the size of the negotiated outcome (the 'pie').

Internal cause. Belief that a person's achievements are caused by his ability or effort.

Internal consistency. The extent to which observations of the same concept (e.g. items of a test) correlate with one another.

Internal locus of control. The belief that the outcomes one obtains (rewards and punishments) are the result of one's own effort.

Internal validity of experiments. Validity referring to experiments in which the obtained effect can be attributed confidently to the independent variable.

Interpersonal Discrimination Test. A measure of cognitive differentiation. In this test, subjects are asked to rate a number of persons from their close environment along ten dimensions such as outgoing-shy, friendly-unfriendly.

Inter-rater reliability. Reliability referring to the correlation between observations made by two different judges.

Interval measurement. Assignment of standard units to objects or judgments.

Introspection. A technique whereby specially trained people carefully observe and analyze their own mental experiences.

Involvement. The level of perceived personal importance and/or interest evoked by a stimulus (e.g. a product) within a specific situation.

Isolation effect. A cognitive simplification of prospects consisting of two or more stages, based on evaluation of a single stage.

James–Lange theory of emotion. A theory according to which emotions are experienced as a result of bodily responses to changes in the environment.

Just noticeable difference (j.n.d.). The point at which two stimuli are detected as different 50 percent of the time.

Knowledge function of attitudes. To structure one's experiences such as to be consistent with one's former knowledge structure.

Latent learning. Any learning that is not evidenced by behavior at the time of the learning. Experiments on latent learning support the concept of cognitive representations.

Learned helplessness. The belief that one's outcomes are independent of one's actions.

Lexicographic attitude model. This model assumes that evaluation of objects occurs in the salience order of attributes.

Life-style. Pattern of behavior characterized by certain values, demographics and buying patterns.

Likert scale. Psychological measurement scale including approval and disapproval categories of judgment regarding attitude or opinion statements.

Locus of causality. The psychological belief that an event was caused by internal or external factors.

Locus of control. The psychological belief of exercising control over the environment.

Macro level studies of behavior. Studies concerned with the economic behavior of large groups, such as whole nations.

Magnitude estimation. Psychophysical measurement technique requiring exact judgments regarding the magnitude of stimuli, e.g. by stating a number or drawing a line of a certain length.

Matched control group. Control group which is similar to the experimental group on a number of variables (e.g. age, gender, family status, etc.).

Matrix of beliefs and evaluations. An inner psychological structure concerning the attributes of environmental stimuli which determines selection of (preference for) possible behavior.

Melioration. Heuristic resulting in switches to behavior that seems currently more effective.

Mental arithmetic. A psychological mechanism to evaluate the balance of different accounts. Money values are frequently not cleared within the same mental account.

Meso level studies of behavior. Studies concerned with the behavior of social groups and organizations.

Micro level studies of behavior. Studies aimed at understanding individual behavior.

Minimaxing regret. Minimizing the maximum expected loss resulting from a choice.

Modal salient attributes. The most frequently mentioned attributes in a sample of individuals.

Mood. A relatively enduring emotional state.

Motivation. A force that energizes and directs behavior.

Multiple-act criterion. A set of behaviors related to the same object. The object is considered the target in attitude measures explaining this criterion.

Multiple item scale. A scale consisting of a number of items measuring the same concept.

Multiplicative power law. Multiplicative expression relating sensation to power functions of a number of objective stimuli.

Naturalistic observation. Observation in real-world settings with no attempt made to manipulate or control the situation.

Need. An excess or deficiency in something related to survival, such as air, food or water.

Need for achievement. The need to accomplish something difficult, to master, manipulate or organize physical objects, human beings or ideas.

Need for cognition. The tendency of individuals to engage in and enjoy cognitive endeavors.

Need principle of distribution. The need principle states that the distribution of a good is considered undesirable if different people's needs are not fulfilled to the same extent.

Negative time preference. A preference for delaying the allocation of resources.

Negotiation. All kinds of activities to resolve social problems, including bargaining.

Negotiation dance. The sequence of offers and counter-offers in negotiation.

Net response strength. The strength of approach behavior relative to the strength of the avoidance behavior.

Nominal measurement. Assignment of categories to objects or judgments.

Normative models of behavior. Models making particular assumptions underlying behavior, e.g. that optimal processing of information precedes behavior.

Norms. Rules that apply to all members of a group.

One-item scale. The measurement of a concept consisting of only one item.

Operant conditioning. A type of learning in which the consequences of behavior lead to changes in the probability of that behavior's occurrence.

Operant response. A behavior shown to acquire positive reinforcement (or avoid negative reinforcement). Reinforcement is contingent on the behavior.

Opponent-process theory. Theory assuming that affect-provoking stimulation brings about contrasting effects or emotions.

Opportunity costs. The cost of using something is the benefit foregone (or the opportunity lost) by not using it in its best alternative (e.g. the opportunity cost of wasted time).

Ordinal measurement. Assignment of a rank order to objects or judgments.

Out-of-pocket costs. Expenses made for the acquisition of commodities.

Overjustification. Loss of intrinsic motivation to perform an activity by giving material rewards. After withdrawal of the rewards, the motivation to perform the activity declines below the original level.

Parallel forms of observations. Observation of the same concept by two similar forms of measurement, e.g. two different variants of a psychological test.

Partial non-response. Non-response to particular questions in an interview or survey, due to unwillingness or lack of knowledge. (Also known as item non-response.)

Payoff matrix. Outcomes of choices in a game, ordered according to the possible choices of oneself and the other people involved in the game.

Perceived instrumentality. Perceived instrumentalities are an individual's beliefs regarding the need satisfying properties of behavioral alternatives.

Perceptual space. Space defined by the psychological dimensions underlying the perception or evaluation of events, activities or other stimuli.

Perceptual standard. Standard of comparison in perceptual judgment or sensation, e.g. one's own income in the perception of other incomes.

Personality. Relatively stable and distinctive patterns of behavior that characterize an individual and his reactions to the environment.

Personalized tokens. Personalized tokens can only be cashed in by the person who earned them and cannot be interchanged.

Phobia. Irrational fear.

Positional negotiation. Negotiation that considers the bargaining positions of the parties, rather than their principles and interests, as fundamental and given.

Positive time preference. A preference for allocation of resources in or near the present.

Posttest. Experimental observation made after manipulation of independent variables.

Posttest-Only Control Group Design. A design including an experimental group and a control group both of which are randomly selected. It controls both for the main effect of testing and for the interaction effect, although it does not measure these effects.

Power law. Stevens (1957) assumed that equal objective stimulus ratios produce equal subjective ratios. From this assumption, one can derive that sensation is linearly related to a stimulus magnitude raised to a power.

Precommitment. A solution to problems of control over one's behavior in the form of binding agreements.

Premack principle. Any response might act as a reward for any other response, provided that the first was the more probable of the two when both were freely available. There is no fixed list of stimuli or activities that can act as rewards or punishments.

Pretest. Experimental observation made before the manipulation of independent variables.

Pretest-Posttest Control Group Design. A design that controls for the effects of testing and maturation, since both the control group and the experimental group are tested twice.

Price-quality relationship. The assumption that the higher the price of a commodity, the better its quality will be.

Primary affective reaction (PAR). An initial affective reaction to a stimulus, assumed to guide a (subconscious) decision as to whether it is necessary, useful or interesting to collect and to process more information about the stimulus (e.g. a product or an ad).

Primary commodity. A primary commodity functions as an unconditioned stimulus, providing positive reinforcement.

Principal negotiation. Negotiation that considers the principles and interests of the parties, rather than their bargaining positions, as fundamental and given.

Prisoner's dilemma game. A game leading to a stable inefficient equilibrium if the players make defective choices. If the players choose cooperatively, the outcomes are higher than with defective choices but are unstable.

Programed instruction. An application of operant conditioning in education. Teaching material is presented in small units, so that learning can proceed with a minimum of error.

Prospect theory. A generalization of the expected utility model assuming subjective probabilities of uncertain prospects and different value functions for gains and losses.

Psychographics. The study of life-styles by observing individual activities, interests, opinions and demographics.

Psychophysics. The experimental study of formal relationships between sensations and stimulus quantities.

Public step good. Public good that is produced only if a critical amount of contributions has been made.

Pure research. Scientific endeavors to understand the world and the human being.

Quasi-experiment. Experiment without full control over all independent variables.

Random selection. A method for selecting subjects whereby each individual has an equal chance of being chosen or assigned to a specific group.

Randomized response. An experimental technique to increase the validity of observations by confounding the response with a random variable (e.g. a chance outcome). The experimenter does not know whether the subject responds to an experimental question or to the chance outcome.

Ratio measurement. Assignment of standard units to objects or judgments relative to a meaningful zero point.

Rational expectations. Expectations that are formed on the basis of all relevant and available information.

Rationality. Economic assumption that generates norms for economic behavior, indicating what is to be expected if well-informed economic agents seek to maximize their gains.

Reactive effects. Unintended, unavoidable response effects produced by an experimental setting.

Reference group. A group of people that is used for comparison in judgments of one's own circumstances. In a sense, the circumstances of people in the reference group serve as perceptual standards in judgment. The reference group has been assumed to consist of people with the same age, education, job, income, family circumstances and living place.

Reference point. Perceptual standard in prospect theory that may shift under the influence of the framing effect.

Reflection effect. The reflection effect changes risk aversion in the domain of positive outcomes into risk seeking in the domain of negative outcomes.

Reformed sinner strategy. Game tactic in which one starts with a series of defective choices, followed by cooperative choices to elicit cooperative choices from the other player.

Regression to the mean. The effect that extreme outcomes due to chance will not be repeated.

Regressive prediction. Prediction that outcomes will tend toward the average.

Reinforcement. A consequence that increases the probability that a behavior will occur.

Reliability. Reliability can be defined as the accuracy and consistency of observations.

Representative consumer. Economic assumption according to which aggregate behavior can be explained from consumers with identical preferences.

Representativeness. This cognitive heuristic concerns probability judgments that an event or object belongs to a particular category.

Reservation price. The ultimate price a negotiator is willing to accept. A negotiator will be indifferent between the reservation price and the BATNA.

Revealed preference. Preference inferred from actual behavior. Repeated choice of A over B reveals that A is preferred over B.

Risk. Aspect of a situation concerning the known probability of outcomes.

Risk attitude. Individual disposition to evaluate uncertain prospects as more or less favorable. This comprises risk aversion and risk seeking.

Risk aversion. The unfavorable evaluation of risky prospects resulting from a concave utility function.

Rod and Frame Test (RFT). A test to measure a subject's susceptibility to environmental influences on his judgment.

Saliency. The saliency of attributes refers to the actual utilization of attributes in the evaluation of choice alternatives.

Satiation point. Point beyond which a reinforcer may no longer be an effective determinant of approach behavior.

Satisfaction of need. Satisfaction of a physical state involving any lack or deficit within the organism.

Satisficing. Behavior in which the individual does not strive for the best alternative by optimally using all available information but is satisfied with the first alternative meeting his expectations.

Schedule of reinforcement. Rules governing partial reinforcement that determine the occasion when a response will be reinforced.

Secondary reinforcer. A stimulus that has become reinforcing through prior association with a reinforcing stimulus.

Self-control. The ability of a person to maintain or alter the course of his or her behavior independently of obvious external influences.

Self-imposed constraints. Restrictions on behavior that are made voluntarily.

Self-monitoring. Tendency to pay attention to other people's opinions about one's behavior.

Self-perception. The individual's awareness of himself.

Self-serving bias. Positive outcomes are attributed to internal causes, whereas negative outcomes are attributed to external causes.

Semantic Differential. Psychological bipolar measurement scale defined with contrasting adjectives.

Sensation Seeking Scale (SSS). A questionnaire to measure the need for stimulation or optimal levels of stimulation.

Shaping. The process of rewarding sequential approximations of desired behavior.

Signal detection theory. A theory of psychophysical judgments regarding weak signals in which non-sensory factors are eliminated. Both correct and incorrect judgments are taken into account.

Silver lining. A process in which the pain caused by bad news is migitated by a little pleasure from good news.

Simulation. A cognitive heuristic referring to the use of examples, scenarios or advice in making judgments.

Single-act criterion. A single act related to a target to be explained from attitudes that correspond with the behavior according to the elements of target and action.

Social comparison. The process by which we evaluate ourselves vis-à-vis others.

Social desiribility. A response set in which the individual's answers are geared to what they think the examiner wants to hear or to presenting themselves in a better light.

Social judgment. Using other people as a reference standard of judgment.

Social learning. In social learning, behavior changes take place by observation and imitation of a model.

Sociobiology. A contemporary view emphasizing that all behavior is motivated by the desire to favor individuals or groups to which one is genetically related (e.g. family or members of one's country).

Sociotropic aspect of consumer confidence. Consumer confidence as indicated by questions regarding the evaluation of the general economic situation.

Solomon Four Group Design. A design including two randomized control groups and two randomized experimental groups. Each of the four groups is given a posttest but only one of each pair is given a pretest. The design controls both for the main effect of testing and for the interaction effect of testing and experimental treatment.

Spontaneous recovery. The process by which the conditioned response recurs after extinction.

Split-half reliability. Reliability judged from the correlation between two halves of a set of observations.

Status quo bias. Doing nothing or maintaining one's current or previous position.

St. Petersburg paradox. A gamble dealing with infinite expected values but nonetheless not preferred to a fixed payoff. The game has been considered by Bernoulli in a scientific journal published in St. Petersburg.

Stable equilibrium. A possible outcome of a game characterized by the fact that neither of the players is willing to change his strategy unilaterally.

Standard of judgment theories of well-being. People judge their well-being relative to standards of reference, such as the well-being of other people or to their own past well-being.

Statistics. The science that deals with the collection and handling of numerical data and with inferences made from such data.

Stimulus discrimination. In classical conditioning, the process in which the organism responds only to the exact, original conditioned stimulus and not to similar stimuli.

Stimulus generalization. In classical conditioning, the phenomenon in which stimuli similar to a conditioned stimulus elicit a similar response without prior learning.

Stochastic preferences. Preferences that have a particular value with only some probability. With stochastic preferences, a certain degree of incompleteness and intransitivity is allowed.

Strategic item. Commodity that induces expenditure associated with related goods and services, e.g. a car leading to expenditure on fuel, taxes, etc.

Strategy. Possible choice in a game.

Stress. The wear and tear in the body due to the demands placed on it.

Subjective interest rate. The measure of the willingness to save a present amount of money in order to receive a greater future amount.

Subjective restrictions. Restrictions within the organism including (internalized) social norms, psychological effort and physical energy, etc. Subjective restrictions may be influenced by social opinions.

Subjective well-being. People's evaluation of their happiness or satisfaction with life.

Sunk costs. Historical costs which should not influence future decisions.

Tactical altruism. Altruistic behavior based on the expectation that other people also feel obliged to cooperative behavior.

Telic theories of well-being. The view that well-being depends on the degree to which terminal values are attained.

Temperament. The more or less consistent way of reacting emotionally.

Terminal values. Psychological end-states of life. Activities can be judged to the extent that they are instrumental in attaining the life values.

Test-retest reliability. Reliability that is assessed by the correlation between results of the same test given on two different occasions.

Thematic Apperception Test (TAT). A projective technique in which the individual tells stories about pictures shown on cards. The stories are then scored by judges on the basis of several criteria.

Thurstone scale. Battery of attitude statements equally spaced along a psychological continuum.

Time-inconsistent preferences. Non-random temporary preference changes.

Time preference. Time preference is exhibited if the distribution of a potential stock of resources to be allocated over future intervals of time is skewed toward or away from the present.

Time series. A series of regular observations over time, e.g. per annum, per season or per month.

Token economy. A technique developed in behavior therapy in which the individual earns tokens that can be exchanged later for desired rewards.

Top-down theory of well-being. Satisfaction with one's life as a whole may induce relatively positive evaluations in specific life domains.

Transformational commodities. Commodities converting a baseline utility level into a utility increase.

Transitivity of preferences. Given three goods (or combinations of goods) A, B and C, any individual who prefers A to B and B to C should also prefer A to C.

Trust game. Experimental game in which defective choice results in a lower payoff than cooperative choice, until the number of defectors becomes critical. If the number of defectors becomes too high, cooperative choice results in a lower payoff than defective choice.

Ultimatum bargaining. Experimental game in which subjects allocate resources to themselves and other persons. The other persons may sanction the allocation result.

Uncertainty. Aspect of a situation concerning unknown or undefined probability of outcomes.

Unconditioned response (UCR). A reflexive response produced by a stimulus in the absence of learning.

Unconditioned stimulus (UCS). A stimulus that causes reflexive or unlearned behavior.

Unit of sensation. Definition regarding the units of a subjective scale of stimulus perception.

Utility. Subjective value of a certain amount of commodities or characteristics.

Utility function of income. Hypothetical relation between utility and income.

Valences. Regions within the life space of an individual that attract or repulse that individual.

Validity. The extent to which a test measures what it is intended to measure.

Value-expressive function of attitudes. To express oneself in terms of attitudes that are consonant with personal values.

Value function. A function defined over gains and losses with respect to some reference point. Its shape may be different for gains and losses.

Variable interval schedule. On this schedule, reinforcement occurs after a specified period of time that varies from one reinforcement to the next.

Variable ratio schedule. On this schedule, reinforcement occurs after a spec-

ified number of non-reinforced responses that varies from one reinforcement to the next.

Vignette. A brief description of several demographic and social characteristics
of a particular person.

Warm glow. The utility obtained from the act of giving per se.

Weber's law. Weber's assumption that the difference threshold is a constant
proportion of stimulus magnitude, which may vary across the stimuli
involved.

Well-being. General happiness or satisfaction with life.

Willingness to accept. Maximum price that one is prepared to pay in order to
avoid a loss or minimum payment required in order to accept a loss.

Willingness to pay. Maximum price that one is prepared to pay in order to
obtain a gain.

Yerkes–Dodson law. Tasks of different complexity are performed best at
different levels of arousal.

REFERENCES

Abramovitch, R., J.L. Freedman and P. Pliner, 1991. Children and money: Getting allowance, credit versus cash, and knowledge of pricing. *Journal of Economic Psychology* 12, 27–45.

Abramson, L.Y., M.E.P. Seligman and J.D. Teasdale, 1978. Learned helplessness in humans: Critique and reformulation. *Journal of Abnormal Psychology* 87, 49–74.

Adams, F.G., 1964. Consumer attitudes, buying plans, and purchases of durable goods: A principal components, time series approach. *The Review of Economics and Statistics* 46, 347–355.

Adams, J.S., 1963. Toward an understanding of inequity. *Journal of Abnormal and Social Psychology* 67, 422–436.

Adams, J.S., 1965. 'Inequity in social exchange'. In: L. Berkowitz (ed.), *Advances in experimental psychology*, Vol. 2. New York: Academic Press. pp. 267–299.

Adams, J.S. and P.R. Jacobsen, 1964. Effects of wage inequities on work quality. *Journal of Abnormal and Social Psychology* 69, 19–25.

Adelbratt, T. and H. Montgomery, 1980. Attractiveness of decision rules. *Acta Psychologica* 45, 177–185.

Ajzen, I. and M. Fishbein, 1977. Attitude-behavior relations: Theoretical analysis and review of empirical research. *Psychological Bulletin* 84, 888–918.

Akerlof, G.A. and W.T. Dickens, 1982. The economic consequences of cognitive dissonance. *The American Economic Review* 72, 307–319.

Akerlof, G.A. and J.L. Yellen, 1990. The fair wage-effort hypothesis and unemployment. *Quarterly Journal of Economics* 105, 255–283.

Alhadeff, D.A., 1982. *Microeconomics and human behavior*. Berkeley, CA: University of California Press.

Alhadeff, D.A., 1982. *Microeconomics and human behavior*. Berkeley, CA: University of California Press.

Allport, G.W., 1967. 'Attitudes'. In: M. Fishbein (ed.), *Readings in attitude theory and measurement*. New York: Wiley. pp. 3–13.

Amsel, A., 1958. The role of frustrative nonreward in noncontinuous reward situations. *Psychological Bulletin* 55, 102–119.

Amsel, A., 1962. Frustrative nonreward in partial reinforcement and discrimination learning: Some recent history and a theoretical extension. *Psychological Review* 69, 306–328.

Anand, P. and C.J. Cowton, 1993. The ethical investor: Exploring dimensions of investment behavior. *Journal of Economic Psychology* 14, 377–385.

Anderson, M.A. and A.H. Goldsmith, 1994. Rationality in the mind's eye: An alternative test of rational expectations using subjective forecast and evaluation data. *Journal of Economic Psychology* 15, 379–403.

Andreassen, P.B., 1987. On the social psychology of the stock market: Aggregate attributional effects and the regressiveness of prediction. *Journal of Personality and Social Psychology* 53, 490–496.

Andreoni, J., 1989. Giving with pure altruism: Applications to charity and Ricardian equivalence. *Journal of Political Economy* 97, 1447–1458.

393

Andreoni, J., 1993. An experimental test of the public-goods crowding- out hypothesis. *American Economic Review* 83, 1317–1327.

Andreoni, J., 1995. Warm-glow versus cold-prickle: The effects of positive and negative framing on cooperation in experiments. *Quarterly Journal of Economics* 110, 1–21.

Andrews, F.M. and R.F. Inglehart, 1979. The structure of subjective well-being in nine western societies. *Social Indicators Research* 6, 73–90.

Andrews, F.M. and A.C. McKennell, 1980. Measures of self-reported well-being: Their affective, cognitive, and other components. *Social Indicators Research* 8, 127–155.

Andrews, F.M. and S.B. Withey, 1976. *Social indicators of well-being*. New York: Plenum.

Andrews, J.D.W., 1967. The achievement motive in two types of organizations. *Journal of Personality and Social Psychology* 6, 163–168.

Antonides, G., 1989. An attempt at integration of economic and psychological theories of consumption. *Journal of Economic Psychology* 10, 77–99.

Antonides, G., 1990. *The lifetime of a durable good: An economic psychological approach.* Dordrecht: Kluwer Academic Publishers.

Antonides, G., 1991. Psychological variables in negotiation. *Kyklos* 44, 347–362.

Antonides, G., 1992. 'A Model of Negotiations for the Sale of a House.' In: S.E.G. Lea, P. Webley and B.M. Young (eds.), *New Directions in Economic Psychology: Theory, Experiment and Application.* Aldershot: Edward Elgar. pp. 260–275.

Antonides, G., 1994. Mental accounting in a sequential Prisoner's Dilemma game. *Journal of Economic Psychology* 15, 351–374.

Antonides, G., 1995. Entrapment in risky investments. *Journal of Socio-Economics* 24, 447–461.

Antonides, G., 1995. The consumer's perceptual product space. Erasmus University Rotterdam: Tinbergen Institute Discussion Paper TI 1995–245.

Antonides, G., K. Farago, R. Ranyard and T. Tyszka, 1996. 'Perceptions of economic activities: A cross-country comparison.' In: G. Antonides, S. Maital and W.F. van Raaij (eds.), *Advances in Economic Psychology.* Chichester: Wiley.

Antonides, G. and A.J.M. Hagenaars, 1989. The distribution of welfare in the household. Papers on Economic Psychology 81. Rotterdam: Erasmus University.

Antonides, G. and H.S.J. Robben, 1995. True positives and false alarms in the detection of tax evasion. *Journal of Economic Psychology* 16, 617–640.

Antonides, G. and N. van der Sar, 1990. Individual expectations, risk perception and preferences in relation to investment decision making. *Journal of Economic Psychology* 11, 227–245.

Antonides, G. and W.F. van Raaij, 1989. Income judgments of the employed and the unemployed. Proceedings of the 14th Colloquium of the International Association for Research in Economic Psychology. pp. 599–613.

Arkes, H.R. and C. Blumer, 1985. The psychology of sunk cost. *Organizational Behavior and Human Decision Processes* 35, 124–140.

Arndt, J., 1979. Family life cycle as a determinant of size and composition of household expenditures. *Advances in Consumer Research* 6, 128–132.

Arts, W., P. Hermkens and P. van Wijck, 1991. Income and the idea of justice: Principles, judgments and their framing. *Journal of Economic Psychology* 12, 121–140.

Atkinson, J.W., 1958. 'Towards experimental analysis of human motivation in terms of motives, expectancies, and incentives'. In: J.W. Atkinson (ed.), *Motives in fantasy, action, and society.* Princeton, NJ: Van Nostrand.

Ausubel, L.M., 1991. The failure of competition in the credit market. *American Economic Review* 81, 50–81.

Ax, A.F., 1953. The physiological differentiation between fear and anger in humans. *Psychosomatic Medicine* 15, 433–442.

Axelrod, R. 1980. Effective choice in the prisoner's dilemma. *Journal of Conflict Resolution* 24, 3–25.

Axelrod, R. 1980. More effective choice in the prisoner's dilemma. *Journal of Conflict Reso-*

lution 24, 379–403.

Axsom, D. and J. Cooper, 1980. 'Reducing weight by reducing dissonance: The role of effort justification in inducing weight loss'. In: E. Aronson (ed.), *Readings for the social animal.* San Francisco: Freeman.

Bagozzi, R.P., 1981. Attitudes, intentions and behavior: A test of some key hypotheses. *Journal of Personality and Social Psychology* 41, 607–627.

Bagozzi, R.P., H. Baumgartner and Y. Yi, 1992. State versus action orientation and the theory of reasoned action: An application to coupon usage. *Journal of Consumer Research* 18, 505–518.

Bandura, A., 1986. *Social foundations of thought and action: A social cognitive theory.* Englewood Cliffs, NJ: Prentice-Hall.

Bandura, A., E.B. Blanchard and B. Ritter, 1969. Relative efficacy of desensitization and modeling approaches for inducing behavioral, affective, and attitudinal changes. *Journal of Personality and Social Psychology* 13, 173–199.

Barber, T.X. and M.J. Silver, 1968. Fact, fiction and the experimenter bias effect. *Psychological Bulletin Monograph Supplement* 70, 1–29.

Bass, F.M. and W.L. Wilkie, 1973. A comparative analysis of attitudinal predictions of brand preferences. *Journal of Marketing Research* 10, 262–269.

Batchelor, R.A., 1986. The psychophysics of inflation. *Journal of Economic Psychology* 7, 269–290.

Batra, R. and M.L. Ray, 1986. Affective responses mediating acceptance of advertising. *Journal of Consumer Research* 13, 234–249.

Batson, C.D., J.L Dyck, J.R. Brandt, J.G. Batson, A.L. Powell, M.R. McMaster and C. Griffitt, 1988. Five studies testing two new egoistic alternatives to the empathy – altruism hypothesis. *Journal of Personality and Social Psychology* 55, 52–77.

Bazerman, M.H., 1984. The relevance of Kahneman and Tversky's concept of framing to organizational behavior. *Journal of Management* 10, 333–343.

Bazerman, M.H., 1994. *Judgment in managerial decision making.* New York: Wiley.

Beaman, A.L., C.M. Cole, M. Preston, B. Klenz and N.M. Steblay, 1983. Fifteen years of foor-in-the-door research. A meta-analysis. *Personality and Social Psychology Bulletin* 9, 181–196.

Bechtel, G.G., P. Vanden Abeele and A.M. DeMeyer, 1993. The sociotropic aspect of consumer confidence. *Journal of Economic Psychology* 14, 615–633.

Becker, G.M. and C.G. McClintock, 1967. Value: Behavioral decision theory. *Annual Review of Psychology* 18, 239–268.

Becker, G.S., 1965. A theory of the allocation of time. *The Economic Journal* 75, 493–517.

Becker, G.S., 1973. A theory of marriage. Part I. *Journal of Political Economy* 81, 813–846.

Becker, G.S., 1974. A theory of marriage. Part II. *Journal of Political Economy* 81, S11–S26.

Becker, G.S., 1981. *A treatise on the family.* London: Harvard Press.

Bem, D.J., 1972. 'Self-perception theory'. In: L. Berkowitz (ed.), *Advances in experimental social psychology*, Vol. 6. New York: Academic Press. pp. 1–62.

Benzion, U., A. Rapoport and J. Yagil, 1988. Discount rates inferred from decisions: An experimental study. Proceedings of the 13th Colloquium of the International Association for Research in Economic Psychology.

Berger, I.E., B.T. Ratchford and G.H. Haines Jr., 1994. Subjective product knowledge as a moderator of the relationship between attitudes and purchase intentions for a durable product. *Journal of Economic Psychology* 15, 301–314.

Berlyne, D.E., 1963, 'Motivational problems raised by exploratory and epistemic behavior'. In: S. Koch (ed.), *Psychology: A study of a science*, Vol. 5. New York: McGraw-Hill. pp. 284–364.

Bernoulli, D., 1738. Specimen theoriae novea de mensura sortis. Commentarii Academiae Scientiarium Imperialis Petropolitanae 6, 175–192. Translated by L. Sommer, 1954. Exposition of a new theory on the measurement of risk. *Econometrica* 22, 23–36.

Bernstein, I.L., 1978. Learned taste aversions in children receiving chemotherapy. *Science* 200, 1302.

Best, A. and A.R. Andreasen, 1976. *Talking back to business: Voiced and unvoiced consumer complaints*. Washington, D.C.: Center for Study of Responsive Law.

Bieri, J., 1955. Cognitive complexity-simplicity and predictive behavior. *Journal of Abnormal and Social Psychology* 51, 263–268.

Birnbaum, M.H., 1981. Thinking and feeling: A skeptical review. *American Psychologist* 36, 99–101.

Blomqvist, H.C., 1989. The 'rationality' of expectations: An experimental approach. *Journal of Economic Psychology* 10, 275–299.

Bohrnstedt, G.W., 1970. 'Reliability and validity assessment in attitude measurement.' In: G.F. Summers (ed.), *Attitude measurement*. Chicago: Rand McNally. pp. 80–99.

Bolle, F., 1992. Why and when to love your enemy. *Journal of Economics Psychology* 13, 509–514.

Bolton, G.E. and E. Katok, 1995. An experimental test of the crowding out hypothesis: The nature of beneficiant behavior. Working paper 295.95. Penn State Department of Management Science.

Bolton, G.E. and R. Zwick, 1993. Anonymity versus punishment in ultimatum bargaining. Working paper, Penn State Department of Management Science.

Bonacich, P., G.H. Shure, J.P. Kahan and R.J. Meeker, 1976. Cooperation and group size in the *N*-person prisoner's dilemma. *Journal of Conflict Resolution* 20, 687–705.

Bower, G.H. and P.R. Cohen, 1982. 'Emotional influences in memory and thinking: Data and theory'. In: M.S. Clark and S.T. Fiske (eds.), *Affect and cognition*. Hillsdale, NJ: Lawrence Erlbaum. pp. 291–331.

Bradburn, N.M., 1969. *The structure of psychological well-being*. Chicago: Aldine.

Brandstätter, H., 1993. Should economic psychology care about personality structure? *Journal of Economic Psychology* 14, 473–494.

Bransford, J.D. and B.S. Stein, 1984. *The ideal problem solver*. New York: Freeman.

Brehm, J., 1956. Postdecision changes in the desirability of alternatives. *Journal of Abnormal and Social Psychology* 52, 384–389.

Brickman, P., D. Coates and R. Janoff-Bulman, 1978. Lottery winners and accident victims: Is happiness relative? *Journal of Personality and Social Psychology* 36, 917–927.

Bronner, A.E. and R. de Hoog, 1984. Computer assisted decision making: A new tool for market research. Paper presented at the ESOMAR-congress, Rome.

Brown, J.S., 1948. Gradients of approach and avoidance responses and their relation to level of motivation. *Journal of Comparative and Physiological Psychology* (December), 450–465.

Bruner, J.S. and C.C. Goodman, 1947. Value and need as organizing factors in perception. *Journal of Abnormal and Social Psychology* 42, 33–44.

Buchanan, J.M., 1965. Ethical rules, expected values and large numbers. *Ethics* 76, 1–13.

Byrne, D., 1966. *An introduction to personality*. London: Prentice-Hall.

Cacioppo, J.T. and R.E. Petty, 1982. The need for cognition. *Journal of Personality and Social Psychology* 42, 116–131.

Cagan, P., 1965. *The effect of pension plans on aggregate saving: Evidence from a sample survey*. New York: Columbia University Press.

Calder, B.J. and B.M. Staw, 1975. Self perception of intrinsic and extrinsic motivation. *Journal of Personality and Social Psychology* 31, 599–605.

Camerer, C. and R.H. Thaler, 1995. Anomalies: Ultimatums, dictators and manners. *Journal of Economic Perspectives* 9, 209–219.

Cameron, P., 1974. Social stereotypes: Three faces of happiness. *Psychology Today* 8, 63–64.

Campbell, A., P.E. Converse and W.L. Rodgers, 1976. *The quality of American life*. New York: Russell Sage Foundation.

Campbell, D.T. and D.W. Fiske, 1959. Convergent and discriminant validation by the multitrait-multimethod matrix. *Psychological Bulletin* 56, 81–105.

Campbell, D.T. and J.C. Stanley, 1963. *Experimental and quasi-experimental designs for research*. Chicago: Rand McNally College.

Cantril, H., 1965. *The pattern of human concerns*. New Brunswick, NJ: Rutgers University Press.

Carmone, F.J. and P.E. Green, 1981. Model misspecification in multiattribute parameter estimation. *Journal of Marketing Research* 18, 87–93.

Christensen-Szalanski, J.J.J., 1984. Discount functions and the measurement of patient values: Womens' decisions during childbirth. *Medical Decision Making* 4, 47–58.

Christie, R. and F.L. Geis, 1970. *Studies in Machiavellism*. New York: Academic Press.

Cialdini, R.B., 1985. *Influence. Science and practice*. London: Harper Collins.

Cohen, A.R., 1960. Attitudinal consequences of induced decrepancies between cognitions and behavior. *Public Opinion Quarterly* 24, 297–218.

Colman, A.M. 1982. *Game theory and experimental games*. Oxford: Pergamon Press.

Combs, B. and P. Slovic, P., 1979. Newspaper coverage of causes of death. *Journalism Quarterly* 56, 837–843.

Cook, K.S. and K.A. Hegtvedt, 1983. Distributive justice, equity, and equality. *Annual Review of Sociology* 9, 217–241.

Coombs, C.H. and G.S. Avrunin, 1977. Single-peaked functions and the theory of preference. *Psychological Review* 84, 216–230.

Cooper, J., 1971. Personal responsibility and dissonance: The role of foreseen consequences. *Journal of Personality and Social Psychology* 18, 354–363.

Cooper, J. and R.H. Fazio, 1984. 'A new look at dissonance theory'. In: L. Berkowitz (ed.), *Advances in experimental social psychology*, Vol. 17. New York: Academic Press. pp. 229–266.

Cooper, J. and S. Worchel, 1970. Role of undesired consequences in arousing cognitive dissonance. *Journal of Personality and Social Psychology* 16, 199–206.

Cooper, J., M.P. Zanna and P.A. Taves, 1978. Arousal as a necessary condition for attitude change following induced compliance. *Journal of Personality and Social Psychology* 36, 1101–1106.

Cooper, P., 1970. 'Subjective economics: Factors in a psychology of spending'. In: B. Taylor and G.Wills (eds.), *Pricing strategy*. Princeton, NJ: Brandon Systems Press.

Cox, J.C. and R.M. Isaac, 1986. 'Incentive regulation: A case study in the use of laboratory experimental analysis in economics'. In: S. Moriarity (ed.), *Laboratory market research*. Norman: University of Oklahoma.

Cronbach, L.J., 1984. *Essentials of psychological testing*. New York: Harper and Row.

Croyle, R. and J. Cooper, 1983. Dissonance arousal: Physiological evidence. *Journal of Personality and Social Psychology* 45, 782–791.

Cude, B.J., 1980. An objective method of determining the relevancy of product characteristics. *Proceedings of the American Council of Consumer Interests*. pp. 111–116.

Daamen, D.D.L. and H.A.M. Wilke, 1994. An anchoring-and-adjustment perspective on salary negotiations. Proceedings of the combined IAREP-SABE conference. Rotterdam: Erasmus University.

Daniel, T.R., 1994. Time preference and saving: An analysis of panel data. Progress Report 20. Tilburg: Center for Economic Research.

Dardis, R. and N. Gieser, 1980. Price and quality of durable goods: Are they more closely related in the seventies than in the sixties? *Journal of Consumer Policy* 4, 238–248.

Davis, F.D., G.L. Lohse and J.E. Kottemann, 1994. Harmful effects of seemingly helpful information on forecasts of stock earnings. *Journal of Economic Psychology* 15, 253–267.

Davis, J.M., 1958. The transitivity of preferences. *Behavioral Science* 3, 26–33.

Dawes, R.M. 1979. The robust beauty of improper linear models in decision making. *American Psychologist* 34, 571–582.

Dawes, R.M. 1980. Social dilemmas. *Annual Review of Psychology* 31, 169–193.

Dawes, R.M. and B. Corrigan, 1974. Linear models in decision making. *Psychological Bulletin*

81, 95–106.

Dawes, R.M., J. McTavish and H. Shaklee, 1977. Behavior, communication and assumptions about other people's behavior in a commons dilemma situation. *Journal of Personality and Social Psychology* 35, 1–11.

Dawes, R.M. and T.L. Smith, 1985. 'Attitude and opinion measurement'. In: G. Lindzey and E. Aronson (eds.), *Handbook of social psychology*, Vol. 1. New York: Random House. pp. 509–566.

Day, R.L. and E.L. Landon Jr., 1976. Collecting comprehensive complaint data by survey research. *Advances in Consumer Research* 3, 263–268.

Deaton, A. and J. Muellbauer, 1981. *Economics and consumer behavior.* Cambridge: Cambridge University Press.

Deci, E.L. and J. Porac, 1978. Cognitive evaluation theory and the study of human motivation. In: M.R. Lepper and D. Greene (eds.), *The hidden costs of reward.* New York: Wiley. pp. 149–178.

Deci, E.L. and R.M. Ryan, 1980. The empirical exploration of intrinsic motivational processes. In: Berkowitz (ed.) *Advances in Experimental Social Psychology*, Vol. 13. New York: Academic Press. pp. 39–80.

Deutsch, M., 1975. Equity, equality and need: What determines which value will be used as the basis of distributive justice? *Journal of Social Issues* 31, 137–149.

Dholakia, R.R. and S.J. Levy, 1987. Effect of recent economic experiences on consumer dreams, goals and behavior in the United States. *Journal of Economic Psychology* 8, 429–444.

Diener, E., 1984. Subjective well-being. *Psychological Bulletin* 95, 542–575.

Drottz-Sjöberg, B.-M., 1991. Risk: How you see it, react and communicate. *European Management Journal* 9, 88–97.

Dutton, D. and A. Aron, 1974. Some evidence for heightened sexual attraction under conditions of high anxiety. *Journal of Personality and Social Psychology* 30, 510–517.

East, R., 1993. Investment decisions and the theory of planned behavior. *Journal of Economic Psychology* 14, 337–375.

Easterlin, R.A., 1974. 'Does economic growth improve the human lot? Some empirical evidence'. In: P.A. David and W.R. Melvin (eds.), *Nations and households in economic growth.* Palo Alto: Stanford University Press. pp. 89–121.

Einhorn, H.J., D.N. Kleinmuntz and B. Kleinmuntz, 1979. Linear regression and process-tracing models of judgment. *Psychological Review* 86, 465–485.

Ekman, G., 1956. Discriminal sensitivity on the subjective continuum. *Acta Psychologica* 12, 233–243.

Ekman, G., 1959. Weber's law and related functions. *Journal of Psychology* 47, 343–352.

Ekman, P., 1980. *The face of men.* New York: Garland STPM.

Ekman, P., 1994. Strong evidence for universals in facial expressions: A reply to Russell's mistaken critique. *Psychological Bulletin* 115, 268–287.

Ekman, P., R.W. Levenson and W.V. Friesen, 1983. Autonomic nervous system activity distinguishes among emotions. *Science* 221, 1208–1210.

Elster, J., 1979. *Ulysses and the sirens.* Cambridge: Cambridge University Press.

Elster, J., 1983. *Sour grapes.* Cambridge: Cambridge University Press.

Elster, J. (ed.), 1986. *The multiple self.* Cambridge: Cambridge University Press.

Engel, J.F., R.D. Blackwell and P.W. Miniard, 1990. *Consumer behavior.* Chicago: The Dryden Press.

Epstein, S., 1979. The stability of behavior: I. On predicting post of the people most of the time. *Journal of Personality and Social Psychology* 37, 1097–1126.

Epstein, S., 1980. The stability of behavior: II. Implications for psychological research. *American Psychologist* 35, 790–806.

Epstein, S. and E.J. O'Brien, 1985. The person-situation debate in historical and current perspective. *Psychological Bulletin* 98, 513–537.

Erev, I. and S. Maital, 1996. A lot of knowledge is a dangerous thing. In: G. Antonides, S. Maital and W.F. van Raaij (eds.), *Advances in Economic Psychology.* Chichester: Wiley.

Etzioni, A., 1988. *The Moral Dimension.* New York: The Free Press.

Feinman, S., 1978. The blind as "ordinary people". *Journal of Visual Impairment and Blindness* 72, 231–238.

Ferber, R., 1973. 'Family decision making and economic behavior: A review'. In: E.B. Sheldon (ed.), *Family economic behavior: Problems and prospects.* Philadelphia: Lippincott. pp. 29–61.

Ferber, R. and R.A. Piskie, 1965. Subjective probabilities and buying intentions. *Review of Economics and Statistics* 47, 322–325.

Festinger, L., 1957. *A theory of cognitive dissonance.* Evanston, IL: Row, Peterson.

Festinger, L. and J.M. Carlsmith, 1959. Cognitive consequences of forced compliance. *Journal of Abnormal and Social Psychology* 58, 203–210.

Fischhoff, B., S. Lichtenstein, P. Slovic, S.L. Derby and R.L. Keeney, 1981. *Acceptable risk.* Cambridge: Cambridge University Press.

Fischhoff, B., P. Slovic, S. Lichtenstein, S. Read and B. Combs, 1978. How safe is safe enough? A psychometric study of attitudes towards technological risks and benefits. *Policy Sciences* 9, 127–152.

Fishbein, M., 1966. 'The relationship between beliefs, attitude and behavior'. In: S. Feldman (ed.), *Cognitive consistency.* New York: Academic Press. pp. 199–223.

Fishbein, M., 1967. 'Attitude and the prediction of behavior'. In: M. Fishbein M. (ed.), *Readings in attitude theory and measurement.* New York: Wiley. pp. 477–492.

Fishbein, M. and I. Ajzen, 1975. *Belief, attitude, intention and behavior.* Reading, Mass.: Addison-Wesley.

Fisher, I. 1930. *The theory of interest.* New York: Macmillan. Reprinted by Kelly, Clifton.

Fisher, R., Ury, W. and B. Patton, 1983. *Getting to yes: Negotiating agreement without giving in.* Boston: Houghton Mifflin.

Fiske, S.T. and S.E. Taylor, 1984. *Social cognition.* New York: Random House.

Foa, U.G., 1971. Interpersonal and economic resources. *Science* 171, 345.

Foa, U.G., L.N. Salcedo, K.Y. Tornblom, M. Garner, H. Glaubman and M. Teichman, 1987. Interrelation of social resources. *Journal of Cross-Cultural Psychology* 18, 221–233.

Folkes, V.S., 1984. Consumer reactions to product failure: An attributional approach. *Journal of Consumer Research* 10, 398–409.

Fordyce, M.W., 1977. The happiness measures: A sixty-second index of emotional well-being and mental health. Unpublished manuscript, Edison Community College, Ft. Myers, Florida.

Fordyce, M.W., 1978. Prospectus: The self-description inventory. Unpublished manuscript, Edison Community College, Ft. Myers, Florida.

Frank, R.H., T. Gilovitch and D.T. Regan, 1993. Does studying economics inhibit cooperation? *Journal of Economic Perspectives* 7, 159–171.

Freedman, J., 1965. Long-term behavioral effects of cognitive dissonance. *Journal of Experimental Social Psychology* 1, 145–155.

Freedman, J.L. and S.C. Fraser, 1966. Compliance without pressure: The foot-in-the-door technique. *Journal of Personality and Social Psychology* 4, 195–202.

Frey, B.S. 1983. The economic model of behavior: Shortcomings and fruitful developments. University of Zürich. (mimeographed).

Frey, B.S., 1993. Motivation as a limit to pricing. *Journal of Economic Psychology* 14, 635–664.

Frey, B.S., 1994. How intrinsic motivation is crowded out and in. *Rationality and Society* 6, 334–352.

Frey, B.S. and I. Bohnet, 1995. Institutions affect fairness: Experimental investigations. *Journal of Institutional and Theoretical Economics* 151, 286–303.

Frey, B.S. and R. Eichenberger, 1994. Economic incentives transform psychological anomalies. *Journal of Economic Behavior and Organization* 23, 215–234.

Frey, B.S. and K. Foppa, 1986. Human behavior: Possibilities explain actions. *Journal of Economic Psychology* 7, 137–160.

Friedman, M., 1953. 'The methodology of positive economics'. In: M. Friedman (ed.), *Essays in Positive Economics*. Chicago: University of Chicago Press. pp. 3–43.

Fuchs, V.R., 1982. 'Time preferences and health : An exploratory study'. In: V.R. Fuchs (ed.), *Economic aspects of health*. Chicago: University of Chicago Press. pp. 93–120.

Furnham, A., 1983. Inflation and the estimated size of notes. *Journal of Economic Psychology* 4, 349–352.

Furnham, A. and A. Lewis, 1986. *The economic mind*. Brighton, Sussex, UK: Wheatsheaf.

Gabor, A. and C.W.J. Granger, 1966. Price as an indicator of quality: Report on an enquiry. *Economica* 46, 43–70.

Galanter, E., 1990. Utility functions for nonmonetary events. *American Journal of Psychology* 103, 449–470.

Gärling, T. and E. Lindberg, 1987. Beliefs about attainment of life satisfaction as determinants of preferences for everyday activities. Proceedings of the 12th Colloquium of the Association for Research in Economic Psychology. pp. 821–830.

Geistfeld, L.V., 1982. The price-quality relationship revisited. *Journal of Consumer Affairs* 16, 334–346.

Geistfeld, L.V., E.S. Maynes and G. Duncan, 1979. Informational imperfections in local consumer markets: A preliminary analysis. *Advances in Consumer Research* 6, 180–185.

Gilovich, T., 1983. Biased evaluation and persistence in gambling. *Journal of Personality and Social Psychology* 44, 1110–1126.

Ginsburg, H. and S. Opper, 1969. *Piaget's theory of intellectual development*. Englewood Cliffs, NJ: Prentice-Hall.

Glatzer, W., 1984. 'Satisfaction with life and alternative measures of subjektive well-being'. In: W. Glatzer and W. Zapf (eds.), *Lebensqualität in der Bundesrepublik*. (In German.) Frankfurt: Campus.

Goedhart, T., V. Halberstadt, A. Kapteyn and B.M.S. van Praag, 1977. The poverty line: Concept and measurement. *Journal of Human Resources* 12, 503–520.

Granbois, D.H., 1977. 'Shopping behavior and preferences'. In: *Selected aspects of consumer behavior – a summary from the perspective of different disciplines*. Washington, D.C.: U.S. Government Printing Office. pp. 259–298.

Gray-Little, B. and N. Burks, 1983. Power and satisfaction in marriage: A review and critique. *Psychological Bulletin* 93, 513–538.

Gredal, K., 1966. 'Purchasing behavior in households'. In: M. Kjaer-Hansen (ed.), *Readings in Danish theory of marketing*. Copenhagen: Einar Harcks Forlag. pp. 84–100.

Green, P.E. and M.T. Devita, 1975. An interaction model of consumer utility. *Journal of Consumer Research* 2, 146–153.

Grift, Y.K., J.J. Siegers and G.N.C. Suy, 1989. *Consumption of time in The Netherlands* (in Dutch). The Hague: SWOKA.

Griliches, Z., 1971. 'Hedonic price indexes for automobiles: An econometric analysis of quality change'. In: Z. Griliches (ed.), *Price indexes and quality change: studies in new methods of measurement*. Cambridge, MA: Harvard University Press.

Guilford, J.P., 1965. *Fundamental statistics in psychology and education*. New York: McGraw-Hill.

Gurin, G., J. Veroff and S. Feld, 1960. *Americans view their mental health*. New York: Basic Books.

Güth, W., R. Schmittberger and B. Schwarze, 1982. An experimental analysis of ultimatum bargaining. *Journal of Economic Behavior and Organization* 3, 367–388.

Güth, W. and R. Tietz, 1990. Ultimatum bargaining behavior – A survey and comparison of experimental results. *Journal of Economic Psychology* 11, 417–449.

Haberfeld, Y., 1992. Pay, valence of pay and gender: A simultaneous equation model. *Journal of Economic Psychology* 13, 93–109.

Haffner, M.E.A., 1989. Image and identity of 'warm' bakers. (In Dutch). Master's thesis, Erasmus University Rotterdam.

Hagenaars, A.J.M., 1986. *The perception of poverty*. Amsterdam: North-Holland.

Hamblin, R.L. 1973. 'Social attitudes: Magnitude measurement and theory'. In: H.M. Blalock Jr. (ed.), *Measurement in the social sciences*. London: Macmillan. pp. 61–121.

Hamburger, H., 1977. 'Dynamics of cooperation in 'take some' games'. In: W.F. Kempf and B.H. Repp (eds.), *Mathematical models for social psychology*. Bern: Huber. pp. 252–276.

Hamburger, H., 1979. *Games as models of social phenomena*. San Francisco: Freeman.

Handy, C.R. and M. Pfaff, 1975. Consumer satisfaction with food products and marketing services. Washington, D.C.: United States Department of Agriculture, Economic Research Service, Agricultural Report No. 281.

Hardin, G.R., 1968. The tragedy of the commons. *Science* 162, 1243–1248.

Harris, D.B., 1963. *Goodenough-Harris drawing test manual*. New York.

Harris, R.J. 1972. An interval-scale classification system for all 2×2 games. *Behavioral Science* 17, 371–383.

Hartman, R.S., M.J. Doane and C.-K. Woo, 1991. Consumer rationality and the status quo. *Quarterly Journal of Economics* 106, 141–162.

Hausman, J.A. 1979. Individual discount rates and the purchase and utilization of energy-using durables. *Bell Journal of Economics* 10, 33–54.

Havlena, W.J. and M.B. Holbrook, 1986. The varieties of consumption experience: Comparing two typologies of emotions in consumer behavior. *Journal of Consumer Research* 13, 394–404.

Hayes, R.H. and W.J. Abernathy, 1980. Managing our way to economic decline. *Harvard Business Review* July-August, 67–77.

Hayes, S.P. Jr., 1950. Some psychological problems of economics. *Psychological Bulletin* 47, 289–330.

Heider, F., 1958. *The psychology of interpersonal relations*. New York: Wiley.

Heise, D.R., 1970. 'The Semantic Differential and attitude research.' In: G.F. Summers (ed.), *Attitude measurement*. Chicago: Rand McNally. pp. 235–253.

Helson, H., 1959. 'Adaptation level theory'. In: S. Koch (ed.), *Psychology: A study of a science*, Vol. 1. New York: McGraw-Hill. pp. 565–621.

Helson, H., 1964. *Adaptation level theory*. New York: Harper and Row.

Hermkens, P.L.J., 1986. Fairness judgments of the distribution of incomes. *Netherlands Journal of Sociology* 22, 61–71.

Hermkens, P.L.J. and F.A. Boerman, 1989. Consensus with respect to the fairness of incomes: Differences between social groups. *Social Justice Research* 3, 201–215.

Herrnstein, R.J., 1990. Rational choice theory: Necessary but not sufficient. *American Psychologist* 45, 356–367.

Herrnstein, R.J. and D. Prelec, 1991. Melioration: A theory of distributed choice. *Journal of Economic Perspectives* 5, 137–156.

Hilgard, E.R., R.C. Atkinson and R.L. Atkinson, 1971. *Introduction to psychology*. New York: Harcourt Brace Jovanovich.

Hill, R., 1963. Judgment and consumership in the management of family resources. *Sociology and Social Research* 47, 460–466.

Hiltrop, J.M., 1988. Mediator tactics and the effectiveness of mediation in the resolution of intergroup conflicts. Proceedings of the 13th Annual Colloquium of the International Association of Research in economic Psychology. Leuven.

Hoch, S.J. and G.F. Loewenstein, 1991. Time-inconsistent preferences and consumer self-control. *Journal of Consumer Research* 17, 492–507.

Hoffman, E., K. McCabe. K. Shachat and V.L. Smith, 1994. Preferences, property rights and anonymity in bargaining games. *Games and Economic Behavior* 7, 346–380.

Hoffman, E., K. McCabe and V.L. Smith, forthcoming. On expectations and the monetary stakes in ultimatum games. *International Journal of Game Theory*.

Hoffman, E., K. Shachat and V.L. Smith, 1992. Preferences, property, rights and anonymity in bargaining games. Working paper, University of Arizona.

Hogg, R.V. and A.T. Craig, 1971. *Introduction to mathematical statistics.* London: Collier-Macmillan.

Holbrook, M.B. and R. Batra, 1987. Assessing the role of emotions as mediators of consumer responses to advertising. *Journal of Consumer Research* 14, 404–420.

Holbrook, M.B. and J. O'Shaughnessy, 1984. The role of emotions in advertising. *Psychology and Marketing* 1, 45–64.

Holmes, T.H. and R.H. Rahe, 1967. The social readjustment rating scale. *Journal of Psychosomatic Research* 11, 213–218.

Humphreys, P.C. and A. Wisudha, 1979. MAUD – an interactive computer program for the structuring, decomposition and recomposition of preferences between multi-attributed alternatives. Decision Analysis Unit. Technical Report 79–2. Uxbridge, Middx.: Brunel University.

Hurvich, L.M. and D. Jameson, 1974. Opponent process as a model of neural organization. *American Psychologist* 29, 88–102.

Iacocca, L., 1984. *Iacocca: An autobiography.* New York: Bantam.

Isen, A.M. and P.F. Levin, 1972. Effect of feeling good on helping: Cookies and kindness. *Journal of Personality and Social Psychology* 21, 384–388.

Izard, C.E., 1994. Innate and universal facial expressions: Evidence from developmental and cross-cultural research. *Psychological Bulletin* 115, 288–299.

Jacoby, J., D.E. Speller and C.K. Berning, 1974. Brand choice behavior as a function of information overload: Replication and extension. *Journal of Consumer Research* 1, 33–42.

Jacoby, J., D.E. Speller and C.A. Kohn, 1974. Brand choice behavior as a function of information overload. *Journal of Marketing Research* 11, 63–69.

James, W., 1950. *The principles of psychology.* New York: Dover. (Original work published 1890.)

Janis, I.L. and S. Feshbach, 1953. Effects of fear-arousing communications. *Journal of Abnormal and Social Psychology* 48, 78–92.

Janis, I.L. and D. Hoffman, 1970. Facilitating effects of daily contact between partners who make a decision to cut down on smoking. *Journal of Personality and Social Psychology* 17, 25–35.

Jasso, G. and P.H. Rossi, 1977. Distributive justice and earned income. *American Sociological Review* 45, 3–32.

Johnson, E., J. Hershey, J. Meszaros and H. Kunreuther, 1993. Framing, probability distortions and insurance decisions. *Journal of Risk and Uncertainty* 7, 35–51.

Johnson, E. and A. Tversky, 1983. Affect, generalization and the perception of risk. *Journal of Personality and Social Psychology* 45, 20–31.

Jones, E.E. and S. Berglas, 1978. Control of attributions about the self through self-handicapping strategies: The appeal of alcohol and the role of underachievement. *Personality and Social Psychology Bulletin* 4, 200–206.

Jones, E.E. and K.E. Davis, 1965. 'From acts to dispositions: The attribution process in person perception'. In: L. Berkowitz (ed.), *Advances in experimental social psychology*, Vol. 2. New York: Academic Press. pp. 219–266.

Jones, E.E. and V.A. Harris, 1967. The attribution of attitudes. *Journal of Experimental Social Psychology* 3, 1–24.

Jones, E.E. and R.E. Nisbett, 1971. *The actor and the observer: Divergent perceptions of the causes of behavior.* Morristown, NJ: General Learning Press.

Jones, E.E. and H. Sigall, 1971. The bogus pipeline: A new paradigm for measuring affect and attitude. *Psychological Bulletin* 76, 349–364.

Jungermann, H., 1988. 'Time preferences: The expectation and evaluation of decision consequences as a function of time'. In: S. Maital (ed.), *Applied behavioural economics*, Vol. 2.

Brighton: Wheatsheaf. pp. 579–592.

Kagel, J., C. Kim and D. Moser, in press. Fairness in ultimatum games with asymmetric information and asymmetric payoffs. *Games and Economic Behavior*.

Kagel, J. and A.E. Roth, 1995. *Handbook of experimental economics*. Princeton: Princeton University Press.

Kahneman, D., J.L. Knetsch and R.H. Thaler, 1986a. Fairness and the assumptions of economics. *Journal of Business* 59, S285–S300.

Kahneman, D., J.L. Knetsch and R.H. Thaler, 1986b. Fairness as a constraint on profit seeking: Entitlements in the market. *American Economic Review* 76, 728–741.

Kahneman, D., J.L. Knetsch and R.H. Thaler, 1990. Experimental tests of the endowment effect and the Coase theorem. *Journal of Political Economy* 98, 1325–1347.

Kahneman, D. and A. Tversky, 1974. Judgment under uncertainty: Heuristics and biases. *Science* 185, 1124–1131.

Kahneman, D. and A. Tversky, 1979. Prospect theory: An analysis of decision under risk. *Econometrica* 47, 263–291.

Kahneman, D. and A. Tversky 1982. The psychology of preferences. *Scientific American* 246, 136–142.

Kahneman, D., A. Tversky and P. Slovic, 1983. *Judgment under uncertainty: Heuristics and biases*. Cambridge: Cambridge University Press.

Kamen, J.M. and R.J. Toman, 1970. Psychophysics of prices. *Journal of Marketing Research* 7, 27–35.

Kammann, R., 1982. Personal circumstances and life events as poor predictors of happiness. Paper presented at the 90th Annual Convention of the American Psychological Association. Washington D.C.

Kapteyn, A., T. Wansbeek, and J. Buyze, 1979. Maximizing or satisficing? *Review of Economics and Statistics* 61, 549–563.

Kapteyn, A. and T. Wansbeek, 1985. The individual welfare function: A review. *Journal of Economic Psychology* 6, 333–363.

Katona, G., 1964. *The mass consumption society*. New York: McGraw-Hill.

Katona, G., 1965. *Private pensions and individual saving*. Ann Arbor MI: University of Michigan.

Katona, G., 1974. Psychology and consumer economics. *Journal of Consumer Research* 1, 1–8.

Katona, G., 1975. *Psychological economics*. New York: Elsevier.

Katz, D., 1960. 'The functional approach to the study of attitudes'. Excerpted from *Public Opinion Quarterly* 24, 163–204. In: M. Fishbein, 1960 (ed.), *Readings in attitude theory and measurement*. New York: Wiley. pp. 457–468.

Kearl, M.C., 1981–1982. An inquiry into the positive personal and social effects of old age stereotypes among the elderly. *International Journal of Aging and Human Development* 14, 277–290.

Keeney, R.L. and Raiffa, H., 1976. *Decisions with multiple objectives: Preferences and value tradeoffs*. New York: Wiley.

Kelley, H.H., 1967. 'Attribution theory in social psychology'. In: D.L. Vine (ed.), *Nebraska symposium on motivation*. Lincoln, Nebraska: University of Nebraska Press. pp. 192–238.

Kelley, H.H., 1972. *Causal schemata and the attribution process*. Morristown, NJ: General Learning Press.

Kelley, H.H. and J.L. Michela, 1980. Attribution theory and research. *Annual Review of Psychology* 31, 457–501.

Kingma, B.R., 1989. An accurate measurement of the crowd-out effect, income effect, and price effect for charitable contributions. *Journal of Political Economy* 97, 1197–1207.

Kirchler, E., 1993. Spouses' joint purchase decisions: Determinants of influence tactics for muddling through the process. *Journal of Economic Psychology* 14, 405–438.

Kirchler, E., 1995. Studying economic decisions within private households: A critical review and design for a 'couple experiences diary'. *Journal of Economic Psychology* 16, 393–419.

Köhler, W., 1925. *The mentality of apes*. New York: Harcourt Brace Jovanovich.

Komorita, S.S. and J.K. Esser, 1975. Frequency of reciprocated concessions in bargaining. *Journal of Personality and Social Psychology* 32, 699–705.

Kothandapani, V., 1971. Validation of feeling, belief and intention to act as three components of attitude and their contribution to prediction of contraceptive behavior. *Journal of Personality and Social Psychology* 19, 321–333.

Kroonenberg, P., 1983. *Three-mode principal component analysis. Theory and applications.* Leyden: DSWO Press.

Kuhl, J., 1982. Action vs. state orientation as a mediator between motivation and action. In: W. Hacker (ed.), *Cognitive and motivational aspects of action.* Amsterdam: North-Holland. pp. 67–85.

Lancaster, K., 1966. A new approach to consumer theory. *Journal of Political Economy* 74, 132–157.

Lancaster, K., 1979. *Variety, equity, and efficiency.* New York: Columbia University Press.

Lange, C.G., 1922. *The emotions.* Baltimore: Williams and Wilkins.

Langer, E.J., 1975. The illusion of control. *Journal of Personality and Social Psychology* 32, 311–328.

LaPiere, R.T., 1967. 'Attitudes versus actions'. In: M. Fishbein (ed.), *Readings in attitude theory and measurement.* New York: Wiley. pp. 26–31.

Larsen, R.J., E. Diener and R.A. Emmons, 1985. An evaluation of subjective well-being measures. *Social Indicators Research* 17, 1–17.

Lastovicka, J.L., 1982. On the validation of lifestyle traits: A review and illustration. *Journal of Marketing Research* 19, 126–138.

Lastovicka, J.L. and E.A. Joachimsthaler, 1988. Improving the detection of personality – behavior relationships in consumer research. *Journal of Consumer Research* 14, 583–587.

Latané, B. and J.M. Darley, 1970. *The unresponsive bystander: Why doesn't he help?* New York: Appleton-Century-Crofts.

Latané, B. and S. Nida, 1981. Ten years of research on group size and helping. *Psychological Bulletin* 89, 308–324.

Lazarus, R.S., 1981. A cognitivist's reply to Zajonc on emotion and cognition. *American Psychologist* 36, 222–223.

Lazarus, R.S., 1982. Thoughts on the relation between emotion and cognition. *American Psychologist* 37, 1019–1024.

Lazarus, R.S., 1984. On the primacy of cognition. *American Psychologist* 39, 124–129.

Lazarus, R.S., 1991. Cognition and motivation in emotion. *American Psychologist* 46, 352–367.

Lea, S.E.G., 1978. The psychology and economics of demand. *Psychological Bulletin* 85, 441–466.

Lea, S.E.G., 1981. Inflation, decimalization and the estimated sizes of coins. *Journal of Economic Psychology* 1, 79–81.

Lea, S.E.G., 1981. Animal experiments on economic psychology. *Journal of Economic Psychology* 1, 245–271.

Lea, S.E.G., R.M. Tarpy and P. Webley, 1987. *The individual in the economy.* Cambridge: Cambridge University Press.

Lehtinen, U., 1974. A brand choice model. Theoretical framework and empirical results. *European Research* 2, 51–83.

Leiser, D. and G. Izak, 1987. The money size illusion as a barometer of confidence? The case of high inflation in Israel. *Journal of Economic Psychology* 8, 347–356.

Leiser, D., G. Sevón and D. Lévy, 1990. Children's economic socialization: Summarizing the cross-cultural comparison of ten countries. *Journal of Economic Psychology* 11, 591–614.

Lepper, M.R. and D. Greene, 1978. Overjustification research and beyond: Toward a means-ends analysis of intrinsic and extrinsic motivation. In: M.R. Lepper and D. Greene (eds.),

The hidden costs of reward. New York: Wiley. pp. 109–148.

Lesourne, J., 1979. 'Economic dynamics and individual behavior'. In: L. Lévy-Garboua (ed.), *Sociological economics*. London: Sage Publications. pp. 29–47.

Levenson, H., 1973. Perceived parental antecedents of internal, powerful others, and chance locus of control orientations. *Developmental Psychology* 9, 268–274.

Levin, I.P., R.D. Johnson and M.L. Davis, 1987. How information frame influences risky decisions: Between subjects and within subject comparisons. *Journal of Economic Psychology* 8, 43–54.

Lewin, K., 1938. *The conceptual representation and the measurement of psychological forces*. Durham: Duke University Press.

Lichtenstein, S., P. Slovic, B. Fischhoff, M. Layman and B. Combs, 1978. Judged frequency of lethal events. *Journal of Experimental Psychology: Human Learning and Memory* 4, 551–578.

Liebrand, W.B.G., D.M. Messick and H.A.M. Wilke, 1992. *Social dilemmas: Theoretical and research findings*. Oxford: Pergamon Press.

Liebrand, W.B.G., H.A.M. Wilke, R. Vogel and F.J.M. Wolters, 1986. Value orientation and conformity. A study using three types of social dilemma games. *Journal of Conflict Resolution* 30, 77–97.

Likert, R., 1970. 'A technique for the measurement of attitudes.' In: G.F. Summers (ed.), *Attitude measurement*. Chicago: Rand McNally. pp. 149–158.

Lindauer, M.S., 1987. Public and investor attitudes in relation to the stockmarket. *Journal of Economic Psychology* 8, 91–107.

Lindqvist, A., 1981. A note on the determinants of household saving behavior. *Journal of Economic Psychology* 1, 39–57.

Lipsey, R.G. and P.O. Steiner 1978. *Economics*. New York: Harper and Row.

Litai, D., 1980. A risk comparison methodology for the assessment of acceptable risk. Unpublished Ph.D. dissertation. Massachusetts Institute of Technology.

Lovell, M.C., 1986. Tests of rational expectations hypotheses. *American Economic Review* 76, 110–124.

Lowe, C. and S. Kassin, 1978. Biased attributions for political messages: The role of involvement. Paper presented at Eastern Psychological Association meeting. Reported in D. Krech, R.S. Crutchfield, N. Livson, W.A. Wilson Jr. and A. Parducci, 1982. *Elements of psychology*. New York: A. Knopf. pp. 716–717.

Lurie, S., 1987. A parametric model of utility for two-person distributions. *Psychological Review* 94, 42–60.

Lynn, M. and A. Grassman, 1990. Restaurant tipping: An examination of three 'rational' explanations. *Journal of Economic Psychology* 11, 169–181.

Maddala, G.S., 1977. *Econometrics*. New York: McGraw-Hill.

Mahone, C.H., 1960. Fear of failure and unrealistic vocational aspiration. *Journal of Abnormal and Social Psychology* 60, 253–271.

Maier, N.R.F., 1931. Reasoning in humans. *Journal of Comparative Psychology* 12, 181–194.

Maier, S.F. and M.E.P. Seligman, 1976. Learned helplessness: Theory and evidence. *Journal of Experimental Psychology: General* 105, 3–46.

Maital, S.L., S. Maital and N. Pollak, 1986. 'Economic behavior and social learning'. In: A.J. MacFadyen and H.W. MacFadyen (eds.), *Economic psychology: Intersections in theory and application*. Amsterdam: North-Holland. pp. 271–290.

Malholtra, N.K., 1982. Information load and consumer decision making. Journal of Consumer Research 8, 419–430.

Mandler, G., 1962. 'Emotion'. In: R. Brown, E. Galanter, E.H. Hess and G. Mandler (eds.), *New directions in psychology*, Vol. 1. New York: Holt. pp. 267–343.

Markowitz, H.M., 1952. Portfolio selection. *Journal of Finance* 6, 77–91.

Maslow, A., 1954. *Motivation and personality*. New York: Harper & Row.

May, K.O., 1954. Intransitivity, utility and the aggregation of preference patterns. *Econometrica*

22, 1–13.

Maynes, E.S., 1975. The concept and measurement of product quality. In: N.E. Terleckyj (ed.), *Household production and consumption.* New York: National Bureau of Economic Research. pp. 529–560.

Maynes, E.S., 1980. Informationally imperfect markets: The consumer's underrecognized problem. Working Paper. New York: Cornell University.

Mazur, J.E., 1975. The matching law and quantifications related to Premack's principle. *Journal of Experimental Psychology: Animal Behaviour Processes* 1, 374–386.

MacFadyen, A.J., 1986. 'Rational economic man: An introduction survey'. In: A.J. MacFadyen and H.W. MacFadyen (eds.), *Economic psychology: Intersection in theory and application.* Amsterdam: North-Holland. pp. 25–66.

MacFadyen, A.J. and H.W. MacFadyen (eds.), 1986. *Economic psychology: Intersection in theory and application.* Amsterdam: North-Holland.

McArthur, L.A., 1972. The how and what of why: Some determinants and consequences of causal attribution. *Journal of Personality and Social Psychology* 22, 171–193.

McClelland, D.C., 1961. *The achieving society.* Princeton, NJ: Van Nostrand.

McClelland, D.C., 1987. *Human motivation.* Cambridge: University of Cambridge.

McClelland, D.C., J.W. Atkinson, R.A. Clark and E.L. Lowell, 1953. *The achievement motive.* New York: Appleton.

McClintock, C.G., R.M. Kramer and L.J. Keil, 1984. 'Equity and social exchange in human relationships'. In: L. Berkowitz (ed.), *Advances in experimental and social psychology,* Vol. 17. New York: Academic Press. pp. 183–228.

McCrae, R.R. and P.T. Costa, 1987. Validation of the five-factor model of personality across instruments and observers. *Journal of Personality and Social Psychology* 52, 81–90.

McKennell, A.C., T. Atkinson and F.M. Andrews, 1978. Structural constancies in surveys of perceived well-being. Working Paper, Uppsala, Sweden.

McNeil, J., 1974. Federal programs to measure consumer purchase expectations, 1946–1973: A post mortem. *Journal of Consumer Research* 1, 1–10.

McQuarrie, E.F., 1988. An alternative to purchase intentions: The role of prior behavior in consumer expenditure on computers. *Journal of the Market Research Society* 30, 407–437.

McSweeney, F.K. and C. Bierley, 1984. Recent developments in classical conditioning. *Journal of Consumer Research* 11, 619–631.

Mehrabian, A. and J.A. Russell, 1974. *An approach to environmental psychology.* Cambridge, MA: MIT Press.

Messick, S.J., 1967. 'The psychology of acquiescence: An interpretation of the research evidence'. In: I.A. Berg (ed.), *Response set in personality assessment.* Chicago: Aldine. pp. 115–145.

Meyer, H.-D., 1992. Norms and self-interest in ultimatum bargaining: The prince's prudence. *Journal of Economic Psychology* 13, 215–232.

Meyer, W., 1982. The research programme of economics and the relevance of psychology. *British Journal of Social Psychology* 21, 81–91.

Miller, G.A., 1956. The magical number seven, plus or minus two: Some limits on our capacity for processing information. *Psychological Review* 63, 81–97.

Miller, G.A., E. Galanter and K.H. Pribram, 1960. *Plans and the structure of behavior.* New York: Holt, Rinehart and Winston.

Miller, N.E., 1959. 'Liberalization of basic S-R concepts: Extensions to conflict behavior, motivation and social learning'. In: S. Koch (ed.), *Psychology: A study of a science,* Vol. 2. New York: McGraw-Hill.

Mills, J., 1958. Changes in moral attitudes following temptation. *Journal of Personality* 26, 517–531.

Mischel, W., 1968. *Personality and assessment.* New York: Wiley.

Mischel, W., 1974. 'Processes in delay of gratification'. In: L. Berkowitz (ed.), *Advances in experimental social psychology,* Vol. 7. New York: Academic Press. pp. 249–292.

Mischel, W., 1984. Convergences and challenges in the search for consistency. *American Psychologist* 39, 351–364.

Mitchell, A., 1983. *Nine American life-styles: Who we are and where we are going*. London: Macmillan.

Mittal, B., 1988. The role of affective choice mode in the consumer purchase of expressive products. *Journal of Economic Pyschology* 9, 499–524.

Monroe, K.B., 1971. Psychophysics of prices: A reappraisal. *Journal of Marketing Research* 8, 248–251.

Monroe, K.B., 1973. Buyers' subjective perceptions of price. *Journal of Marketing Research* 10, 70–80.

Mueller, E., 1963. Ten years of consumer attitude surveys: Their forecasting record. *Journal of the American Statistical Association* 58, 899–917.

Munnell, A.H., 1974. *The effect of social security on personal saving*. Cambridge, MA: Ballinger.

Murray, H.A., 1938. *Explorations in personality*. New York: Oxford University Press.

Musgrave, A., 1981. Unreal assumptions in economic theory: The F-twist untwisted. *Kyklos* 34, 377–387.

Muth, J.F., 1961. Rational expectations and the theory of price movements. *Econometrica* 129, 315–335.

Nakhaie, M.R., 1993. Knowledge of profit and interest among children in Canada. *Journal of Economic Psychology* 14, 147–160.

Neale, J.M. and R.M. Liebert, 1973. *Science and behavior*. Englewood Cliffs, NJ: Prentice-Hall.

Neale, M.A. and M.H. Bazerman, 1991. *Cognition and rationality in negotiation*. New York: The Free Press.

Nisbett, R.E., 1968. Taste, deprivation, and weight determinants of eating behavior. *Journal of Personality and Social Psychology* 10, 107–116.

Nunnally, J.C., 1978. *Psychometric theory*. New York: McGraw-Hill.

Odink, J.G. and J.S. Schoorl, 1984. *Introduction to microeconomics* (In Dutch). Groningen: Wolters-Noordhoff.

Offerman, T, J. Sonnemans and A. Schram, forthcoming. Value orientations, expectations, expectations and voluntary contributions in public goods. *Economic Journal*.

Ölander, F., 1977. Can consumer dissatisfaction and complaints guide public consumer policy? *Journal of Consumer Policy* 1, 124–137.

Ölander, F. and C.M. Seipel, 1970. Psychological approaches to the psychology of saving. Urbana, IL: Bureau of economics and business research, University of Illinois.

Oliver, R.L., 1980. A cognitive model of the antecedents and consequences of satisfaction decisions.*Journal of Marketing Research* 17, 460–469.

Olshavsky, R.W. and D.H. Granbois, 1979. Consumer decision making – fact or fiction? *Journal of Consumer Research* 6, 93–100.

Olson, M., 1965. *The logic of collective action*. Cambridge MA: Harvard University Press.

Oppewal, H. and E. Tougariova, 1992. A three-person ultimatum game to investigate effects of differences in need, sharing rules and observability on bargaining behavior. *Journal of Economic Psychology* 13, 203–213.

Organization for Economic Cooperation and Development, 1982. *The OECD list of Social Indicators*. Paris: OECD.

Orne, M.T. and K.E. Scheibe, 1964. The contribution of nondeprivation factors in the production of sensory deprivation effects: The psychology of the panic button. *Journal of Abnormal and Social Psychology* 68, 3–12.

Ortona, G. and F. Scacciati, 1992. New experiments on the endowment effect. *Journal of Economic Psychology* 13, 277–296.

Osgood, C.E., G.J. Suci and P. Tannenbaum, 1957. *The measurement of meaning*. Urbana, IL: University of Illinois Press.

Oskamp, S., 1971. Effects of programmed strategies on cooperation in the prisoner's dilemma and other mixed-motive games. *Journal of Conflict Resolution* 15, 225–259.

Overlaet, B., 1991. Merit criteria as justification for differences in earnings. *Journal of Economic Psychology* 12, 689–706.

Payne, J.W. and M.L. Braunstein, 1971. Preferences among gambles with equal underlying distributions. *Journal of Experimental Psychology* 87, 13–18.

Peterson, C. and M.E.P. Seligman, 1984. Causal explanations as a risk factor for depression: Theory and evidence. *Psychological Review* 91, 347–374.

Peterson, C., A. Semmel, C. von Baeyer, L.Y. Abramson, G.I. Metalsky and M.E.P. Seligman, 1982. The attributional style questionnaire. *Cognitive Therapy and Research* 6, 287–299.

Peterson, S.P. and R.J. Reilly, 1991. The rationality of expectations: The Blomqvist experiment reconsidered. *Journal of Economic Psychology* 12, 527–533.

Petty, R.E. and J.T. Cacioppo, 1986. 'The elaboration likelihood model of persuasion'. In: L. Berkowitz (ed.), *Advances in experimental social psychology*, Vol. 19. New York: Academic Press. pp. 123–205.

Phares, E.J. 1978. 'Locus of control'. In: H. London and J.E. Exner Jr. (eds.), *Dimensions of personality*. New York: Wiley. pp. 263–304.

Pieters, R.G.M., 1988. 'Attitude-behavior relationships'. In: W.F. van Raaij, G.M. van Veldhoven and K.E. Wärneryd (eds.), *Handbook of economic psychology*. Dordrecht: Kluwer Academic Publishers. pp. 147–204.

Pieters, R.G.M. and W.F. van Raaij, 1988. 'The role of affect in economic behavior'. In: W.F. van Raaij, G.M. van Veldhoven and K.E. Wärneryd (eds.), *Handbook of economic psychology*. Dordrecht: Kluwer Academic Publishers. pp. 1–41.

Pinson, C. 1978. 'Consumer cognitive styles: Review and implications for marketers'. In: E. Topritzhofer (ed.), *Marketing*. Wiesbaden, Gabler. pp. 163–184.

Pliner, P., P. Darke, R. Abramovitch and J.L. Freedman, 1994. Children's consumer behavior in a store with unattractive merchandise: The 'caveat emptorium'. *Journal of Economic Psychology* 15, 449–465.

Plutchik, R., 1980. *Emotion: A psychoevolutionary synthesis*. New York: Harper and Row.

Poiesz, T.B.C., 1989. The image concept: Its place in consumer psychology. *Journal of Economic Psychology* 10, 457–472.

Poiesz, T.B.C. and J. von Grumbkow, 1988. 'Economic well-being, job satisfaction, income evaluation and consumer satisfaction: An integrative attempt'. In: W.F. van Raaij, G.M. van Veldhoven and K.E. Wärneryd (eds.), *Handbook of economic psychology*. Dordrecht: Kluwer Academic Publishers. pp. 570–593.

Pollack, I., 1952. The information of elementary auditory displays. *Journal of the Acoustical Society of America* 24, 745–749.

Praet, P. and J. Vuchelen, 1984. The contribution of E.C. consumer surveys in forecasting consumer expenditures: An econometric analysis for four major countries. *Journal of Economic Psychology* 5, 101–104.

Premack, D., 1965. 'Reinforcement theory'. In: D. Levine (ed.), *Nebraska symposium on motivation 1965*. Lincoln, NE: University of Nebraska Press. pp. 123–188.

Premack, D., 1971. 'Catching up with common sense or two sides of a generalization: Reinforcement and punishment'. In: R. Glaser (ed.), *The nature of reinforcement*. New York: Academic Press. pp. 121–150.

Pruitt, D.G., 1970. Motivational processes in the decomposed prisoner's dilemma game. *Journal of Personality and Social Psychology* 14, 227–238.

Pruitt, D.G., 1983. Strategic choice in negotiation. *American Behavioral Scientist* 27, 167–194.

Pruitt, D.G. and M.J. Kimmel, 1977. Twenty years of experimental gaming: Critique, synthesis, and suggestions for the future. *Annual Review of Psychology* 28, 363–392.

Purohit, D., 1995. Playing the role of buyer and seller: The mental accounting of trade-ins. *Marketing Letters* 6, 101–110.

Raiffa, H., 1982. *The art and science of negotiation*. Cambridge MA: Harvard University Press.

Rainwater, L., 1974. *What money can buy: The social meaning of poverty.* New York: Basic Books.

Rapoport, A. and A.M. Chammah, 1965. *Prisoner's dilemma: A study in conflict and cooperation.* Ann Arbor, MI: University of Michigan Press.

Rapoport, A. and A.M. Chammah, 1966. The game of chicken. *American Behavioral Scientist* 10, 10–28.

Rapoport, A. and M. Guyer, 1966. A taxonomy of 2 × 2 games. *General Systems* 11, 203–214.

Rapoport, A. and T.S. Wallsten, 1972. Individual decision behavior. *Annual Review of Psychology* 23, 131–176.

Ratchford, B.T., 1975. The new economic theory of consumer behavior: An interpretive essay. *Journal of Consumer Research* 2, 65–75.

Ratchford, B.T., 1979. Operationalizing economic models of demand for product characteristics. *Journal of Consumer Research* 6, 76–85.

Ray, M.L. and R.B. Batra, 1983. Emotions and persuasion in advertising: What do we do and don't know about affect. *Advances in Consumer Research* 10, 543–548.

Rescorla, R.A., 1968. Probability of shock in the presence and absence of CS in fear conditioning. *Journal of Comparative and Physiological Psychology* 66, 1–5.

Rescorla, R.A., 1988. Pavlovian conditioning. It's not what you think it is. *American Psychologist* 43, 151–160.

Ritchie, J.R.B. 1974. An exploratory analysis of the nature and extent of individual differences in perception. *Journal of Marketing Research* 11, 41–49.

Rokeach, M., 1973. *The nature of human values.* New York: The True Press.

Rosenberg, M.J., 1956. Cognitive structure and attitudinal affect. *Journal of Abnormal and Social Psychology* 53, 367–372.

Rosenberg, M.J., 1960a. 'An analysis of affective-cognitive consistency'. In: C.I. Hovland and M.J. Rosenberg (eds.), *Attitude organization and change.* New Haven, Conn.: Yale University Press. pp. 15–64.

Rosenberg, M.J., 1960b. Cognitive reorganization in response to the hypnotic reversal of attitudinal effect. *Journal of Personality* 28, 39–63.

Rosenthal, R. and K.L. Fode, 1963. The effect of experimenter bias on the performance of the albino rat. *Behavioral Science* 8, 183–189.

Ross, L., 1977. 'The intuitive psychologist and his shortcomings: Distortions in the attribution process'. In: L. Berkowitz (ed.), *Advances in experimental social psychology*, Vol. 10. New York: Academic Press. pp. 174–214.

Ross, M. and G.J.O. Fletcher, 1985. 'Attribution and social perception'. In: G. Lindzey and E. Aronson (eds.), *Handbook of social psychology*, Vol. 2. New York: Random House. pp. 73–122.

Rossiter, J.S. and L. Percy, 1987. *Advertising and promotion management.* New York: McGraw-Hill.

Rotter, J.B., 1966. Generalized expectancies for internal versus external control of reinforcement. *Psychological Monographs* 80 (1).

Russell, J.A., 1980. A circumplex model of affect. *Journal of Personality and Social Psychology* 39, 1161–1178.

Russell, J.A., 1994. Is there universal recognition of emotion from facial expression? A review of the cross-cultural studies. *Psychological Bulletin* 115, 102–141.

Russell, J.A. and Mehrabian, 1977. Evidence for a three-factor theory of emotions. *Journal of Research in Personality* 11, 273–294.

Saccuzzo, D.P., 1987. *Psychology.* Boston: Allyn and Bacon.

Safilios-Rothschild, C., 1976. A macro- and micro-examination of family power and love: An exchange model. *Journal of Marriage and the Family* 42, 31–44.

Samuelson, W. and R. Zeckhauser, 1988. Status quo bias in decision making. *Journal of Risk and Uncertainty* 1, 7–59.

Santrock, J.W., 1988. *Psychology.* Dubuque, Iowa: Brown.

Saris, W.E., C. Bruinsma, W. Schoots and C. Vermeulen, 1977. The use of magnitude estimation in large scale survey research. *Mens en Maatschappij* 52, 369–395.

Savage, L.J., 1954. *The foundation of statistics*. New York: Wiley.

Sawry, W.L., J.J. Conger and E.S. Turrell, 1956. An experimental investigation of the role of psychological factors in the production of gastric ulcer in rats. *Journal of Comparative and Physiological Psychology* 49, 457–461.

Sawyer, J. 1965. The altruism scale: A measure of co-operative, individualistic, and competitive interpersonal orientation. *American Journal of Sociology* 71, 407–416.

Scanzoni, J. and K. Polonko, 1980. A conceptual approach to explicit marital negotiation. *Journal of Marriage and the Family*, February, 31–44.

Schachter, S. and J.E. Singer, 1962. Cognitive, social and physiological determinants of emotional state. *Psychological Review* 69, 379–399.

Schlosberg, H., 1954. Three dimensions of emotion. *Psychological Review* 61, 81–88.

Schmöelders, G. and B. Biervert, 1972. 'Level of aspiration and consumption standard: Some general findings'. In: B. Strümpel, J.N. Morgan, and E. Zahn (eds.), *Human behavior in economic affairs*. Amsterdam: Elsevier. pp. 213–227.

Schoemaker, P.J.H., 1982. The expected utility model: Its variants, purposes, evidence and limitations. *Journal of Economic Literature* 20, 529–563.

Schwarz, N. and G.L. Clore, 1983. Mood, misattribution, and judgments of well-being: Informative and directive functions of affective states. *Journal of Personality and Social Psychology* 45, 513–523.

Schwarz, N. and F. Strack, 1987. 'Cognitive and affective processes in judgments of subjective well-being: A preliminary model'. In: H. Brandstätter and E. Kirchler (eds.), *Economic Psychology*. Linz: Rudolf Trauner Verlag. pp. 439–447.

Schwarz, N., F. Strack, D. Kommer and D. Wagner, 1987. Soccer, rooms and the quality of your life: Mood effects on judgments of satisfaction with life in general and with specific domains. *European Journal of Social Psychology* 17, 69–79.

Scitovsky, T., 1976. *The joyless economy*. Oxford: Oxford University Press.

Scott, W.A., 1957. Attitude change through reward of verbal behavior. *Journal of Abnormal and Social Psychology* 55, 72–75.

Seligman, C., M. Bush and K. Kirsch, 1976. Relationship between compliance in the foot-in-the-door paradigm and size of first request. *Journal of Personality and Social Psychology* 33, 517–520.

Sevón, G. and S. Weckström, 1988. Conceptions of economic events and actors. Proceedings of the 13th Colloquium of the International Association for Research in Economic Psychology.

Shaw, M.L.G., 1979. *On becoming a personal scientist*. London: Academic Press.

Shechter, M., 1988. 'Incorporating anxiety induced by environmental episodes in life valuation'. In: S. Maital (ed.), *Applied behavioral economics*, Vol. 2. Brighton: Wheatsheaf. pp. 529–536.

Shefrin, H.M. and M. Statman, 1985. The disposition to sell winners too early and ride losers too long: Theory and evidence. *Journal of Finance* 40, 777–790.

Shefrin, H.M. and M. Statman, 1994. Behavioral portfolio theory. Working Paper, University of Santa Clara.

Shefrin, H.M. and R.H. Thaler, 1988. The behavioral life-cycle hypothesis. *Economic Inquiry* 26, 609–643.

Sherman, S.J. and E. Corty, 1984. 'Cognitive heuristics'. In: R.S. Wyer Jr. and T.S. Srull (eds.), *Handbook of social cognition*, Vol. 1. Hillsdale, NJ: Erlbaum. pp. 189–286.

Sheth, J.N. and W. Talarzyk, 1973. Perceived instrumentality and value importance as determinants of attitudes. *Journal of Marketing Research* 9, 6–9.

Siegel, S., 1956. *Nonparametric statistics for the behavioral sciences*. New York: McGraw-Hill.

Siegel, S., 1957. Level of aspiration and decision making. *Psychological Review* 64, 253–262.

Simon, H.A., 1955. A behavioral model of rational choice. *Quarterly Journal of Economics* 69, 99–118.

Simon, H.A., 1959. Theories of decision-making in economics and behavioral science. *American Economic Review* 49, 253–283.

Simon, H.A., 1963. 'Economics and psychology'. In: S. Koch (ed.), *Psychology: A study of a science*, Vol. 6. New York: McGraw-Hill. pp. 685–723.

Simon, H.A., 1978. Rationality as process and as product of thought. *American Economic Review* 68, 1–16.

Simon, H.A., 1980. The behavioral and social sciences. *Science* 209, 72–78.

Simon, H.A., 1984. On the behavioral and rational foundations of economic dynamics. *Journal of Economic Behavior and Organization* 5, 35–55.

Sims, J.H. and D.D. Baumann, 1972. The tornado threat: Coping styles of the North and the South. *Science* 176, 1386–1391.

Sjöberg, L. 1987. 'Economic acts and reasons in everyday life'. In: H. Brandstätter and E. Kirchler (eds.), *Economic Psychology*. Linz: Rudolf Trauner Verlag. pp. 449–458.

Sjöberg, L. and G. Torell, 1993. The development of risk acceptance and moral evaluation. *Scandinavian Journal of Psychology* 34, 223–236.

Sjöberg, L. and E. Winroth, 1986. Risk, moral value of actions and mood. *Scandinavian Journal of Psychology* 27, 191–208.

Skinner, B.F., 1948. *Walden II*. New York: Macmillan.

Skinner, B.F., 1954. The science of learning and the art of teaching. *Harvard Educational Review* 24, 86–97.

Skinner, B.F., 1968. *The technology of teaching*. New York: Appleton-Century-Crofts.

Slovic, P., B. Fischoff and S. Lichtenstein, 1977. Behavioral decision theory. *Annual Review of Psychology* 28, 1–39.

Slovic, P., B. Fischoff and S. Lichtenstein, 1977. Behavioral decision theory perspectives on risk and safety. *Acta Psychologica* 56, 183–203.

Slovic, P., B. Fischoff and S. Lichtenstein, 1978. Accident probabilities and seat belt usage: A psychological perspective. *Accident Analysis & Prevention* 10, 281–285.

Slovic, P., B. Fischoff, S. Lichtenstein, B. Corrigan and B. Combs, 1977. Preference for insuring against probable small losses: Implications for the theory and practice of insurance. *Journal of Risk and Insurance* 44, 237–258.

Slovic, P., B. Fischhoff and S. Lichtenstein, 1984. Behavioral decision theory perspectives on risk and safety. *Acta Psychologica* 56, 183–203.

Solomon, R.L., 1949. An extension of control group design. *Psychological Bulletin* 46, 137–150.

Solomon, R.L., 1980. The opponent-process theory of acquired motivation. The costs of benefits and the benefits of pain. *American Psychologist* 35, 691–712.

Sondak, H. and M.H. Bazerman, 1989. Matching and negotiation processes in quasi-markets. *Organizational Behavior and Human Decision Processes* 44, 261–280.

Span, P., 1973. Information processing complexity as an aspect of cognitive style. (in Dutch). Dissertation, University of Utrecht.

Spielberger, C.D., 1976. 'The nature and measurement of anxiety'. In: C.D. Spielberger and R. Diaz-Guerrero (eds), *Cross-cultural anxiety*. Washington D.C.: Hemisphere.

Sproles, G.B., 1977. New evidence on price and product quality. *Journal of Consumer Affairs* 11, 63–77.

Stacey, B.G., 1982. Economic socialization in the pre-adult years. *British Journal of Social Psychology* 21, 159–173.

Stanley, T.D., 1994. Silly bubbles and the insensitivity of rationality testing: An experimental illustration. *Journal of Economic Psychology* 15, 601–620.

Starbuck, W.H., 1963. Level of aspiration. *Psychological Review* 70, 51–60.

Starr, C., 1969. Social benefit versus technological risk. *Science* 165, 1232–1238.

Statman, M. and D. Caldwell, 1987. Applying behavioral finance to capital budgeting: Project terminations. *Financial Management* (Winter), 7–15.

Sternberg, S., 1966. High-speed scanning in human memory. *Science* 153, 652.

Stevens, S.S. 1957. On the psychophysical law. *Psychological Review* 64, 153–181.

Stevens, S.S. and E.H. Galanter, 1957. Ratio scales and category scales for a dozen perceptual continua. *Journal of Experimental Psychology* 54, 377–411.

Stigler, G.J., 1950. The development of utility theory. *Journal of Political Economy* 58, 307–327, 373–396.

Stigler, G.J., 1961. The economics of information. *Journal of Political Economy* 69, 213–225.

Stigler, G.J., 1984. Economics: The imperial science? *Scandinavian Journal of Economics* 86, 301–313.

Strickland, L.H., R.J. Lewicki and A.M. Katz 1966. Temporal orientation and perceived control as determinants of risk taking. *Journal of Experimental Social Psychology* 2, 143–151.

Stroebe, W. and B.S. Frey, 1982. Self-interest and collective action: The economics and psychology of public goods. *British Journal of Social Psychology* 21, 121–137.

Stroeker, N.E., 1995. Second-hand markets for consumer durables. Ph.D. dissertation. Rotterdam: Erasmus University.

Strotz, R.H., 1955–1956. Myopia and inconsistency in dynamic utility maximization. *Review of Economic Studies* 23, 165–180.

Strümpel, B. 1976. *Economic means for human needs*. Ann Arbor, MI: University of Michigan.

Stuart, O.D.J., 1984. A note on the measurement, quantification and use of consumer confidence. *Journal of Economic Psychology* 5, 125–138.

Sullivan, H.S., 1949. The theory of anxiety and the nature of psychotherapy. *Psychiatry* 12, 3–13.

Svenson, O. and G. Karlsson, 1989. Decision-making, time horizons, and risk in the very long-term perspective. *Risk Analysis* 9, 385–399.

Svenson, O. and G. Nilsson, 1986. Mental economics: Subjective representations of factors related to expected inflation. *Journal of Economic Psychology* 7, 327–349.

Taylor, L.D., 1975. Commentaries on Ratchford, "The new economic theory of consumer behavior: An interpretive essay." *Journal of Consumer Research* 2, 76–77.

Thaler, R.H., 1979. Individual intertemporal choice: A preliminary investigation. Research memorandum (mimeographed).

Thaler, R.H., 1980. Toward a positive theory of consumer choice. *Journal of Economic Behavior and Organisation* 1, 39–60.

Thaler, R.H., 1985. Mental Accounting and consumer choice. *Marketing Science* 4, 199–214.

Thaler, R.H., 1986. The psychology and economics conference handbook: Comments on Simon, on Einhorn and Hogarth, and on Tversky and Kahneman. *Journal of Business* 59, S279–S284.

Thaler, R.H., 1988. Anomalies: The ultimatum game. *Journal of Economic Perspectives* 2, 195–206.

Thaler, R.H., 1992. *The winner's curse*. New York: The Free Press.

Thaler, R.H. and H.M. Shefrin, 1981. An economic theory of self-control. *Journal of Political Economy* 89, 392–406.

Theil, H. and R.F. Kosobud, 1968. How informative are consumer buying intentions surveys? *Review of Economics and Statistics* 50, 50–59.

Thomas, E.A.C. and W.E. Ward, 1979. Time orientation, optimism, and quasi-economic behavior. Stanford University (mimeographed).

Thurstone, L.L., 1970. 'Attitudes can be measured.' In: G.F. Summers (ed.), *Attitude measurement*. Chicago: Rand McNally. pp. 127–141.

Tietz, R., 1992. 'An endowment effect in market experiments.' In: S.E.G. Lea, P. Webley and B.M. Young (eds.), *New directions in economic psychology*. Aldershot: Edward Elgar. pp. 99–121.

Tolman, E.C., 1948. Cognitive maps in rats and men. *Psychological Review* 55, 189–208.

Tolman, E.C., 1951. 'A psychological model'. In: T. Parsons and E.A. Shils (eds.), *Toward a general theory of action.* New York: Harper & Row. pp. 279–361.

Tolman, E.C., 1959. 'Principles of purposive behavior'. In: S. Koch (ed.), *Psychology: A study of a science*, Vol. 2. New York: McGraw-Hill. pp. 92–157.

Treisman, M., 1988. 'The St. Petersburg paradox and the expectation heuristic'. In: S. Maital (ed.), *Applied behavioral economics*, Vol. 2. Brighton, Wheatsheaf. pp. 668–676.

Tsal, Y., 1985. On the relationship between cognitive and affective processes: A critique of Zajonc and Markus. *Journal of Consumer Research* 10, 428–441.

Tullock, G., 1974. Does punishment deter crime? *Public Interest* 36, 103–111.

Turner, C.F., 1978. 'Why do surveys disagree? Some preliminary hypotheses and some disagreeable examples'. In: C.F. Turner and E. Martin (eds.), *Surveying subjective phenomena*, Vol. 2. pp. 159–214.

Tversky, A., 1972. Elimination by aspects: A theory of choice. *Psychological Review* 79, 281–298.

Tversky, A. and Griffin, 1991. Endowment and contrast in judgments of well-being. In: R.J. Zeckhauser (ed.), *Strategy and choice*. Cambridge, MA: MIT Press. pp. 297–318.

Tyszka, T., 1994. How do people perceive economic activities? *Journal of Economic Psychology* 15, 651–668.

Uhl, J., 1970. Retail food prices: A study in consumer perception. Unpublished Paper, First meeting of the Association for Consumer Research, Amherst.

Ulen, T.S., 1988. Cognitive imperfections and the analysis of law. Proceedings of the 13th Colloquium of the International Association for Research in Economic Psychology.

Unger, L.S., 1991. Altruism as a motivation to volunteer. *Journal of Economic Psychology* 12, 71–100.

Van de Stadt, H., G. Antonides and B.M.S. van Praag, 1984. Empirical testing of the expected utility model. *Journal of Economic Psychology* 5, 17–29.

Vanden Abeele, P., 1983. The index of consumer sentiment: Predictability and predictive power in the EEC. *Journal of Economic Psychology* 3, 1–17.

Van der Pligt, J. and E.C.M. van Schie, 1990. Frames of reference, judgement and preference. *European Review of Social Psychology* 1, 61–80.

Van der Sar, N.L. and B.M.S. van Praag, 1993. The evaluation question approach: A method of measuring attitudes. *Journal of Economic Psychology* 14, 183–201.

Van Dijk, E. and M. Grodzka, 1992. The influence of endowments asymmetry and information level on the contribution to a public step good. *Journal of Economic Psychology* 13, 329–342.

Van Herwaarden, F.G., A. Kapteyn and B.M.S. van Praag, 1977. Twelve thousand individual welfare functions. *European Economic Review* 9, 283–300.

Van Herwaarden, F.G. and A. Kapteyn, 1979. Empirical comparison of the shape of welfare functions. *Economics Letters* 3, 71–76.

Van Praag, B.M.S., 1968. *Individual welfare functions and consumer behaviour.* Amsterdam: North-Holland.

Van Praag, B.M.S., S. Dubnoff and N.L. van der Sar, 1988. On the measurement and explanation of standards with respect to income, age and education. *Journal of Economic Psychology* 9, 481–498.

Van Praag, B.M.S., T. Goedhart and A. Kapteyn, 1980. The poverty line – a pilot survey in Europe. *Review of Economics and Statistics* 62, 461–465.

Van Praag, B.M.S., A. Kapteyn and F.G. van Herwaarden, F.G., 1979. The definition and measurement of social reference spaces. *Nederlands Journal of Sociology* 15, 13–25.

Van Raaij, W.F. 1981. Economic Psychology. *Journal of Economic Psychology* 1, 1–24.

Van Raaij, W.F. 1984. Micro and macro economic psychology. *Journal of Economic Psychology* 5, 385–401.

Van Raaij, W.F., 1986. 'Developments in consumer behavior research'. In: B. Gilad and S. Kaish (eds.), *Handbook of behavioral economics*, Vol. A. Greenwich, JAI Press. pp. 67–88.

Van Raaij, W.F., 1986. 'Causal attributions in economic behavior'. In: A.J. Macfadyen and

H.W. MacFadyen (eds.), *Economic psychology*. Amsterdam: North-Holland. pp. 353–379.

Van Raaij, W.F., 1988. 'Information processing and decision making. Cognitive aspects of economic behaviour'. In: W.F. Van Raaij, G.M. van Veldhoven and K.E. Wärneryd (eds.), *Handbook of economic psychology*. Dordrecht: Kluwer Academic Publishers. pp. 74–106.

Van Raaij, W.F. and H.J. Gianotten 1990. Consumer confidence, expenditure, saving and credit. *Journal of Economic Psychology* 11, 269–290.

Van Raaij, W.F., G.M. van Veldhoven and K.E. Wärneryd (eds.), 1988. *Handbook of economic psychology*. Dordrecht: Kluwer Academic Publishers.

Van Witteloostuijn, A., 1990. Learning in economic theory: A taxonomy with an application to expectations formation. *Journal of Economic Psychology* 11, 183–207.

Van Witteloostuijn, A., 1991. Economic psychology and socio- economics. An essay on discourse strategies and research potentials. In: G. Antonides, W. Arts and W.F. van Raaij (eds.), *The consumption of time and the timing of consumption*. Amsterdam: North-Holland. pp. 232–242.

Van Witteloostuijn, A., 1993. Review of "G. Antonides, Psychology in Economics and Business: An Introduction to Economic Psychology, 1991." *De Economist* 141, 177–178.

Veenhoven, R., 1984a. *Conditions of happiness*. Dordrecht: Reidel.

Veenhoven, R., 1984b. *Data-book on happiness*. Dordrecht: Reidel.

Veenhoven, R., 1987. National wealth and individual happiness. Proceedings of the 12th Colloquium of the International Association for Research in Economic Psychology. pp. 867–881.

Veevers, J.E. 1971. Drinking attitudes and drinking behavior: An exploratory study. *Journal of Social Psychology* 85, 103–109.

Veldscholte, C.M., G. Antonides and P. Kroonenberg, 1995. Converging perceptions of economic activities between East and West. Erasmus University Rotterdam, Tinbergen Institute Discussion Paper TI 1-95-192.

Verplanck, W.S., 1955. The control of the content of conversation: Reinforcement of statements of opinion. *Journal of Abnormal and Social Psychology* 51, 668–676.

Viscusi, W.K., 1979. *Employment hazards*. Cambridge, MA: Harvard University.

Vlek, C. and P.-J. Stallen, 1980. Rational and personal aspects of risk. *Acta Psychologica* 45, 273–300.

Vlek, C. and W.A. Wagenaar, 1979. 'Judgment and decision under uncertainty'. In: J.A. Michon, E.G.J. Eijkman and L.F.W. de Klerk (eds.), *Handbook of psychonomics*, Vol. 2. Amsterdam: North-Holland.

Vodopivec, B., 1992. A need theory perspective on the parallellism of attitude and utility. *Journal of Economic Psychology* 13, 19–37.

Von Neumann, J. and O. Morgenstern, 1947. *Theory of games and economic behavior*. Princeton: Princeton University Press.

Wagner, H.M., 1969. *Principles of operation research*. Englewood Cliffs, NJ: Prentice-Hall.

Wallraff, G., 1985. *Ganz Unten*. Witsch: Kiepenheuer.

Walster, E., G. Berscheid and G.W. Walster, 1973. New directions in equity research. *Journal of Personality and Social Psychology* 23, 151–176.

Walster, E. and G.W. Walster, 1975. Equity and social justice. *Journal of Social Issues* 31, 21–43.

Ward, S., 1974. Consumer socialization. *Journal of Consumer Research* 1, 1–14.

Wärneryd, K.E., 1988. 'Economic psychology as a field of study'. In: W.F. van Raaij, G.M. van Veldhoven and K.E. Wärneryd (eds), *Handbook of Economic Psychology*. Dordrecht: Kluwer Academic Publishers. pp. 2–41.

Wärneryd, K.E., 1988. 'The psychology of innovative entrepreneurship'. In: W.F. van Raaij, G.M. van Veldhoven and K.E. Wärneryd (eds.), *Handbook of economic psychology*. Dordrecht: Kluwer Academic Publishers. pp. 404–447.

Wärneryd, K.E., 1994. Demystifying rational expectations theory through an economic-psychological model. IAREP-SABE proceedings. Erasmus University, Rotterdam.

Wärneryd, K.E. and K. Westlund, 1993. Ethics and economic affairs in the world of finance.

Journal of Economic Psychology 14, 523–539.

Warr, P., 1984. 'Job loss, unemployment and well-being'. In: V.L. Allen, and E. van de Vliert (eds.), *Role transitions*. New York: Plenum. pp. 263–285.

Watson, J.B. and R. Raynor, 1920. Emotional reactions. *Journal of Experimental Psychology* 3, 1–14.

Weber, M., 1930. *The Protestant ethic and the spirit of capitalism*. (Translated by T. Parsons.) New York: Scribner. (Originally published in 1904.)

Webley, P. and S.E.G. Lea, 1993. Towards a more realistic psychology of economic socialization. *Journal of Economic Psychology* 14, 461–472.

Weiner, B., 1974. 'Achievement motivation as conceptualized by an attribution theorist'. In: B. Weiner (ed.), *Achievement motivation and attribution theory*. Morristown, NJ: General Learning Press. pp. 3–48.

Weiner, B., 1985. An attributional theory of achievement motivation and emotion. *Psychological Review* 92, 548–573.

Weinstein, M.C. and R.J. Quinn, 1983. Psychological considerations in valuing health risk reductions. *Natural Resources Journal* 23, 659–673.

Wells, W.D. 1975. Psychographics: A critical review. *Journal of Marketing Research* 12, 196–213.

Wells, W.D., 1981. How advertising works. Working paper. Chicago, IL: Needham, Harper and Steers Advertising.

Westbrook, R.A., 1980. A rating scale for measuring product/service satisfaction. *Journal of Marketing* 44, 68–72.

Wilkie W.L., 1986. *Consumer behavior*. New York: Wiley.

Wilkie, W.L. and E.A. Pessemier, 1973. Issues in marketing's use of multi-attribute attitude models. *Journal of Marketing Research* 10, 428–441.

Wills, T.A., 1981. Downward comparison principles in social psychology. *Psychological Bulletin* 90, 245–271.

Wilson, W., 1967. Correlates of avowed happiness. *Psychological Bulletin* 67, 294–306.

Winston, G.C., 1980. Addiction and backsliding. A theory of compulsive consumption. *Journal of Economic Behavior and Organization* 1, 295–324.

Winter-Ebmer, R., 1994. Motivation for migration and economic success. *Journal of Economic Psychology* 15, 269–284.

Witkin, H.A., R.B. Dijk, H.F. Faterson, D.R. Goodenough and S.A. Karp, 1962. *Psychological differentiation*. London: Wiley.

Witkin, H.A., D.R. Goodenough and P.K. Oltman 1979. Psychological differentiation: Current status. *Journal of Personality and Social Psychology* 37, 1127–1145.

Wortman, C. and R. Silver, 1982. Coping with undesirable life events. Paper presented at the 90th Annual Convention of the American Psychological Association. Washington D.C.

Yates, J.F., 1972. Individual time preference (delayed gratification) behavior: A review and a model. Ann Arbor, MI: University of Michigan. Unpublished manuscript.

Yerkes, R.M. and J.D. Dodson, 1908. The relation of strength of stimulus to rapidity of habit-formation. *Journal of Comparative Neurology and Psychology* 18, 459–482.

Zajonc, R.B. 1980. Feeling and thinking. *American Psychologist* 35, 151–175.

Zajonc, R.B., 1984. On the primacy of affect. *American Psychologist* 39, 117–123.

Zajonc, R.B. and H. Markus, 1982. Affective and cognitive factors in preferences. *Journal of Consumer Research* 9, 123–131.

Zanna, M.P and J. Cooper, 1974. Dissonance and the pill: An attribution approach to studying the arousal properties of dissonance. *Journal of Personality and Social Psychology* 29, 703–709.

Zillman, D., 1978. 'Attribution and misattribution of excitatory reactions'. In: J.H. Harvey, W. Ickes and R.F. Kidd (eds.), *New directions in attribution research*, Vol. 2. Hillsdale, NJ: Erlbaum. pp. 335–368.

Zuckerman, M. 1978. 'Sensation seeking'. In: H. London and J.E. Exner Jr. (eds.), *Dimensions of personality*. New York: Wiley. pp. 487–559.

Zuckerman, M. 1979. *Sensation seeking*. Hillsdale, NJ: Erlbaum.

Zuckerman, M. 1979. Attribution of success and failure revisited, or: The motivational bias is alive and well in attribution theory. *Journal of Personality* 47, 245–287.

Zullow, H.M., 1991. Pessimistic rumination in popular songs and newsmagazines predict economic recession via decreased optimism and spending. *Journal of Economic Psychology* 12, 501–526.

AUTHOR INDEX

SUBJECT INDEX

425